HANDBOOKS

RIO DE JANEIRO

MICHAEL SOMMERS

Contents

Maps

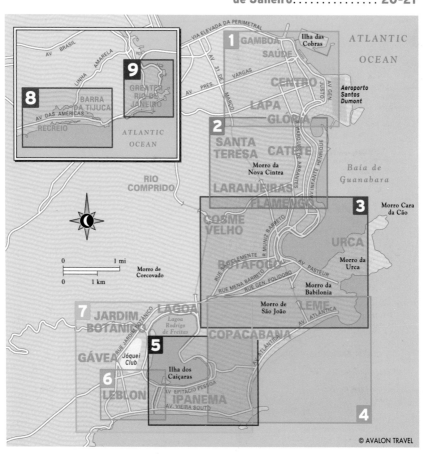

✪ SIGHTS

1 CIDADE DO SAMBA
5 IGREJA DO MOSTEIRO DE SÃO BENTO
6 ILHA FISCAL
9 PALÁCIO ITAMARATY
11 IGREJA NOSSA SENHORA DA CANDELÁRIA
21 ESPAÇO CULTURAL DA MARINHA
23 ARCO DO TELLES AND TRAVESSA DO COMÉRCIO
24 IGREJA NOSSA SENHORA DO CARMO DA ANTIGA SÉ
25 PRAÇA XV DE NOVEMBRO
25 ILHA DE PAQUETÁ
28 PAÇO IMPERIAL
29 PALÁCIO TIRADENTES
31 MUSEU HISTÓRICO NACIONAL
34 REAL GABINETE PORTUGUÊS DE LEITURA
56 ◖ IGREJA DA ORDEM TERCEIRA DE SÃO FRANCISCO DA PENITÊNCIA
57 CONVENTO E IGREJA DE SANTO ANTÔNIO
61 ◖ THEATRO MUNICIPAL
63 MUSEU NACIONAL DE BELAS ARTES
64 PALÁCIO GUSTAVO CAPANEMA
65 BIBLIOTECA NACIONAL
66 CINELÂNDIA
74 CATEDRAL METROPOLITANA
89 ARCOS DA LAPA
94 ESCADARIA SELARÓN
97 PASSEIO PÚBLICO
100 ◖ MUSEU DE ARTE MODERNA

◖ RESTAURANTS

7 RUBRO CAFÉ
8 SENTAÍ
10 CASA PALADINO
17 CAIS DO ORIENTE
19 BRASSERIE ROSÁRIO
20 RIO MINHO
26 BISTRÔ DO PAÇO
30 ALBAMAR
33 SÍRIO E LIBANÊS
35 ◖ CONFEITARIA COLOMBO
36 EÇA
44 CASA CAVÉ
50 MANGUE SECO
58 SHIN MIURA
82 ◖ NOVA CAPELA
95 ADEGA FLOR DE COIMBRA
101 LAGUIOLE

◖ NIGHTLIFE

2 THE WEEK
3 TRAPICHE GAMBOA
4 CABARET KALESA
16 ADEGA DO TIMÃO
22 BOTECO CASUAL
40 NOVA ESTUDANTINA
42 ◖ CENTRO CULTURAL CARIOCA
45 ELITE
47 ◖ RIO SCENARIUM
54 CINE IDEAL
55 BAR LUIZ
67 AMARELINHO
73 VILLARINO
76 CASA DA MÃE JOANA
80 CLUB SIX
83 BAR BRASIL
84 CARIOCA DA GEMA
85 ESTRELA DA LAPA
86 CASA BRASIL MESTIÇO
90 CABARET CASANOVA
91 ◖ LAPA 40°
92 CLUBE DOS DEMOCRÁTICOS
93 SEMENTE
99 CLUBE SANTA LUZIA

◖ ARTS AND LEISURE

12 CASA FRANÇA-BRASIL
13 ◖ CENTRO CULTURAL BANCO DO BRASIL
14 CENTRO CULTURAL DOS CORREIOS
18 GALERIA PAULO FERNANDES
38 A GENTIL CARIOCA
39 CENTRO DE ARTE HÉLIO OITICICA
41 TEATRO JOÃO CAETANO
43 CENTRO CULTURAL CARIOCA
51 TEATRO CARLOS GOMES
60 CAIXA CULTURAL
62 THEATRO MUNICIPAL
68 CENTRO CULTURAL DA JUSTIÇA
69 TEATRO RIVAL
70 ◖ CINE ODEON BR
72 CENTRO EXCURSIONISTA DO RIO DE JANEIRO
78 FUNDIÇÃO PROGRESSO
87 ◖ TEATRO ODISSÉIA
88 CIRCO VOADOR
96 SALA CECÍLIA MEIRELES
98 VIVO RIO

Morro da Previdência

GAMBOA

Palácio Itamaraty

Presidente Vargas

Central do Brasil

Praça Major Valô

Praça Procópio Ferreira

Central

Real Gabinete Português de Leitura

Praça da República

Praça Tiradentes

LAPA

SEE MAP 2

SIGHTS

5	MUSEU CHÁCARA DO CÉU	32	PARQUE DO FLAMENGO
6	PARQUE DAS RUÍNAS	35	PALÁCIO DO CATETE
8	MUSEU DO BONDE	38	MUSEU DE FOLCLORE EDISON CARNEIRO
30	IGREJA NOSSA SENHORA DA GLÓRIA DO OUTEIRO	39	PARQUE DO CATETE
		46	PALÁCIO DAS LARANJEIRAS AND PARQUE GUINLE

RESTAURANTS

7	ALDA MARIA DOCES PORTUGUESES	26	CASA DA SUÍÇA
9	ASIA	29	BARRACUDA
10	ESPÍRITO SANTA	33	ESTAÇÃO REPÚBLICA
11	ADEGA DO PIMENTA	52	BAR DO SERAFIM
13	SOBRENATURAL	58	MAJÓRICA
16	JASMIM MANGA	60	LAMAS
24	APRAZÍVEL	63	SENAC BISTRÔ
		66	PORÇÃO RIO'S

NIGHTLIFE

1	GOYA BEIRA	50	CASA ROSA
2	BURACO DA LACRAIA	62	BELMONTE
14	BAR DO MINEIRO	64	J CLUB
17	ARMAZÉM SÃO THIAGO		

ARTS AND LEISURE

21	CINE SANTA TERESA	54	RIO HIKING
27	MARLIN YACHT	57	TRILHARTE ECOTURISMO
28	SAVEIRO'S TOUR	61	CENTRO CULTURAL ARTE SESC
36	ESPAÇO MUSEU DA REPÚBLICA	65	CASA DE ARTE E CULTURA JULIETA DE SERPA
45	OI FUTURO		
51	CASA ROSA		
53	ESPAÇO RIO CARIOCA		

SHOPS

12	LA VEREDA	55	MARACATU BRASIL
25	GETÚLIO DAMADO	56	PÉ DE BOI

HOTELS

3	CASA AMARELO	37	HOTEL RIAZOR
4	RIO HOSTEL SANTA TERESA	40	HOTEL IMPERIAL
15	CASTELINHO 38	41	HOTEL FLORIDA
18	POUSADA CASA ÁUREA	42	HOTEL REGINA
19	POUSADA PITANGA	43	THE MAZE INN
20	HOTEL SANTA TERESA	44	SCORIAL RIO
22	SOLAR DE SANTA	47	CASA 579
23	MAMA RUÍSA	48	RIO 180°
31	BARON GARDEN	49	ANANAB GUESTHOUSE
34	HOTEL INGLÊS	59	PAYSANDU HOTEL

SANTA TERESA

Museu do Bonde

LARANJEIRAS

Morro da Nova Cintra

Parque Eduardo Guinle

Praça Del Prete

Praça Duque Costa

0   200 yds
0   200 m

DISTANCE ACROSS MAP
Approximate: 1.9 mi or 3.1 km

SEE MAP 1

SEE MAP 3

LADEIRA DOS MEIRELLES

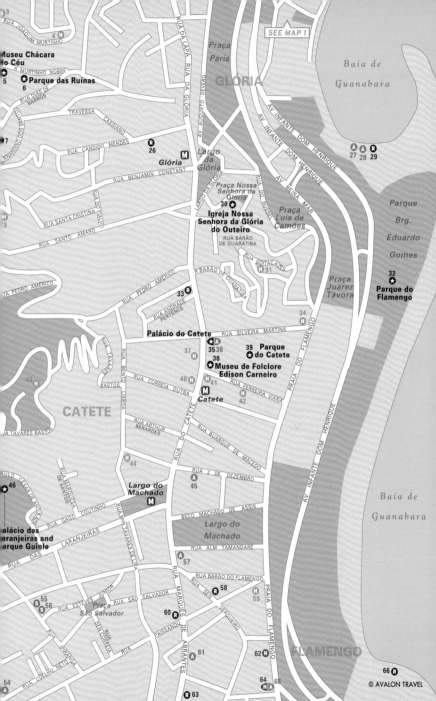

Baía de
Guanabara

Praça
Paris

GLÓRIA

SEE MAP 1

Museu Chácara
do Céu

Parque das Ruínas

RUA JOAQUIM MURTINHO

R. MURTINHO NOBRE

RUA DIAS DE BARROS

TRAVESSA CASSIANO

RUA DA LAPA

RUA DA GLÓRIA

AV AUGUSTO SEVERO

AV INFANTE DOM HENRIQUE

AV INFANTE DOM HENRIQUE

27 28 29

RUA CANDIDO MENDES

26

Glória

Largo
da
Glória

RUA BENJAMIN CONSTANT

RUA SANTA CRISTINA

RUA DO FIALHO

RUA SANTO AMARO

Praça Nossa
Senhora de
Glória

30

Igreja Nossa
Senhora da Glória
do Outeiro

RUA BARÃO
DE GUARATIBA

Praça
Luis de
Camões

AV BEIRA MAR

Parque
Brg.
Eduardo
Gomes

RUA DA SANTA

RUA DO RUSSEL

RUA PEDRO AMERICO

R BARÃO DE GUARATIBA

33

RUA ANDRADE
PERTENCE

RUA GOITACAZES

31

Praça
Juarez
Távora

32

Parque do
Flamengo

34

RUA TAVARES
BASTOS

RUA BENTO LISBOA

Palácio do Catete

RUA SILVEIRA MARTINS

37
35 36
38

39 Parque
do Catete

Museu de Folclore
Edison Carneiro

RUA CORREIA DUTRA

40 41

RUA FERREIRA VIANA

43

CATETE

Catete

42

PRAIA DO FLAMENGO

RUA ARTHUR
BERARDES

RUA DO CATETE

RUA BUARQUE DE MACEDO

AV INFANTE DOM HENRIQUE

46

44

RUA MARQUESA
DE SANTOS

RUA 2 DE DEZEMBRO

45

Largo do
Machado

RUA GAGO COUTINHO

RUA JANGADEIROS

RUA TAVARES DE LIRA

BECO MACHADO DE ASSIS

Largo do
Machado

Baía de
Guanabara

Palácio das
Laranjeiras and
Parque Guinle

RUA LARANJEIRAS

RUA DAS

RUA ALM TAMANDARÉ

57

RUA BARÃO DO FLAMENGO

55
56

RUA ESTEVES JUNIOR

RUA SÃO SALVADOR

Praça
São Salvador

60

58

RUA SEN

RUA TERQUEIRO

59

RUA MARQUES DE ABRANTES

PAISSANDU

61

62

PRAIA DO FLAMENGO

FLAMENGO

66

54

RUA COELHO NETO

RUA SENT CORREA

63

64 65

© AVALON TRAVEL

Largo do Boticário
1 2

COSME VELHO

3 Corcovado

4 Museu Internacional de Arte Naïf

SEE MAP 2

LARANJEIRAS

RUA DA COSME VELHO

RUA GEN. GLICÉRIO

RUA JUÇANÃ

RUA MUNDO NOVO

Praça Chaim Weizmann

RUA B. TÁVORA

RUA OSWALDO CRUZ

RUA MARQUES DE OLINDA

RUA BARÃO DE ITAMBI

PRAIA DE BOTAFOGO

AV. INFANTE DOM HENRIQUE

S SHOPS
11   BOTAFOGO PRAIA SHOPPING
16   ARTÍNDIA
24   COBAL DO HUMAITÁ
33   BISCOITO FINO
33   SHOPPING RIO SUL

H HOTELS
2 CASA 32
18   VILA CARIOCA HOSTEL

RUA ASSUNÇÃO

RUA BAMBINA

RUA VISC. DE OURO PRÊTO

RUA NATAL

PRAIA DE BOTAFOGO

Praça Radial Sul

10 N

Fundação Casa de Rui Barbosa
13

A 12

RUA SÃO CLEMENTE

11 S

BOTAFOGO

14

RUA SÃO CLEMENTE

RUA DA MATRIZ

Museu do Índio
15
16

RUA DONA MARIANA

RUA CONDE DE IRAJÁ

17 Museu Villa-Lobos

RUA SOROCABA

RUA PAULO

RUA VOLUNTÁRIOS DA PÁTRIA

18

RUA PROF. ÁLVARO RODRIGUES

19
20 N
Botafogo M
A 21

22

23

RUA MARTINS FERREIRA

RUA REAL GRANDEZA

24 S

RUA VOLUNTÁRIOS DA PÁTRIA

RUA SÃO JOÃO

R. H. NOVAES
26

RUA MENA BARRETO

RUA T. GUIMARÃES
27

28

RUA ARNALDO QUINTELA

29 R

RUA DE CARAVELAS

25

RUA VISCONDE DE SILVA

RUA VISC.

RUA GEN. POLIDORO

RUA ÁLVARO RAMOS

A 31

RUA P. GUIMARÃES

RUA REAL GRANDEZA

Cemitério São João Batista

TÚNEL VELHO

Morro de São João

0   400 yds
0   400 m

DISTANCE ACROSS MAP
Approximate: 2.8 mi or 4.1 km

Praça Ver. Rocha Leão

RUA SANTA CLARA

RUA DÉCIO VILARES

RUA SIQUEIRA CAMPOS

RUA TONELERO

© AVALON TRAVEL

SIGHTS

1	LARGO DO BOTICÁRIO	8	PRAIA DA URCA	36	PISTA CLAUDIO COUTINHO
3	CORCOVADO	9	PÃO DE AÇÚCAR	37	PRAIA VERMELHA
4	MUSEU INTERNACIONAL DE ARTE NAÏF	13	FUNDAÇÃO CASA DE RUI BARBOSA		
5	MUSEU CARMEN MIRANDA	15	MUSEU DO ÍNDIO		
		17	MUSEU VILLA-LOBOS		

RESTAURANTS

22	MUSEU DA CADEIRA	29	ADEGA DO VALENTIM	35	ZOZÔ
25	CARÊME	30	MIAM MIAM		
28	YORUBÁ	34	SORVETE BRASIL		

NIGHTLIFE

| 6 | BAR URCA | 10 | CHAMPANHERIA OVELHA NEGRA | 20 | DRINKERIA MALDITA |
| 7 | GAROTA DA URCA | | | 26 | CASA DA MATRIZ |

ARTS AND LEISURE

12	CENTRO DE ESCALADA LIMITE VERTICAL	21	ESTAÇÃO BOTAFOGO	31	CASA DE DANÇA CARLINHOS DE JESUS
14	PINAKOTHEKE CULTURAL	23	ESPAÇO CULTURAL MAURICE VALANSI	32	CANECÃO
19	ESPAÇO UNIBANCO DE CINEMA	27	LURIXS ARTE CONTEMPORÂNEA		

SEE MAP 3

Morro de
São João

SEE MAP 7

TÚNEL VELHO

DISTANCE ACROSS MAP
Approximate: 1.8 mi or 2.9 km

0   300 yds
0   300 m

Praça Ver.
Rocha Leão

Cardeal
Arcoverde

Praça Cardeal
Arcoverde

Praça
Edmundo
Bitencourt

Siqueira
Campos

TÚNEL
VAZ

COPACABANA

Praça
Serzedelo
Correia

Praia de
Copacabana

Morro dos
Cabritos

Praia

Cantagalo

AV. HENRIQUE DODSWORTH

RUA PROF. GASTÃO BAHIANA

Morro do
Cantagalo

TÚNEL PREF.
SÁ FREIRE ALVIM

RUA ALMIRANTE
GONÇALVES

RUA SAINT ROMAN

RUA SÁ FERREIRA

Morro do
Pavão

RUA SOUSA LIMA

SEE MAP 5

RUA VISC. DE PIRAJÁ

Praça
Gen. Osório

RUA PRUDENTE DE MORAIS

IPANEMA

AV. VIEIRA SOUTO

AV. VIEIRA SOUTO

Praça do
Arpoador

RUA FRANCISCO OTAVIANO

Forte de
Copacabana

Praça Cel.
Eugenio Franco

◎ SIGHTS

1	PEDRA DO LEME	21 ◖ PRAIA DE COPACABANA	57 FORTE DE COPACABANA

◎ RESTAURANTS

2 MARIUS CRUSTÁCEOS	14 AMIR	41 COPA CAFÉ
3 DA BRAMBINI	16 CIPRIANI	42 ◖ SIRI MOLE PRAIA
4 SHIRLEY	18 ◖ PÉRGULA	44 O CARANGUEJO
5 D'AMICI	24 A POLONESA	45 LE BLÉ NOIR
6 MISS TANAKA	34 THE BAKERS	55 LE PRÉ CATELAN
11 AZUMI	40 CAFEÍNA	

◎ NIGHTLIFE

7 BOSSA LOUNGE	27 FOSFOBOX	50 ATLÂNTICO
8 CERVANTES	30 ALLEGRO BISTRÔ MUSICAL	51 BUNKER
25 CAFÉ E BAR PAVÃO AZUL	46 LA CUEVA	52 LE BOY
26 ADEGA PÉROLA	47 BIP BIP	53 LA GIRL

◎ ARTS AND LEISURE

19 PEQUENA GALERIA 18	37 GALERIA MOVIMENTO	54 MARCIA BARROZO DO
32 SPECIAL BIKE	43 ROXY	AMARAL GALERIA DE ARTE

◎ SHOPS

13 BOSSA NOVA & CIA	28 ◖ SHOPPING DOS	33 LIDADOR
23 BARATOS DA RIBEIRO	ANTIQUÁRIOS	35 CHARUTARIA LOLLÔ
	31 ◖ MODERN SOUND	

◎ HOTELS

9 ◖ STONE OF A BEACH	20 ASTORIA PALACE	39 SESC COPACABANA
10 CASA DA VALESKA	22 OLINDA OTHON CLASSIC	48 SOUTH AMERICAN
12 ROYAL RIO PALACE	29 HOTEL SANTA CLARA	COPACABANA
15 ◖ DAYRELL OURO VERDE	36 HOTEL TOLEDO	49 PORTINARI DESIGN HOTEL
17 ◖ COPACABANA PALACE	38 OTHON CALIFORNIA	56 SOFITEL RIO DE JANEIRO

0   200 yds
0   200 m
DISTANCE ACROSS MAP
Approximate: 1.9 mi or 3.1 km

SEE MAP 7

SEE MAP 7

Parque da Catacumba

Lagoa Rodrigo de Freitas

Ilha dos Caiçaras

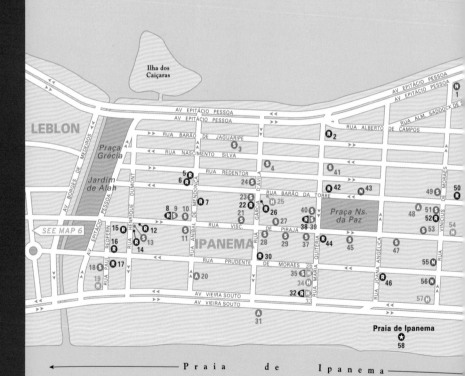

LEBLON

Praça Grécia

Jardim de Alah

AV. EPITÁCIO PESSOA
AV. EPITÁCIO PESSOA

RUA BARÃO DE JAGUARIPE
RUA NASCIMENTO SILVA
RUA REDENTOR

RUA ALBERTO DE CAMPOS

RUA ALM. SADDOCK DE S

RUA BARÃO DA TORRE

IPANEMA

RUA VISC. DE PIRAJÁ

RUA PRUDENTE DE MORAES

AV. VIEIRA SOUTO
AV. VIEIRA SOUTO

Praça Ns. da Paz

SEE MAP 6

Praia de Ipanema
58

← Praia de Ipanema →

ATLANTIC OCEAN

✪ SIGHTS

58	PRAIA DE IPANEMA	83	PRAIA DO ARPOADOR

⊘ RESTAURANTS

2	STRAVAGANZE	17	OSTERIA DELL'ANGOLO	44	POLIS SUCOS
5	GERO	22	VIA SETE	46	ZAZÁ BISTRÔ TROPICAL
6	ESPLANADA GRILL	26	MIL FRUTAS CAFÉ	50	SATYRICON
7	FORNERIA	26	ALESSANDRO E FREDERICO CAFÉ	52	MINIMOK
8	BAZZAR			60	OPIUM
12	FONTES	30	DELÍRIO TROPICAL	72	CASA DA FEIJOADA
14	MARGUTTA	32	GALANI	76	BRASILEIRINHO
15	GULA GULA	38	ARMAZÉM DO CAFÉ	78	FASANO AL MARE
16	TEN KAI	42	LÍQUIDO	82	AZUL MARINHO

◑ NIGHTLIFE

1	DAMA DE FERRO	56	VINICIUS PIANO BAR	65	DEVASSA
43	BARONNETI	63	GALERIA CAFÉ	67	A BOFETADA
55	GAROTA DE IPANEMA	65	LOUNGE 69	77	MISTURA FINA
				79	LONDRA

⊙ ARTS AND LEISURE

20	GALERIA DE ARTE IPANEMA	48	JUST FLY	70	BIKE & LAZER
31	ESCOLINHA DE SURF PAULINHO DOLABELLA	62	ESTAÇÃO LAURA ALVIM	71	SILVIA CINTRA GALERIA DE ARTE
		64	LAURA MARSIAJ ARTE CONTEMPORÁNEA	74	ESTÚDIO GUANABARA

⊜ SHOPS

3	CARE BODY & SOUL	27	GILSON MARTINS	45	MONICA PONDÉ
4	ALESSA	28	JELLY	45	FARM
9	LIVRARIA DA TRAVESSA	29	CONTEMPORÂNEO	47	LIGA RETRÔ
10	SOBRAL JOIAS	35	BRASIL & CIA	49	MARIA BONITA
11	TOTEM	37	SEMENTEIRA	51	TOCA DE VINICIUS
13	SOLLAS	39	RESERVA	53	LETRAS E EXPRESSÕES
18	0-21 MÓVEIS CARIOCA	40	BRAZILIAN SOUL	68	OUSADIA
21	H. STERN	41	VIRZI	73	FEIRA HIPPIE
23	ANTONIO BERNARDO	45	FOCH	75	A CENA MUDA
24	VERVE	45	GLORINHA PARANAGUÁ	84	GALERIA RIVER

⌂ HOTELS

19	HOTEL PRAIA IPANEMA	54	VERMONT HOTEL	69	YAYA HOTEL
25	IPANEMA BEACH HOUSE	57	SOL IPANEMA	80	FASANO RIO
33	CAESAR PARK	59	THE MANGO TREE	81	ARPOADOR INN
34	EVEREST PARK HOTEL	61	IPANEMA PLAZA		
36	IPANEMA INN	66	IPANEMA SWEET		

SEE MAP 4

Morro do
Pavão

ALBERTO DE CAMPOS

69

NASCIMENTO SILVA

RUA SÓUSA LIMA

RUA FRANCISCO SÁ

RUA BARÃO DA TORRE

67

68 70

RUA VISC. DE PIRAJÁ

66 74
71

65
72 73

RUA PRUDENTE DE MORAES

60 61
62 64
63

77

RUA GOMES CARNEIRO

RUA RAINHA ELISABETH DA BÉLGICA

78 79 80

RUA DE CASTILHOS

RUA FARME DE AMOEDO

RUA TEIXEIRA DE MELLO

RUA JANGADEIROS

Praça
Gen.
Osório

75

76

RUA BARÃO

RUA JOAQUIM NABUCO

AV. VIEIRA SOUTO

AV. VIEIRA SOUTO

RUA BULHÕES CARVALHO

RUA RAUL POMPÉIA

AV. N.S. DE COPACABANA

AV. ATLÂNTICA

ATLANTIC
OCEAN

Praça Cel.
Eugenio
Franco

RUA FRANCISCO OTAVIANO

84

81
82

AV. FRANCISCO BHERING

Praça do
Arpoador

Praia do
Arpoador
83

Parque Garota
de Ipanema

Praia do Arpoador

SEE MAP 7

☼ SIGHTS
- 40 PRAIA DE LEBLON
- 45 PARQUE DO PENHASCO DOIS IRMÃOS

℞ RESTAURANTS
- 1 ARATACA
- 3 VEGETARIANO SOCIAL CLUBE
- 4 UNIVERSO ORGÂNICO
- 6 SAWASDEE
- 7 CAFÉ SEVERINO
- 11 ZUKA
- 12 SUSHI LEBLON
- 13 CELEIRO
- 14 CARLOTA
- 18 GARCIA & RODRIGUES
- 19 AQUIM
- 20 PIZZARIA GUANABARA
- 22 KONI STORE
- 24 BB LANCHES
- 26 TALHO CAPIXABA
- 27 KURT
- 28 FELLINI
- 30 GIUSEPPE GRILL
- 32 BIBI SUCOS
- 33 DEGRAU
- 36 RÁSCAL
- 43 ANTIQUARIUS

◐ NIGHTLIFE
- 5 ACADEMIA DA CACHAÇA
- 25 JOBI
- 31 BRACARENSE
- 41 BAR D'HOTEL
- 44 MELT
- 46 MIRANTE DO LEBLON

◭ ARTS AND LEISURE
- 9 ARTE EM DOBRO
- 21 DIVE POINT
- 29 A! BODY TECH

◉ SHOPS
- 2 COBAL DO LEBLON
- 8 ARGUMENTO
- 10 GRANADO
- 15 ISABEL CAPETO
- 16 ESCH CAFÉ
- 23 BECO DAS VIRTUDES
- 23 DAQUI
- 35 GARAPA DOIDA
- 37 MARIA OITICICA
- 37 SHOPPING LEBLON
- 37 CONSTANÇA BASTO
- 37 AÜSLANDER
- 38 CLUB CAPELLI
- 38 RIO DESIGN LEBLON

◉ HOTELS
- 17 RITZ PLAZA
- 34 LEMON SPIRIT HOSTEL
- 39 MARINA PALACE
- 42 MARINA ALL-SUITES

RUA MÁRIO RIBEIRO
RUA MÁRIO RIBEIRO

Praça Ns. Auxiliador

RUA RODRIGO OCTÁVIO
RUA RODRIGO OCTÁVIO

AV. BARTOLOMEU MITRE
AV. BARTOLOMEU MITRE

RUA JUQUIÁ

RUA CAP. CÉSAR DE ANDRADE

Largo da Memória

RUA DES. ALFREDO RUSSEL

RUA CONDE BERNADOTTE

RUA JOÃO LIRA

Praça Baden Powell

RUA HUMBERTO DE CAMPOS

LEBLON

RUA JOÃO DE BARROS

RUA PROF. ARTHUR RAMOS

Praça Antero de Quental

RUA GEN. VENÂNCIO FLORES

SEE MAP 7

RUA DIAS FERREIRA

RUA GEN. ARTIGAS

RUA GEN. SAN MARTIN

AV. BARTOLOMEU MITRE

RUA ATAULFO DE PAIVA

RUA J. MONTEIRO

RUA VISC. DE ALBUQUERQUE

Praça Rubem Braga

Praça Rubem Dario

45 Parque do Penhasco Dois Irmãos

RUA APEANA

AV. DELFIM MOREIRA
AV. DELFIM MOREIRA

40 Praia de Leblon

P r a i a

AV. NIEMEYER 46

© AVALON TRAVEL

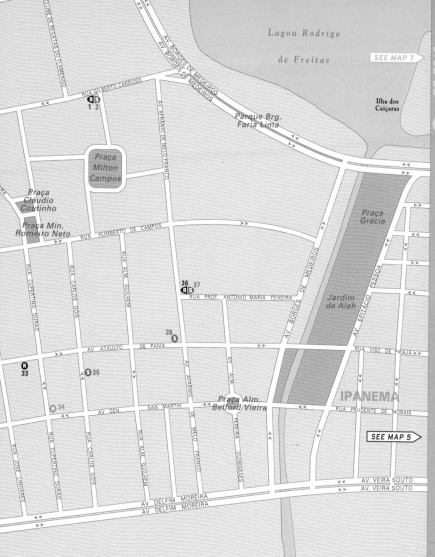

Lagoa Rodrigo
de Freitas

SEE MAP 7

Ilha dos
Caiçaras

CLUBE DE REGATAS DO FLAMENGO

AV. BORGES DE MEDEIROS
AV. BORGES DE MEDEIROS

RUA GILBERTO CARDOSO

1 2

AV. AFFRANIO DE MELO FRANCO

Parque Brg.
Faria Lima

Praça
Milton
Campos

Praça
Cláudio
Coutinho

Praça Min.
Romeiro Neto

RUA HUMBERTO DE CAMPOS

RUA CUPERTINO DURÃO

RUA CARLOS GÓIS

RUA ALM. GUILHEM

RUA ALM. GUILHEM

Praça
Grécia

AV. BORGES DE MEDEIROS

AV. EPITÁCIO PESSOA

36 37
RUA PROF. ANTONIO MARIA TEIXEIRA

Jardim
de Alah

38

AV. ATAULFO DE PAIVA

RUA VISC. DE PIRAJÁ

AV. AFFRANIO

AV. ALM.

R
33

35

PEREIRA

DE MELO FRANCO

GUIMARÃES

IPANEMA

M 34

AV. GEN. SAN MARTIN

Praça Alm.
Belford Vieira

RUA PRUDENTE DE MORAIS

SEE MAP 5

RUA JOSÉ LINHARES

RUA CUPERTINO DURÃO

RUA CARLOS GÓIS

RUA ALM. GUILHEM

AV. DELFIM MOREIRA
AV. DELFIM MOREIRA

AV. VEIRA SOUTO
AV. VEIRA SOUTO

d e   L e b l o n

A T L A N T I C   O C E A N

0   100 yds
0   100 m

DISTANCE ACROSS MAP
Approximate: 1.2 mi or 1.9 km

*Parque Nacional
da Tijuca*

⊙ SIGHTS
1 PARQUE LAGE
16 ⓒ JARDIM BOTÂNICO
28 PLANETÁRIO
33 LAGOA RODRIGO DE FREITAS
37 PARQUE TOM JOBIM
38 PARQUE DA CATACUMBA
39 FUNDAÇÃO EVA KLÁBIN

® RESTAURANTS
2 OLYMPE
3 66 BISTRÔ
4 BRÁZ
5 MR. LAM
8 DA GRAÇA
11 QUADRIFOGLIO
13 ⓒ ROBERTA SUDBRACK
15 ESCOLA DO PÃO
21 BACALHAU DO REI

Ⓝ NIGHTLIFE
12 CAROLINE CAFÉ
14 SATURNINO
20 BRASEIRO DA GÁVEA
30 ⓒ 00
31 DRINK CAFÉ
35 ⓒ PALAPHITA KITCH
36 BAR LAGOA

Ⓐ ARTS AND LEISURE
18 ⓒ JÓQUEI CLUB
19 NIRVANA
22 GALERIA ANNA MARIA NIEMEYER
24 MERCEDES VIEGAS ARTE CONTEMPORÂNEA
25 ⓒ INSTITUTO MOREIRA SALLES (IMS)
29 GALPÃO DAS ARTES
32 ESTAÇÃO DO CORPO
34 RIO WAKE CENTER

Ⓢ SHOPS
6 ATELIÊ ALICE FELZENSZWALB
7 O SOL
9 DONA COISA
10 PARCERIA CARIOCA
17 BABILÔNIA FEIRA HYPE
23 SHOPPING DA GÁVEA

Ⓗ HOTELS
26 LA MAISON
27 GÁVEA TROPICAL BOUTIQUE HOTEL

JARDIM BOTÂNICO

RUA PERI

RUA PACHECO LEÃO

Jardim

Botânico

Jardim ⊙ Botânico 16

Ⓢ 17

RUA MAJ. RUBENS VAZ

Praça Santo Dumont
19 Ⓐ
20 Ⓝ

18 Ⓐ

Jóquei Club

22 23 Ⓐ Ⓢ
® 21

24 Ⓐ

To Museu Histórico da
Cidade do Rio de Janeiro

GÁVEA

RUA JOÃO BORGES

RUA MARQUES DE SÃO VICENTE

RUA VIA.... GOV. BERARDO....

RUA RODRIGO OCTÁVIO

MÁRIO RIBEIRO

Praça Ns. Auxiliadora

Planetário 28 ⊙
30 Ⓝ Ⓐ 29

Largo da Memória

LEBLON

ESTRADA SANTA MARINHA

25 Ⓐ

FRANÇA

LEONEL

RUA VISC. DE ALBUQUERQUE

RUA COCADA

RUA DIAS FERREIRA

Praça Antero de Quental

AV. PADRE LEONEL

AV. ATAÚLFO DE PAIVA

AV. GEN. SAN MARTIN

27 Ⓗ
26 Ⓗ

AV. DELFIM MOREIRA

0   400 yds
0   400 m

DISTANCE ACROSS MAP
Approximate: 1.1 mi or 1.7 km

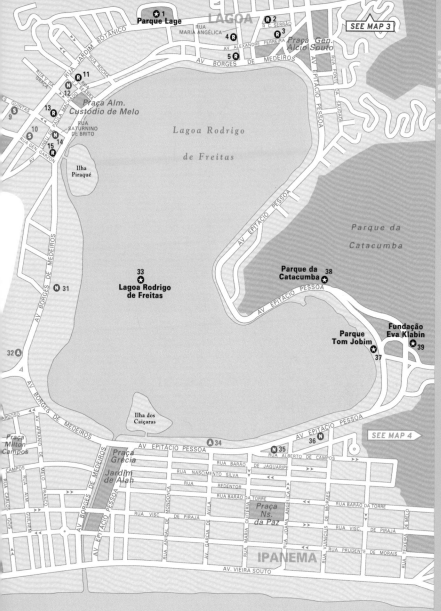

© AVALON TRAVEL

✪ SIGHTS

6	BOSQUE DA BARRA	14	PRAIA DO RECREIO
9	SÍTIO ROBERTO BURLE MARX	15	PRAIA DA BARRA DA TIJUCA
11	CASA DO PONTAL	18	PRAIA DO PEPÊ
12	PRAINHA AND PRAIA DE GRUMARI	21	PRAIA DO JOÁ

ℝ RESTAURANTS

3	QUINTA	7	ANTIQUARIUS GRILL
5	FIAMETTA	10	476

ⒶARTS AND LEISURE

1	PROJETO MERGULHAR	17	ESCOLA DE SURF RICO DE SOUZA
2	TRILHAS DO RIO	19	K-08 KITESURF CLUB
4	CITIBANK HALL	20	RIO WIND SURF

Ⓢ SHOPS

8	BARRA SHOPPING

Ⓗ HOTELS

13	RIO SURF N STAY	22	LA SUITE
16	SHERATON BARRA HOTEL AND SUITES		

ESTRADA

VARGEM GRANDE

Morro do Morro

3
ℝ RUA LUCIANO GALLET

RUA AGAPANTO

Camorim

Rio Centro

Autódromo Jacarepa

Lagoa de Jacarepa

ESTRADA DOS BANDEIRANTES

AV. O PALME

5
ℝ

AV. DAS AMÉRICAS

RECREIO

Parque Ecológico de Marapendi

ESTRADA BENVINDO DE NOVAIS

AV. AS DA SILVEIRA

Lagoa da Marapendi

AV. SALVADOR ALLENDE

To ✪9 Sítio Roberto Burle Marx
and ℝ10 476

AV. DAS AMÉRICAS

AV. GLAUCIO G.

Parque Ecológico Chico Mendes

AV. SERNAMBETIBA   AV. LUCIO COSTA

Casa do Pontal

11
✪

RUA OITO

13
Ⓗ

✪ 14
Praia do Recreio

AV ESTADO DA GUANABARA

12
✪

Prainha and Praia de Grumari

ATLANTIC

To **A**1 Projeto Mergulhar

RUA FRANCISCO SALES

A2

CIDADE DE DEUS

AV. DE JACAREPAGUÁ

ANIL

AV. GOV. CARLOS LACERDA

ESTRADA DOS BANDEIRANTES

URICICA

Morro da Panela

Morro do Pinheiro

AV. ENG. SOUSA FILHO

ITANHANGÁ

ESTRADA DAS FURNAS

ELARDO BUENO

A4 BARRA DA TIJUCA

AV. AYRTON SENNA

Clube da Aeronáutica/ Aeroporto de Jacarepaguá

Lagoa da Tijuca

Itanhangá Golf Club

ESTRADA DA BARRA DA TIJUCA

SEE MAP 9 ▷

Bosque da Barra

Barra Shopping

6 ★

7 **R** **S** 8

To Gávea and Vidigal

AV. DAS AMÉRICAS

Lagoa de Marapendi

AV. PREF. DULCIDO CARDOSO

TÚNEL DO JOÁ

AV. CANAL DE MARAPENDI

H 16

AV. MIN. IVAN LINS

JOÁ

AV. SERNAMBETIBA/ AV. LÚCIO COSTA

15

A 17

Praia da Barra da Tijuca

18 ★

A 19 **A** 20

AV. DO PEPÊ

22 **H**

21 ★

Praia do Pepê

Praia do Joá

OCEAN

0 ——————— 1 mi

0 ——————— 1 km

DISTANCE ACROSS MAP
Approximate: 14 mi or 23 km

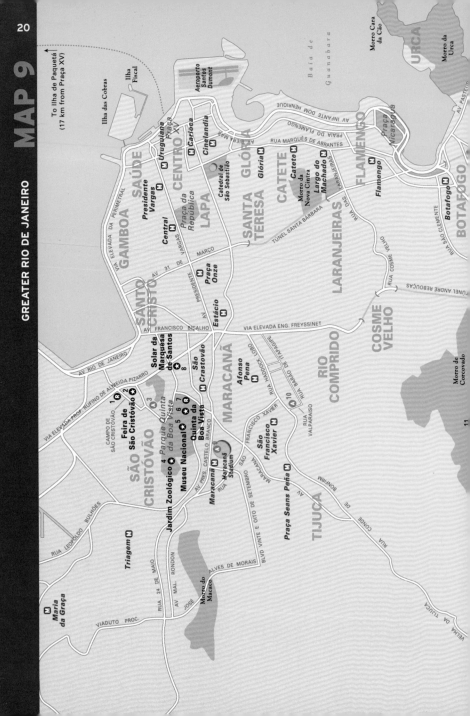

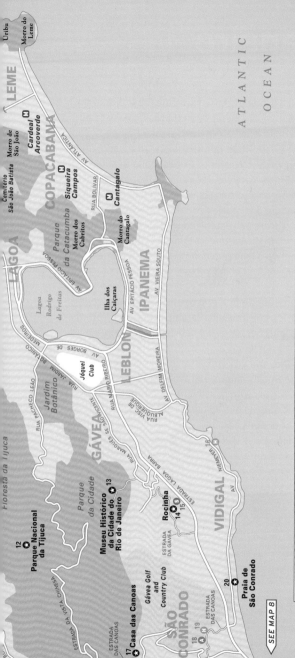

DISTANCE ACROSS MAP
Approximate: 8 mi or 13 km

0 — 1 mi
0 — 1 km

SIGHTS

2 FEIRA DE SÃO CRISTÓVÃO
4 JARDIM ZOOLÓGICO (RIOZOO)
5 MUSEU NACIONAL
6 QUINTA DA BOA VISTA
8 SOLAR DA MARQUESA DE SANTOS
11 MUSEU DO AÇUDE

12 PARQUE NACIONAL DA TIJUCA
13 MUSEU HISTÓRICO DA CIDADE DO RIO DE JANEIRO
14 ROCINHA
17 CASA DAS CANOAS
20 PRAIA DE SÃO CONRADO

7 QUINTA DA BOA VISTA

RESTAURANTS

1 ADEGÃO PORTUGUÊS

ARTS AND LEISURE

3 JEEP TOUR
9 MARACANÃ

10 COMPANHIA DA ESCALADA
18 SUPER FLY

SHOPS

15 SÃO CONRADO FASHION MALL

HOTELS

16 SHERATON RIO HOTEL AND TOWERS

19 FAVELA RECEPTIVA

SEE MAP 8

© AVALON TRAVEL

Discover
Rio de Janeiro

Rio de Janeiro is one of those rare cities that is so legendary, even if you've never been there, it's easy to automatically conjure up its postcard sights: Pão de Açúcar, the statue of Cristo Redentor atop lush Corcovado, and the sweeping white crescent of Copacabana beach.

Referred to by Cariocas (residents of Rio) as the Cidade Maravilhosa, Rio has an incomparable setting squeezed between the Baía de Guanabara and dramatic mountains covered in native Atlantic forest. Here you can take advantage of Rio's natural splendors by swimming, surfing, hang gliding, or hiking through the Parque Nacional da Tijuca. Or just simply sprawl on the beach and sip a lime *caipirinha* in the Zona Sul neighborhoods of Copacabana, Ipanema, or Leblon, all famed for their stunning white-sand beaches.

As a capital of the Portuguese empire and the first Brazilian republic, the city also boasts a glorious mishmash of architecture. Its Centro is a treasure trove of baroque churches, imperial palaces, and monumental buildings and squares.

Music is everywhere in Rio, and yes, there's even dancing in the streets, especially during the world-famous extravaganza known as Carnaval. Nighttime, especially, sizzles with possibilities. Join the throngs of music lovers in the historic *bairros* of Lapa and Santa Teresa to listen to live *chorinho, forró,* and, of course, samba.

Rivaling Rio's musical richness is the contagious *alegria* (joyfulness) of its inhabitants. Life flows to a different rhythm in Rio, and the *alegria* you'll find will leave you wanting more.

Planning Your Trip

▶ WHERE TO GO

Centro

Rio's historic downtown commercial district is a chaotic but intoxicating mixture of soaring high-rises and glorious remnants of the city's past. Cobblestoned alleys, baroque churches, and sweeping 19th-century boulevards flanked by belle epoque palaces pay homage to Rio's prestige as seat of the Brazilian empire and first capital of the republic.

Lapa

Nicknamed Rio's Montmartre, once-thriving Lapa spent most of the 20th century very down and out until *sambistas,* revelers, and night owls of all stripes resurrected this historic *bairro,* transforming it into bohemian central with the highest concentration of nightlife options in all of Rio. By day the narrow streets in the shadow of its iconic aqueduct, the Arcos da Lapa, are quiet and atmospheric; at night the neighborhood comes alive.

Santa Teresa

Perched on a hilltop above Centro, overlooking the Baía de Guanabara, the leafy, bucolic neighborhood of Santa Teresa is one of Rio's most charming, with winding cobblestoned streets, palatial manors, and the clang-clang of the beloved *bonde* (streetcar) shuttling residents and tourists up and down its hills. Long a haven of artists (and more recently, of expats), Rio's up-and-coming hood hasn't lost an iota of its original charm.

Glória and Catete

The formerly posh 19th-century residential

historic houses in downtown

bairros of Glória and Catete have lost their sheen, but their picturesque streets and squares and handful of historic monuments make them worth a visit. Particular highlights include the splendid hilltop Igreja Nossa Senhora da Glória do Outeiro and the Palácio da Catete, the former presidential palace, with its oasis-like park.

Flamengo and Laranjeiras

Sweeping in a grand arc along the Baía de Guanabara, Flamengo was Rio's most sophisticated address in the 19th and early 20th centuries, as evidenced by its tree-lined avenues lined with elegant belle epoque and art deco buildings. Still one of Rio's most elegant *bairros,* it boasts Carioca's most popular playground, the Parque do Flamengo, where you'll find the Museu de Arte Moderna and the Museu Carmen Miranda. Nearby, Laranjeiras is a lovely and largely unexplored residential neighborhood with some impressive architecture of its own.

IF YOU HAVE . . .

- **TWO DAYS:** Sprawl on the beaches of Copacabana and Ipanema, straddle the heights of Corcovado or Pão de Açúcar, stroll through the lush Jardim Botânico, and samba the night away in the bars of bohemian Lapa.

- **THREE DAYS:** Add the charming *bairro* Santa Teresa and the churches and museums of Centro.

- **ONE WEEK:** Add the Museu de Arte Moderna (MAM), shopping in Ipanema and Leblon, a bike ride around Lagoa Rodrigo de Freitas, a boat excursion around the Baía de Guanabara, hang gliding from Pedra Bonita, and a side trip to either Petrópolis, Búzios, or Paraty.

Botafogo, Cosme Velho, and Urca

Lively Botafogo is a bustling traditional Carioca neighborhood untouched by tourism with not much to see, but a fair amount to do. Adjacent Cosme Velho is an attractive residential neighborhood whose main claim to fame is being the access point for a ride up to the majestic heights of Corcovado. Overlooking the Baía de Guanabara, tiny Urca is also mainly residential, but its small cluster of streets sit in the imposing shadow of Pão de Açúcar.

Copacabana and Leme

Its mid-20th-century glamour days may be long gone, but the world's most legendary urban beach still seduces. Crowded Copa is Brazil's most densely populated neighborhood and the high-rise hotels along Avenida Atlântica's famous mosaic boardwalk keep rising. Tourism aside, Copa (and adjacent Leme) is incredibly vibrant and just plain fun. And no matter how crowded it gets, the 4.5-kilometer (3-mi) crescent of dazzling white sand backed by mountains is absolutely stunning.

Ipanema

Ipanema gave birth to the bossa nova, and decades later all the cool, sensual, easy-breezy hedonism associated with its languorous rhythms applies to this eternally hip and relaxed beach *bairro*. Ipanema's white-sand beach is one of the neighborhood's main

view of Pão de Açúcar from Praia do Flamengo

Praia do Arpoador in Ipanema

draws, but its shady side streets are rife with sophisticated boutiques, restaurants, bars, and cafés that keep Cariocas and foreigners entertained day and night.

Leblon

Although its beach—more popular with families than with hipsters—is essentially a continuation of Ipanema beach, Leblon has a style and attitude all its own. Separated from Ipanema by the evocatively named Jardim de Alah, Leblon is a little more chic and discrete than its bohemian neighbor, but no less charming. Its tranquil side streets are filled with cutting-edge boutiques and its bar and restaurant scene rivals (if not surpasses) that of Ipanema.

Gávea, Lagoa, and Jardim Botânico

This trio of upscale, largely residential neighborhoods may not have beach access, but all three are perched around the cobalt-blue Lagoa Rodrigo de Freitas, the playground of Zona Sul residents who religiously work out and kick back around its picturesque 7.5-kilometer (4.5-mi) shoreline. Guarding over

these *bairros* are dramatic mountains covered in the lush Floresta da Tijuca, whose exotic flora can be observed up close in the Jardim Botânico and the Parque Lage.

Barra da Tijuca and Recreio

In the Zona Oeste, the sprawling beach neighborhood of Barra da Tijuca (referred to as Barra) is an over-developed sprawl of condos, mega–shopping centers, and highways. Barra's saving grace is its long, wild, and windswept beach that attracts surfers and extreme-sports aficionados. An extension of Barra, Recreio dos Bandeirantes is equally popular but less developed. The furthest beaches, Prainha and Praia de Grumari, are gorgeously untamed.

Greater Rio de Janeiro

One of Rio's toniest neighborhoods is the tiny Zona Oeste enclave of São Conrado, whose luxury condos and hotels share breathtaking views with residents of neighboring Rocinha, Rio's largest *favela*. Residents of both can glimpse the Parque Nacional da Tijuca, an enormous swathe of native Atlantic forest. Rio's sprawling Zona Norte district also has

the colonial town of Paraty

its share of *favelas,* as well as the vast Parque Quinta da Boa Vista, the colorful Feira de São Cristóvão, and the headquarters of Rio's most traditional samba schools.

Excursions from Rio de Janeiro

Only an hour from Rio, Petrópolis is ideal for those who crave sophisticated amenities and majestic mountain scenery. Nearby, orchid-laced hiking trails wind through native Atlantic forest at the Parque Nacional Serra dos Órgãos. East of the city, the pulsating, upscale resort town of Búzios offers beautiful sandy beaches, with calm pools for snorkeling and big waves for surfers. South along the Costa Verde—named for the verdant mountains that provide a striking backdrop to the unspoiled beaches—highlights include the island paradise of Ilha Grande and the beautifully preserved colonial town of Paraty.

▶ WHEN TO GO

Due to its tropical climate, Rio makes a perfect escape at any time of year. High season—bracketed by the twin mega-*festas* of Réveillon (New Year's Eve) and Carnaval (Feb.–Mar.)—coincides with the Southern Hemisphere's summer (and Brazilians' vacations). If you come during this time, expect high prices, high temperatures, and lots of humidity. For either Carnaval or Réveillon, be aware that prices soar and advance reservations are a must. Summer is also the rainy season, but brief tropical downpours merely interrupt otherwise sunny weather. The winter months, particularly July and August, are characterized by longer rainy periods (of up to two or three days), which are often accompanied by strong winds and temperatures in the vicinity of 15°C (59°F). Otherwise, temperatures are quite moderate (25–30°C, 77–86°F).

Búzios is one of Rio's most stylish weekend getaways.

► BEFORE YOU GO

Passports and Visas

If your country requires Brazilians to have travel visas, you will have to get a visa from the nearest Brazilian consulate before entering Brazil. To date, citizens of Canada, the United States, and Australia require visas. Citizens of the United Kingdom (and other European Union countries) and New Zealand don't need visas, but do need a passport that is valid for six months and a return ticket. Upon arrival, they'll be given a 90-day tourist visa.

All visitors who arrive in Brazil and go through customs will receive an entry form, which you should *not* lose. You'll need to hand it back to the Polícia Federal when leaving the country. Should you want to extend your stay, you can renew your visa, 15 days before it expires, at the visa section of the Polícia Federal headquarters in any major city. The fee for renewal is the equivalent of US$10. If you overextend the 180-day limit, you won't be deported, but you will pay a fine.

Vaccinations

There are no necessary vaccines if you're visiting Rio. However, if you're going to be traveling around other parts of Brazil yellow fever is recommended, and in some cases, required. It is absolutely essential for visiting the Amazon region, but there have also been isolated, yet recent, occurrences in the Pantanal, Brasília, and even Minas Gerais and Bahia. Other recommended vaccines include hepatitis A, hepatitis B, typhoid, and rabies shots.

Transportation

The majority of visitors to Rio arrive by air at the Aeroporto Internacional Tom Jobim, also known as Galeão. International flights generally arrive in the morning, sometimes via São Paulo. A second small airport, Aeroporto Santos Dumont, located downtown, is mostly used by passengers taking the Rio–São Paulo air shuttle. Those traveling by cruise ship will dock downtown, at the terminal located in Centro.

If you're traveling by bus from other cities in Brazil or from Buenos Aires, or Montevideo, you'll arrive at the Rodoviária Novo Rio, Rio's main bus terminal, which is quite close to downtown. Bus service throughout Brazil is very extensive and the buses themselves range from decent (*ônibus comun*) to downright comfortable (*ônibus executivo* and *semi-leito*).

There are a lot of options for getting around the city itself. Rio has a very extensive and inexpensive public transportation system, consisting of an efficient Metrô and a bus system that boasts over 400 lines. Taxis are often the best way to get around Rio. Taxi service is reasonably priced and for specific trips you can often bargain a fixed price with your driver. Driving in the city itself is not recommended; renting a car only makes sense for excursions outside of the city.

Pão de Açúcar

Explore Rio de Janeiro

▶ THE BEST OF RIO

It's possible to experience a sampling of the best that Rio de Janeiro offers in a week. Rio's best is not just about sightseeing; it's about eating, drinking, swimming, samba-ing, adventure sports like hang gliding, and, most important of all, chilling out.

Day 1

After landing in Rio de Janeiro, go straight to your Zona Sul hotel, stash your bags, lather up with sunscreen, and recover from the long flight with a nap on Ipanema beach. Take refuge from the midday sun at one of the healthy per-kilo restaurants in Ipanema, such as Delírio Tropical or Líquido, and maybe do some boutique browsing.

In the mid-to-late afternoon, take a bus or taxi to Cosme Velho. Check out the art on display at the Museu Internacional de Arte Naïf and take a quick peek at the picturesque neo-colonial houses at the nearby Largo do Boticário before taking the train ride up to Corcovado for a view of Baía de Guanabara as the city lights come on.

Return to your hotel and then head out for a light but creative dinner at Zuka in Leblon. Stop off for a nightcap overlooking the sea at the romantic Bar d'Hotel, where the view will serve as a potent reminder that you really are in Rio.

Day 2

After breakfast at your hotel, hit the beach. Copacabana beach is lovely in the morning and walking all the way from Pedra do Leme to the Forte de Copacabana is a great workout, not to mention a fine excuse to ogle the diverse parade of humanity that frequents

Henrique Lage's palace courtyard at Parque Lage

this famous stretch of sand. When you feel the urge, stop for an *água de coco* (coconut water) or beer at a beach kiosk, or use your hunger as an excuse to check out the glorious Copacabana Palace—its Pérgula restaurant overlooking the pool serves a fabulous breakfast (and weekend brunch).

Those who save their appetite for lunch can hop a bus or cab to Jardim Botânico and indulge in a meal prepared by Roberta Sudbrack, one of Brazil's most creative chefs, at her eponymous, contemporary restaurant. Next, spend a couple of leisurely hours strolling beneath imperial palms at Jardim Botânico. Have a *cafezinho* and pastry at the park's café or walk a few blocks for coffee in the palatial courtyard café of the Escola de Artes Visuias, situated in the verdant Parque Lage. From here, it's only a shortish walk (or very quick cab ride) to the Lagoa Rodrigo

TOP 10 BEACHES

Life in Rio is inseparable from the city's many beaches, and you'll find strips of sand to suit your every whim. Here is a list of 10 beaches that you can count on to correspond with your mood and fulfill your desires – whatever they may be.

- If you feel like watching amazing pick-up soccer...head to **Praia do Flamengo,** where local teams play all day and all night in front of the iconic hump of Pão de Açúcar.

- For a more sedate scene...head to **Praia do Leme,** whose tranquil strip of sand is traditionally frequented by an older crowd as well as local families.

- If you feel like eating and drinking and watching the world go by...head to a kiosk bar on **Copacabana,** easily the most diverse and democratic of all Rio's beaches.

- If you're feeling sporty...head to **Praia do Pepê,** at the beginning of Praia da Barra, where you can surf, windsurf, and kitesurf on the waves or play volleyball, *futebol,* or *futevôlei* (a hybrid of both) in the sand.

- If you'd like to discover a secret hideaway... head to **Praia do Joá,** an exquisite and out-of-the-way little beach that is a favorite beach of Cariocas in the know.

- If you're feeling flirtatious (and you're straight)...head to "Coquierão," the strip of **Ipanema** beach surrounding **Posto 9** that is a magnet for artists, hipsters, and beautiful folk in general.

- If you're feeling flirtatious (and you're gay)...head to the strip of **Ipanema** beach surrounding **Posto 8** that is a magnet for gay men.

- For a nice family-friendly beach...head to **Leblon.** The area around Posto 12, known as "Baixo Bebê," has changing facilities as well as a playground for tots.

- For a non-touristy beach...head to Urca's bucolic and oft-overlooked **Praia Vermelha,** a lovely crescent of a beach in the shadow of Pão de Açúcar.

- If you want to get away from it all...head to the beautifully untamed beaches of **Prainha** and **Praia de Grumari** (although keep in mind that even these get crowded on summer weekends).

Ipanema beach

the elegant belle epoque Confeitaria Colombo

de Freitas and Parque dos Patins, where you can rent a bike and circle the entire lagoon. Once you've returned the bike, have a happy-hour drink at Palaphita Kitch, a lagoon-side lounge with an Amazonian ambience (and menu).

Since you're right behind Ipanema, consider dinner at Zazá Bistrô Tropical or the less expensive Alessandro e Frederico Café, followed by some light clubbing at Lounge 69.

Day 3

After getting in a quick hour of sun on the beach, as long as it's not the weekend (when downtown is dead) or Monday (when museums are closed), take a bus or Metrô to Cinelândia or Praça XV and spend the morning exploring the historic Centro. Wander the narrow streets around Rua Ouvidor and Arco do Telles, pop into baroque churches, and check out a couple of the scads of museums and cultural centers (top picks include the Paço Imperial, the Centro Cultural Banco do Brasil, and the Museu Nacional de Belas Artes). Don't forget to stop for a *cafezinho* at the belle epoque Confeitaria Colombo and step inside the Theatro Municipal for a guided tour of its opulent interior.

Have lunch at the Bistrô do Paço, and then take the *bonde* (tram) up to the hilltop neighborhood of Santa Teresa to visit the Museu Chácara do Céu. Wander the cobblestoned streets and linger in a traditional *botequim* such as Bar do Mineiro.

Dine on creative Brazilian fare at Aprazível and then take a minibus or cab down the hill to Lapa. Experience its famous bohemian nightlife at clubs such as Teatro Odisséia, Lapa 40°, and Carioca da Gema.

Day 4

Take a bus or cab to Urca. Climb the Pista Claudio Coutinho, a path that winds up towards Pão de Açúcar, and which you can manage without a guide. If you're feeling ambitious, scale the iconic hump itself, or else settle for taking the cable car to the summit.

Back down on solid land, spend some time chilling on Praia Vermelha before taking a bus or cab to nearby Parque do Flamengo. Have lunch with a view of the Baía de Guanabara at Laguiole, which is located in the Museu de Arte Moderna (MAM). After lunch check out the museum's Brazilian modern and contemporary art. Very close by is the Marina da Glória, from where boat tours of the Baía de Guanabara depart (Marlin Yacht's sunset tour is highly romantic).

Back on dry land, it's only a short bus or cab ride to Rua Voluntários da Pátria in Botafogo, lined with art-house cinemas such as Espaço Unibanco de Cinema and Estação Botafogo. If you're not in the mood to see a film, head straight to Miam Miam for Brazilian comfort food in a cool setting. Alternatively, you can skip the movie (and even dinner) and head to nearby Cobal do Humaitá, a lively market filled with restaurants and bars. Have a nightcap at the alternative club Casa da Matriz, which is also in Botafogo—but you'll need to take a cab there.

Day 5

After breakfast, take a bus or taxi to the Rodoviária Novo Rio, where buses depart every 20 minutes to Petrópolis, in the mountains an hour from Rio. Spend the day strolling around the imperial city and visiting attractions such as the Museu Imperial, Catedral de São Pedro de Alcântara, and the Casa de Santos Dumont. Pay homage to Petrópolis's regal past by treating yourself to lunch or a lavish high tea at the Museu Imperial's Bistro Petit Palais.

Return to Rio at the end of the day, and head to Copacabana for dinner at a traditional seafood restaurant such as O Caranguejo or Shirley. Afterwards, drop by Bip Bip to hear a live samba jam or Bossa Lounge for more mellow melodies. If you have energy for dancing, hop in a cab to check out Copa's alternative club scene. Both decades-old La Cueva and the more recent Fosfobox attract an eclectic GLS (gay, lesbian, and sympathizers) crowd.

Day 6

Your last full day in Rio should be spent doing what Rio is best known for: chilling out. Spend the morning on Copacabana or Ipanema beach working on your tan.

Since you can't leave town without having tasted the national dish, for lunch head to Ipanema's Casa da Feijoada to get your fill of beans and *caipirinhas*. For dessert, spring for a tropically flavored ice cream at Mil Frutas Café and/or a coffee at Armazém do Café. Hit the boutiques along Ipanema's Rua Visconde de Pirajá.

In the late afternoon, return to Ipanema beach. Nab a table at Azul Marinho in front of Praia do Arpoador and enjoy a cocktail and a seafood dish while you watch the sunset. Afterwards, should you feel like a last-night's nightcap in Ipanema, ensconce yourself in a sofa at the Fasano Al Mare's happening bar, Londra, or make a small trek up the street to Devassa, whose own microbrewery beer is considered the best in the city.

Day 7

Since most international flights leave in the early evening, it's best to spend your last day in relaxation and preparation mode. For a light lunch, head to Leblon for a healthy meal at the Zona Sul's high temple of *comida natural*, Celeiro. Reward yourself by indulging in a delicious pastry at Kurt or Talho Capixaba. Afterwards, take some time to wander around Leblon's pretty streets before heading back to your hotel to depart for the airport.

the art deco Edifício Itahy building in Copacabana

RIO ON THE CHEAP

Like any big city, Rio has its greasy spoons and seedy neighborhoods where you can get by on very little. The challenge to doing Rio on a budget is to find venues that have both cheap prices and charm. Taking the following recommendations into consideration will help you enjoy the city to the hilt without breaking the bank.

CHEAP DIGS

- Take advantage of the Rio's new outcrop of charming guesthouses, bed-and-breakfasts, and hostels, such as **The Maze Inn, Casa da Valeska, Stone of a Beach, Ipanema Beach House,** and **The Mango Tree.** Many hostels have nicely furnished double rooms that are cheaper and more homey than staying in a sub-standard hotel.

- Consider staying in **non-beach neighborhoods,** such as Santa Teresa, Flamengo, Cosme Velho, or Laranjeiras. These traditional *bairros* are attractive, historically interesting, and refreshingly untouristy. In Copacabana, Ipanema, and Leblon, consider staying off the beach.

CHEAP EATS

- Rio's many **per-kilo restaurants** allow you to eat as much or as little as you want, of whatever you want. Try **Estação República** and **Delírio Tropical.**

- If you're in **Centro,** many **museums** and **cultural centers,** such as **Paço Imperial, Casa França-Brasil, Centro Cultural dos Correios,** and **Museu de Arte Moderna (MAM),** boast cafés and/or bistros that have creative menus at reasonable prices.

- If you're in the **Zona Sul,** take advantage of the abundance of **juice bars.** Some of the best are **BB Lanches, Bibi Sucos,** and **Polis Sucos.** Aside from healthy (and filling) juices and *vitaminas*, most serve healthy (and filling) *sanduíches naturais.*

- Classic Rio bars, known as *botequins,* serve home-cooked daily lunch specials as well as a wide variety of delicious *petiscos*

fresh fruit for sale in the street

(appetizers), one or two portions of which can easily sub as a meal. Stop into **Casa Paladino, Bar do Serafim, Nova Capela, Bar do Mineiro, Bar Luiz,** or **Cervantes.**

- Many of Rio's top **gourmet restaurants,** including **Roberta Sudbrack, Gero,** and **Fasano Al Mare,** offer **weekday "executive" lunch menus** that are considerably less expensive than their regular dinner menus.

CHEAP ARTS AND ENTERTAINMENT

- Most of Rio's **museums and cultural centers are free** or cost next to nothing. Those that are privately operated almost always have a free admission day.

- If you plan to go **clubbing,** you can often get discounts on the cover charge by **arriving early** and/or by **showing up with a flyer,** which you can print from club websites or pick up in bars, fashion boutiques, and hostels around town.

- There are many places to hear great **live music** for free or next to nothing. Every Wednesday at noon, the **Teatro João Caetano** features top samba and *choro* performers for R$1, while the **Theatro Municipal** offers a lunchtime *meio-dia* (noon) opera series and Sunday-morning (11 A.M.) concerts for R$1.

► CARNAVAL PARTY PLANNER

Rio isn't the only Brazilian city to host Carnaval, but its signature parades, balls, and *escolas de sambas* (samba schools), combined with the non-stop merrymaking have made it one of the most spectacular festivals in the world. What visitors often don't know is that there are many ways to celebrate Carnaval aside from showing up at the Sambódromo. Private or public, tony or tacky, traditional or vanguard, diurnal, nocturnal, or 24 hours nonstop, there are Carnaval-esque festivities to suit every whim and budget.

The Sambódromo

The most famous Carnaval event consists of the *desfiles* (parades) of the top *escolas de samba* (known as the Grupo Especial, or Special Group). These take place in a massive concrete stadium called the Sambódromo. Designed by Oscar Niemeyer, it can seat 90,000 people. *Desfiles* are held on the Sunday and Monday nights of Carnaval (from 9 P.M. to 6 A.M.) and involve 14 *escolas de samba* that compete against each other.

On each night, the *escolas* have between 85 and 95 minutes to strut their stuff for a table of judges who award points for various aspects of their performances, among them choreography, costumes, floats, decorations, *samba de enredo* (theme song), and percussion. The final results are absolutely spectacular, a kaleidoscope of whirling and twirling sequins and feathers and gaudy, flamboyant color. If you miss the competition itself, on the following Saturday you can catch the eight top schools perform in the championship parade, which also takes place at the Sambódromo. In fact, tickets to this "best of" compilation event are much cheaper than those for the *desfiles*.

If you're not content merely being a spectator, you can join the parade as a full-fledged member of the *escola de samba*. Most samba schools allow foreigners to purchase their *fantasias* (costumes)—either via their websites or upon arrival—and join in the fun.

Street Carnaval

In recent years there has been a revival of the many neighborhood and resident association *blocos* and *bandas* that traditionally took to the streets and let loose in an explosion of music and merrymaking. Although *bloco*

escola de samba at the Sambódromo

Carnaval's main event is the *desfile* (parade) of Rio's traditional samba schools.

costumes aren't as ornate as those of the *escolas de samba,* some are highly inventive and downright hilarious. Many men—both gay and straight—dress in drag. If you want to join in the fun, all you have to do is appear at the *blocos* headquarters on the day and time of their parades. Check to see if you're expected to don the *bloco's* traditional colors or to purchase a T-shirt (sold on the spot). Festivities usually kick off in the afternoon and last far into the night.

Centro is home to some of the city's most traditional *blocos*. Among the most popular are Bafo de Onça; Bloco Cacique de Ramos, and Cordão do Bola Preta. Santa Teresa features the Carmelitas de Santa Teresa; Glória has the Banda da Glória; and Botafogo features Barbas, Bloco de Segunda, and Dois Pra Lá, Dois Prá Cá. Copa's most famous *bloco* is Bip Bip, many of whose members are professional musicians, while Ipanema has some of the most wildly alternative groups, among them Símpatia É Quase Amor, Banda de Ipanema, and the highly popular Banda Carmen Miranda.

The City of Rio also organizes outdoor shows and festivities. Rio Folia takes place around the Arcos da Lapa and features an eclectic alternative mixture of various Brazilian musical tendencies. Bailes de Cinelândia's outdoor *bailes* make an effort to revive Rio's traditional Carnaval balls of yore with a roster of top singers and samba bands animating crowds that often exceed 50,000.

Meanwhile, those who don't actually make it in to the Sambódromo needn't feel excluded, since right outside is a recently inaugurated open-air space known as Terreirão do Samba (or "Samba Land") where nightly samba performances are held, starting the weekend before Carnaval and continuing every night during the festivities. It's also here that the mega-*festa* on the Saturday following Carnaval is held, coinciding with the Parade of Champions in which the victorious samba schools do a repeat performance.

Carnaval Balls

The extravagant Carnaval balls of yesteryear are alive and well at Rio's clubs and hotels. Live samba bands supply the rhythms, and costumes are de rigueur. The most famous and fabulous event (costumes or formal wear required) is the Magic Ball held at the Copacabana Palace on Saturday night, which attracts an international throng of rich and gorgeous people, for whom R$1,500 (the average price of a ticket) is chump change.

Tickets to most other balls, however, are in a much more affordable range of R$30–50. Those held at the Scala club on every night during Carnaval are some of the wildest and most spectacular, culminating on the last night with the immensely popular Gala Gay. Many other clubs also organize *bailes* in which men can go all-out with their cross-dressing fantasies. Among the most legendary are those held nightly at Copacabana's famous gay club Le Boy.

Since the one thing Cariocas don't take lightly is Carnaval, no matter where you go, you'll be expected to show up in a seriously extravagant costume.

► NATURE LOVER'S RIO

What sets Rio apart from other great cities is its tropical climate and the fact that it's hemmed in between dazzling white-sand beaches and jungle-carpeted mountains. Whether you prefer to contemplate nature calmly or experience it in all its adrenaline-spiking intensity, Rio can satisfy all your outdoors desires. Mix and match options for radical relaxation and adventures depending on your mood, with healthy, organic eating options in between. Whether you decide to follow the path of least or most resistance, you'll come away feeling toned, healthy, refreshed, and rejuvenated.

Day 1

Start off your day with a leisurely walk along Ipanema beach. Buy an *água de coco* at any beachside kiosk and then get some sun. Have lunch in Ipanema, which has some great inexpensive organic restaurants, such as Líquido and Fontes. Or take a bus (or cab) to Leblon, where you can lunch at acclaimed organic eateries such as Celeiro or Universo Orgânico. If you're fond of natural beauty products, stop by Granado, a century-old pharmacy with its own line of natural products made from native fruits and flowers.

From Leblon, you're only a tunnel away from São Conrado. Take a taxi to the launchpad atop Pedra Bonita and then hang glide all the way down to Praia do Pepino. If you're not up to the adrenaline rush, hang out on Praia do Pepino and watch others commit folly, or continue along in the cab to secluded Praia do Joá (remembering to ask the driver to pick you up again).

Another alternative is to go straight from Leblon (by bus or cab) to Praia do Pepê at the beginning of Barra da Tijuca, where sports fans can indulge in an afternoon of surfing, windsurfing, kitesurfing, or *futevôlei*.

Return to the Zona Sul and have dinner at eclectic Zazá Bistrô Tropical.

Day 2

In the mood for some pampering? Take a bus or cab to the Jóquei Club in Gávea and spend

tropical flowers in bloom

the morning at Nirvana, where after taking a yoga, capoeira, or bio-gymnastics class you can get a massage or holistic treatment at the spa. After lunch at the on-site organic restaurant, get a taxi to travel via the Horto Florestal to Corcovado. Make sure you get the driver to stop at scenic lookout points such as the Vista Chinesa and the Mesa do Imperador before you arrive at the statue of the Cristo Redentor, where you're treated to a breathtaking view of the city. From here take the train down to Cosme Velho and, after checking out the bucolic Largo do Boticário, walk 30 minutes through the leafy *bairros* of Cosme Velho and Laranjeiras to Largo do Machado.

A more active alternative to this day is to sign up for a hiking or biking tour that takes you through the Parque Nacional da Tijuca, with stops for swimming in waterfalls and/or climbing of spectacular outcrops such as the Bico do Papagaio or the Pedra da Gávea.

No matter what you do, at the end of the day you won't be far (by taxi) from the bucolic *bairro* of Santa Teresa, where you can combine a short walk with dinner at Aprazível, which boasts a lovely garden and bewitching city views.

Day 3

To take advantage of this day's activities you'll need to rent a car or hire a taxi for the day. From the Zona Sul, drive west to the splendidly isolated beaches of Prainha and/or Praia de Grumari. Surfers will be in heaven, but the botanically inclined can take advantage of walking trails that weave through the conservation park of native *restinga* that backs both beaches. In order to have lunch at Quinta, an Arcadian eatery lost in the jungle that serves meals prepared with fresh, local ingredients, you'll have to make this trip between Friday and Sunday. A more rustic alternative (open Wed.–Sun.) is 476, which also boasts an impressive incredible natural setting.

After lunch, visit the Sítio Roberto Burle Marx, home of the famous artist and landscaper (advance reservations are necessary), before driving or taxiing back to Ipanema's Praça Nossa Senhora da Paz. From here, do some sustainable shopping; Maria Oiticica makes stunning jewelry out of polished Amazonian seeds, while Sementeira is a great place to pick up stylish beach and yoga attire made from natural fibers.

Perusing and purchasing done, you can walk to Praia do Arpoador. Grab a table at Azul Marinho and watch the sun set, and then stick around to feast on raw oysters, fresh crab, and other seafood specialties.

sunset on Ipanema beach

SIGHTS

Rio's setting is incomparable: The city is squeezed between the Baía de Guanabara and dramatic mountains covered in native Atlantic forest. Although this tropical metropolis of six million is both urban and urbane, every street seems to end in an explosion of towering green or a soothing slice of blue. And this 500-year-old city is hardly lacking in impressive architecture—Rio was not only the capital of the Brazilian empire, but, until 1960, of its republic as well. As a result, its downtown is a treasure trove of baroque churches, imperial palaces (many of which have been converted into cultural centers), and monumental buildings and squares. What's left of Rio's colonial past and most of its churches and museums are concentrated in its old downtown core, known as Centro.

However, you'll find plenty of vestiges of late 19th- and early 20th-century architecture in the bohemian neighborhoods of Lapa and hilltop Santa Teresa as well as the formerly grand but still bustling *bairros* of Glória, Catete, Flamengo, Botafogo, Laranjeiras, Urca, and Cosme Velho, the latter two home to the iconic landmarks Pão de Açúcar and Corcovado.

History—of a more recent variety—is also present in the Zona Sul neighborhoods of Copacabana, Ipanema, and Leblon; all three famed for the stunning white-sand beaches that serve as playgrounds for Cariocas and tourists from all walks of life. It was here that bossa nova was born and the bikini made its mark. Despite all the beautiful people, Zona Sul retains a relaxed casualness that is typical

© MICHAEL SOMMERS

SIGHTS

HIGHLIGHTS

LOOK FOR **🌑** TO FIND RECOMMENDED SIGHTS.

🌑 Most Lavish Baroque Church: Blindingly beautiful, the exquisitely sculpted altars and naves of the **Igreja da Ordem Terceira de São Francisco da Penitência** are slathered in 400 kilos (880 pounds) of pure gold (page 43).

🌑 Best Modern Museum: Aside from its quality exhibits and terrific collection of modern Brazilian art, the **Museu de Arte Moderna** (MAM) occupies a landmark modernist building by Affonso Eduardo Reidy with gardens landscaped by Burle Marx and a view of Baía de Guanabara. Equally cool are the museum's café and design shop (page 45).

🌑 Most Splendid Public Building: Modeled after Paris's Opéra Garnier, Rio's **Theatro Municipal** was built 100 years ago as the showpiece of the Haussman-inspired Centro of the Brazilian republic. To this day, it is Rio's premier theater (page 49).

🌑 Best Panoramic City View: There are many runners-up, but nothing equals the thrill of standing atop **Corcovado,** beneath the outstretched arms of the **Cristo Redentor,** and gazing out over the city (page 60).

🌑 Most Unforgettable Ride: Touristy? Yes. But nobody should turn down the chance to gasp at the breathtaking surroundings from the glass-sided cable car that travels up to **Pão de Açúcar** (page 62).

🌑 Most Spectacular Urban Beach: The gorgeous sweeping arc of sugary sand at **Praia de Copacabana,** a microcosm of Rio that offers proof that democracy is alive and well and getting a suntan (page 67).

🌑 Hippest Urban Beach: Stunning **Praia de Ipanema** isn't just filled with beautiful bronzed bodies modeling the latest (and skimpiest) in beachwear; it's the beach scene to end all beach scenes (page 70).

🌑 Best Natural Refuge: The 200-year-old **Jardim Botânico** offers welcome shade and respite amidst imperial palms, rare orchids, giant Amazonian lily pads, and carnivorous plants (page 72).

🌑 Worth the Trek: Brazil's most extensive, and absolutely fascinating, collection of popular folk art is on display at the **Casa do Pontal,** a sprawling house surrounded by bucolic gardens (page 75).

🌑 Best Get-Away-From-It-All Beaches: Framed by lushly carpeted mountains, the adjacent beaches of **Prainha and Praia de Grumari** offer few signs of civilization aside from wave-seeking *surfistas* (page 76).

🌑 Best Urban Jungle: Brazil's largest urban park, the **Parque Nacional da Tijuca,** consists of 3,200 hectares of lush, tropical jungle replete with hiking trails, lookout points, and refreshing waterfalls where you can stop for or a dip (page 81).

© CHRISTIAN KNEPPER/EMBRATUR

Cristo Redentor

of Rio. In addition to the beaches, shopping, restaurants, nightlife, and most hotels—as well as access to the Floresta da Tijuca forest—are all located in the more upscale Zona Sul neighborhoods, which also include Lagoa (surrounding the Lagoa Rodrigo de Freitas), Jardim Botânico (named after the famous botanical gardens), and Gávea. West of Gávea the newer middle-class beach neighborhoods of São Conrado, Barra da Tijuca, and Recreio dos Bandeirantes stretch along the coast for kilometers, mixing endless condos and shopping malls with wide stretches of beach popular with the surf set. The area north of Centro is known as the Zona Norte. This vast urban zone is a mixture of traditional working-class neighborhoods, commercial and industrial districts, and *favelas,* and encompasses the Rodoviária Novo Rio (bus station) and Aeroporto Internacional Tom Jobim (Galeão),

as well as the *bairro* of São Cristóvão and Maracanã soccer stadium.

Despite Rio's sprawl, getting around the Centro and Zona Sul neighborhoods, in particular, is fairly easy. An excellent Metrô service links the Zona Norte, Centro, Flamengo, Botafogo, and Copacabana, and an efficiently integrated Metrô–express bus service allows you to easily access other neighborhoods including Cosme Velho, Ipanema, Leblon, Gávea, Jardim Botânico, São Conrado, and Barra. Throughout the city, numerous buses run at all hours of the day (safe) and night (less safe depending on where you are). Walking is a wonderful way to explore the city. During the day it's quite safe to stroll around (with the exception of Centro on the weekends). At night more care should be taken, although most Zona Sul neighborhoods are quite bright and busy until at least 10 P.M.

Centro   Map 1

The Centro refers to Rio's historic downtown commercial district. Narrow cobblestoned alleys, grand baroque churches, turn-of-the-20th-century Parisian-inspired avenues and architecture, and the ubiquitous high-rises and urban chaos of a 21st-century megalopolis make up a bewildering if often fascinating patchwork. Although some areas are sorely neglected, many museums and cultural centers have opened or have been revamped as part of an effort to revitalize the area. Meanwhile, stylish bistros have joined some of the city's most traditional bars and cafés. As an antidote to the upscale beach culture of Zona Sul, pockets of the Centro are quite interesting, particularly if you want to get a sense of Rio's rich past.

Despite the traffic, navigating the area is quite easy on foot. Centro is also well served by buses from both the Zona Sul and Zona Norte (take anything marked Centro, Praça XV, or Praça Mauá) and by Metrô (the most convenient stations are Cinelândia, Carioca,

Uruguaiana, Presidente Vargas, and Praça Onze). Although during the day and into the early evening Centro is usually jam-packed, at night and on weekends the area is as quiet as a ghost town and quite unsafe to stroll around. If you're thinking of taking in an exhibition or performance during these times, it's best to take a taxi.

ARCO DO TELLES AND TRAVESSA DO COMÉRCIO
Praça XV de Novembro
Directly across Praça XV from the Paço Imperial, you'll notice an impressive stone arch (Arco do Telles) that marks the entrance to the Travessa do Comércio (also known as the Beco de Telles), a cobblestoned alley lined with rather elegant 19th-century buildings. The stone gateway was built in 1743 by the wealthy Telles de Menezes family as a covered passageway to connect two wings of the opulent family digs. Although the house burned down in a 1790 fire, the imposing

SIGHTS

© MICHAEL SOMMERS

Arco do Telles

Arco survived. Wandering down the Travessa do Comércio, the equally narrow and atmospheric Rua Visconde de Itaboraí, and Rua do Ouvidor allows you to get a sense of what Rio was like in the 18th and 19th centuries. Home to wealthy merchants and, later on, to beggars and prostitutes, these twisting cobblestoned streets today house a vibrant collection of traditional restaurants and bars (many of which have been around for decades) where workers from the neighborhood congregate for a quick lunch or an after-work beer or *caipirinha.* Of particular note is Rio Minho (Rua do Ouvidor 10), a Portuguese tavern dating back to 1884 that is Rio's oldest functioning restaurant. Also of historical interest is No. 13 Travessa do Comércio, where a discreet sign signals the childhood residence of one Maria do Carmo Miranda da Cunha, who would later adopt the stage name Carmen Miranda.

BIBLIOTECA NACIONAL
Av. Rio Branco 219, tel. 21/3095-3879 or 21/3095-3811, www.bn.br
HOURS: Mon.-Fri. 9 A.M.-8 P.M., Sat. 9 A.M.-3 P.M.
The largest library in Latin America, and the eighth-largest in the world, Rio's Biblioteca Nacional boasts some 13 million tomes—the first of which were brought to Brazil by Dom João VI in 1808. Completed in 1910, the building is an eclectic fusion of neoclassical and art nouveau styles. You don't have to be a serious bibliophile to opt for a guided tour (R$2) of the grandiose interior (tours weekdays at 11 A.M., 1 P.M., and 3 P.M.) with its glorious marble staircase flanked by a pair of motivational bronze statues representing intelligence and studiousness. Among the rare treasures in the library's collection are two first editions of Luis de Camões 1572 classic of Portuguese literature, *Os Lusíadas,* a pair of German Mainz Bibles, printed on parchment in 1462, and original correspondence of the Brazilian imperial family.

CIDADE DO SAMBA
Rua Rivadávia Correia 60, tel. 21/2213-2503, www.cidadedosambarj.globo.com
HOURS: Tues.-Sat. 10 A.M.-5 P.M.
COST: R$10
Inaugurated in 2005, Cidade do Samba is an inspired collaboration between Rio's City

IT HAPPENED IN RIO . . .

Many of the crucial moments in Brazil's 500-year-old history took place in Rio, refuge of the Portuguese monarchy, capital of the only empire in the Americas, and capital of the Brazilian republic. All of these key historic roles molded and shaped Rio and left their marks upon the city as did smaller but no less significant cultural events:

· In **1555,** the Portuguese began building Rio's oldest fortress, the **Fortaleza de Santa Cruz.** Constructed out of granite and whale oil, it guarded the entrance to the Baía de Guanabara and prevented Rio from becoming either a French or Dutch colony.

· In **1808,** having fled Napoleon's forces, Portuguese king Dom João VI installed his royal court and family at the stately 18th-century palace that subsequently became known as the **Paço Imperial.**

· In **1822,** Dom João VI's son and prince-regent, Pedro IV, became Pedro I, "Emperor and Perpetual Defender of Brazil," in a sumptuous coronation ceremony held at the equally sumptuous 18th-century baroque **Igreja Nossa Senhora do Carmo da Antiga Sé.**

· In **1889,** emperor Dom Pedro II threw Brazil's last and most lavish imperial ball at the splendid neo-gothic palace built on the **Ilha Fiscal.** Six days later, the Brazilian republic was proclaimed and the emperor went into exile.

· In **1894,** the opulent **Confeitaria Colombo** ushered in a new belle republican epoque. Politicians, intellectuals, and artists, including Ruy Barbosa and Heitor Villa-Lobos, flocked to the art nouveau café, still famed for its Portuguese pastries and *cafezinhos.*

· In **1909,** Rio's grand **Theatro Municipal** was inaugurated amidst much pomp. Modeled after Paris' Opéra Garnier, the grand theater was meant to be the centerpiece of the new Haussmann-inspired Centro. In its early

years, it attracted legendary performers such as Sarah Bernhardt, Isadora Duncan, and Nijinsky.

· In **1917,** Ernesto dos Santos, the grandson of slaves and a composer popularly known as Donga, created the first samba ever to be recorded, "Pelo Telefone." Donga performed it during the **Festa da Penha,** one of Rio's most popular *festas,* held in front of the colonial Igreja da Nossa Senhora da Penha.

· In **1923,** barely 30 years after the blasting of a tunnel through the mountains gave birth to the *bairro* of Copacabana, the **Copacabana Palace** was inaugurated. Modeled after the grand hotels of the French Riviera such as the Negresco and Ritz-Carlton, the gleaming art deco palace was touted as the most sumptuous hotel in South America. Its fame was a magnet for Carioca high society and millionaires and movie stars from around the globe and jump-started Copa's reign of glamour.

· In **1954,** president Getúlio Vargas shot himself in the bedroom of the **Palácio da Catete,** the official presidential residence located in a 19th-century palace in Catete. It's now home to the Museu da República, where you can visit the room where Vargas did the deed – the smoking revolver and the silk pajamas he was wearing are on display.

· In **1962,** Tom Jobim and Vinicius de Moraes were sitting outside at their favorite Ipanema bar when they saw a "tall and tan and young and lovely girl from Ipanema" walking by on the way to the beach. Obviously inspired, they right away set to work on the song that would take the world by storm and transformed the terms "bossa nova" and "Ipanema" into household words. In homage of the historic event, the Bar Veloso changed its name to **Garota de Ipanema.**

SIGHTS

Hall and Liesa, the league of samba schools, that aims to give the city's signature rhythm its due. A vast complex created out of abandoned dockside warehouses, "Samba City" functions both as an industrial workshop and a tourist attraction. In terms of the former, the fourteen Grupo Especial *escolas* have ample space to store materials, sew costumes, and build their magnificent *carros alegóricos* (floats). If you visit between November and Carnaval, you can prowl around on a metal catwalk suspended over the ateliers and watch the schools' master artisans at work. In the center of the complex, an outdoor courtyard exhibits elaborate costumes from Carnavals of yore, shelters snack bars and boutiques hawking Carnaval paraphernalia, and features live performances both during the day, and more spectacularly on Thursday nights, when samba schools take turns strutting their stuff for tourists during a combined show and buffet that costs R$150. Since this area is only starting to undergo revitalization, make sure you take a taxi here.

CINELÂNDIA
Praça Floriano and Av. Rio Branco
One of Centro's main thoroughfares is Avenida Rio Branco. Turn-of-the-20th-century photos reveal it to be a grand European-style avenue flanked with imposing neoclassical buildings and shaded by a canopy of trees. It was here that the city's artists, intellectuals, and fashionable elite came to promenade. Originally called Avenida Central, it cut a swatch of modernity through the labyrinth of crumbling mansions, flophouses, and brothels that had dominated the district since colonial times. Although most of this traffic-laden avenue has been disfigured by ugly modern high-rises, the stretch that opens up onto the monumental Praça Floriano has retained many of its magnificent buildings, among them the Theatro Municipal, the Biblioteca Nacional, and the Museu Nacional de Belas Artes—an architectural ensemble that reveals how grand Rio must have been in the early 20th century. Due

to the presence of the old Câmara Municipal (City Hall) on its northwestern edge, the Praça has also historically been the congregating point for protest marches and political manifestations.

The area encompassing Praça Floriano is known as Cinelândia: In the 1920s, there were ambitious plans to turn this elegant plaza into a Carioca version of Broadway—only instead of theaters, movie palaces were built, including Rio's first cinemas. Only one of these glamorous deco palaces is still intact—the Cine Odeon BR—while the rest were snatched up by churches such as the Igreja Universal de Deus (Universal Kingdom of God). The many cafés scattered around Praça Floriano still draw an eclectic mixture of Cariocas who drop by during happy hour. The most famous of them all, Amarelinho, dates back to the 1920s.

CONVENTO E IGREJA DE SANTO ANTÔNIO
Largo da Carioca, tel. 21/2262-0129
HOURS: Mon. and Wed.-Fri. 8 A.M.-6:30 P.M., Tues. 6:30 A.M.-7:30 P.M., Sat. 8-11 A.M. and 4-6 P.M., Sun. 9-11 A.M.
COST: Free
Built in the early 1600s to house Franciscan monks, the convent and church devoted to Santo Antônio constitute one of Rio's oldest surviving buildings. Although most of the church has been modified over the years, you can admire some baroque works and a splendid sacristy panel of blue and white Portuguese azulejos (ceramic tiles) illustrating the life of Santo Antônio. Although its picturesque hilltop perch lends the church a majestic authority, there are definitely more impressive and intact examples of baroque religious architecture you can gape at while trolling around Centro, starting with the neighboring Igreja da Ordem Terceira de São Francisco da Penitência. The convent has many original paintings, sculptures, and ceramic azulejos, but to see them you'll have to make an appointment.

ESPAÇO CULTURAL DA MARINHA
Av. Alfred Agache, tel. 21/2233-9165,
www.mar.mil.br/dphdm/ecm/ecm.htm
HOURS: Tues.-Sun. noon–5 P.M.
COST: Free

Along the waterfront in Rio's former customs house, the Navy Cultural Center will definitely appeal to boating buffs and fans of maritime history. On display are detailed models of all kinds of Brazilian seafaring crafts—from picturesque *jangadas,* the iconic wooden sailboats still ubiquitous along the coastlines of the Brazilian Northeast, to the elegant royal barge used to transport the imperial family around the Baía de Guanabara. Kids, in particular, will have fun clambering about on the World War II–era torpedo destroyer and a cool 1970s submarine, both moored outside the main building. Meanwhile, landlubbers can pore over antique maps and gape at oodles of buried treasure rescued from sunken ships in the Baía de Gaunabara. Boat tours to the Ilha Fiscal depart from the quay in front of the Espaço Cultural.

◖ IGREJA DA ORDEM TERCEIRA DE SÃO FRANCISCO DA PENITÊNCIA
Largo da Carioca 5, tel. 21/2262-0197
HOURS: Tues.-Fri. 9 A.M.–noon and 1-4 P.M.
COST: R$2

Far more impressive than the Convento and Igreja de Santo Antônio next door is the interior of this church, which is one of Rio's most sumptuous baroque jewels. You're sure to be blinded by the sheer amount of pure gold on display—400 kilos (880 pounds), to be precise. While the church itself took 115 years to build (construction began in 1657), the last 30 years were almost exclusively dedicated to covering the beautifully sculpted cedar altars and naves in gold. A pioneering example of Brazilian baroque, the Igreja de São Francisco set the standard for churches to come. Its architect, Francisco Xavier de Brito, was a major influence on Aleijadinho (The Little Cripple), the genius mulatto sculptor from Minas Gerais whose work adorns the churches of his home

state's colonial gold-mining towns, and who is considered Brazil's greatest baroque artist. The rich ceiling frescoes glorifying Saint Francis of Assisi were painted by Caetano Costa Coelho and mark one of the earliest instances of perspective painting in Brazil. If you're not a big church fan, but want to get at least a glimpse of the singular style that is Brazilian baroque, this is the church to see.

IGREJA DO MOSTEIRO DE SÃO BENTO
Rua Dom Geraldo 68, tel. 21/2291-7122,
www.osb.org.br
HOURS: Daily 8-11 A.M. and 2:30-6 P.M.
COST: Free

Located north of Praça Mauá, Rio's most magnificent example of baroque architecture, this 17th-century monastery devoted to Nossa Senhora de Montserrat crowns the Morro de São Bento. The austere facade masks a startlingly lavish interior featuring delicately carved naves and columns, altars embellished with flocks of expressive angels, and cherubs covered in gold dust. Instead of being blindingly ostentatious, the excessive gold has a warm and burnished hue, the result of soft lighting used to preserve the precious artwork (which include some exceptionally fine sculpted saints and painted panels). On Sunday morning you can take part in the 10 A.M. mass in which the Benedictine monks chant Gregorian hymns accompanied by the church organ. Make sure you arrive early if you want a seat. The oasis-like cloisters can only be viewed on special occasions such as Palm Sunday and Corpus Christi. At other times, the monks have the leafy courtyard all to themselves. Access to the monastery is via an elevator located at Rua Dom Geraldo 40.

IGREJA NOSSA SENHORA DA CANDELÁRIA
Praça Pio X, tel. 21/2233-2324
HOURS: Mon.-Fri. 7:30 A.M.-4 P.M., Sat. 8 A.M.-noon, Sun. 9 A.M.-1 P.M.
COST: Free

Rio's most famous church is located on the site

© MICHAEL SOMMERS

Igreja Nossa Senhora da Candelária

of the city's first chapel, built in the 16th century. Begun in 1775, the present church took over 100 years to complete, which accounts for its eclectic mixture of baroque, renaissance, and neoclassical elements. The interior is filled with a splendid and multihued array of marble, along with decorative elements such as doors made from finely wrought bronze. Ceiling panels recount the legend of the original church's construction by a shipwrecked captain whose life was miraculously saved. Although not one of Rio's most attractive churches, it is the largest and most celebrity infested; it is aggressively sought after by Rio's rich and famous bent on receiving all the pomp and paparazzi they dream of on their wedding day.

IGREJA NOSSA SENHORA DO CARMO DA ANTIGA SÉ

Rua Sete de Setembro 15, tel. 21/2242-7766
HOURS: Church Mon.-Fri. 7 A.M.-4 P.M., Sat.-Sun.
10 A.M.-2 P.M.; museum Mon.-Fri. 11 A.M.-3 P.M., Sat.-Sun.
10 A.M.-2 P.M.
COST: Church free, museum R$8
Completed in 1761, this baroque church served

as Rio's royal chapel as well as the city's principal cathedral until 1977. Many of the city's major religious commemorations—including Emperor Pedro I's coronation and the baptisms and marriages of Emperor Pedro II—were celebrated here. Although the exterior retains little of its original facade, the interior is a rococo feast, with altars richly decorated in silver and a splendid panel of Nossa Senhora do Carmo that was returned to all its original splendor after a major overhaul completed in 2008. To take in the full effect of its riches, time your visit to coincide with the sound and light show (Mon.–Fri. 1:30 and 5:30 P.M., Sat.–Sun. 10 A.M. and 1 P.M., R$5). Next door, the **Igreja da Ordem Terceira do Carmo** (Rua Primeiro de Março, tel. 21/2242-4828, Mon.–Fri. 8 A.M.–4 P.M., Sat. 8 A.M.–noon) also boasts a resplendent baroque interior with the requisite slatherings of gold and panels rendered in blue and white Portuguese azulejos. In the main altar, observe Christ's seldom-depicted great-grandmother, Saint Emerenciana, shown with her daughter Anne, granddaughter, Mary, and of course, the infant Jesus.

ILHA DE PAQUETÁ

Baía de Guanabara, 17 km by boat from Praça XV, www.ilhadepaqueta.com.br
COST: R$4.50 regular ferry (R$9.50 on weekends), R$17 catamaran
Located in the Baía de Guanabara, the small Ilha de Paquetá has been a favorite Carioca getaway since Dom João VI began coming here in the early 19th century. He was responsible for building the Capela de São Roque, around which the lively five-day Festival de São Roque takes places in August. On most weekends and holidays the island is routinely packed with families from the Zona Norte who crowd the (polluted) beaches and seaside bars. If you do want to take a dip, the cleanest of the island's 11 beaches are supposedly Praia da Moreninha, Praia da Imbuca, and Praia de José Bonifácio, where you can stop for lunch or ice cream at the century-old Hotel Lido (tel. 21/3397-0182, www.hotellido.portalpaqueta.com.br). During the week, though, the

island makes for a relaxing day trip, particularly during the off-season. Tranquility reigns and the slightly dilapidated colonial buildings retain their allure—albeit slightly faded. Although much of the original Mata Atlântica (native Atlantic rainforest) that once covered the island was decimated by aristocratic landowners of the 18th and 19th centuries who cultivated fruit and timber, patches of lush greenery still remain. Since no vehicles are allowed, you can easily (and cheaply) rent a bike and pedal around. For a more old-fashioned, albeit touristy, means of transportation you can hire a horse and buggy (R$40 for an hour tour). The trip in itself is worthwhile for the splendid views of Rio and the bay. Ferries (tel. 0800/4004-3113, www.barcassa.com.br) leave at two-hour intervals daily 7 A.M.–11 P.M. from the Estaçáo das Barcas at Praça XV de Novembro. The trip takes a little over an hour. If you're in a hurry, speedy but less picturesque catamarans (tel. 0800/4004-3113, www.barcassa.com.br) will get you there in half the time, with several departures and returns a day (although in 2008 service was temporarily suspended). Maps and information are available at the Paqueturi kiosk (daily 11 A.M.–5 P.M.) opposite the ferry terminal.

ILHA FISCAL

Av. Alfredo Agache, tel. 21/2233-9165

HOURS: Thurs.-Sun. 1, 2:30, and 4 P.M. (tours depart from Espaço Cultural da Marinha)

COST: R$8 adult, R$4 senior and student

From the waterfront, behind Praça XV, lie the Ilha das Cobras and the Ilha Fiscal. Originally known as the Ilha dos Ratos (Island of Rats) due to the fact that numerous rats sought refuge here from the snakes that inhabited neighboring Ilha das Cobras (Island of Snakes), Ilha Fiscal's welcome name change came about in the 19th century when the Finance Ministry lobbied the emperor for the right to build a customs house on the island. The result, dreamed up by engineer Adolpho José del Vecchio, was a neo-gothic castle straight out of a medieval fairy tale. Actually, del Vecchio's somewhat arcane inspiration for the domed

and turreted pistachio-hued palace were the 14th-century castles of the French province of Auvergne. Indeed, the extravagant edifice guarding the Baía de Guanabara enchanted Cariocas, among them Dom Pedro II, who described it as a "delicate jewel box." The emperor was on hand to inaugurate the building in early 1889 and, shortly after, in November, he hosted there what would go down in history as Brazil's last and greatest imperial ball. Over 5,000 lavishly dressed guests descended upon the island. They waltzed and polka-ed the night away while indulging in exotic delicacies, imported wines, and other appetite-assuaging activities—the discovery of intimate apparel strewn haphazardly around the island caused a great deal of salacious commentary in the press. The ball was an imperial swan song—six days later, the Brazilian republic was proclaimed and, from the same quays that had whisked Dom Pedro II to the Ilha Fiscal, the emperor now set sail to Europe.

In 1913, Ilha Fiscal was handed over to the navy (which had coveted the island from the beginning), which administers the island to this day. After extensive restoration work completed in 2001, the castle is as dazzling (and more pistachio-hued) than ever. Guided tours (by boat or van across the causeway) last around two hours and leave from the Espaço Cultural da Marinha. Highlights include the English stained-glass windows featuring portraits of Dom Pedro II and his wife, Isabel, and the Ceremonial Wing, where a dining room and salon outfitted in period furnishings conjure up the grandeur of the last ball. On weekends, tours easily get booked up; try to buy your tickets in advance.

◼ MUSEU DE ARTE MODERNA

Av. Infante Dom Henrique 85, tel. 21/2240-4944, www.mamrio.com.br

HOURS: Tues.-Fri. noon-6 P.M., Sat.-Sun. noon-7 P.M.

COST: R$5 adult, free child under 12

Housed in a stunning modernist steel, concrete, and glass creation overlooking the Baía de Guanabara, the Museu de Arte Moderna (MAM) was completed in 1958 and is considered to be architect Affonso Eduardo Reidy's masterpiece. Its elegant ensemble houses one of Brazil's most interesting and important collections of 20th-century art. A smattering of pieces by international artists such as Brancusi, Henry Moore, and Xul Solar commingle with key works by leading national figures such as Anita Malfatti, Tarsila do Amaral, Lasar Segall, Emiliano Di Cavalcanti, Candido Portinari, Ivan Serpa, and Antônio Dias, many of which were donated by Gilberto Chateaubriand, a wealthy Maecenas and Brazil's largest private art collector. A visit here is highly recommended if you want to get a grip on modern and contemporary Brazilian art—the fact that the works are showcased in such an extravagantly spacious venue (often quite empty) with such scenic surroundings enhances the experience considerably. Aside from hosting some quality temporary exhibits, the museum also has a cinematheque that screens art films, a great design store, and a bright and attractive café with a great collection of international magazines. For a bona fide meal, tuck into the elegant fare served at Laguiole.

MUSEU HISTÓRICO NACIONAL

Praça Marechal Âncora, tel. 21/2550-9260, www.museuhistoriconacional.com.br
HOURS: Tues.-Fri. 10 A.M.-5:30 P.M., Sat.-Sun. 2-6 P.M.
COST: R$6 adult, R$3 senior and student

This sprawling museum occupies three historic buildings: the 17th-century Forte de Santiago, an 18th-century arsenal, and an ammunitions depot. As such, there is ample space to showcase the 250,000 artifacts on display, ranging from carriages to canyons. Amidst this vast collection are some truly precious objects, like the pen that Princesa Isabel used to sign the Abolition of Slavery in 1888. There are also marvelous glass vials and medicine bottles from the imperial pharmacy, Emperor Dom Pedro II's throne (and a chess set owned by his father, Pedro I), and the largest coin collection in Latin America. The reorganized and spruced-up collection does a fine job of illustrating Brazil's rich history, dating from the

© MICHAEL SOMMERS

Paço Imperial

arrival of the first Europeans in 1500 to the declaration of the republic in 1889. If you're looking for an introduction to Brazil's past, a visit to this museum is highly recommended.

MUSEU NACIONAL DE BELAS ARTES
Av. Rio Branco 199, tel. 21/2240-0068,
www.mnba.gov.br
HOURS: Tues.-Fri. 10 A.M.-6 P.M., Sat.-Sun. noon-5 P.M.
COST: R$4 adult Tues.-Sat., free adult Sun., free senior and child under 12 Tues.-Sun.

Built in 1908, this neoclassical temple devoted to art originally housed Rio's national school of fine arts, before being converted into a somewhat somber and stodgy old-school European museum by Getúlio Vargas in 1937. It has a modest collection of European works, but you should really focus your attention on the national collection, which provides an excellent overview of Brazilian painting. The collection of 19th-century works is particularly strong and features artists such as Victor Meireles and Pedro Américo, who painted Brazilian historical events with epic flair and drama. More unusual and original for foreigners are the early- to mid-20th-century painters who, departing from European influences, experimented with new and distinctly Brazilian styles and subject matter. Among those represented are Anita Malfatti, Candido Portinari, Lasar Segall, and Alfredo Volpi. There is also an interesting gallery displaying Brazilian folk art, and the museum hosts traveling exhibitions as well.

PAÇO IMPERIAL
Praça XV de Novembro 48, tel. 21/2533-4491,
www.pacoimperial.com.br
HOURS: Tues.-Sun. noon-6 P.M.
COST: Free

Built in 1743, the stately bleached-white Paço (Palácio) Imperial originally served as a residence for Portugal's colonial viceroys and governors. It then housed the Portuguese court itself when Dom João VI fled Napoleon's forces in 1808. When the royal palace moved north to the Palácio da Quinta da Boa Vista (today the Museu Nacional), the Paço Imperial continued to host receptions and events. Today,

its cool and cavernous rooms house interesting temporary exhibits of contemporary art. Overlooking the internal courtyard is a lovely café-bistro, the Bistrô do Paço, and the more sophisticated Atrium restaurant as well as the Livraria Imperial, a used bookstore; Arlequim, a CD store specializing in jazz, classical, and MPB (Música Popular Brasiliero, i.e. classic Brazilian pop music), and a small cinema that shows independent and repertory films.

PALÁCIO GUSTAVO CAPANEMA
Rua da Imprensa 16, tel. 21/2220-1490
HOURS: Mon.-Fri. 9 A.M.-3 P.M.
COST: Free

One of Rio's most iconic modernist landmarks, the Palácio Gustavo Capanema has an impeccable pedigree. Built between 1937 and 1943, the architectural team in charge of its execution was led by Lúcio Costa and Oscar Niemeyer (in his first commission), the talented brains who dreamed up the space-age capital of Brasília, and Affonso Eduardo Reidy, who would later design Rio's remarkable Museu de

© MICHAEL SOMMERS

Palácio Gustavo Capanema

Arte Moderna. The entire proceedings were watched over by none other than the Swiss-French modernist guru Le Corbusier, who served as a consultant. Constructed to house the Ministry of Education and Health, the building is sustained by a handful of slender columns that mirror the smooth trunks of imperial palms surrounding the building. The offices on the 2nd floor maintain their fabulous original furnishings—conical lamps, carpets patterned with futuristic swirls, streamlined leather chairs, and gorgeously un-officelike colors such as pumpkin and eggplant—but can only be visited by appointment since they are currently government offices. You can, however, admire Roberto Burle Marx's gardens, the curvaceous sculptures of Bruno Giorgi, and the marvelous blue-and-white azulejo panels executed by artist Candido Portinari. On the ground floor, you can also check out temporary art exhibits and poke into the Livraria Mário de Andrade that specializes in books by and about Brazilian authors and artists.

PALÁCIO ITAMARATY

Av. Marechal Floriano 196, tel. 21/2223-1284 or 21/2263-2828 (museum)
HOURS: Mon.-Fri. 10 A.M.-5 P.M., advance reservations needed for museum tours
COST: Free

Not far from Central Station, the lovely pink neoclassical building known as the Palácio Itamaraty seems out of place amidst the high-rises and zooming traffic along Avenida Vargas. Built by the Baron of Itamaraty in the 1850s, the palace was purchased in 1889 by the new republican government and served as the official residence for Brazil's first presidents: Marechal Deodoro, Floriano Peixoto, and Prudente de Moraes. In 1899, it was transformed into the Ministry of Foreign Affairs and for decades diplomats and ambassadors glided around its polished parquet corridors and imbibed cocktails at the elegant parties hosted in the courtyard garden with its mirrored pool and rows of slender imperial palms. Today, while it still functions as an outpost of Brasília's main ministry office, the palace also contains a variety

of interesting treasures shared by the Arquivo Histórico, with its collection of rare diplomatic letters and documents; the Mapoteca, featuring thousands of globes, atlases, and maps of Brazil dating back to the 16th century (the oldest of which are adorned with highly fantastical illustrations of sea monsters, noble savages, and Edenic landscapes); and the Museu Histórico e Diplomático, with an eclectic array of historical artifacts and decorative arts ranging from the expressive depictions of life in 19th-century Rio by the famed French engraver Jean-Baptiste Debret to period furniture and knickknacks belonging to the Itamaraty and imperial families. Museum tours are available in English.

PALÁCIO TIRADENTES

Rua 1ero de Março, tel. 21/2588-1251
HOURS: Mon.-Sat. 10 A.M.-7 P.M., Sun. noon-5 P.M.
COST: Free guided tours

Built on the site of Rio's old city jail, this imposing neoclassical edifice topped by a grand dome and accessorized with somber statues representing Independence and Republic was constructed in the early 1920s to house the

© MICHAEL SOMMERS

main entrance of the Palácio Tiradentes

National Assembly. Deputies congregated here from 1930 until the capital moved to Brasília in 1960, although during the days of the Vargas dictatorship the assembly was shut down and the building served as headquarters for the Department of Propaganda. These days, it is occupied by Rio's State Legislative Assembly. Political-history buffs might want to tour the palace with guides (who speak English as well as Portuguese). There are some interesting period photos, but all the text is in Portuguese. During the week, you can venture up to the 2nd floor and peer down at the politicos at work (or not). The stained-glass windows in the giant overhead skylight depict the city skies exactly as they were at 9:15 P.M. on November 15, 1889—the precise moment at which the Brazilian republic was declared. As for the palace's name, it pays homage to Brazilian independence hero Tiradentes, who was jailed here prior to his execution in 1792 and who is represented by the wildly bearded statue located at the entrance. Take a free guided tour or feel free to check out the palace on your own.

PRAÇA XV DE NOVEMBRO

Btwn. Rua 1ero de Março and Av. Alfredo Lagache

Historically, Praça XV comprised the symbolic heart of Centro, and since most buses pass by this large plaza it's a practical starting point to exploring the surrounding neighborhood. The *praça* itself is surrounded by some of the Centro's most important historical monuments, including the Palácio Tiradentes, the Igreja de Nossa Senhora do Monte do Carmo, and the former royal palace, the Paço Imperial, for which the plaza served as a large public patio (it was originally known as the Largo do Paço). At the far end, along the waterfront, is the Estação de Barcas (formerly the main city passenger docks) where you can catch a boat to Niterói or Ilha de Paquetá.

The square's full name, Praça XV de Novembro, refers to November 15, 1899, the day upon which Brazil's first president, Marechal Deodoro de Fonseca, stood and declared Brazil to be a republic. Since then, countless significant historical events have taken place here—among them the crowning of Brazil's two emperors, Pedro I and Pedro II, and the abolition of slavery in 1888. On Thursday and Friday a colorful street market fills the square with vendors hawking everything from food and handicrafts to antique stamps and coins. The unusual pyramid-capped well, hewn out of marble and granite, dates back to 1789 and is the work of Mestre Valentim, the mulatto son of a Portuguese diamond merchant and an African slave. Considered one of the foremost sculptors and wood carvers in colonial Brazil, he executed many public commissions in the city.

REAL GABINETE PORTUGUÊS DE LEITURA

Rua Luís de Camões 30, tel. 21/2221-3138, www.realgabinete.com.br

HOURS: Mon.-Fri. 9 A.M.–6 P.M.

COST: Free

Even if you don't read Portuguese, you'll still be bowled over by the Royal Portuguese reading room, which dates back to 1837. The unusual facade with its stylized sailors' knots, seashells, and Moorish motifs are typical of Manueline style, which was popular in Portugal during the reign of Manuel I (1495–1521), but is rarely seen elsewhere. Inside is one of the largest libraries of works in the Portuguese language. It's worth taking a peek at the stunning reading room with its jacaranda tables, 23 meter-high ceiling crowned with a stained-glass window skylight, and seemingly endless polished wood bookshelves reminiscent of a medieval library.

◖ THEATRO MUNICIPAL

Praça Floriano, tel. 21/2299-1677, www.theatromunicipal.rj.gov.br

HOURS: Mon.-Fri. 1-5 P.M., tours depart every hour

COST: Tours R$10 adult, free senior and child under 5

If, when you first set eyes upon the Theatro Municipal, you immediately think of Paris, it's probably because this splendid theater was modeled after Paris's Opéra Garnier. Meant to be a showpiece of the ultra-modern Haussman-inspired Centro of the brand-new republic,

SIGHTS

© MICHAEL SOMMERS

reading room of the Real Gabinete Português de Leitura

the theater was designed by Francisco Pereira Passos, son of Rio's ambitious mayor Francisco Pereira Passos (yes, there were charges of nepotism when he won the commission) and French architect Albert Guilbert. Its choice location was selected so that one could gaze out at the Baía de Guanabara from the majestic staircase (a privilege since thwarted by the erection of high-rises that block the view).

Since its inauguration in 1909, Brazil's premier theater has played host to some of the world's most prestigious orchestras, opera, dance, and theater companies as well as legends such as Sarah Bernhardt, Isadora Duncan, Nijinsky, Maria Callas, Caruso, and Stravinsky. The interior is a sumptuous feast of marble, bronze, and gold with ample glitter provided

by gilded mirrors and crystal chandeliers. Onyx banisters line the grand marble staircase and there are some wonderful mosaic frescoes and stained-glass windows. Decidedly, the most exotic feature is Assírio, a restaurant (no longer in operation) that is straight out of a tale from *One Thousand and One Nights*. Located in the basement, it has an over-the-top Cecil B. de Mille decor with Pompeii-style mosaic floors, walls covered in glossy 3-D enamel frescoes of pseudo Babylonian, Egyptian, and Persian motifs, and a ceiling supported by stone pillars topped with bull's heads. The only way to see the theater is to see a show or take a guided tour. If you're without the time or inclination to take in a performance, take the guided tour (it's best to reserve in advance).

Lapa

Map 1

One of Rio's most traditional and notorious neighborhoods, Lapa has had many incarnations. It was originally a beach (known as the Spanish Sands) before being paved over and made into a rather posh 19th-century residential neighborhood. The Passeio Público evokes what Lapa must have been like when it was still a swank *bairro* where well-to-do families strolled beneath the shady trees of this elegant park.

By the turn of the 20th century, Lapa's fortunes had declined. Middle-class families migrated south and a colorful collection of gangsters, tricksters, low-lifes, prostitutes, bohemians, and *sambistas* started moving in. They created a wildly bohemian underground scene that become the stuff of Carioca legend. During the 1930s, Lapa was not unlike New York's Harlem. However, as the century wore on, its buildings became increasingly dilapidated and disreputable and crime escalated. Until the late 1990s, the neighborhood was very down-and-out. Then, unexpectedly, a renaissance began to take hold of Lapa. Nightly samba jams were held beneath the arches of Lapa's colonial aqueduct. A row of antiques stores opened along the Rua do Lavradio. Inspired by Barcelona's Gaudí, a Chilean artist named Selarón began covering a steep 215-step staircase to the neighborhood of Santa Tereza with a bright mosaic of ceramic plate fragments (many sent to him from all four corners of the globe). But most of all, Lapa became famous for its intensely vibrant nightlife, where Cariocas from all walks of life congregate to eat, drink, and dance the night away.

Although Lapa's fortunes have recently taken a turn for the better, it is still somewhat seedy around the edges. During the day it's quiet, even a bit deserted in places. At night, although its main streets are teeming with people, it's potentially dodgy if you don't take care (and cabs). Nonetheless, it's a wonderfully atmospheric slice of old Rio that shouldn't be missed.

ARCOS DA LAPA

Near Av. Mem de Sá

Lapa's most iconic landmark is the Arcos da Lapa, a distinctly Roman 42-arch aqueduct constructed during the 18th century. Originally known as the Aqueduto da Carioca, the Arcos was built in order to resolve the problem of Rio's chronically poor water supply. Linking the Morro de Santa Teresa with the Morro de Santo Antônio (where the Catedral Metropolitana now stands), the aqueduct carried freshwater from the Rio Carioca to the residents of Centro, who gathered at the great well at Largo de Carioca with their buckets and basins. In 1896, the Arcos got a new lease on life as a viaduct over which *bondes* (trams) travel, providing transport to the elegant hillside neighborhood of Santa Teresa. The arches also play an integral role in Lapa's famed nightlife; beneath them *sambistas* hold court, jamming the night away as revelers strut their stuff.

CATEDRAL METROPOLITANA

Av. República de Chile 245, tel. 21/2240-2669, www.catedral.com.br

HOURS: Daily 7:30 A.M.–5:30 P.M.

COST: Free, museum R$2

You can spot this soaring 75-meter-high (246-foot) cone-shaped pyramid from quite a distance. Built between 1964 and 1976, the Catedral Metropolitana took over the role of Rio's municipal cathedral from the 18th-century Nossa Senhora do Carmo da Antiga Sé in 1979. While it's a bit raw and *Brave New World*–like on the outside, the interior's sense of spaciousness coupled with pared-down minimalism is conducive to contemplation (to wit: of the 20,000 souls that have the capacity to fill this church). If you visit on a sunny day, you'll be bewitched by the psychedelic patterns of gold, green, blue, and yellow that are refracted through the four immense stained-glass windows. A small Museu de Arte Sacra includes objects such as the baptismal fonts used to christen the emperors' offspring and the gold roses Princesa Isabel received from Pope Leo XII after abolishing slavery.

ESCADARIA SELARÓN
Rua Joaquim Silva at the corner of Rua Teotônio Regadas, www.selaron.net

This surreal and dramatic Gaudí-esque staircase is the inspired and ongoing work of Chilean artist Jorge Selarón, who after traveling the world decided to settle in Rio in 1983. Rising from Lapa's Rua Joaquim Silva all the way up to the Convento de Santa Teresa, the 250 steps are covered with fragments of mirrors and azulejos, or colored tiles, which have been gathered by the artist from over 60 countries as well as from garbage dumps and construction sites around Rio. When he first began this project in the early '90s, Selarón meant to honor the Brazilian people with his use of the national colors, green, yellow, and blue. However, as the years have passed he has amplified his chromatic scheme significantly, incorporating dishes, tiles, and ceramics sent to him by eager collaborators from all over the world. Moreover, whenever the staircase is "finished," Selarón begins reworking it, claiming that his obsessive oeuvre will only end on the day of his death (although lately he has

also begun paving a new area at the foot of the Arcos da Lapa).

PASSEIO PÚBLICO
Rua do Passeio Público
HOURS: Daily 7:30 A.M.–9 P.M.

The Passeio Público evokes Lapa's initial incarnation as a fashionably upscale neighborhood. Originally the site of a lake, the subsequent landfill was made into a European-style park at the behest of Governor Vasconcelos e Sousa, supposedly in order to gain the affections of a fetching young girl who lived in the neighborhood. The design was carried out by master planner and sculptor Mestre Valentim, whose surviving works include a granite obelisk and the *Chafariz dos Jacarés*, a fountain decorated with bronze alligators. (Subsequent alterations were carried out in the 1860s by noted French landscaper Auguste Glaziou.) Completed in 1783, the Passeio was Rio's first public leisure area, an elegant oasis for well-to-do families to while away an afternoon in the shade. At that time, the Aterro de Flamengo had not yet been built and the Baía de Guanabara came right up to its edges. In recent decades, the park has suffered some poorly planned interventions and the gardens have become somewhat dilapidated.

Santa Teresa   Map 2

It would be a shame to come to Rio de Janeiro and not visit the utterly charming, bucolic hilltop neighborhood of Santa Teresa, one of the city's oldest residential *bairros*. In the 19th century, wealthy Cariocas built gracious villas along its narrow winding streets, with terraces and balconies overlooking the lush green mountains and blue waters of the Baía de Guanabara. The views are still alluring—as is the neighborhood, which is why after a long period of decline many artists began to move in, snatching up the dilapidated villas for a song and transforming them into ateliers and galleries. After an initial revival in the 1960s

and '70s, a second revitalization began to take place in 2005, resulting in the trickling in of boutique hotels and fashionable bistros as well as improved security (surrounded by *favelas,* Santa Teresa has traditionally had a somewhat dodgy reputation, particularly at night).

Thanks to efforts spearheaded by neighborhood artists, Santa Teresa has gradually evolved into a vibrant community. Many small-scale artistic and musical events take place in "Santa" on a regular basis. Among the most popular is an event known as Portas Abertas (www.viavasanta.com.br). Held twice a year—on weekends in May and November—Santa Teresa's "Open

Doors" event involves over 100 resident artists, who literally open the doors to their homes and studios so you can view their work (and their often fantastic living spaces).

The easiest, and by far most diverting, way to get to Santa Teresa is to hop aboard the old-fashioned *bonde* (trolley) that clangs its way up the hills from Centro. *Bondes* leave from the Estação Carioca (Rua Professor Lélio Gama, tel. 21/2240-5709, departures every 20 minutes daily 6 A.M.–10 P.M., R$1), located near the Carioca Metrô station. The ride itself is wonderfully scenic; the *bonde* passes over the Arcos da Lapa before climbing up the steep hills of Santa Teresa, continuing until it finally clatters to a halt at the charming Largo dos Guimarães. Although security on the open-sided *bondes* has been beefed up due to numerous thefts, you'll want to keep visible valuables to a minimum.

MUSEU CHÁCARA DO CÉU

Rua Murtinho Nobre 93, tel. 21/2507-1932, www.museuscastromaya.com.br

HOURS: Wed.-Sun. noon-5 P.M.
COST: R$2 adult Thurs.-Sun., free adult Wed., free senior and child under 12 Wed.-Sun.

The Museu Chácara do Céu is one of Rio's most lovely museums. Surrounded by a beautiful hilltop garden designed by noted landscaper Roberto Burle Marx, the museum is located in a very attractive modernist house commissioned in 1957 by Raymundo Castro Maya, a wealthy business magnate with a great eye for art. His impressive private collection includes the works of some fine Brazilian masters, such as Alberto Guignard, Emiliano Di Cavalcanti, and Candido Portinari. Also exhibited are sketches and paintings of Brazil created by visiting Europeans, most notably Jean-Baptiste Debret, a French painter whose watercolors portray 19th-century Cariocas from all walks of life. The international collection, which mingles ancient Chinese ceramics with European masters, took a serious hit during Carnaval 2006, when thieves entered the museum and made off with a Monet, Picasso, Matisse, and Dalí in broad daylight.

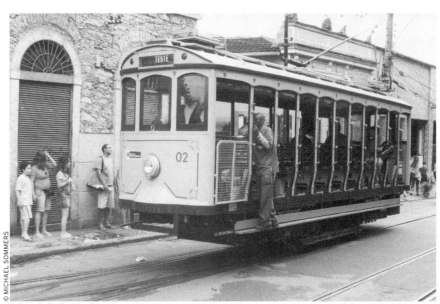

© MICHAEL SOMMERS

a *bonde* in Santa Teresa

FAVELAS

One of Rio's and Brazil's most complex and pervasive social phenomena, *favelas* are far more complicated than their inadequate English translation "slums" would suggest. The first *favelas* in Rio de Janeiro developed in the late 1890s. The federal government had offered land to demobilized soldiers from Northeastern Brazil so that they could settle on Rio's vacant slopes. When the government went back on its word, the soldiers occupied the promised land and baptized it Morro da Favela – *favela* is a tough thorny plant native to the semi-arid Northeast. Subsequent *favelados* were freed slaves who immigrated to Rio in search of work and settled on the hillsides surrounding Centro and the wealthier commercial and residential *bairros*. Rio grew, and so did its *favelas*, as poor Brazilians from all over the country migrated to the city in the hopes of finding work. Today Rio has over 600 *favelas*, which are home to between 20 and 25 percent of the city's population. Unfortunately, they are growing at a much faster rate than the rest of the city.

Rio's *favelas* are notorious for several reasons. The first is their proximity to Rio's most upscale neighborhoods. The largest ones are almost literally perched right on top of the wealthiest Zona Sul *bairros* (ironically, this means that *favela* residents enjoy far more privileged views than their rich neighbors below). There is also the fact that most are controlled by cocaine cartels, with twofold results. On one hand, the drug lords maintain order and security within the *favela* in return for residents' loyalty. However, other consequences include easy access to drug use and to drug dealing as a way of life, as well as the violent shoot-outs between drug lords and the police who frequently invade the hillsides. Tragically, innocent victims getting caught in the crossfire is a common occurrence.

Some *favelas* are utterly desolate places where entire families live in miniscule shacks cobbled together out of scrap materials, without electricity, running water, or sewage systems. Built precariously on steep hills, homes are easily destroyed – and residents injured or killed – due to rainstorms and landslides. However, over time, quite a few *favelas* have developed into highly organized communities with day care, medical clinics, and even Internet cafés and DVD rentals. Residents are not all destitute. Many have (low-paying) jobs in the surrounding neighborhoods and live in concrete or cinder-block houses (some of them 2–3 stories high) with fridges, stoves, TVs, and air-conditioners. More importantly, they enjoy a sense of community spirit and engage in grassroots activism.

Historically, the government treated *favelas* as blighted areas (they weren't even indicated on maps) and the elite and middle-class guiltily ignored them (while employing many *favela* dwellers as nannies, cooks, and housekeepers). However, in the last two decades, as it's been recognized that *favelas* won't go away, this thinking has shifted significantly. Projects such as Favela Bairro have been instrumental in helping to begin integration of these communities into the city's urban fabric. *Favelas* are increasingly included on city maps and *favelados* are being given legal titles to their property.

More recently, *favelas* have also started attracting tourists, who are curious to see firsthand how Brazil's very significant other half lives. While it's dangerous to wander alone into a *favela*, tours are available with guides who know the lay of the land. Several companies have jumped on the *favela* tour bandwagon, but the most experienced and knowledgeable is **Favela Tour** run by Carioca Marcelo Armstrong. Although some might be scared of potential danger or leery of the

© MICHAEL SOMMERS

favelas are part of Rio's urban tapestry

voyeuristic aspects of touring a poor neighborhood, Armstrong is well-known within the communities. He vouches for both visitors' safety and the fact that residents appreciate foreigners getting a firsthand glimpse at a neighborhood that is about much more than the reductionist clichés of drugs, violence, and poverty. Furthermore, aside from the tours pumping some money into the local community, if *favelas* become more of a tourist destination then police will be forced to diminish their often aggressive behavior towards *favela* residents.

Indeed, *favela* tourism seems to be on this rise. Aside from offering trips into Rocinha

with local English-speaking *motoboys* (delivery boys on motorcycles), **Be a Local** also takes visitors to *favela* parties where they can dance the night away to the pounding strains of local funk. In the last couple of years, even *favela* accommodations have caught on. Perched above Catete, British artist Bill Nadkarn operates the **Maze Inn,** a popular bed-and-breakfast whose labyrinthine architecture blends into the surrounding *favela* of Tavares Bastos, while **Favela Receptiva** organizes lodgings with residents of Vila Canoas and Vila da Pedra Bonita, two *favelas* overlooking the luxurious *bairro* of São Conrado.

MUSEU DO BONDE
Rua Carlos Brandt 14, tel. 21/2242-2354
HOURS: Daily 9 A.M.-4:30 P.M.
COST: Free

Just around the corner from Largo dos Guimarães, in an old depot, is this small museum devoted to Santa Teresa's iconic *bondes* (whose name comes from the public bonds sold to pay for them). Old tickets, conductors' uniforms, and models of *bondes* past—including the original donkey-driven vehicles—are worth a quick glance. For many residents of Santa these trams constitute an important link to Rio proper, and their welfare is sacred: Emotions run high when rumors of privatization occasionally surface. Moreover, prototypes of new and improved *bondes* are viewed with suspicion, despite the fact that their modern mechanical systems will be hidden beneath the traditional *bonde* shell that has been declared historic patrimony.

PARQUE DAS RUINAS
Rua Murtinho Nobre 169, tel. 21/2252-1039
HOURS: Tues.-Sun. 8 A.M.-8 P.M.

Adjacent to the Museu Chácara do Céu is this small leafy park, built around the atmospheric ruins of a palace that belonged to Laurinda Santos Lobo, a wealthy and notoriously elegant Carioca who was a generous patron of the arts during the early 1900s and held legendary literary salons. Using lots of glass and iron, the palace's vestiges have been ingeniously transformed into a cultural center that features art exhibits, musical performances, and other cultural happenings (including magic shows for kids). A small café offers magnificent views of Pão de Açúcar and Corcovado.

Glória and Catete   Map 2

In the mid-19th century, the neighborhoods of Glória and Catete were considered outskirts of Rio. Their proximity to Centro and the Baía de Guanabara lured Rio's burgeoning upper-middle classes, and they remained fashionable addresses until the mid-20th century. Since then the area has lost much of its luster, but Catete in particular is quite lively, with lots of local bars and restaurants as well as a handful of interesting sights.

IGREJA NOSSA SENHORA DA GLÓRIA DO OUTEIRO
Praça Nossa Senhora da Glória, tel. 21/2225-2869, www.outeirodagloria.org.br
HOURS: Mon.-Fri. 9 A.M.-noon and 1-5 P.M.,
Sat.-Sun. 8 A.M.-noon
COST: Free, museum R$2

The *bairro* Glória is named after the dazzling white Igreja Nossa Senhora da Glória do Outeiro, which is perched dramatically atop the Morro da Glória. Visiting the church involves a steep climb up the Ladeira da Glória or a less exhausting ride up the restored 1940s funicular (whose access is at Rua do Russell 300). This early baroque church (built between 1714 and 1739) is one of the most stunning in Rio, and a personal favorite of the Brazilian royal family (many princes and princesses were baptized here). Boasting an unusual octagonal shape, the interior is adorned with marvelous blue-and-white Portuguese azulejo panels of Biblical scenes by reputed artist Mestre Valentim. If the church is closed, you can ask for the keys at the **Museu da Imperial Irmandade de Nossa Senhora da Glória** (on Praça Nossa Senhora da Glória in the annex of the church, tel. 21/2557-4600, Mon.–Fri. 9 A.M.–5 P.M., Sat.–Sun. 9 A.M.–1 P.M.), a small museum with religious art, ex votos, and some personal belongings of the Empress Tereza Cristina. Note the unusually slapstick work of French artist Félix Émile Taunay, who painted a portrait of Dom Pedro II falling off his horse.

MUSEU DE FOLCLORE EDISON CARNEIRO

Rua do Catete 181, tel. 21/2285-0441,
www.museudofolclore.com.br
HOURS: Tues.-Fri. 11 A.M.-6 P.M., Sat.-Sun. 3-6 P.M.
COST: R$2 adult Thurs.-Sun., free adult Wed., free
senior and child under 12 Tues.-Sun.

Adjacent to the Palácio do Catete, this modest-sized museum possesses an interesting collection of Brazilian folk art and artifacts that gives you a sense of a traditional day-in-the-life in various regions throughout Brazil. Objects on display are organized according to themes such as daily life, religion, popular *festas*, work, and art and include exhibits such as life-size reproductions of a *casa de farinha* (manioc flour mill) from the Amazonian state of Pará and a typical Northeastern marketplace. Aside from the permanent collection, there are frequent temporary exhibits. Among some of the major figures whose work can be glimpsed are Mestre Vitalino, from the arid interior of Pernambuco, who excelled at disarmingly expressive clay miniatures of people and scenes from the Northeastern Sertão; Nhô Caboclo, also from Pernambuco, renowned for his highly imaginative sculptures fashioned out of wood, scrap metal, and other found objects; and Bahian-born Waldomiro de Deus, one of Brazil's most prolific and original *naif* painters. After viewing the ingenious works on display, you'll be hard-pressed not to take away a souvenir from the small gift shop.

PALÁCIO DO CATETE

Rua do Catete 153, tel. 21/2558-6350,
www.museudarepublica.org.br
HOURS: Tues.-Fri., Sat.-Sun. 2-6 P.M.
COST: Free, museum R$6 but free Wed. and Sun.

Upon the proclamation of the Brazilian republic in 1889, the new government was in sudden need of an administrative palace. Instead of building one from scratch, it was decided to purchase a (very grand) one that already existed on Rua do Catete, which had been built in 1858 by the Baron of Nova Friburgo, a rich coffee magnate and imperial crony with extravagant taste. Henceforth, the palace—also known as the Palácio das Águias in reference to the five brooding bronze *águias* (eagles) perched atop its facade—became the official residence of Brazil's presidents. It remained so until 1960, when president number 18, Juscelino Kubitschek, moved the capital to Brasília.

Kubitschek was also responsible for transforming his opulent former digs into the **Museu da República.** A more or less interesting collection of presidential photos, documents, and objects (the presidential dinner service is pretty fab) as well as sumptuous furnishings conjure up the history of republican Rio. The highlight is the apartment where president Getúlio Vargas lived—and died. Seemingly frozen in time from the day he shot himself in 1954, it features the smoking revolver along with his silk striped pajamas with the fatal bullet hole. In spite (or because of) the morbid aspect, it is one of the Rio sights most visited by Brazilians. The palace itself, with its stained-glass windows, shiny parquet floors, and lavish marble fixtures, is quite grand and definitely worth a gape. In the Salão Nobre, classical music concerts are held every Wednesday at noon (invitations are available one hour before). The Palácio also shelters a small bookstore and an art-house cinema.

PARQUE DO CATETE

Rua do Catete 153
HOURS: Daily 8 A.M.-9 P.M.

Surrounding the Palácio do Catete and extending all the way from the Rua do Catete down to the Praia do Flamengo, the very elegant Parque do Catete is an oasis of green decked out with imperial palms, cascades and fish ponds, and serpentine paths designed by French landscaper Paul Villon. Providing welcome shade are a host of native fruit trees including mango, carambola (star fruit), tamarind, and avocado. The grounds include an exhibition space, a theater, and a small café. Various cultural events are often held here, including a photography fair that takes places the last Sunday of every month.

Flamengo and Laranjeiras   Map 2

Stretching along the Baía de Guanabara from Centro to the tunnel that leads to Copacabana is the sprawling and attractive *bairro* of Flamengo. In the 19th and early 20th centuries, it was one of Rio's most posh residential neighborhoods. To this day, many of the wide avenues and tree-lined side streets still conserve an impressive number of gracious belle epoque mansions and elegant art deco apartment buildings, some of which housed foreign embassies back in the day when Rio was still Brazil's capital. In the mid-20th century, Rio's rich and fashionable elite began to abandon the area for the newly minted glamour of the Zona Sul.

Squeezed between Flamengo, Catete, and Cosme Velho is the equally lovely *bairro* of Laranjeiras, whose name attests to its rural origins when orchards of "orange trees" reigned. Although there are few specific sights to be seen there, Laranjeiras is one of Rio's oldest, and most charming, neighborhoods.

While you'll undoubtedly glimpse snatches of Flamengo (and adjacent Botafogo) as you're careening back and forth between Centro and the Zona Sul, its worthwhile to wander the area's streets if you have time to spare. Less chaotic than Centro and far less touristy than the Zona Sul, these neighborhoods offer an appealing and colorful slice of Carioca life. Apart from numerous traditional bars and restaurants, the area has a few sights that are worth checking out and shelters one of Rio's most extensive and popular recreational spaces, the Parque do Flamengo.

PALÁCIO DAS LARANJEIRAS AND PARQUE GUINLE

Rua Paulo César de Andrade 407, tel. 21/2299-5689

HOURS: Palace Tours Tues. and Thurs. 2 and 3 P.M. (reserve in advance)

COST: Free

Overlooked by most tourists (and many Cariocas), this grandiose hilltop palace was built at the beginning of the 20th century by local scion Eduardo Guinle. Subsequently known as the Palácio das Laranjeiras, today it serves as the state governor's residence. As such, if you want to traipse around the lavishly upholstered apartments you'll need to make an appointment. The original palace park, known as Parque Guinle (whose main entrance is from Rua Gago Coutinho), was designed by French landscaper Gochet and its winding walkways, swan-dotted lagoons, and ornate wrought-iron gates guarded by sphinxes, winged lions, and cherubs add a touch of European charm to the tropical shrubbery that was planted by Roberto Burle Marx in the early 1950s. The fabulous modernist apartment complexes overlooking the park area were also designed at this time by Le Corbusier disciple Lúcio Costa (who later planned Brasília). Aside from the slender pillars upholding the structures, the most notable features are the geometrically patterned ceramic sunshades tinted coral pink, lemony yellow, and baby blue. To this day, the lusted-after apartments cost an arm and a leg. Cool and refreshing, the park itself is quite safe due to the presence of palace security guards.

PARQUE DO FLAMENGO

Av. Infante Dom Henrique

In 1960, much of Flamengo's beach disappeared beneath tons of earth. This radical landfill was part of an ambitious project to create a vast public park on prime oceanfront real estate. Extending from the Aeroporto Santos Dumont all the way to the Praia de Botafogo, to this day Parque do Flamengo is often referred to as Aterro do Flamengo—the Flamengo Landfill (barely anyone remembers that the park's official name is Parque Brigadeiro Eduardo Gomes). Spearheading this massive undertaking was a formidable woman named Maria Carlota de Macedo Soares. A vanguard intellectual from one of Rio's most traditional families, "Lota" was the lover of American poet Elizabeth Bishop (who, at the time, lived with Lota in Rio). A great fan of modernism and a self-taught architect, Lota sought out the talents

© MICHAEL SOMMERS

exterior of the Museu de Arte Moderna (MAM) in Parque do Flamengo

feature an abundance of native species from all over Brazil (a radical concept at the time). In terms of palm trees alone, there are more than 4,400 representing 50 species, among them the rare *Corypha umbraculifera,* which flowers just once and then promptly dies (many bit the dust in 2004). She also insisted the park have all-night lighting so that Cariocas could take refreshing nighttime strolls or play a nocturnal game of soccer or tennis.

Today this sweeping ribbon of green is Rio's most popular playground. It contains running, cycling, and skateboard paths, various playing fields, a children's park, a puppet theater, and an area reserved for model planes. It is also home to two museums, the **Museu de Arte Moderna (MAM)** and the **Museu Carmen Miranda;** the Marina da Glória, from where swan-like launches and schooners set sail for points up and down Rio's lovely coast; and the rather somber **Monumento aos Mortas de Segunda Guerra Mundial,** which pays homage to the lives of Brazilian soldiers lost during World War II, with a statue by modernist master Alfredo Ceschiatti guarding a mausoleum where former combatants were laid to rest. On Sundays and holidays, part of Avenida Infante Dom Henrique is closed to traffic and Cariocas descend in droves upon the park. On weekend evenings outdoor concerts featuring top names in Brazilian music are often held here.

of leading landscape designer Roberto Burle Marx and architect Affonso Eduardo Reidy. Battling bureaucracy and machismo (her all-male crew and colleagues balked at taking orders from a woman), she was able to carry out most (though not all) of the original project. A great plant lover, Lota insisted that the park

Botafogo, Cosme Velho, and Urca   Map 3

Like neighboring Flamengo, Botafogo began life as bucolic getaway where wealthy Cariocas built seaside weekend palaces in which to escape from the stress of Centro. In its heyday, the lovely white crescent beach of Botafogo was the equivalent of Ipanema today. Although it remains lovely from an aesthetic viewpoint (and serves as very scenic soccer fields), the pollution factor is such that nobody would dream of bathing in its waters these days. Since the mid-20th century, the neighborhood has also lost its former sheen, suffering from an onslaught of

verticalization with its share of modern highrises and shopping centers. However, its leafy side streets are tranquil and stuffed with cinemas, cultural centers, bookstores, restaurants, and bars that are prized by Cariocas and largely ignored by tourists.

To the north of Botafogo, Cosme Velho is a pretty residential neighborhood that winds its way up the hills towards Corcovado. At the Estação Cosme Velho, hordes of tourists line up to catch the mini-train that whisks them up the mountain to the outstretched arms of

SIGHTS

Cristo Redentor, which in 2007 was elected as one of the New Seven Wonders of the World by a global jury of cybervoters.

Squeezed onto a promontory facing Botafogo and sheltering Pão de Açúcar—one of Rio's most celebrated landmarks—the tiny residential neighborhood of Urca has resisted much of the urban mayhem characteristic of Rio's other beachside *bairros*. Neglected by tourists, unmarred by developers, and ignored by *assaltantes* (thieves), it is a lovely place to stroll around, take in some magnificent views, and watch local fisherman cast their lines off into the Baía de Guanabara.

◖ CORCOVADO

Rua Cosme Velho 513, tel. 21/2558-1329, www.corcovado.com.br

HOURS: Trains depart Estação do Corcovado every 30 minutes daily 8:30 A.M.–6:30 P.M.

COST: Entrance R$13 adult, free child under 5; train R$36 adult (round-trip fare including R$5 entrance fee), free child under 5

Even before you arrive in Rio, the word will be rolling around on your tongue: "Corcovado"—and not just because it's the title of one of the best-known and most languorous bossa nova tunes of all times (penned by João Gilberto and sung, in English, by his then wife Astrud Gilberto). One of Rio's most instantly recognizable and oft visited icons, "Hunchback" (the English translation lacks the lyrical sonority of its Portuguese name) mountain rises straight up from the center of Rio to a lofty height of 700 meters (2,300 feet). Equally iconic is the 30-meter (100-foot) art deco statue of **Cristo Redentor** (Christ the Redeemer), his outstretched arms enveloping the surrounding city, that crowns Corcovado's sheer granite face. The statue, a gift from France to commemorate 100 years of Brazilian independence in 1921, didn't actually make it up to the top of the mountain until 1931. Since then, however, it has become a true beacon, visible from almost anywhere in the city. It is particularly striking at night when, due to a powerful illumination system, the Cristo glows like an otherworldly angel against the darkened sky.

© MICHAEL SOMMERS

Cristo Redentor atop Corcovado

Needless to say, the views from the top of Corcovado are utterly breathtaking. They're even more impressive than those preferred from Pão de Açúcar (which is half the size).

The most scenic—and fun—way to get to the top of Corcovado is by taking the 19th-century cog-wheel train from the Estação de Ferro do Corcovado, which was inaugurated in 1884 by Dom Pedro II. The crazily steep ride takes 20 minutes and treats you to stunning views of the beaches of Zona Sul and the Lagoa Rodrigo de Freitas. Once you get off the train, you reach the Cristo by walking up a flight of 220 steep steps. (If you're feeling lazy, opt for the escalator or panoramic elevator.) From Corcovado station, you can also take a registered van (make sure it is registered) for R$36 or hail a taxi to the top—which, aside from the fare, will cost an additional R$5 per passenger. Avoid weekends, when the road becomes clogged with traffic and the train lines are long. It's best to beat the crowds by heading up early on a weekday morning, when you'll have the added privilege of seeing Rio bathed in golden light. Obviously you should choose a clear day for your visit.

FUNDAÇÃO CASA DE RUI BARBOSA
Rua São Clemente 134, tel. 21/3289-4600, www.casaruibarbosa.gov.br
HOURS: Museum Tues.-Fri. 9 A.M.-5:30 P.M., Sat.-Sun. 2-6 P.M.; gardens Mon.-Fri. 8 A.M.-6 P.M., Sat.-Sun. 9 A.M.-6 P.M.
COST: Museum R$2 adult Tues.-Sat., free adult Sun., free senior and child under 12 Tues.-Sun.; gardens free adult, senior, and child

One of Brazil's most important public figures, Rui Barbosa (1849–1923) was a prolific and influential journalist, jurist, and statesman. Born and raised in Salvador, Bahia, he then moved to Rio where his abolitionist writings were instrumental in the passage of the Lei Áurea that ended slavery. A fervent republican, he also contributed to Brazil's first constitution. The gracious neoclassical mansion where he resided was the first private house in Brazil to be transformed into a museum (in 1930). Aside from the elegant rooms whose carefully preserved period pieces conjure up life in turn-of-the-20th-century Rio, the Fundação possesses an important library and archive of historical manuscripts as well as a rambling garden, shaded by trees bearing fruit such as mangos, *pitangas,* and even lychees, that's a favorite playground of local children.

LARGO DO BOTICÁRIO
Rua Cosme Velho 822

Hidden amidst a small patch of Mata Atlântica (native Atlantic rainforest), this charming square of pastel painted houses resembles a colonial-era movie set. Named for former resident Joaquim Luís da Silva Souto, who happened to be the royal family's *boticário* (apothecary), the seven houses, which originally date back to the early 1800s, received neocolonial makeovers in 1920. Regardless, the ensemble is quite enchanting, a sensation that is enhanced by the gurgling waters of the Rio Carioca, in whose supposedly magical waters the Tamoio people regularly bathed in order to up their beauty

and virility quotient. Across the street, you can't miss the grand, if sadly dilapidated, Solar dos Abacaxis, a 19th-century mansion notable for its cotton-candy-pink facade as well as the series of wrought-iron *abacaxis* (pineapples) adorning its balconies.

MUSEU CARMEN MIRANDA
Av. Rui Barbosa (in front of 560), tel. 21/2299-5586, www.funarj.rj.gov.br
HOURS: Tues.-Fri. 11 A.M.-5 P.M., Sat.-Sun. 1-5 P.M.
COST: Free

Although Carmen Miranda died tragically in 1955 at the age of 46, the legend of the "Lady in the Tutti Frutti Hat" lives on in this small, weirdly bunker-like complex designed by Affonso Eduardo Reidy and located in the midst of the Parque do Flamengo.

Born in Portugal but raised in Rio, Carmen rose to fame in the 1930s, coinciding with the birth of Brazil's recording industry and the transformation of radio from a corner-store phenomenon to a nationwide unifier. As a result of these technological advances, a repertory of infectious sambas penned by leading composers of the day such as Josué de Barros, Assis Valente, Ary Barroso, and Dorival Caymmi, and her irrepressible charm (which compensated for a merely adequate voice), Carmen became such a major star that, in 1939, she was whisked off to Broadway by Lee Schubert. After taking New York by storm (Saks' windows were filled with mannequins sporting turbans and platform shoes), Carmen headed to Hollywood and starred in a series of garish Technicolor musicals at 20th Century Fox. Her popularity was such that by the mid-1940s she was the top-paid actress in Hollywood.

Fashionistas, drag queens, and fans of the Golden Age of Hollywood will adore this gloriously kitschy shrine featuring Carmen memorabilia. Highlights include her infamous sky-high platform shoes—Miranda was a tiny 1.52 meters (5 feet) tall—outrageous gowns, gaudy costumes, jewelry, and of course, the inimitable headdresses topped with tropical fruit.

MUSEU DO ÍNDIO
Rua das Palmeiras 55, tel. 21/2286-8899,
www.museodoindio.org.br
HOURS: Tues.-Fri. 9 A.M.-5:30 P.M., Sat.-Sun. 1-5 P.M.
COST: R$3

Occupying a handsome 19th-century mansion in Botafogo, this museum was founded in 1953 by noted Brazilian anthropologist Darcy Ribeiro. Linked to FUNAI, Brazil's national foundation of indigenous affairs, it possesses an extremely important collection of artifacts reflecting Brazil's diverse native peoples. Among the objects on display are hunting and cooking implements, traditional costumes, musical instruments, and religious talismans. These are accompanied by interesting multimedia displays that provide a good introduction to the social, religious, and economic life of various tribes. The headdresses fashioned out of the Technicolor plumage of Amazonian parrots and toucans are drop-dead gorgeous. Kids will enjoy checking out the authentic dwellings dispersed amidst the garden. The museum shop sells an attractive (and decently priced) array of authentic handicrafts.

MUSEU INTERNACIONAL DE ARTE NAÏF
Rua Cosme Velho 561, tel. 21/2205-8612,
www.museunaif.com.br
HOURS: Tues.-Fri. 10 A.M.-6 P.M., Sat.-Sun. noon-6 P.M.
COST: R$8

A two-minute walk uphill from the Estação do Corcovado, this small but compelling museum lodged in a colonial mansion lays claim to having the world's largest collection of art *naïf* (works created by artists with no formal training). The delightfully expressive and colorful paintings do a fine job of conjuring up many elements of popular Brazilian culture: including *futebol*, Carnaval, and scenes from daily life, all the while capturing an essential verve and spontaneity that is very Brazilian. Although most of the works exhibited (spanning five centuries) are by self-taught Brazilian artists, there are international works from over 100 countries. A small boutique sells *naïf* art from contemporary artists.

MUSEU VILLA-LOBOS
Rua Sorocaba 200, tel. 21/2266-3845,
www.museuvillalobos.org.br
HOURS: Mon.-Fri. 10 A.M.-5:30 P.M.
COST: R$8

Fans of erudite music may interested in visiting the former residence of Heitor Villa-Lobos (1887–1959), considered one of the most important New World composers and definitely the most prolific and well-known Brazilian composer of all time. Villa-Lobos revolutionized classical music by integrating popular and regional Brazilian forms such as samba and *choro* together with African and indigenous influences and instruments and sounds from nature (bird calls were a favorite) into his compositions. Aside from a trio of rooms that recount his career and showcase personal effects, a small library contains sheet music, correspondence, books, films, and recordings of many of his symphonies, operas, and film scores.

◖ PÃO DE AÇÚCAR
Av. Pasteur 520, tel. 21/2461-2700,
www.bondinho.com.br
HOURS: Daily 8 A.M.-10 P.M.
COST: R$35 adult, R$17.50 child 6-12, free child under 6

Rio's equivalent of Paris's Eiffel Tower and New York's Statue of Liberty is the monumental chunk of granite guarding the entrance to the Baía de Guanabara known as Pão de Açúcar. No matter how many times you contemplate this rugged natural sculpture, the sensation is one that will definitely take your breath away. Rio's original inhabitants, the Tupi, referred to it as *pau-nh-acugua* (high, pointed, mountain), which is something of an understatement. When the Portuguese arrived on the scene, both the Tupi term and the mountain itself reminded them of a *pão de açúcar* (sugar loaf), a conical mound of sugar made by pouring liquid cane juice into a rounded mould and leaving it to harden. The name stuck and today Pão de Açúcar is one of Rio's most recognized icons.

© MICHAEL SOMMERS

Pão de Açúcar

As can be imagined, the panoramic views of Rio and the Baía de Guanabara glimpsed from the top of Pão de Açúcar are quite stupendous. You can reach the summit by taking a glass-sided cable car up the mountain—an unforgettably scenic journey with two stops. The first is at Morro da Urca, a 210-meter (690-foot) mountain where there is a restaurant and some small shops. The second stop is at the actual 396-meter (1,300-foot) summit of Pão de Açúcar. From here, trails lead through the lush forest with its tiny *mico* monkeys and rare wild orchids.

Cable cars depart for the top every 30 minutes from Praia Vermelha. Make sure the day is a clear one, but to avoid long lineups steer clear of weekends, holidays, and peak hours (10 A.M.–3 P.M.). If you're in a romantic frame of mind—or would like to be—make the trip in the late afternoon. The sunset and twilight, with the lights of Rio glittering in the dusk against the mountain silhouettes, are truly bewitching.

PISTA CLAUDIO COUTINHO
Entrance from Praia Vermelha

While some are content merely to gaze upon the lush hump that is Pão de Açúcar from above or below, others want to walk all over it. The easiest way to do so is by following this 2-kilometer (1-mi) *pista* (trail) that weaves through jungly Mata Atlântica. *Mico* monkeys and brightly feathered birds are frequent companions; the views across the bay are breathtaking, but the walk itself won't leave you out of breath. From the Pista Claudio Coutinho, two more-difficult trails allow you to actually climb up and around Morro da Urca and Pão de Açúcar, but these should only be attempted with a guide.

PRAIA DA URCA
Av. Portugal

Smaller and less exclusive than Urca's most coveted beach, Praia Vermelha, Praia da Urca nonetheless has its appeal. Although the fact that its sands are lapped by the waters of the Baía de Guanabara means it's no good for bathing, the views are pretty bewitching. During the week the rampart-like stone walls lining the seaside are sprinkled with amateur fisherman casting off and reeling in, but come the weekend suntanned scenesters flock to the area en masse to cavort, drink beer, and listen to improvised samba sessions. That the beach has become a major hangout is a source of contention for Urca's vocal residents' association (AMOUR), who are also none too pleased about the fact that the once-glamorous 1930s Cassino da Urca that fronts the beach—and where Carmen Miranda famously performed before heading to Hollywood—is going to become the latest outpost of the European Design Institute.

PRAIA VERMELHA
Praça General Tibúrcio, access via Av. Pasteur

During the week, you'd be justified for mistaking this charming little crescent of a beach lined with a bucolic park and deco villas for a secluded Côte d'Azur fishing village. Of course, when you're forced to factor in the

backdrop of mountains that includes a looming Pão de Açúcar, the comparison (not unhappily) ends. It's little wonder that (much to the chagrin of local residents) it has become a hip destination for Rio's beach cognoscenti. Incredibly it was less than a century ago, with the construction of Urca's first roads in the late 1920s, that Cariocas could first actually leave their footprints in the soft sand here. Prior to this time, the beach functioned during colonial times as part of a defensive outpost guarding the entrance to the Baía de Guanabara. Indeed the military legacy is alive and well in the number of high-ranking officers who inhabit the vicinity as well as the Instituto Militar de Engenharia, the Escola Naval, and Círculo Militar da Praia Vermelha, a clubhouse whose terrace shaded by almond trees is an idyllic spot for a beer (civvies are welcome too). On Thursday and Saturday evenings, live performances of *choro,* samba, and MPB often take place. Praia Vermelha is also where you catch the *bonde* that whisks you up to the top of Pão de Açúcar.

Copacabana and Leme   Map 4

Although its glamour days are long gone, Copacabana still manages to live up to its legend as the world's most famous strip of white sand. Originally a tiny fishing village, it didn't gain neighborhood status until the 1891 dynamiting of the Túnel Velho through the mountains opened up the deserted beaches of the Zona Sul to the beginnings of urbanization. With the construction of the Copacabana Palace, a Mediterranean-style luxury hotel, in 1923, the wealthy and fabulous came flocking. A slew of striking deco apartment buildings soon rose up along the beachfront's Avenida Atlântica. Before long "Copa" was not just *the* place to live but *the* place to party. Tycoons, movie stars, royalty, and the international jet set transformed its sweeping carpet of sand into their personal playground.

A Copa address became so coveted that by the 1960s and '70s the long but narrow neighborhood (hemmed in by mountains) was the most densely populated urban area in the world. To this day, Copa is not unlike a tropical Manhattan: People fork out absurd amounts of money to live in one of the thousands of closet-sized apartments located in the ugly high-rises that have mushroomed in the streets behind the oceanfront. The most populous of them all is the Edifício Richard, located at Rua Barata Ribeiro 194, which has 507 apartments (45 per floor).

While many of Rio's rich and fashionable have since moved on to the more chic neighborhoods of Ipanema and Leblon, Copa has become—for better or worse—one of Rio's most eclectic, vibrant, and democratic

ART DECO RIO

Rio has been called the art deco capital of the Southern Hemisphere. It's estimated that the city boasts more than 400 deco gems, in various states ranging from immaculate to decadent. Although you'll catch sight of impressive individual examples throughout older parts of the city – the most famous being the statue of the **Cristo Redentor** – the greatest and most glorious concentration of edifices can be found in Copacabana, since Copa's birth as a *bairro* in the 1920s and '30s coincided with the deco rage that was taking the world by storm. The first residences that sprang up in the shadow of the Copacabana Palace all adopted the streamlined style that symbolized modernity and elegance.

If you take a walk between Avenida Atlântica and Rua Barata Ribeiro, along the streets that surround the Praça do Lido, such as Rua Ministro Viveiros de Castro, Rua Ronaldo de Carvalho, Rua Fernando Mendes, and Rua República do Peru, you'll come across dozens of sleek and sophisticated residential buildings. Among the most striking is the 1932 **Edifício Itahy** (Av. Nossa Senhora da Copacabana 252), which features a brilliant malachite-green wrought-iron entrance with stylized depictions of marine plants. Also remarkable is the 1935 **Edifício Ypiranga** (Av. Atlântica 3170), an aerodynamic baby-blue building with incredible curves where architect Oscar Niemeyer once had his office.

Other standouts in Copacabana include: on **Av. Atlântica** – Ed. Labourdette (no. 1880) and Ed. Embaixador (no. 3170); on **Av. Nossa Senhora da Copacabana** – Ed. Comodoro (no. 162), Ed. Solano (no. 166), Ed. Ouro Preto (no. 174), and Ed. Ceará (no. 209); on **Rua Viveiros de Castro** – Ed. Tuyuti (no. 100), Ed. Orion (no. 104), Ed. América (no. 110), and Ed. Alagoas (no. 122); on **Rua Ronald de Carvalho** – Ed. Ribeiro Moreira (no. 21), Ed. Petronio (no. 45), and Ed. Guahy (no. 181); on **Rua Fernando Mendes** – Ed. Brasil (no. 19), Ed. Amazonas (no. 25), and Ed. Irapuan (no.

31). Also in Copa is Rio's sole surviving art deco cinema, the **Roxy** (Av. Nossa Senhora de Copacabana 945); inaugurated in 1938, this glamorous movie palace with its sweeping staircase still continues to screen films.

Outside of Copa, you'll find some beautiful examples of deco in Flamengo, notably **Edifício Biarritz** (Praia de Flamengo 268) that inevitably attracts gazes from those walking or whizzing by the Parque do Flamengo, as well as two residential buildings on **Rua Payssandu:** Ed. Payssandu (no. 93) and the Casa Marajoara (no. 319). In Centro, famous examples of deco include the imposing train station, **Estação Central do Brasil** (Praça Cristiano Otóni), and the more modern branch of the famous 19th-century café and pastry shop **Casa Cavé** (Rua Sete de Setembro 133).

Edifício Biarritz overlooks Praia do Flamengo

© MICHAEL SOMMERS

neighborhoods, a place where street kids and millionaires, models and muscle men, doormen and nannies from Northeast Brazil and American tourists from the deepest, darkest Midwest all rub shoulders. While during the day senior citizens swarm the beaches and the dozens of bakeries along the main drag of Avenida Nossa Senhora de Copacabana, by night the stretch of Avenida Atlântica towards Ipanema is a hot spot for prostitutes and for the (many foreign) johns who travel to Copa in search of more piquant forms of R&R. There is also the complicated situation that four major *favelas* cover the steep hills behind the middle-class condos. Shoot-outs between drug traffickers and police mean that it's not uncommon for shots to ring out (and stray bullets to fly).

Although Copa is not the safest place in the world, the oceanfront is well policed and if you're aware, smart, and don't flash your valuables, you will be fine. It's best to stick to well-populated areas, particularly at night, and it is also advisable to take a taxi at night unless you're strolling beneath the well-lit hotel exteriors on Avenida Atlântica. Despite its darker and seedier sides, Copacabana is full of a vibrancy and diversity that is unrivaled by any other Rio neighborhood. Although its glamour has definitely faded, it's hard to resist the charm of the local restaurants and traditional bars that co-exist alongside the multitude of 24-hour gyms and juice bars. Copa may be a little decadent and tacky in places, but it is also, quite simply, fun. And whatever you may think of the *bairro* itself, there is no denying the allure of its beach, the magnificent crescent-shaped sweep of sand that is a world unto itself.

FORTE DE COPACABANA

Corner of Avenida Atlântica and Rua Francisco Otaviano, tel. 21/2521-1032, www.fortedecopacabana.com
HOURS: Tues.-Sun. 10 A.M.–5 P.M.
COST: R$4 adult, R$2 senior and child under 12, free child under 6

Built on the site of the Igreja Nossa Senhora de Copacabana that served as a sanctuary for Our Lady of Copacabana, patron saint of sailors and fishermen, this sturdy whitewashed fortress was erected in 1914 in order to defend the Baía de Guanabara from potential attacks. As you can see for yourself, Krupp, the German

© MICHAEL SOMMERS

Praia de Copacabana

arms manufacturer contracted to build the fort, took its mission seriously; the walls are 12 meters (39 feet) thick in some places and the giant swiveling cannon is capable of firing up to distances of 25 kilometers (16 mi). Occupied by the Brazilian army, the well-preserved interior houses the Museu Histórico do Exército, whose pretty feeble collection of army paraphernalia will probably only interest military buffs. Much more enticing are the views of Copacabana beach and the bay. You can gaze upon them from the Café do Forte, operated by Confeitaria Colombo; an idyllic place for breakfast or late-afternoon tea. In recent summers, the fort has become extremely animated due to the presence of a giant Ferris wheel, musical performances en plein air, and an outpost of the legendary Ibiza "sunset bar," Café del Mar on its grounds.

PEDRA DO LEME
Caminho dos Pescadores

Looming primitively over the Praia do Leme, this imposing rock shaped like a ship's hull *(leme)* is the inspiration for the name of the beach and neighborhood of Leme. Steep climbing trails lead to the top, where the 18th-century **Forte Duque de Caxias** stands guard over a magnificent landscape (access to the fort is via Praça Almirante Júlio de Noronha, a 20-minute walk, Sat.–Sun. 10 A.M.–5 P.M., R$3). Meanwhile, the narrow walkway that winds around the Pedra, known as the Caminho dos Pescadores, is a favorite cast-off point for amateur and professional fishing enthusiasts and offers terrific views of the entire length of Copacabana in all its sweeping grandeur. Sprinkled around are a handful of kiosks that serve fish and seafood as well as beer and *água de coco*. Sundays are particularly lively due to the samba jam sessions that take place here.

◖ PRAIA DE COPACABANA
Av. Atlântica btwn. Av. Princesa Isabel and Rua Francisco Otaviano

Urban beaches don't get any more dazzling than this 4.5-kilometer (2.8-mi) strip that stretches in a magnificent arc from the Pão de Açúcar to the Forte de Copacabana. The sand is sugary fine and white and is a striking contrast to the blue of the open Atlantic and the hypnotically wavy white-and-black mosaic promenade that separates it from busy Avenida Atlântica. More than just affording a great view or acting as an outdoor tanning salon, the *praia* of Copacabana is a way of life. From dawn to dusk there is always something happening on Copa's beach—whether it's an early-morning yoga class for seniors, a *Vogue* photo shoot, an early-evening volleyball practice for preteen girls, or midnight hookers on the prowl for foreign tourists. The beach is also a meeting spot and a pick-up place. You can get a tan or a tattoo, drink a *caipirinha* at a fancy *barraca* or an icy *água de coco* sold by one of the many hundreds of *ambulantes* who hawk everything from bags of the strangely addictive Globo biscuits to transistor radios. Of course, in a pinch, you can go swimming—the chilly temperatures coupled with an undercurrent demand caution—but you can also do so much more.

Like the neighborhood itself, Copacabana beach is actually very stratified and different points are occupied by different "tribes." The 1-kilometer (0.6-mi) stretch closest to the tunnel that leads to Botafogo—between Morro do Leme and Avenida Princesa Isabel—is actually known as Praia do Leme (the small attractive residential *bairro* behind it is known as Leme as well). Leme is popular with families and older residents. The stretch of Copacabana in front of the Copacabana Palace is fashionable with gay men and transvestites. The patch near Rua Santa Clara is popular with jocks: particularly fans of *futebol* and *futevôlei* (a Brazilian version of volleyball in which no hands are allowed). Closer to Ipanema, Postos 5 and 6 (*posto* refers to the beacon-like lifeguard posts) draw an eclectic mix of seniors and *favela* kids. At the very end in front of the Forte de Copacabana is a fisherman's colony, one of the oldest and most traditional in Rio. Here, you can watch *pescadores* haul in their catch and mend their nets.

Ipanema

Map 5

The most coveted—and expensive—slice of beachfront property in Rio de Janeiro is without a doubt the area from which the first chords of "A Garota de Ipanema" ("The Girl from Ipanema") were set down by two bohemian poets. The years was 1962 and Tom Jobim and Vinicius de Moraes were enjoying ice-cold *chope* (draft beer) at their favorite neighborhood bar when one of many enticingly bronzed and bikinied young Cariocas sashayed by on the way to the beach and inspired the languorously cool bossa nova jewel. The song that seduced the world also summed up the seductive charm of what had become Rio's hippest, most happening beach *bairro*. Since the swinging '60s, Ipanema has been a magnet for a cosmopolitan yet funky mix of artists, musicians, and leftist intellectuals, along with a rich and trendy crowd who consistently fall prey to the lovely neighborhood with its shady tree-lined streets, fashionable bistros, bars, and boutiques, and magnificent white sands.

Together, Ipanema and Leblon constitute one long and captivating beach divided by the narrow Jardim de Alah canal, which separates both neighborhoods and links the Lagoa Rodrigo de Freitas to the ocean. Ipanema begins at the Pedra do Arpoador, a dramatic rock jutting into the sea, and Leblon ends at the twin-headed Morro de Dois Irmãos, a fantastically shaped mountain—covered by lush tropical forest as well as the *favela* of Vidigal—that really does poetically conjure up the heads of "Two Brothers." During the week, the beaches are fairly tranquil, but when the weekend rolls around the sand is a sea of bronzed, bikinied bodies, engaging in varied activities from playing *futevôlei* to smoking illicit joints. On Sundays, the main oceanfront drags of Avenida Viera Souto (Ipanema) and Avenida Delfim Moreira (Leblon) are closed to traffic and the

© MICHAEL SOMMERS

Ipanema and Leblon beaches

BEACH DOS AND DON'TS

In Rio, the beach is a fundamental part of life and lifestyle. Although it all appears incredibly laid-back, the truth is that Cariocas have developed a very sophisticated *cultura de praia*, with habits and codes that it's worth taking note of if you want to blend in.

· **Don't** wear a bathing suit from home: Chances are you're going to be hopelessly out of style. Rio's cutting-edge bikini and *sunga* (the male version of a bikini) styles are always light years ahead of the rest of the world, and since prices are generally affordable, **do** purchase one (or several) on location.

· If you're female, **do** know that Cariocas (even very large ones) are not at all shy about revealing an awful lot of flesh (although the days of the *fio dental* – dental floss – thong have mercifully passed). However, you **don't** want to take your top off. Aside from a brief headline-making phase on Ipanema a few summers ago – when a few women's toplessness led to the police enforcing decades-old decency laws – topless sunbathing is a no-no. Moreover, Cariocas are very proud of their tan lines.

· If you're male, **don't** don a Speedo-style bathing suit – these are for Olympic swimmers. For the last couple of years, stylish *sungas* have been modeled on men's full briefs. **Do** know that surfing shorts are for surfing or for wearing over your bathing suit as you go to and from the beach, but definitely not for lounging around on the sand or swimming.

· On the way to and from the beach, **do** wear flip-flops (Havaianas are the coolest) and **don't** wear shoes. Females should cover up (lightly) with a lightweight top and micro shorts or skirts. Walking to and from the beach, males can flaunt their bare chests, but otherwise should wear a T-shirt.

· **Don't** take any valuables to the beach and don't leave your possessions unguarded. Take a beach bag instead of a purse. If

late afternoon on Ipanema beach

© MICHAEL SOMMERS

you're alone, **do** ask a respectable-looking neighbor to keep an eye on your stuff while you take a dip.

· **Don't** bring a towel to the beach (even if you're staying in a swanky hotel with very plush ones). *Kangas* (a rectangular piece of thin, brightly colored cotton that can be worn as a wrap or used as a beach towel) are lighter and de rigueur. They are sold all over the beaches. If you want more comfort, rent a chair.

· **Don't** schlep food or drinks to the beach; you'll look like a bag person. Rio's beaches are terrifically well serviced by *ambulantes*, vendors who sell all sorts of drinks and snacks (both healthy and unhealthy).

· Rio's beaches have strong currents in places. **Don't** go swimming if a red flag is flying. Only go in the water in areas where locals are already swimming.

· **Don't** get a sunburn. Not only will you suffer on your vacation, and contribute to possible skin cancer, but the red-lobster look is definitely uncool and will brand you as a foolish gringo.

whole area becomes a massive outdoor recreational scene where, between sips of *água de coco* and ice-cold beer, you can inspect the latest styles in flip-flops and beachwear.

◖ PRAIA DE IPANEMA
Av. Vieira Souto btwn. Rua Francisco Otaviano and Av. Epitácio Pessoa

Ipanema beach is more than just one of the world's most gorgeous urban beaches. It's the living embodiment of a lifestyle, a culture, and a state of mind whose seductive guiding principles of modernism and hedonism have left their mythical imprint on the rest of Brazil and the world. Although straighter and narrower than Copacabana's wide crescent, the 3-kilometer (2-mi) strip of sugary sand lined with *barracas* festooned with chilled green coconuts and a cycling and running lane overflowing with the athletically inclined is no less scenic nor varied in its human fauna.

Like Copa, Ipanema is divided into tribal territories. The area around Posto 8 (off Rua Farme de Amoedo), signaled by a giant rainbow flag, is a magnet for gay men, while Posto 9 (the patch between Rua Maria Quitéria and Rua Joana Angêlica, known as Coqueirão due to the presence of an extremely tall coconut palm) has long been the territory of artists, hipsters, and intellectuals who would rather flaunt their leftist viewpoints. Further along, the area around Posto 10 is nicknamed Cap Ferrat. The allusion to the French Riviera pretty much describes the crowd: a little more conservative and a lot more rich (the Brazilian equivalent of the Skip and Muffy set, referred to in Portuguese as Mauricinhos and Patricinhas).

PRAIA DO ARPOADOR
Av. Francisco Bhering

The narrow 500-meter (0.3-mi) stretch of golden sand that extends from the Forte de Copacabana to the intersection of Rua Francisco Otaviano and Avenida Vieira Souto is known as the Praia do Arpoador. *Arpoador* means harpoon and, according to local legend, whale hunters used to brandish them fiercely from the slippery slopes of the Pedro do Arpoador, the giant rock anchoring the beach. These days, habitués are more likely to brandish surfboards. Due to some impressive wave actions, Arpoador is *surfista* central and you'll see buffed boys (and the odd girl) catching swells at all hours of the day (and night, due to the 24-hour spotlights). Meanwhile, on late golden afternoons, locals ritually congregate, crab-like, along the Pedra to witness (and collectively applaud) the magnificent sunsets.

Leblon — Map 6

Leblon is slightly more sedate, tranquil, and residential (and richer), but no less appealing than neighboring Ipanema. Like Ipanema, by day much of life revolves around the beach. As a result, it carries off the impressive feat of being both incredibly chic and disarmingly casual. To wit: The sight of tattooed surfer boys, barefoot and dripping wet, carrying their boards past the discreetly jeweled millionaires ensconced at the terraces of five-star restaurants is extremely common.

PARQUE DO PENHASCO DOIS IRMÃOS
Rua Aperana, tel. 21/2503-2799
HOURS: Daily 8 A.M.-6 P.M.

Often overlooked by both locals and tourists, this chunk of jungle paradise located at the foot of Morro de Dois Irmãos makes for a relaxing break. Walking trails lead to a quartet of lookouts, each of which offers different but spectacular panoramic views of Rio's iconic sights. From the Mirante do Anfiteatro, you can look out at Vidigal and the Cagarras islands; the Mirante da Sede and Mirante do Sétimo Céu give you a sweeping view of Leblon and Ipanema beaches with Niterói in the distance; and the Mirante da Lagoa gazes out at the Lagoa Rodrigo de Freitas and Jardim Botânico stretching all the way to Botafogo. Weekends are popular with families, while during the week you can expect to find some New Age gurus meditating in synch with the beating of the waves.

PRAIA DE LEBLON
Av. Delfim Moreira btwn. Av. Borges de Medeiros and Av. Visconde de Albuquerque

Narrower than Ipanema, Leblon's beach, which sits in the magnificent shadow of the Morro de Dois Irmãos, has the advantage of being slower-paced and more tranquil than Ipanema. Families prize the beach, especially in the areas around Posto 11 and Posto 12; the latter is known as Baixo Bebê due the number of young couples and their tots who congregate around the playground and diaper-changing facilities. The far end is popular with residents of Vidigal, the neighboring hillside *favela* that, when lit up at night, appears to be covered with thousands of twinkling dragon flies. For a stunning view of the entire beach, follow Avenida Niemeyer in the direction of Vidigal to the Mirante do Leblon, a lookout point at the foot of the Morro de Dois Irmãos.

Gávea, Lagoa, and Jardim Botânico   Map 7

Although less hip and happening than Ipanema and neighboring Leblon, Gávea is an attractive, well-to-do neighborhood with lots of pretty tree-lined streets. The upper residential portions climb up towards jungle-clad mountains crowned by the dramatic Pedra da Gávea, an immense slab of rock that resembles a prehistoric giant's coffee table (and is a favorite jump-off point for hang gliders). The neighborhood's flatter expanses—known as Baixa (Lower) Gávea—are riddled with bars and restaurants and segue into the neighborhood known as Lagoa that rings the Lagoa Rodrigo de Freitas, a placid lagoon whose emerald shores, replete with walking and cycling trails, sports facilities, and kiosk bars, comprise one of Rio's favorite open-air playgrounds.

Adjacent to Gávea and also bordering the Lagoa is the lush upscale neighborhood of Jardim Botânico. While its wealthy residents may lack sea views, they are handsomely rewarded by being in between the jungly slopes of Corcovado and the exotic flora of one of the world's best botanical gardens. Aside from possessing some of the city's chicest restaurants and bars, Jardim Botânico is where the Globo television network has its Rio headquarters, ensuring the presence of lots of celebs (and paparazzi).

FUNDAÇÃO EVA KLABIN
Av. Epitácio Pessoa 2480, tel. 21/2523-3471, www.evaklabin.org.br
HOURS: Tues.-Sun. 2-6 P.M.
COST: R$16 adult, R$8 senior and student, free Tues.

The daughter of a Lithuanian paper and cellulose magnate who made his fortune in São Paulo, Eva Klabin (1903–1991) was more than just an idle heiress. Like her father and sister Ema (who has a Fundação of her own in Sampa), she was a philanthropist and passionate art collector who at a young age went trolling around Europe and Asia for treasures, which she then brought home to decorate the exquisite 1930s Norman-style house—one of the first mansions built on the shore of the Lagoa—in which she lived in high style. Following the death of her husband, Klabin became a notorious night owl. She regularly hosted lavish midnight dinners and parties for artists, intellectuals, scions, and even visiting VIPs such as Henry Kissinger and the Rockefellers. The flower arrangements were always designed by close pal Roberto Burle Marx, while the art collection—whose growth demanded the construction of new wings in neoclassical style—was organized in different salons according to themes. The Renaissance room, for example, is hung with Tintorettos and Boticellis, while the Egyptian room is awash in antiquities that include the mummy of a cat. Klabin's personal favorite was the English room, where she would curl up with a glass of whiskey on a comfy sofa and an Agatha Christie mystery, taking time out to contemplate the Gainsborough and Reynolds portraits around her. With no heirs of her own, Klabin bequeathed her house and its possessions to the City of Rio. Although meandering through the elegantly furnished rooms on your own is a rewarding experience for lovers of ancient and classical art (though temporary exhibits of contemporary works are also held here), guided tours are available at 2 and 4 P.M.

© MICHAEL SOMMERS

imperial palms at the Jardim Botânico

JARDIM BOTÂNICO

Rua Jardim Botânico 1008, tel. 21/3874-1808, www.jbrj.gov.br
HOURS: Daily 8 A.M.–5 P.M.
COST: R$4 adult, free senior and child under 7

A 340-acre urban oasis—it's been scientifically proven that the temperature is always a bit cooler here than elsewhere in this often humid city—Rio's Botanical Garden offers an unparalleled green mix of native Atlantic forest, lagoons covered with giant Vitória-Régia lily pads, and over 8,000 plant species. Many of them—pineapples, cinnamon, and tea among others—were introduced here prior to their cultivation in the rest of Brazil. Created by Dom João I—who planted the park's signature double row of imperial palms—the Jardim Botânico is a wonderfully tranquil refuge during the week (on weekends, it fills up with Cariocas and their kids). Highlights include the scent garden, the cactus garden, and the fabulous *orquidário,* featuring over

1,000 species of wild orchids. Kids (and adults) with a fondness for the mildly gruesome will enjoy the carnivorous plant collection. Also enchanting is the Jardim dos Beija-Flores, where 50 shrubs that attract *beija-flors* (hummingbirds) ensure a constant gathering of these tiny jewel-like birds with their seemingly motorized wings. In 2008, in commemoration of its 200-year birthday, the gardens received the gift of a Museu do Meio Ambiente (daily 10 A.M.–5 P.M.), an eco-museum dedicated to tackling timely environmental issues confronting both the world and Brazil. Near the park entrance is a pretty café and a great gift shop with lots of eco-souvenirs. Also on the premises is the Espaço Tom Jobim, a cultural center devoted to the author of "The Girl from Ipanema," who loved the Jardim Botânico as if it were his backyard. Aside from a rich collection of documents, photos, videos, and recordings, the theater hosts performances of jazz, samba, and MPB every other Saturday.

LAGOA RODRIGO DE FREITAS

Av. Borges de Medeiros

If you go strolling amidst the shady streets of Ipanema and Leblon, you'll approach a vast saltwater lagoon ringed by luxury villas and apartment buildings set against the backdrop of mountains, including the famed and fabulous Corcovado. Already-svelte Cariocas get sportily dressed to the nines and power walk, jog, and cycle around the lagoon until they break a sheen. The less athletically inclined (but still nicely decked out) prefer to sip an *água de coco* or *caipirinha* at one of the many kiosks, all of which serve food and drink. Also surrounding the *lagoa* are a variety of posh private clubs, skating parks, tennis courts, and a heliport. In the evening, live music is often played at the kiosks (the best of which are near the Parque dos Patins and the Corte do Cangalo).

PARQUE DA CATACUMBA

Av. Epitácio Pessoa 3000, tel. 21/2247-9949
HOURS: Tues.-Sun. 8 A.M.-5 P.M.

This park gets its name from the fact that indigenous groups buried their dead upon the Morro dos Cabritos, the hillside that the park sits on, which rises up from the Copacabana side of the Lagoa Rodrigo de Freitas. Providing a contrast to the placid lagoon and the shady sprinkling of fruit trees are some 30 large-scale sculptures made by renowned artists such as Carybé, Bruno Giorgi, and Victor Brecheret. A steep but short trail leads up to the Mirante do Saco, which offers splendid panoramic views of the Lagoa, the Morro de Dois Irmãos, the Pedra da Gávea, and the beaches of Ipanema and Leblon. On Sunday afternoons, the park's outdoor amphitheater sometimes hosts free concerts.

PARQUE LAGE

Rua Jardim Botânico 414, tel. 21/2527-2397,
www.rio.rj.gov.br/fpj/pqlage.htm
HOURS: Daily 8 A.M.-5 P.M.

Since it is only a few blocks from the Jardim Botânico, the Parque Lage is often overlooked by tourists on the prowl for delights of a verdant nature. Big mistake. In the park designed by 19th-century English landscaper John Tyndale the winding paths snake around small ponds and through the lush tropical landscape that covers the lower slopes of Corcovado. For kids, there is a small playground and an aquarium along with the thrill of catching sight of monkeys and brightly colored birds. When the white gauzy clouds that sometimes glide by the mountains threaten to shroud the treetops, you'll feel as if you're walking in a cloud forest. The early-20th-century mansion of Henrique Lage, a wealthy industrialist, and his opera singer wife, Gabriela, was designed by Italian architect Mario Vrodet. Its stately marble facade presents a striking contrast to the exuberant tropical landscape. The internal courtyard with its stately arcades and turquoise pool reflecting the mountains is Alhambra-esque. Even better is the fact that you can throw yourself onto a tatami mat and indulge in cakes and coffee at the Café do Laje. Today, the palace houses the Escola de Artes Visuais, an art school where temporary exhibits are often held.

PARQUE TOM JOBIM

Av. Epitácio Pessoa and Av. Borges de Medeiros

Zona Sul residents' second-favorite playground (number one is the beach) is the Lagoa Rodrigo de Freitas. Walking, jogging, cycling, or skateboarding around its 7.4-kilometer (4.5-mi) perimeter is how many residents stay in shape (or sane) and catch up on essential gossip. The green area surrounding the lagoon's shores, known as the Parque Tom Jobim, embraces a number of tony private athletic and social clubs (many dating back to the 1940s) as well as celebrated drink and snack *quiosques* where (mellow) live music is often performed. There's also a well-maintained ensemble of playgrounds, exercise equipment, sport and game facilities, picnic areas, and (generally clean) bathrooms with showers.

Within Parque Tom Jobim are several mini-parks. In the shadow of Copacabana's Morro do Cantagalo, **Parque do Cantagalo** is sports central with a soccer field; volleyball, tennis, and basketball courts; and a baseball diamond.

Those who want to exercise their romantic impulses can rent swan-shaped *pedalinhos* (pedal boats) and leisurely tool around the lagoon with a loved one. In Leblon, behind Jardim de Alah, the **Parque das Taboas** also has tennis and soccer facilities as well as a ramp for skateboarders to strut their stuff. Serving Amazonian fare amidst Amazonian decor, the Palaphita Kitch *quiosque* is the ideal place for whiling away a few hours. Other popular *quiosques* are clustered together in the **Parque dos Patins** behind Gávea's Jóquei Clube; among the most popular are Café del Lago (pasta and pizza), Arab (falafels and *esfihas*), and Sushi Bar Lagoa (sushi). To work off the calories, Parque dos Patins also has various sports facilities including bike rental outlets and a kids' playground and roller-skating rink.

PLANETÁRIO
Rua Vice-Gov. Rubens Berardo 160, tel. 21/2274-0046, www.rio.rj.gov.br/culturas

HOURS: Tues.-Fri. 10 A.M.-7 P.M., Sat.-Sun. 3-9 P.M.
COST: R$6 adult, R$3 senior and anyone under 21

A classic outing for parents with kids is a visit to Latin America's most "modern" planetarium, with not one but two domes devoted to celestial matter. From the Universarium VIII, you can gaze out at the universe and boggle your brain trying to take count of the 9,000 stars that are visible on a clear night (Tues.–Thurs. 6:30 and 8:30 P.M.). The more modest Spacemaster contents itself to simulate the movement of some 6,500 heavenly bodies, projected onto the inside of the cupola (Sat.–Sun. 4 and 5:30 P.M. children; 7 P.M. adults only). The galactic good times continue at the Museu do Universo, which houses a few dozen interactive exhibits dealing with intergalactic phenomena. Depending on your disposition you can extend your visit late into the night at 00, an eternally fashionable restaurant-bar-club conveniently located on the premises.

Barra da Tijuca and Recreio   Map 8

After Leblon, Rio's coastal road, Avenida Niemeyer, goes through a long tunnel that burrows beneath the Morro de Dois Irmãos, whose slopes are home to one of Rio's largest *favelas*, Vidigal. Although from a socioeconomic perspective the successive beach neighborhoods are considered extensions of the Zona Sul, geographically they are part of the Zona Oeste, since they are situated west of Copacabana, Ipanema, and Leblon. These sprawling neighborhoods are much more recent and lack the history and charm of the Zona Sul. While their beaches are attractive and unspoiled, the neighborhoods themselves offer little aside from a collection of soulless restaurants, bars, and gigantic shopping malls where the middle classes and *novo ricos* (nouveau riche) hang out. None of these neighborhoods are laid out with pedestrians in mind. Cars rule, but the coastline is also well served by buses from the Zona Sul with destinations marked Barra and Recreio.

After the tiny but wealthy enclave of São Conrado, another long tunnel leads to the mega-developed, super-suburban Miami-like *bairro* of Barra da Tijuca (known simply as Barra). Thirty years ago, this 16-kilometer (10-mi) stretch of coastline was little more than a long wild sweep of white sand with a few *barracas*. Now it is the playground for Rio's middle classes, who alternate days spent on the beaches and at the many *shoppings* with nights in the many bars, clubs, and *shoppings* in the *bairro*. In fact, Barra was modeled after an American suburb, and as a result getting around without a car is near impossible, although buses career up and down the main autobahn-like drag of Avenida das Américas and, to a lesser extent, along the parallel-running Avenida Sernambetiba, which follows the ocean.

Barra's one saving grace is its beach, which remains amazingly unspoiled, particularly during the week. On weekends, however, the sands sizzle with lots of young tanned and toned bodies in a partying frame of mind. The trendiest strip, at the beginning of the Barra (between Postos 1 and 2), is known as Praia do Pepê (access from Av. do Pepê). Although the surf is rough, you can swim here. You can also engage in all varieties of sports in the water and on the sand.

Barra da Tijuca becomes more deserted the further west you travel. Eventually it turns into the 11-kilometer-long (7-mi) beach known as Recreio dos Bandeirantes, whose untamed surroundings and rough waves are a magnet for Rio's surfing crowd. Particularly attractive is the small and secluded Prainha beach, at the end of Recreio. The spectacular waves and presence of several renowned surfing academies make it a mecca for wave junkies. Even more deserted is Grumari, whose reddish sands are framed by spectacular mountains covered in lush native Atlantic forest. Both Prainha and Grumari are located in protected nature reserves. Despite the fact that they can't be reached by bus, they can fill up on the weekends with Cariocas seeking a quick back-to-nature fix.

BOSQUE DA BARRA
Av. das Américas 6000, tel. 21/3151-3428
HOURS: Tues.-Sun. 8 A.M.-5 P.M.

A welcome antidote to Barra's increasingly urban landscape of malls and condos is this municipal conservation area. Its mission is to safeguard and study the original ecosystem of the region known as *restinga*, an exotic mixture of vegetation that includes various species of trees, bushes, vines, bromeliads, and ferns and is home to creatures such as cranes, capybaras, and sloths. The park is well equipped with paths for walking, jogging, and cycling as well as a playground carved out of tree trunks, and a picnic area that fills up on weekends.

⬛ CASA DO PONTAL
Estrada do Pontal 3295, tel. 21/2490-3278,
www.popular.art.br/museucasadopontal
HOURS: Tues.-Sun. 9:30 A.M.-5 P.M.
COST: R$10 adult, R$5 senior, free child under 5

In the late 1940s, a curious designer and art collector from France, named Jacques Van de Beuque, began traveling throughout Brazil (especially the Northeast). Aside from curing his wanderlust, he discovered a fantastically rich folk-art tradition of which nobody—not even Brazilians—was aware. To preserve and promote these works, he returned to Rio and built a vast house set amidst shady green gardens, located inland from Recreio beach. Today, the Casa de Pontal shelters the largest collection of Brazilian folk art in the country. The 5,000 works on display include a fabulous array of *figurinhas de barro,* wonderfully vivid clay figures of popular Northeastern characters (including bandits and barflies) created by masters such as Pernambuco's Mestre Vitalino. Also dazzling are the extravagantly embroidered and sequinned *boi* (bull) costumes worn by celebrants of traditional *bumba-meu-boi festas,* which take place during June in São Luís, Maranhão. Although it takes a while to get there (buses run from the Zona Sul), it's really worth viewing this collection to get a sense of the richness and variety, not to mention the ingenious improvisational nature, of Brazil's popular artistic traditions in which everything from palm fibers, fabric scraps, and wire to tin cans, sand, and bread crumbs is ripe with creative possibilities.

PRAIA DA BARRA DA TIJUCA
Av. Sernambetiba

Rio's longest beach runs for 18 kilometers (11 mi) and is quite a vision, with sweeping white sands and emerald-green waters. While you don't have to worry about pollution, you do have to be concerned about the roughness of the waves, unless of course, you happen to practice windsurfing, kitesurfing, or plain old surfing—in which case you'll be in heaven. Rio's *surfistas* congregate en masse along the entire length of the beach, but a particularly nirvanic spot is a 1-kilometer (0.5-mi) patch right in the middle (close to Av. Serrnambetiba 3100) where waves rise to heights of two meters (7 feet) and championships are often held. Barra's sands are also beloved by athletes who keep in top shape by running after balls of all kinds: Frescoball, volleyball, soccer, and *futevôlei* are all endemic and you'll find nets, goal posts, and sweaty guys and girls in enviable shape along the entire expanse of beach. Barra's beach is well equipped with *quiosques* selling drinks and *água de coco,* bathroom and shower facilities, and a bike path. The first 6 kilometers (4 mi) are the most urbanized, but even on weekends it never gets as packed as the beaches of the Zona Sul. Beware of the traffic, however, which can be really intense on weekends and in the summer. With this in mind, save yourself some hassle and arrive early (i.e., before 10 A.M.).

PRAIA DO JOÁ
Access via Estrada da Joatinga

The hip, insiders' beach du jour during the summer, Praia do Joá has all the usual trappings of a fabulous secret: 1) It's tricky to get to—tourists will have to take a taxi, which will set you back around R$20 from Ipanema, and subsequent access, via a condominium complex, involves a mildly treacherous descent down a rocky cliffside of Morro da Joatinga; 2) The small beach is so narrow that between the months of April and October it's swallowed up by the sea; 3) Due to the remote location, prices at the two beach *barracas* are a little steeper than elsewhere; 4) It's very charming.

PRAIA DO PEPÊ
Av. Sernambetiba

At the very beginning of Barra beach, a 1.5-kilometer (1-mi) stretch of sand between Posto 1 and Posto 2 known as Praia do Pepê is Barra's epicenter of cool. A blend of hot surfers, *novela* actors, and radical sports daredevils, all impeccably tanned, buffed, and bikinied, stay active by indulging in myriad forms of surfing as well as soccer, volleyball, and *futevôlei.* The combination of strong winds, coarse sand (less slippery than the soft, silky variety), and rough waves make it a paradise for sports on both water and land. The name of the beach, as well as this stretch of Avenida Sernambetiba, commonly known as Avenida do Pepê, pay homage to Pedro Paulo Lopes, a beloved adventure-sports junkie who was the first to colonize the area by opening up a *barraca* selling juices and healthy sandwiches. Although Pepê died in a 1991 hang-gliding accident, his memory and ethos live on, as does his famous Barraca do Pepê (www.pepe.com.br), near Posto 1, which serves as an unofficial clubhouse for beach regulars.

PRAIA DO RECREIO
Av. Sernambetiba

Basically an extension of Barra, Praia do Recreio has the advantage of being (for now) less urbanized, and swathes of this 2-kilometer (1-mi) strip are backed not by creeping condos but by native vegetation known as *restinga*. The central portion is the most developed, with enough bars and *quiosques* to keep the bohemian crowd in *águas* other than the rough ones that attract legions of surfers. However, other patches are very tranquil, particularly the western extremity that is known as Praia da Macumba. Quite untamed, Macumba has soft sands surrounded by green forest and swept by strong winds that beckon surfers (numerous surfing academies are located here). A gigantic boulder separates the untamed surfing zone from more protected waters that are ideal for bathing.

◖ PRAINHA AND PRAIA DE GRUMARI
Av. Estado da Guanabara

If you're looking for unspoiled paradise within Rio's perimeter, a heavenly pair of beaches just west of Recreio fit the bill. They're wild, windswept, and surrounded by an environmentally protected landscape of mountains lushly carpeted in native *restinga*—the only trappings of civilization are a couple of rustic *barracas* hawking drinks and sunscreen. With easier access, Prainha is the darling of surfers due to its consistently strong winds and rollers that seem to last forever before breaking. Grumari is dramatic, with soft reddish sand and jade-green waters that are alternately calm and choppy. The portion closest to Prainha is favored by surfers, while the furthest extreme is where tour buses and cars battle for parking space. On weekends, particularly in the summer, both beaches are packed with an eclectic combination of local residents, tour groups, hipsters, hippies, and Zona Sul families fleeing the city. In fact, lineups are common on the picturesque final route to Grumari. To ensure a place in the sun (and a parking space), arrive early (i.e., before 11 A.M.). Both beaches are surrounded by nature parks with easy hiking trails. While there's not much to eat on the beaches themselves, if you have a car you can head to the surrounding settlements of Barra de Guaratiba, further along the coast, and Vargem Grande, located inland, for a handful of fine restaurants set amidst bucolic natural surroundings where you can easily while away a Saturday or Sunday afternoon.

SÍTIO ROBERTO BURLE MARX

Estrada da Barra de Guaratiba 2019, tel. 21/2410-1412
HOURS: Guided visits daily 9:30 A.M. and 1 P.M. by appointment
COST: R$4 adult, free senior and child under 7

The idyllic Sítio Roberto Burle Marx is another attraction worth the time and effort to get to. Between 1949 and 1994, this bucolic country estate was the primary residence of renowned landscape architect Roberto Burle Marx, whose most famous projects in Rio include the Parque do Flamengo and Copacabana's iconic black-and-white mosaic "wave" promenade. The surrounding nursery and gardens—featuring more than 3,500 plant species collected from Brazil and around the world—were designed with great flair. Indeed, it was said about Marx—who was also a painter—that he used plants as other artists used paint. The colonial house (originally part of a coffee plantation) and adjoining atelier have been transformed into a museum where you can admire the artist's works, possessions, and rich collection of Brazilian folk art. If you don't have a car, take the bus marked Marambaia-Passeio that passes through the Zona Sul.

Greater Rio de Janeiro   Map 9

SÃO CONRADO

Separated from Gávea by an immense tunnel that cuts right through the mountains, São Conrado is a small and very posh neighborhood full of luxury high-rise condominiums and a fancy shopping mall. In a disarming contrast, these chic edifices gaze directly onto Rio's biggest and most notorious *favela*, Rocinha, where brick and cement dwellings cover the otherwise jungle-carpeted Morro de Dois Irmãos. Although Rio is all about glaring contradictions and brutal extremes, nowhere else is the divide between rich and poor so prominently, fascinatingly, and perversely apparent. São Conrado's main draw is the small and spectacular Praia do Pepino (Cucumber Beach), where hang gliders burn off their adrenaline after taking off from the neighboring peaks of Pedra da Gávea and Pedra Bonita.

CASA DAS CANOAS

Estrada das Canoas 2310, tel. 21/3322-3581,
www.niemeyer.org.br/canoas/canoas.htm
HOURS: Tues.-Fri. 1-5 P.M.
COST: R$10 adult, R$5 student, free senior and child under 10

Aside from its beach and its *shopping*, São Conrado's only noteworthy attraction is this landmark modernist house commissioned in 1951 by architect Oscar Niemeyer for himself and his family. The house is truly magnificent: Its flowing bends and curves harmonize perfectly with the exuberant natural surroundings, and cool pools and statues abound. Inside, a permanent exhibit devoted to the architect features furniture, drawings, and maquettes. Hours can change, so call first to confirm.

PRAIA DE SÃO CONRADO

Av. Prefeito Mendes de Morais btwn. Av. Niemeyer and the Túnel São Conrado, tel. 21/3874-1808, www.jbrj.gov.br

Stretching from the end of Avenida Niemeyer to the entrance to the São Conrado tunnel, the strikingly beautiful 3-kilometer-long (2-mi) beach of São Conrado is mostly frequented by residents and tourists who check into the Sheraton Rio Resort as well as surfers attracted by the big breakers (which make swimming difficult). Magnificently framed by the natural sculptures of Pedra da Gávea, Pedra Bonita, and the Morro de Dois Irmãos, and with a surreal backdrop in which highrise condos mingle with the cubist conglomeration of shacks in Rocinha, this a beach where it's hard to close your eyes, particularly if you head to the southern end of the beach, known as Praia do Pepino. This is where the thrill-seeking hang gliders land after diving, Icaruslike, off Pedra Bonita.

ROCINHA

Estrada da Gávea

Billed as the world's biggest *favela,* with over 200,000 residents, Rocinha's name is as famously Carioca as *bairros* such as Copacabana and Ipanema. In fact, the vast labyrinth of houses, shops, schools, day cares, banks, DVD rental stores, and even its own TV station is looking to become a bonafide *bairro,* as part of a fairly recent tactic of integrating *favelas* into the urban fabric as opposed to pretending they don't exist. Although you'll hear stories about gringo grad students, artists, and thrill-seekers who live in Rocinha, tourists who don't know the codes nor the terrain shouldn't venture forth on their own. For better or worse, Rocinha has lately become a hot tourist destination. An increasing number of local tour guides offer group and individual tours to the *favela,* and while these may provide some insights as to how the other half

lives, the jury is still out as to whether this form of tourism is beneficial, exploitative, or a little bit of both.

ZONA NORTE

As you travel from the Tom Jobim international airport to Centro or Zona Sul you'll pass through Rio's sprawling Zona Norte district. For the most part, there is no reason to see more of it than the glimpse afforded from your bus or taxi window. The area is a mixture of industrial and commercial areas combined with working-class and poor residential neighborhoods and some large *favelas.* Poverty and drug-related violence has made large pockets extremely unsafe. The exception are the Feira de São Cristóvão, a traditional Northeastern market, and the Quinta da Boa Vista (which is fairly close to Centro and easily accessible by Metrô), a vast park with some interesting sights, among them the Museu Nacional. If you have some extra time to kill while in Rio, you can combine the Zona Norte attractions into a day trip.

FEIRA DE SÃO CRISTÓVÃO

Pavilhão de São Cristóvão, São Cristóvão, tel. 21/3860-9976, www.feiradesaocristovao.org.br
HOURS: Tues.-Thurs. 10 A.M.-4 P.M., 24 hours from Fri. 10 A.M. to Sun. 10 P.M.
COST: R$1

Recently renovated and rebaptized as the Centro Luiz Gonzaga de Tradições Nordestinas, this massive outdoor market reunites people from Brazil's Northeastern states, many of whom migrated to Rio for work but still get homesick for the food, drink, music, and sheer animation of their home states. The *feira* has 700 *barracas* (stalls), where vendors hawk typical products ranging from handwoven hammocks from Ceará and leather hats and sandals from the sunbaked Sertão to jars of herb-infused *cachaças,* hot peppers, and amber-colored *dendê* (palm) oil from Bahia. Tuesday–Thursday, you'll find lots of places to eat typical lunches. The good times don't really roll, however, until the weekends, when *nordestino* expats and fun-loving Cariocas congregate to listen to performances of *forró* (country-like music featuring fiddle, accordion, and percussion) and *repentistas* (musical preachers) as well as samba and MPB. From Friday morning until Sunday night, the *barracas* stay open around the clock. To get to the *feira*, take any bus marked São Cristóvão leaving from the Zona Sul. By night, take a taxi.

JARDIM ZOOLÓGICO (RIOZOO)

Parque Quinta da Boa Vista, São Cristóvão,
tel. 21/3878-4200, www.rio.rj.gov.br/riozoo
HOURS: Tues.-Sun. 9 A.M.-4:30 P.M.
COST: R$6 adult, free senior and child under one meter

Located within the sprawl of Parque Quinta da Boa Vista, Rio's zoo shelters more than 2,000 mammals, birds, and reptiles, many of them native to Brazil. Among the most interesting are the extremely distinctive *urubu rei* (king vulture), *tamanduá bandeira* (giant anteater), and the exquisitely leonine *mico leão dourado* (golden lion tamarin), all of which are tragically close to extinction. The feline section is very popular due to splendid inhabitants such as native jaguars and ocelots as well as more far-flung Himalayan and Siberian tigers. Another big draw is the Casa Noturna, an area in which simulated night allows you to observe creatures that only come to life after dark. Part of the zoo's mission is the rescue of endangered animals. Penguins and sea lions that find themselves washed up on Rio's coastline find a temporary refuge here, as do giant sea tortoises that measure up to 1 meter (3 feet) in length. Should you seek refuge as well, you'll find it at the snack bar, the *sorveteria,* or the picnic area.

MUSEU NACIONAL

Parque Quinta da Boa Vista, São Cristóvão,
tel. 21/2562-6040, www.museunaciona.ufrj.br
HOURS: Tues.-Sun. 10 A.M.-4 P.M.
COST: R$3

Brazil's oldest scientific museum and the largest natural history museum in Latin America, the Museu Nacional was originally known as the Museu Real due to the fact that the enormous and somewhat eclectic collection was started by Dom João VI in the 1820s. Shortly after the emperor went into exile following the declaration of the republic, the collection moved into the Palácio de São Cristóvão, the former imperial digs located in the Quinta da Boa Vista park. Visitors to the museum should exercise discrimination, because there's a lot of stuff to weed through. The archaeological section focuses on prehistoric Latin American peoples, but you can also check out the Egyptian artifacts (including some ornate mummies) that Dom Pedro I picked up for a song at auction, and the Empress Teresa Cristinas's collection of Greco-Roman pieces. The ethnological collection has some interesting artifacts related to Brazil's indigenous cultures. Among the highlights in the mineral section is the Bendigo Meteorite, which landed in the state of Bahia in 1888, and is the heaviest metallic mass known to have crashed through the planet's atmosphere.

QUINTA DA BOA VISTA

Av. Pedro II btwn. Rua Almirante Baltazar and Rua Dom
Meinrado, São Cristóvão, tel. 21/2232-4398
HOURS: Daily 5 A.M.-6 P.M.
COST: R$4 adult, free senior and child under 7

A former sugar plantation, the Quinta da Boa Vista was where Brazil's imperial family took up residence between 1822 to 1889. Befitting royalty, the expansive grounds designed in 1869 in pure romantic style by French landscaper Auguste Glaziou feature lots of parkland festooned with Greek and Romanesque bronze and marble statues, flower gardens, grottoes, lakes, a restaurant, and even a zoo. An alley lined with *sapucaias* leads to Palácio de São Cristóvão, a stately neoclassical palace where the emperor and his family lived. It was here that both Dom Pedro II and his daughter, Princesa Isabel, were born. Today, it is home to the Museu Nacional. To get to the Quinta da Boa Vista, take the Metrô to São Cristóvão. If you're in search of peace and tranquility, avoid weekends, but during the week refrain from wandering off into isolated areas since safety can be an issue.

SOLAR DA MARQUESA DE SANTOS

Av. Pedro II 293, São Cristóvão, tel. 21/2332-4513,
www.funarj.rj.gov.br
HOURS: Tues.-Sun. 11 A.M.-5 P.M.

Built in the early 1820s, this grand neoclassical mansion was a gift from Dom Pedro I to his mistress and great love, Dimitilia de Castro Canto e Melo, aka the Marquesa dos Santos; she lived here from 1826 to 1829. Today, it functions as the Museu do Primeiro Reinado, with a collection of books, documents, and artifacts related to the reign of Dom Pedro I (1822–1831) that is likely to interest only historians. Romantics will probably get more of a charge out of peering at the Marquesa's personal effects and sighing over the door and window arches—at the emperor's behest, they were decorated with hearts meant to symbolize his undying passion.

PARQUE DA CIDADE
MUSEU HISTÓRICO DA CIDADE DO RIO DE JANEIRO

Estrada de Santa Marinha, tel. 21/2512-2353,
www.rio.rj.gov.br/culturas
HOURS: Tues.-Fri. 10 A.M.-4 P.M., Sat.-Sun. 10 A.M.-3 P.M.

Tucked away within the Parque da Cidade, a leafy park crisscrossed by streams and walking paths, the former 19th-century estate of the Marquis of São Vicente has been through several renovations and now houses temporary and permanent exhibits that trace the history of Rio de Janeiro from colonial to republican times. Aside from some dusty maquettes and old photographs, there are plenty of period objects including art works, furnishings, and dishes rescued from the Paço Imperial. Near the main house, the Capela de São João Baptista (that can only be visited by appointment) is infamous for its fresco of the life of St. John, in which Bahian painter Carlos Bastos used the likenesses of famous 1970s personages—the uproar was such that the work was never finished. Even if you're not terribly curious about Rio's past, the mansion, with its slender iron columns supporting wide verandas, combined with the surrounding park, offers

a bucolic getaway for a couple of hours. It's recommended to take a cab there (and have the driver pick you up) since getting there and back involves a trek through the outskirts of the *favela* of Rocinha.

FLORESTA DA TIJUCA

Although the dense tropical forest that covers Rio's jagged mountains possesses a distinctly primeval quality, the truth is that by the 19th century the original Atlantic forest that had existed for thousands of years had been almost completely cleared away to make way for sugar and coffee plantations. The deforestation was so dire that by the mid-1800s, Rio was facing an ecological disaster that menaced the city's water supply. Fortunately, inspired emperor Dom Pedro II had a green conscience. In 1861 he ordered that 3,200 hectares be replanted with native foliage—the first example of government mandated reforestation in Brazil's history. Over time, the forest returned to its original state and today this urban jungle boasts an astounding variety of exotic trees and animals ranging from jewel-colored hummingbirds to monkeys, squirrels, and armadillos.

Within the Floresta lies the Parque Nacional da Tijuca, a veritable oasis in the midst of the city with walking trails, waterfalls, grottoes, and lookout points that offer stunning views of the city.

MUSEU DO AÇUDE

Estrada do Açude 764, Alto da Boa Vista,
tel. 21/2492-2119, www.museuscastromaya.com.br
HOURS: Tues.-Sun. 11 A.M.-5 P.M.
COST: R$2 adult, free senior and child under 12,
free adult Thurs.

Completely engulfed by the jungly Floresta da Tijuca, the Museu do Açude occupies a turn-of-the-20th-century neoclassical villa built as a summer residence for wealthy industrialist Raymundo Ottoni de Castro Maya. Beautifully decorated with antiques and Portuguese azulejo panels, it now houses Castro Maya's impressive art collection, a treasure trove that runs the gamut from ancient Oriental sculptures and East India Company porcelain to works by contemporary Brazilian artists such as Hélio de Oiticica and Ligia Clark. Many pieces are so large that they are displayed (to great effect) amidst the lovely grounds. If you're around on the last Sunday of the month, consider dropping by for brunch in the garden, accompanied by live music.

C PARQUE NACIONAL DA TIJUCA

Main entrance on Praça Afonso Viseu,
tel. 21/2492-2253
HOURS: Daily 8 A.M.–5 P.M.

Within the Floresta da Tijuca lies the largest urban park in Brazil, the Parque Nacional da Tijuca, a particularly refreshing destination during the dog days of summer. The park has various walking trails—many of them quite easy—and waterfalls as well as grottoes and many lookout points that offer stunning views of the city. The most spectacular of these are the **Mesa do Imperador** (Emperor's Table—where Dom Pedro II liked to picnic with members of his court) and the **Vista Chinesa.** Another highlight is the charming **Capela Mayrink,** with panels painted by the talented modernist artist Candido Portinari.

The easiest way to explore the park is by car. If you don't have access to one, take a taxi: You can usually negotiate with drivers to drop you off and pick you up for a reasonable rate. You can also take a guided jeep or hiking tour. If you want to venture in on your own, take the Metrô to Saens Pena and then a bus going to Barra da Tijuca that stops at Alta da Boa Vista. Organized hiking tours are also offered. A few hundred meters past the entrance is a visitors center where you can buy a map (although trails are well marked). Robberies are increasingly common, so be careful not to venture too far off the beaten track and don't go alone. It's safer to visit on weekends, when the park is more crowded. Near the entrance are three restaurants and a café. Or if you want, bring along food for a picnic.

SIGHTS

RESTAURANTS

In keeping with a city of its size, sophistication, and diversity, Rio has an impressive restaurant scene featuring the best of so-called *alta* and *baixa culinária* (high and low cuisine). *Alta* cuisine has really taken off in Rio since the 1990s. In particular, the neighborhoods of Ipanema, Leblon, Jardim Botânico, and, to a lesser extent, Centro have seen a rise in stylish eateries owned and operated by some of the most vanguard chefs in the country. While some focus on international cuisine, others innovatively marry traditional European cooking techniques with distinctive Brazilian ingredients, creating a *nouvelle cuisine tropicale*.

Many traditional neighborhood *churrascarias* and *botequins* offer up tasty *comida caseira* (home cooking) ranging from hearty *caldos* (soups), robust sandwiches, and barbecued chicken and beef, to the classic Saturday *feijoada*, in which the famed Brazilian stew of beans, pork, and sausages is garnished with sautéed *couve* (kale), *farofa* (crunchy manioc flour), and orange slices. The obligatory libation is, of course, the *caipirinha*, made with *cachaça*, sugar, crushed ice, and lime.

Although carnivores fare well in Rio, fish and seafood lovers will be equally spoiled. In keeping with Cariocas' fame as a body-conscious bunch, there are also numerous vegetarian, organic, and all-around healthy eateries—many of them self-service per-kilo buffets where diners can control their weight down to the last gram—particularly in the Zona Sul. Propitiously located between the beaches and seemingly endless number of gyms, juice bars serve up dozens of varieties of

HIGHLIGHTS

LOOK FOR 🎔 TO FIND RECOMMENDED RESTAURANTS.

🎔 **Most Sumptuous Café:** For a rare glimpse into how the upper classes lived a century ago, stop in for a *cafezinho* at the opulent belle epoque **Confeitaria Colombo** in Centro (page 85).

🎔 **Best Late-Night Meal:** A classic Lapa *boteco* that's been in business since 1903, **Nova Capela** is a favored pit stop for the samba-'til-3 A.M. crowd that can't get enough of the specialty: roasted kid with broccoli rice (page 88).

🎔 **Most Scenic Supper:** Rio is hardly lacking in fine restaurants with great views, but Santa Teresa's charming **Aprazível** combines creative Brazilian cuisine and a daring wine list with stunning views of the city and Baía de Guanabara (page 90).

🎔 **Best Family-Friendly *Churrascaria*:** **Porção Rio's** has a fantastic array of barbecued meats, plus an all-you-can-dream-of buffet with options to tempt the pickiest of eaters – salads, sushi, seafood, and lots of mouthwatering desserts. The spacious restaurant's location in the Parque do Flamengo guarantees lots of room to run around (page 93).

🎔 **Best Bahian Beach Food:** There's nowhere more appropriate to sample Bahian fish and seafood specialties such as *acarajé* and *moqueca* than right on the beach, at the Copacabana kiosk operated by **Siri Mole Praia** (page 96).

🎔 **Most Lavish Brunch:** You know you're living it up when your day begins by piling your plate to the ceiling with blinis, caviar, raw oysters, and foie gras at **Pérgula,** the Copacabana Palace's glamorous poolside café (page 97).

🎔 **Best *Feijoada* Fix:** Choosing the "best" *feijoada* in a city where the national dish of beans and salted meat is as essential as water is a contentious move, but the fact that **Casa da Feijoada** serves it every single day (with all the fixings) and is consistently packed from noon to midnight means they're doing something right (page 102).

🎔 **Best Dessert:** Nothing beats the heat like the pure bursts of tropical flavor that come in a scoop of **Mil Frutas Café** ice cream (page 104).

🎔 **Best Vegetarian Meal:** The dozens of freshly made salads prepared daily at Leblon's **Celeiro** are so good that hard-core carnivores line up along with figure-watching models and celebs (page 114).

🎔 **Foodie Favorite:** One of Brazil's most innovative chefs, **Roberta Sudbrack,** relies on fresh local ingredients to create contemporary dishes that astonish the senses. A meal at her eponymous restaurant in Jardim Botânico is a culinary event (page 116).

© MICHAEL SOMMERS

the belle epoque interior of the Confeitaria Colombo

fresh fruit juices, vitamin drinks, and healthy *sanduiches naturais.*

Aside from restaurants, bars and *botequins* are also great places to eat. Menus invariably feature a satisfying array of *petiscos* (appetizers) that, depending on your willpower, will either tide you over between meals or leave you contentedly stuffed. In recent times, a new crop of charming cafés has sprung up, many of them located in the city's cultural centers, cinemas, and *livrarias* (bookstores). In addition to gourmet coffee and delicious bistro-style meals, the desserts tend to be quite fabulous. As you'll witness everywhere from the street *barracas* in Lapa to the *padarias* (bakeries) in Copa, Cariocas have a pronounced sweet tooth, and satisfying sugar cravings is absurdly easy.

Although Rio's top restaurants are not at

PRICE KEY

- $ Entrées less than R$25
- $$ Entrées R$25–R$50
- $$$ Entrées more than R$50

---

all cheap, the prices are quite decent when compared to the equivalents in major North American and European cities. As such, it's definitely worth your while to splurge once or twice (also know that many top restaurants offer more reasonably priced weekday *menus executivos* for lunch). You can then atone for your sins by seeking out more reasonably priced culinary experiences at the city's beach *barracas,* bars, bakeries, and bookstores.

Centro   Map 1

The restaurants in Centro, Rio's commercial and financial hub, cater overwhelmingly to a clientele of workers and executives. As such, the majority are open only on weekdays and for lunch. Options are hardly lacking: You'll find scores of cheap per-kilo places, *lanchonetes* (snack bars) serving sandwiches, and basic restaurant-bars serving basic "PFs" *(prato feitos)*—which generally consists of a portion of beef or chicken with rice, fries, and a measly salad for around R$6–8. Quality varies. In general, you get what you pay for, although traditional *botecos* serve *comida caseira* that is inexpensive and very tasty. At the other end of the spectrum, as executive palates have become more educated, an increasing number of sophisticated bistros and fine restaurants have opened. Many are located around the atmospheric cobblestoned streets of Rua do Ouvidor and Rua do Rosário, where you'll also find a handful of Rio's oldest restaurants (many of them Portuguese) that have changed little in the hundred years they've been in business. Finally, a large number of the area's cultural centers (most of which

are housed in historic buildings) boast cafés and bistros that combine attractive settings with creative and very affordable menus that are ideal for snacks or light meals.

BISTROS AND LIGHT FARE
BISTRÔ DO PAÇO $

Praça XV 48, tel. 21/2262-3613, www.bistro.com.br
HOURS: Mon.-Fri. 11:30 A.M.-7:30 P.M., Sat.-Sun. noon-7 P.M.

Looking out onto a whitewashed courtyard inside the Paço Imperial, this cozy stone-walled cavern offers a tranquil oasis from the surrounding noise, heat, and traffic of Centro. Lunch is a rapid but tasteful affair with delicious salads, sandwiches, and daily specials. The homemade quiches are particularly good— try the version with sweet potato, ginger, and saffron, which is usually served on Wednesday. At around 1 P.M. the place gets quite crowded with hungry execs. Late afternoons are more conducive to lingering, especially with a plate of the irresistible bittersweet-chocolate Brazilnut torte in front of you.

BRASSERIE ROSÁRIO 💲💲

Rua do Rosário 34, tel. 21/2518-3033,
www.brasserierosario.com.br

HOURS: Mon.-Fri. 11 A.M.-10 P.M., Sat. 11 A.M.-7 P.M.

This brasserie is a gourmet café, delicatessen, bakery, wine cellar, and bistro all rolled into one very attractive high-ceilinged, stone-walled building dating from the 1860s. Light eaters can choose from myriad antipasti, salads, and unusual sandwiches made with freshly baked breads, while those with serious hunger pangs can attack the likes of artichoke herb risotto or grilled bass served with couscous and topped with a basil froth. Don't leave without sampling the pastries. The petits-fours made with *castanha-de-caju* (cashews) are downright sublime.

CAFÉS AND SNACKS
CASA CAVÉ 💲

Rua Sete de Setembro 137, tel. 21/2222-0533

HOURS: Mon.-Fri. 9 A.M.-7 P.M., Sat. 9 A.M.-1 P.M.

Surely when French émigré Auguste Charles Cavé first opened a Parisian-style tea salon in 1860, he never imagined that at the dawn of the 21st-century locals would still be thronging the charming little tea house in search of their mille-feuille fix. French patisseries aside, most of the other mouthwatering sweets flaunting their caloric forms from behind the glass display case are of Portuguese origin (whose recipes were created by convent nuns). Particularly irresistible are the cinnamon-dusted *pastéis de nata* (custard tarts) and *toucinho do céu* (a rich, velvety egg and almond tart).

the elegant art deco interior of Casa Cavé

🅒 CONFEITARIA COLOMBO 💲

Rua Gonçalves Dias 32, tel. 21/2232-2300,
www.confeitariacolombo.com.br

HOURS: Mon.-Fri. 8 A.M.-8 P.M., Sat. 10 A.M.-5 P.M.

This disarmingly elegant belle epoque café offers one of the few remaining examples of how grand life must have been if you were an aristocrat in turn-of-the-20th-century Rio. Stepping off the gritty narrow street and into the dazzling interior provides a living definition of the word contrast. The interior—outfitted with French stained glass, Portuguese azulejos, and immense Belgian mirrors with jacaranda frames—resonates with Old World charm. More than a century after it opened, Colombo is still a Rio institution: While working Cariocas cluster around the bar chasing pastries with *cafezinhos,* slack-jawed tourists can take *chá da tarde* (high tea) in the salon or indulge in the Saturday-afternoon *feijoada,* accompanied by live samba and *choro.*

RUBRO CAFÉ 💲

Rua da Quitanda 191, tel. 21/2516-0610,
www.rubrocafe.com.br

HOURS: Mon.-Fri. 7 A.M.-8 P.M.

Ideally located in the foyer of the Centro do Comércio do Café (the 100-year-old regulating body of Brazil's prize crop), this airy, modern café is where the people who really *know* about coffee go to get their caffeine fix. More than 20 gourmet coffee drinks are served as well as breakfast fare, sandwiches, salads, and desserts. Rubro is the name of the delicious house blend, which you can also buy to take home with you.

CONTEMPORARY

CAIS DO ORIENTE ⑨⑨

Rua Visconde de Itaboraí 8, tel. 21/2233-2531, www.caisdooriente.com.br

HOURS: Sun.-Mon. noon-4 P.M., Tues-Sat. noon-midnight

Ambience is everything at Cais do Oriente, located in a stunningly renovated 19th-century warehouse. Actually there are several ambiences to choose from: the palmy open-air patio, the mezzanine lounge with a stage for live music performances, and the main salon, which is sumptuously decorated with antiques, Oriental carpets, and gigantic mirrors. The menu, as varied as the surroundings, offers a mishmash of Asian and Mediterranean dishes prepared with a contemporary twist. The overall sensation is otherworldly.

EÇA ⑨⑨⑨

Av. Rio Branco 128, tel. 21/2524-2401, www.hstern.com.br/eca/

HOURS: Mon.-Fri. noon-4 P.M.

You have to walk past a lot of bling to get to Eça, located in the basement of H. Stern jewelers. This elegant restaurant is singlehandedly responsible for the arrival of contemporary cuisine in Rio's business district. Celebrated Belgian chef Frédéric de Maeyer brings a Gallic sensibility and sense of inventiveness to the kitchen. The results—such as tuna with goat-cheese sorbet and arugula or fresh fish in a pistachio crust with leek risotto—are sophisticated and surprising. For dessert, Maeyer gets (understandably) nationalistic, and resorts to Belgian chocolate for the preparation of airy soufflés and tortes.

LAGUIOLE ⑨⑨⑨

Av. Infante Dom Henrique 85, Museu de Arte Moderna, tel. 21/2517-3129

HOURS: Mon.-Fri. noon-5 P.M.

The deft and adventurous creations of Pedro de Artagã, one of Rio's most promising culinary talents, are totally in keeping with Laguiole's location on the 3rd floor of Rio's MAM. Reflecting the museum's iconic modernism, the restaurant is strikingly minimalist with squeaky-clean lines and sleek white furniture providing an ideal canvas for inventions such as langoustine *bobó* with asparagus tempura or tender slices of filet mignon layered with pears roasted in balsamic vinegar and served with tropical fruit chips. Oenophiles take note: The wine cellar—with more than 400 vintages—is considered one of the best in the city. Dessert-aholics beware: The chocolate mousse cigars are sublime. As a bonus, all diners receive free admission to the museum.

JAPANESE

SHIN MIURA ⑨⑨⑨

Av. Rio Branco 156, Loja 324, 3rd fl., tel. 21/2262-3043

HOURS: Mon.-Fri. 11 A.M.-3 P.M.

Japanese food traditionalists may grimace at the notion of semi-grilled tuna sushi with foie gras and honey-soy sorbet or tuna tartare with ginger chips and avocado. However, adventurous palates can't help but be entranced by chef Nao Hara's daring application of Chinese, French, and Italian touches to unorthodox creations whose startling colors and textures are as provocative as their taste. For "best of" sampling, opt for the *esqueminha,* or chef's tasting menu, which allows you to savor numerous creations based on the size of your table (and your pocketbook). The small dining room is a bit tricky to find—hidden away inside a nondescript mall named Shopping Avenida Central.

MIDDLE EASTERN

SÍRIO E LIBANÊS ⑨

Rua Senhor dos Passos 217, tel. 21/2224-1629

HOURS: Mon.-Fri. 11 A.M.-6 P.M., Sat. 11 A.M.-4 P.M.

With its unassuming retro air, this humble oasis amidst the bazaar-like agitation of the Saara neighborhood serves up delicious and hearty portions of Lebanese specialties for an extremely nice price. You can grab a quick bite at the counter—the crunchy beef-stuffed kibbes are especially good–or else take a seat in the dining room and treat yourself to a banquet. The house specialty, *carneiro ao sírio e libanês,* is tender lamb stuffed with crushed chick peas and cashews, stewed in a sauce flavored with fresh mint.

SEAFOOD
ALBAMAR 💲💲
Praça Marechal Âncora 184, tel. 21/2240-8428, www.albamar.com.br
HOURS: Daily 11 A.M.-6 P.M.

One of Rio's most traditional restaurants, Albamar was getting worn and frayed around the edges until Luiz Incao, the former chef at the Copacabana Palace, took over as chef in early 2009. Despite early growing pains, things are definitely looking up. Incao has added his flavor to the menu, which emphasizes fish and crustaceans. The setting—inside a tower that is the only remnant of Rio's once-grandiose municipal market—is unbeatable. From this lofty aerie, the views of the city and Baía de Guanabara are captivating. Sunday lunch is a singular experience.

RIO MINHO 💲💲
Rua do Ouvidor 10, tel. 21/2509-2338
HOURS: Mon.-Fri. 11 A.M.-3 P.M.

Rio's oldest restaurant still in existence hasn't changed much since it first opened its doors in 1884, and it's often overlooked—except by a faithful posse of business execs and a few intrepid tourists. The small traditional eatery is famed for its *sopa Leão Veloso,* a heady bouillabaisse-like stew of shrimp and fish heads flavored with leeks and cilantro; it was named after a diplomat. As a young man, present owner Ramon Dominguez was turned down for a job at the restaurant; undeterred, he waited decades to buy it along with the Anexo next door, where Dominguez serves smaller (and cheaper) portions.

SENTAÍ 💲💲
Rua Barão do São Félix 75, tel. 21/2233-8358, www.sentai.com.br
HOURS: Tues.-Sun. 11 A.M.-5 P.M.

Despite the dodgy location—behind the Central do Brasil train station—crustacean-loving

RESTAURANTS

Rio Minho is Rio's oldest restaurant still in operation.

© MICHAEL SOMMERS

Cariocas in the know swear by the delicious grilled lobster, lobster *moqueca,* lobster *pastéis* (turnovers), and other mouthwatering recipes served at this humble but typical old-style Centro eatery. It goes by the nickname Rei da Lagosta (Lobster King), but if you're not in the mood for lobster there are other fish in the sea to feast upon as well as a smattering of meat dishes.

TRADITIONAL
CASA PALADINO $

Rua Uruguaiana 224, tel. 21/2263-2094
HOURS: Mon.-Fri. 7 A.M.-8:30 P.M., Sat. 8 A.M.-noon

Over a century old, this venerable old *boteco* happily looks its age, with original fixtures and glossy ceiling-high cabinets crammed with bottles containing all types of national and imported brews and beverages. At lunchtime this atmospheric place is packed with workers addicted to the simple but succulent home-cooked offerings that range from cold-cut sandwiches on crunchy rolls to omelettes (*bacalhau* and shrimp are two of the most popular). An alternative to the midday frenzy is stopping by later in the afternoon for a languorous beer or shot of *cachaça.*

Lapa   Map 1

Renowned for its bohemian ways, Lapa really comes into its own at night, which is also when you're more likely to find more appetizing sustenance. *Botecos* are much more prevalent than restaurants, and all bars, night clubs, and live-music venues serve *petiscos* and even meals, which range from traditional bar grub to more trendier (and expensive) creations. If you really want to dig into a full-fledged meal, however, your best bet is seeking out the most traditional *botequins* in the *bairro*—a few of them have been around for close to a century. Thick with historic atmosphere, they offer generous portions of traditional *comida caseira* at affordable prices.

BRAZILIAN
NOVA CAPELA $

Av. Mem de Sá 96, tel. 21/2252-6228
HOURS: Daily 11 A.M.-5 A.M.

Dating from 1903, Nova Capela is the only one of Lapa's old-time *botequins* that stays open into the wee hours, and over the years it's become the classic pit stop after sambaing the night away at Lapa's neighboring clubs and dance halls. For serious hunger pangs, the classic choice is the house specialty: *cabrito com arroz-de-brocolis* (roasted kid with broccoli rice), which has become

a culinary institution and goes down very nicely at 4 A.M.

PORTUGUESE
ADEGA FLOR DE COIMBRA $$

Rua Teotônio Regadas 34, tel. 21/2224-4582
HOURS: Mon.-Sat. noon-2 A.M., Sun. noon-6 P.M.

Tradition runs high at this 70-year-old Portuguese eatery where original decorative flourishes include barrels of wine, glistening clusters of plastic grapes, and a sign prohibiting *beijos ousados* (daring kisses). The menu is pretty traditional as well and features what Portuguese do best: *bacalhau*. Before plunging into the entrées, order a portion of crunchy *bolinhos*. Among the Adega's many famous regulars over the years was the modernist painter Candido Portinari, who couldn't get enough of the *sopa à lisboeta,* a hearty soup made with butter beans. To drink, choose from over 30 varieties of Portuguese wine.

SEAFOOD
MANGUE SECO $$

Rua do Lavradio 23, tel. 21/3852-1947,
www.manguesecocachacaria.com.br
HOURS: Mon.-Thurs. 11 A.M.-midnight,
Fri.-Sat. 11 A.M.-2 A.M.

Before becoming a street, the area around Rua

do Lavradio was a *mangue* (mangrove swamp). In Brazil *mangues* are rife with freshwater crabs, and at Mangue Seco crabs rule—as evidenced by the crustacean-stuffed aquarium located near the entrance along with the *toc toc* of clients using tiny mallets to hammer away at shells. For a more sustaining meal, tuck into a fish or seafood *moqueca* (stew). The fact that one of the proprietors is the president of the Brazilian Academy of Cachaça explains the incredible diversity of *cachaça* on display. Savor it pure or in a *caipirinha*—in the evenings, you can do so upstairs amidst performances of *choro* and samba.

Santa Teresa   Map 2

Santa's ongoing metamorphosis into Rio's hip, alternative arts *bairro* is gradually spilling over into its restaurant scene. Local entrepreneurs and artists and an increasing number of European expats have been transforming the century-old mini-palaces and mansions into gourmet eateries, many of which feature imaginative Brazilian fare. The charming, bucolic atmosphere—often coupled with staggering views of the bay and city below—seduce both tourists and Cariocas. Meanwhile, Santa's residents and artists often head to a handful of charming decades-old *botecos,* which continue to serve up *petiscos* and *comida caseira* at much more affordable prices.

ASIAN
ASIA 💲💲💲
Rua Almirante Alexandrino 256, tel. 21/2224-2014, www.asia-rio.com
HOURS: Wed.-Sun. noon-11 P.M.
Riding the tide of Asian eateries that have been taking Rio by storm, Asia opened in 2006, billing itself as Rio's first Pan-Asian

© MICHAEL SOMMERS

Asia and Espírito Santa occupy adjoining houses in Santa Teresa.

restaurant. The owners are English and Malaysian and their distinctive backgrounds are reflected in the impeccable decor of the four floors of this handsomely renovated mansion, overflowing with terraces, which effortlessly mingles sleek Euro minimalism with rich ethnic accents of the Orient. The ambitious menu juggles Chinese dim sum with Malaysian satays and Thai curries. While some of the fare might be a novelty for Cariocas, North American diners might balk at the steep prices charged for a humble stir fry or bowl of wonton soup.

BRAZILIAN
APRAZÍVEL $$$

Rua Aprazível 62, tel. 21/2508-9174,
www.aprazivel.com.br
HOURS: Thurs.-Sat. noon-1 A.M., Sun. 1-7 P.M.

Aprazível—Portuguese for delightful—is the perfect name for this restaurant whose rustic jacaranda tables fill the warm, honey-colored interior of a bucolic villa. Even more appealing are those that spill out onto the veranda and lush tropical garden, both of which offer panoramic views of the Baía de Guanabara. The cuisine riffs on the traditional fare of Minas Gerais—yielding dishes such as *galinhada caipira* (organic chicken seasoned with sausage and garnished with braised kale and banana) and *rainha do baião* (tilapia bathed in cilantro-scented olive oil and served with okra and tangy *coalho* cheese). The wine menu, designed by American expat and indie filmmaker Jonathan Nossiter (who made the excellent wine documentary *Mondovino*), focuses on unsung local vintages. Since the restaurant fills up on weekends, reservations are recommended.

ESPÍRITO SANTA $$

Rua Almirante Alexandrino 264, tel. 21/2508-7095,
www.espiritosanta.com.br
HOURS: Mon.-Wed. 11:30 A.M.-6 P.M., Thurs.-Sat.
11:30 A.M.-midnight, Sun. 11:30 A.M.-7 P.M.

There's no need to journey to the Amazon to savor exotic ingredients such as piranha, mozzarella made from the Ilha do Marajó's buffalo

herds, and fruits such as *jambu, taperabá,* and *cupuaçu.* Amazonian chef Natacha Fink uses these and many other delicacies at this innovative restaurant housed in a coral-colored 1930s villa with a lovely terrace. Start off with crab claws served with *jambu* vinaigrette, then move on to sole stuffed with shrimp in a *taperabá* sauce, accompanied by hearts of palm. Save room for desserts such as crisp fritters filled with guava, cashews, and *cupuaçu.* Exotic *caipirinhas* are made with artisanal *cachaças.*

SOBRENATURAL $$

Rua Almirante Alexandrino 432, tel. 21/2224-1003
HOURS: Mon.-Thurs. noon-midnight,
Fri.-Sun. noon-1 A.M.

The delicious fish and seafood served at this unpretentious and laid-back restaurant are caught daily by owner Carlos Moura and inspire the preparation of simple home-style Brazilian dishes such as seafood paella and fish *moqueca* (a Bahian stew that uses coconut milk, tomatoes, cilantro, and lime) with shrimp sauce. The generous portions are enough to feed two

© MICHAEL SOMMERS

Sobrenatural is famed for its fresh seafood.

or three. On the weekends, call ahead or you'll risk waiting in line for a table.

CAFÉS AND SNACKS

ALDA MARIA DOCES PORTUGUESES $
Rua Almirante Alexandrino 116, tel. 21/2232-1320, www.aldadocesportugueses.com.br
HOURS: Tues.-Sun. 2-7 P.M.
From her lovely house decorated with traditional blue and white azulejos, Alda Maria sells Portuguese sweets and pastries that she makes using recipes passed down by her grandmother. Neighborhood favorites include *dom-rodrigo* (an angel-haired ensemble of sweetened egg-yolk strands and almonds) and *papo de anjo* (whipped egg yolks, baked and then boiled in sugar syrup). Cholesterol-phobics beware; invented centuries ago in Portuguese convents, most of these pastries rely heavily on eggs (Alda Maria claims she cracks more than 800 a week).

JASMIM MANGA $
Largo do Guimarães 143, tel. 21/2242-2605, www.jasmimmangacafe.com.br
HOURS: Wed.-Mon. 10 A.M.-10 P.M.
A great way to start the day off in Santa Teresa

is to head to this charming cyber café, right next to Santa's only cinema. A trio of computers are tucked away in an upstairs mezzanine. Along with coffee and pastries, it serves eight versions of breakfast: from the beggar's banquet of baguette and café au lait to an all-out feast involving a cornucopia of tropical fruits, specialty breads, herbed butters, and frozen cappuccinos. An added bonus is the fact that late risers don't lose out—in a Carioca rarity, breakfast is served all day long.

GERMAN

ADEGA DO PIMENTA $$
Rua Almirante Alexandrino 296, tel. 21/2224-7554
HOURS: Mon.-Fri. 11:30 A.M.-10 P.M., Sat. 11:30 A.M.-8 P.M., Sun. 11:30 A.M.-6 P.M.
This cozy little German-style tavern dishes up hearty portions of authentic Bohemian grub: *eisbein* (pork cheeks), sauerkraut, sausages, and on weekends even a German version of *feijoada* that uses white beans. For dessert, apple strudel and cheesecake are both good choices. At times, the *froideur* of the waitstaff matches the iciness of the *chope,* but that hardly fazes the locals who have haunted the place for years.

Glória and Catete — Map 2

Apart from *lanchonetes* and bars serving run-of-the-mill fare, there are very few notable restaurants in either of these *bairros.*

PER-KILO BUFFET

ESTAÇÃO REPÚBLICA $
Rua do Catete 104, tel. 21/2225-2650
HOURS: Mon.-Sat. 11 A.M.-midnight, Sun. 11 A.M.-11 P.M.
Just across the street from the Palácio and Parque do Catete, this cheery and spacious per-kilo restaurant is nothing special, but it does have an enormous range of offerings that will make it difficult for even the pickiest of eaters to refrain from piling their plate high with food. To boot, its extended hours are quite rare for a self-service place.

Carnivores will appreciate the *churrasqueira,* featuring juicy barbecued meats, while more diet-conscious souls can take refuge in salads and sushi.

SEAFOOD

BARRACUDA $$$
Av. Infante Dom Henrique, Loja 6, tel. 21/2265-4641, www.restaurantebarracuda.com.br
HOURS: Mon.-Sat. noon-midnight, Sun. noon-6 P.M.
Located at the Marina da Glória, Barracuda takes its location seriously. The decor is heavy-handed, with wooden beams redolent of a ship's hold and walls adorned with kitschy nautical equipment. Thankfully, there are also expertly prepared fish and seafood dishes

such as *bacalhau no tacho à Julio;* cod baked to golden perfection in olive oil with potatoes, peppers, and onions. Although it's not listed on the menu, regulars swear by the highly original *feijoada de polvo,* in which the classic *feijoada* is made over with white beans, red wine, and octopus. The ambience may be a far cry from Riviera chic, but the prices are quite in sync with those of Cannes.

SWISS
CASA DA SUIÇA 🄂🄂🄂
Rua Cândido Mendes 157, tel. 21/2252-5182, www.casadasuica.com.br
HOURS: Mon.-Fri. noon-3 P.M. and 7 P.M.-midnight, Sat. 7 P.M.-1 A.M., Sun. noon-4 P.M. and 7-11 P.M.

One of the more unexpected culinary presences in Rio is this decades-old Swiss restaurant housed in the Swiss Consulate. To date, the (Austrian) chef's biggest challenge has been to convince Cariocas that there's more to Swiss cuisine than fondue. His attempts to prove otherwise result in dishes such as pork stuffed with ham and emmenthal and filet mignon with oysters. However, in spite of Rio's tropical heat, the fondues—particularly the classic cheese with herb version served with chunks of fresh pears and mushrooms—are in high demand. While the cozy dining salons ooze Old World charm, on "winter" Sundays the delightful back garden is *the* place to stuff yourself on raclette.

Flamengo and Laranjeiras   Map 2

The most interesting eating options in this *bairro* are the handful of alluringly retro *botequins* and restaurants that have survived from the area's early-20th-century heyday. Anything but trendy, these are great places to savor tasty, traditional fare that has become the Carioca equivalent of comfort food.

BRAZILIAN
LAMAS 🄂🄂
Rua Marquês de Abrantes 18, tel. 21/2556-0799, www.tempero.com.br/lamas
HOURS: Daily 9:30 A.M.-3 A.M.

Although Lamas has changed addresses several times since it first opened in 1874, everything about the place—from the food and suave bow-tied waiters to the retro ambience—is suffused with an aura of Rio's dining past. The front is a *botequim* where you can enjoy an icy *chope,* while the restaurant is located at the back. The food is honest, solid fare without surprises. Most famous are the succulent filet mignons. Try the *filé à francesa,* served with matchstick potatoes and green peas flavored with diced ham and

onions. After a night of drinking, the *canja* (homemade chicken soup) is an excellent way to ward off a hangover.

CHURRASCARIAS
MAJÓRICA 🄂🄂
Rua Senador Vergueiro 11-15, tel. 21/2205-6820
HOURS: Sun.-Thurs. noon-midnight, Fri.-Sat. noon-1 A.M.

Majórica is one of Rio's best *churrascarias.* Its classic no-nonsense decor, in which slabs of meat and a massive charcoal *churrasqueira* are prominent features, betray the fact that this is one of Rio's oldest and most traditional *churrascarias.* Juicy cuts of prime beef such as T-bone, *picanha* (rump), and filet mignon will make your mouth water. Traditional garnishes such as potato soufflé, french fries, *farofa* (toasted manioc flour) with eggs and banana, and *arroz maluco* ("crazy rice" that features bacon, parsley, and matchstick potatoes) are served separately. In honor of his Catalonian heritage, the proprietor serves an excellent paella on Wednesdays. On weekends, avoid the immense family lineups by arriving after 3 P.M.

◖ PORCÃO RIO'S ❺❺❺

Av. Infante Dom Henrique, Parque do Flamengo,
tel. 21/3389-8989, www.porcao.com.br

HOURS: Sun.-Thurs. 11 A.M.-midnight,
Fri.-Sat. 11 A.M.-1 A.M.

Meat in all its succulent glory is truly the raison d'être of Porcão Rio's. Its *rodízio de carne* (rotation of meat) is an ingenious Brazilian culinary tradition: Waiters circulate the dining room brandishing various just-grilled cuts of meat, and clients choose what they want. Started by two Gaúcho brothers from Brazil's most carnivorous state of Rio Grande do Sul, Porcão has become an institution, as well as a popular (and fairly pricy) chain. Growth, however, hasn't spoiled the quality of the food or service. In fact, aside from mouthwatering cuts of beef, the price—R$68 per person—includes unlimited trips to the fabulous buffet, which includes everything from salads and seafood to sushi. The restaurant also features a seaside view, located right in front of Pão de Açúcar. Its popularity with local families and *turistas* means that weekends can get very crowded.

CONTEMPORARY
SENAC BISTRÔ ❺

Rua Marquês do Abrantes 99, tel. 21/3138-1540,
www.senacbistro.com.br

HOURS: Tues.-Sat. noon-4 P.M. and 7 P.M.-midnight,
Sun. noon-5 P.M.

Sharing digs with the Centro Cultural Arte Sesc, Senac Bistrô is located in a splendid mansion constructed by wealthy Czech magnate Fred Figner in 1912. Part of the Senac restaurant school, this model restaurant offers contemporary bistro fare with Brazilian accents prepared with meticulous care (after all, the chefs are being graded for their efforts). A typical starter may consist of pumpkin balls stuffed with sun-dried beef, served with gratinéed hearts of palm, followed by an entrée of cashew-crusted stone bass garnished with banana puree. Prices are quite affordable, especially the R$25 weekday *executivo* lunch menu. Since their futures depend upon it, the young waitstaff-in-training are also extremely (sometimes overly) solicitous.

PORTUGUESE
BAR DO SERAFIM ❺❺

Rua Alice 24, Loja A, tel. 21/2225-2843

HOURS: Mon.-Sat. 8 A.M.-midnight, Sun. 10 A.M.-6 P.M.

Tucked away on a quiet street in the pretty residential neighborhood of Laranjeiras, this favorite corner *boteco* has changed little since it first opened in 1944. Amidst barrels and bottles of wine, old posters and yellowing newspaper clippings, and the odd *futebol* jersey, regulars congregate to nibble on perennially crunchy *bolinhos de bacalhau* washed down with icy *chope,* or the house *cachaça, coquinho do Juca,* infused with coconut. Among the hearty (and somewhat heavy) menu offerings are *bacalhau* and a potent *rabada* (oxtail stew) with watercress that makes locals' mouths water. On Friday a *feijoada complete* is served.

RESTAURANTS

© MICHAEL SOMMERS

The Senac Bistrô is operated by the Senac restaurant school.

Botafogo, Cosme Velho, and Urca   Map 3

These traditional residential neighborhoods are best known for their decades-old *botequins* and Portuguese *tascas* that serve up tried-and-true *comida caseira*, but as Botafogo's nightlife has blossomed so has the (still quite modest) culinary scene.

BRAZILIAN
YORUBÁ $$

Rua Arnaldo Quintela 94, tel. 21/2541-9387
HOURS: Wed.-Sun. 7 P.M.-midnight, Sat.-Sun. noon-7 P.M.

Chef Neide Santos has a flair for preparing traditional Afro-Bahian recipes with an uncommonly light and sophisticated touch. Whet your appetite with crunchy *acarajés* made from pureed black-eyed beans, deep fried in palm oil, before sampling a savory Bahian *moqueca* of *siri mole* (soft-shell crab) swimming in tomatoes, cilantro, and coconut milk, or *ewa*, grilled fish seasoned with dried shrimp and okra and dusted with toasted manioc flour. To cleanse your palate, opt for the tapioca *sorvete* or pleasantly acidic tamarind *doce*. Lodged inside a run-down old house with prison-like bars on the windows and touristy tchotchkes on the walls, the ambience is sadly less appetizing than the menu.

CAFÉS AND SNACKS
SORVETE BRASIL $

Av. Pasteur 520, tel. 21/2543-3615,
www.sorvetebrasil.com.br
HOURS: Daily 9 A.M.-9 P.M.

The icing on the cake that is a ride up to the top of Pão de Açúcar is stopping for an ice cream cone at this *sorveteria* located inside the Estação de Bondinho (tram station). Nothing helps the back-down-to-Earth transition better than a scoop of fig-and-walnut or lime meringue *sorvete*. There is another outlet in Ipanema at Rua Maria Quitéria 74, Loja C (tel. 21/2247-8404).

RODÍZIO

Rodízio (rotation) refers to a type of restaurant in which you pay a set price and then choose food from trays proffered by waiters who circle endlessly between the kitchen and the dining room. Since you can feast until you're full, it's recommended that you go on an empty stomach. Most often, you'll find *rodízio* in *churrascarias*, where an endless parade of freshly grilled meat will make the rounds. All it takes is the slightest signal to a waiter and the appetizing piece of meat that was on a skewer will be on your plate. Other popular forms of *rodízio* include pasta, pizza, and sushi.

CHURRASCARIAS
ZOZÔ $$$

Av. Pasteur 520, tel. 21/2542-9665,
www.zozorio.com.br
HOURS: Daily noon-midnight

Zozô offers an innovative, less-hectic twist on the classic Brazilian *rodízio* system of waiters swirling around and brandishing skewers of barbecued meat in your face: From a vast menu, select whatever *churrasco* offerings suit your fancy—spareribs, tender *picanha* and *maminha* steaks, grilled fish—and then have them served to you in whatever order you see fit. The R$69 fixed price covers the entire menu as well as a smashing salad and sushi bar and an in-your-face view of Praia Vermelha and Pão de Açúcar through the restaurant's glass walls and ceiling.

CONTEMPORARY
MIAM MIAM $$

Rua General Góes Monteiro 34, tel. 21/2244-0125,
www.miammiam.com.br
HOURS: Tues.-Fri. 7:30 P.M.-12:30 A.M., Sat. 8 P.M.-1:30 A.M.

With a name that's the Brazilian equivalent

of "yum yum," this tiny but very cozy and romantic café-bar is appetizing on all fronts. In 1998, 21-year-old Roberta Ciasca went backpacking through Europe and ended up at the Cordon Bleu cooking school in Paris. In 2006, when she decided to convert her grandmother's turn-of-the-20th-century house into a restaurant, her creative comfort food—such as arugula rolls stuffed with roast beef and parmesan, or chicken pancakes with asparagus, mushrooms, emmenthal, and tarragon—quickly seduced the city's gourmets as well as a young hipster crowd who appreciate the eccentrically retro decor as well as the creative drinks menu (try the *caipivodca*, made with fresh pineapple, mint, and a shot of hot pepper).

FRENCH
CARÊME ●$●
Rua Visconde de Caravelas 113, tel. 21/2537-2274
HOURS: Tues.-Sat. 8 P.M.-midnight
Flávia Quaresma is one of Brazil's most renowned chefs, with a slew of best-selling cookbooks and her own TV show. If you want to see what all the fuss is about, head to her latest eatery, Carême, a cozy little Parisian-style bistro with a small number of daily specials (along with the weather conditions in Paris) written on a blackboard. Classics such as filet mignon in red-wine sauce served with golden potatoes, mushrooms, bacon, and onions share menu space with more unusual recipes such as roasted lamb in a cocoa pepper sauce served on polenta and *cupuaçu bavaroise* topped with cashew sorbet. On Wednesday night there is a specially priced tasting menu for gourmands on a tight budget.

MUSEU DA CADEIRA ●$
Rua Martins Ferreira 48, tel. 21/2527-4044
HOURS: Mon.-Fri. noon-3 P.M. and 7 P.M.-midnight, Sat. 7 P.M.-midnight
This eclectic space inside the Espaço Cultural Maurice Valansi combines a café, restaurant, bookstore, and—as its name suggests—a highly original chair museum,

FOOD BY WEIGHT (COMIDA POR QUILO)

Highly popular and very affordable are restaurants serving *comida por quilo*, where you make choices from a self-service buffet and then pay for your food by weight. You'll find kilo restaurants all over Rio. They range from very basic (and sometimes unappetizing) to banquet-like extravaganzas featuring fine cuisine. Natural-food restaurants serving health food also usually operate on a per-kilo system. There are also dessert options, and complimentary coffee and tea are usually offered at the end of the meal. The best thing about per-kilo restaurants is that you can choose exactly what and how much you want to eat. This is particularly useful for solo travelers. Unfortunately, most kilo restaurants are only open for lunch. An average meal in a kilo restaurant will set you back R$8-20, depending on the sophistication of the food and your appetite.

whose collection of 200-plus *cadeiras* scattered around include major Brazilian furniture designers such as Joaquim Tenreiro and the Campana brothers as well as international stars such as Le Corbusier, Charles and Ray Eames, and Philippe Starck. Admire the upholstery while savoring the likes of duck with mushrooms in caramelized vinegar. If you're simply in the mood for a snack, the crepes are a good choice.

PORTUGUESE
ADEGA DO VALENTIM ●$
Rua da Passagem 178, tel. 21/2527-4044
HOURS: Daily noon-midnight
The interior of this rustic and slightly somber restaurant is a dead ringer for a typical Lisbon or Porto *tasca;* its tiled walls are lined with bottles of Portuguese wine and plaintive strains of fado float in the background. The home-cooked dishes are served in hearty and

generous portions that feed two or even three. *Bacalhau* is popular enough to warrant 20 different versions. The robust white bean and sausage *cozido* (stew) is tasty, but will leave you in a stupor. Lighter fare includes grilled sardines and the risotto-like *arroz com lulas* (squid). Speaking of Lulas, Brazil's president considers this place his favorite restaurant in Rio.

Copacabana and Leme
Map 4

Although it's not much of a gourmet destination, Copa's eating options are as numerous and varied as its inhabitants. Of course everyone wants a meal with a view, but do yourself a favor and steer clear of all the overpriced, mediocre tourist traps along Avenida Atlântica (fortunately, there is a hint of change in the air with the recent opening of stylish contemporary eateries such as Miss Tanaka and Copa Café). Although Cariocas are divided over the shiny new *quiosques* placed at intervals along the beach—many prefer the more rustic, traditional *barracas* dangling with green coconuts and furnished with plastic stools—some of them are branches operated by reputed restaurants and bars (Siri Mole, Bar Luiz, Caroline Café) that offer decent food with unbeatable views. If you've got money to burn, you can eat fabulous food in fabulous style at grand hotels such as the Copacabana Palace and Sofitel, but if you're willing to turn your back on the beach you'll find plenty of traditional neighborhood eateries and drinking holes, particularly in more tranquil, residential Leme; many specialize in seafood and/or Italian fare. Meanwhile, for a snack or a light meal, calorie counters will find a phenomenal number of juice bars, and calorie addicts will salivate at the staggering quantity of cafés and pastry shops.

ASIAN
AZUMI 😊😊😊
Rua Ministro Viveiros de Castro 127, tel. 21/2541-4294
HOURS: Sun. and Tues.-Thurs. 7 P.M.-midnight, Fri.-Sat. 7 P.M.-1 A.M.
Rio's most traditional Japanese restaurant forsakes all trends and focuses on pure flavors and impeccable preparation of classical Japanese fare. The small space is divided into a sushi bar at the front and a back area reserved for *robatas*, or grilled dishes. Specialties include sushi made with sea urchin eggs, *kanitama* (crab omelette with sweet-sour sauce), and *yamaimo bainiko* (chopped acara fish with Japanese plum). The prices aren't cheap, but considering the quality of the food this is definitely the best Japanese food deal in town.

MISS TANAKA 😊😊
Av. Atlântica 974, tel. 21/2275-3589
HOURS: Daily noon-1 A.M.
Since restaurateur Graça Tanaka moved her cult Jardim Botânico restaurant to Leme in 2007 it has become all the rage. Its popularity is a consequence not only of the deliriously kitschy decor featuring wacky floral chandeliers and a cornucopia of Buddha statues, but also of her revamped menu starring unusual dishes such as skewered shrimp and sugarcane with hot sauce and tuna seared in a poppyseed crust with fried rice noodles and curried fruit. Save room for the dessert: The chocolate mousse with crystallized ginger is guaranteed to excite the most zen palates.

BRAZILIAN
🄲 SIRI MOLE PRAIA 😊😊
Av. Atlântica, Quiosque 32 (in front of Rua Bolivar), tel. 21/3684-6671
HOURS: Mon. 3 P.M.-midnight, Tues.-Sun. 9 A.M.-midnight
There's no better place to truly savor Bahian cuisine than at a beachside eatery. With this in mind, head to Siri Mole Praia, an oceanfront kiosk that's an offshoot of the classic Siri Mole (Rua Franciscano Otaviano 50, Copacabana, tel. 21/2267-0894). For a snack, order the crunchy *acarajés* stuffed with dried shrimp,

CAFFEINE FIX

All those clichés you've heard about Brazil as the land of coffee are true. *Café* is seemingly everywhere, and Brazilians always seem to be drinking it – for the most part with vast amounts of sugar or sweetener *(adocante)*. Sometimes it's served pre-sweetened, so if you want your coffee black, ask for it *sem açúcar.* Instead of the big mugs of silty watered-down stuff popular with the Starbucks generation, Brazilians like their *café* small and potent. In fact, served as espresso or in little plastic cups (if you're drinking one from the vendors who sell thermoses of the stuff in the streets of Centro), it is popularly known as *cafezinho* (little coffee). *Cafezinhos*

can be enjoyed all day long, and they usually are, often accompanied by some type of sweet or savory pastry. And no meal is complete without one, although if you order a *cafezinho* with your dessert (as opposed to after), people will look at you funny. In the morning and in the evening *leite* (milk) is sometimes added.

The best of Brazil's coffee was typically exported, but in the last few years a gourmet coffee scene has begun to emerge. Rio in particular has many cafés where you can savor organic and exclusive blends from all over Brazil (although the best beans are from Minas), as well as purchase beans to take home with you.

caruru (seasoned okra), and *vatapá* (a puree featuring shrimp, cashews, and coconut milk). For a light bite, choose from the refreshing seafood starters and salads, or else go whole hog and order a famous *moqueca,* a succulent fish or seafood stew cooked with tomatoes, coconut milk, cilantro, lime, and *dendê* (palm oil). The most popular are made with *siri mole* (soft-shelled crab), lobster, or shrimp.

CAFÉS AND SNACKS
THE BAKERS ⬤
Rua Santa Clara 86-B, tel. 21/3209-1212, www.thebakers.com.br
HOURS: Mon.-Fri. 9 A.M.-8 P.M., Sat. 9 A.M.-5 P.M.
Modeled loosely on old-style New York Jewish delis whose windows flaunt calorie-rich cakes and freshly baked bread (including expertly braided challah), The Bakers is an ideal spot for a light meal or a sandwich. Served on Italian ciabatta bread, the New York, New York packs a wallop with smoked Canadian ham, green apple, provolone, and blackberry chutney. It's also hard to escape without some sort of sugar fix. Particularly irresistible are the Bakers *brigas,* a signature version of *brigadeiro,* an immensely popular Brazilian dessert that resembles a gooey chocolate-fudge truffle.

CAFEÍNA ⬤
Rua Constante Ramos 44, tel. 21/2547-8561, www.cafeinabistro.com.br
HOURS: Daily 8 A.M.-11:30 P.M., Sat. 8 A.M.-1:30 A.M.
This lively little café's sidewalk tables make excellent perches for people-watching. Even if you already had breakfast in your hotel, the pastries, breads, and coffee (culled from the finest plantations in São Paulo, Minas Gerais, and southern Bahia) are so good you might want seconds (an inspired variation of cappuccino, *café mineiro,* features espresso with a shot of artisanal *cachaça* and a dollop of chantilly). For light meals there are fresh salads, creative sandwiches (try the roast beef with caramelized onions, gruyère, and a terrine of fine herbs) and daily specials. There's also an outlet on Rua Barata Ribeiro 507 (tel. 21/2547-4390), along with three others in Ipanema and Leblon.

⬛ PÉRGULA ⬤⬤⬤
Av. Atlântica 1702, tel. 21/2545-8744, www.copacabanapalace.com.br
HOURS: Daily 7 A.M.-midnight
It's hard to get more glam than the Copacabana Palace's poolside café overlooking the beach: Amidst models, magnates, and barefoot *turistas,* you can stop by for a leisurely meal or cocktail session. Breakfast (daily until 10:30 A.M.) is

an extravagant affair with over 100 options to choose from, but it pales in comparison to the lavish Sunday brunch (12:30–4:30 P.M.) where you can pile your plate sky-high with caviar, raw oysters, and freshly made foie gras, and wash it down with a glass of champagne. The price is unsurprisingly steep (R$170 per person for brunch), but it's worth every *centavo* to feast (and feel, if just for a while) like a millionaire. Lunch and dinner specialties range from the rarified (guinea fowl in truffle sauce) to the mundane (a classic club sandwich), but are all impeccably prepared and served.

CONTEMPORARY
COPA CAFÉ ⓈⓈ
Av. Atlântica 3056, Loja B, tel. 21/2235-2947
HOURS: Daily 7 P.M.–2 A.M.

The suave and intimate Copa Café has brought a welcome touch of hipness to the sometimes excessively tacky tourism of Avenida Atlântica. In the duskily lit downstairs bar-lounge, an alternative GLS (gay, lesbian, and sympathizers) crowd sips cocktails, nibbles on gourmet burgers (try the lamb burger in red-wine sauce topped with fresh mint jelly), and warms up for the night's adventures with sultry DJ-spun tunes. Meanwhile, upstairs is given over to contemporary dining with refined dishes such as duck cooked in vanilla-steeped port with Moroccan couscous and langoustine risotto with curried apples and ginger.

FRENCH
LE BLÉ NOIR ⓈⓈ
Rua Xavier da Silveira 19-A, tel. 21/2267-6969
HOURS: Mon.-Thurs. 7:30 P.M.–1 A.M., Fri.-Sat. 7:30 P.M.–2 A.M.

Owner and chef Alain Caro hails from Brittany, the very cradle of crepes, and he obviously has a way with a skillet. The delicate, crisp-edged sweet and savory offerings that emerge from his kitchen are made with *blé noir* (black flour, also known as sarrasin/buckwheat flour) and filled with an astonishing variety of creative (not to mention refined) fillings, such as wine-seared scallops cooked with mushrooms and hearts of palm. For dessert, the mini crepes stuffed with vanilla ice cream and topped with fresh fruit, toasted almond, and melted chocolate are out of this world. If you view crepes as glorified pancakes you'll be shocked by the prices, but aficionados will come away satisfied.

LE PRÉ CATELAN ⓈⓈⓈ
Av. Atlântica 4240, tel. 21/2525-1160, www.sofitel.com
HOURS: Mon.-Sat. 7:30–11:30 P.M.

Considered one of the finest hotel restaurants in the world, Sofitel's gastronomic temple is presided over by French master chef Roland Villard, the man many credit with introducing haute cuisine to Brazil. The ceremony begins the moment you are escorted into the sleek dining room with its color-changing spotlights and breathtaking views of Copacabana. Aside from the classic trappings of French haute cuisine—truffles, foie gras, fish, and game, all masterfully prepared with cream, wine, herbs, and butter—Villard's exposure to the exotica of his adopted homeland has resulted in more unusual creations, such as the celebrated grilled *tambaqui* (an Amazonian fish) in thyme sauce, served with a cloud-like mousse of smoked manioc. The patisseries, dreamed up by pastry chef Dominique Guérin, are paraded throughout the dining room in a glass box and you can eat as many as you want.

ITALIAN
CIPRIANI ⓈⓈⓈ
Av. Atlântica 1702, tel. 21/2545-8747, www.copacabanapalace.com.br
HOURS: Mon.-Sat. 12:30–3 P.M. and 7 P.M.–midnight

Cipriani's lack of a seafront view is more than compensated for by the glamorous vision of the Copacabana Palace's cinematographic *piscina* (for those who reserve a poolside table). Everything at this sumptuous restaurant is a class act, from the gleaming Italian silver, shimmering crystal, thick damask tablecloths, and heady aroma of fresh flowers to the stellar service and the flawless Northern Italian cuisine. Although master chef Francesco Carli is faithful to the classics, he isn't afraid to subvert traditional recipes with Brazilian elements—as witnessed by the beef *tournedos* bathed in *jaboticaba* sauce, accompanied by a velvety black-bean puree and a manioc tartlet. Make sure you dress to fit in with the opulent surroundings—shorts and flip-flops are prohibited.

DA BRAMBINI ⑤⑤

Av. Atlântica 514-B, tel. 21/2752-4346, www.dabrambini.com.br
HOURS: Daily noon–1 A.M.

This intimate trattoria overlooking the sea serves up delicious Northern Italian fare that attracts neighborhood regulars as well as fashionistas (despite the distinctly unfashionable decor). The fresh homemade pastas are outstanding, particularly the tortelli with pears and walnuts in a gorgonzola sauce and spaghetti bathed in a langoustine sauce. Also highly recommended are veal dishes and the *risotto brambini,* which features the unusual marriage of shrimp and *abacaxi* (pineapple) flambéed in cognac and served ceremoniously in a hollowed-out *abacaxi.* The incomparable *profiteroles* provide a happy ending to any meal.

D'AMICI ⑤⑤⑤

Rua Antônio Vieira 18-B, tel. 21/2541-4477, www.damicirestaurante.com.br
HOURS: Daily noon–1 A.M.

One of the city's best-kept Italian secrets, this refined and discreet eatery is a favorite lunch spot for execs and politicians, not to mention socialites who swear by the robust portions and eclectic menu. Specialties run the gamut from simple classics (melt-in-your-mouth osso buco and lasagna bolognesa) to more sophisticated and daring dishes such as ostrich carpaccio and wild boar roasted with herbs in a wine sauce. The sommelier is one of Rio's finest. Although it's not listed on the menu, the *petit gâteau de goiabada* (guava jelly) served with a white-cheese sorbet is pretty sublime. Interestingly, the four *amici* who own the restaurant aren't from Italy, but from the Northeastern state of Ceará.

MIDDLE EASTERN

AMIR ⑤⑤

Rua Ronald de Carvalho 55-C, tel. 21/2275-5596, www.amirrestaurante.com.br
HOURS: Sun.-Thurs. noon–11 P.M., Fri.-Sat. noon-midnight

The ornate Middle Eastern trappings appear to be ripped out of a tale from *One Thousand and One Nights,* but despite the richness of the colors and fabrics on display the Lebanese fare on Amir's menu is quite affordable—yet the portions generous enough to feed a very famished sultan. The *combinado* plate is a "best of" platter overflowing with appetizers such as hummus, baba ghanoush, tabbouleh, falafel, and stuffed grape leaves that pave the way for main events such as *shawarma,* succulent cuts of beef and lamb grilled over charcoal. On weekends, Moroccan couscous makes a special appearance on the menu.

POLISH

A POLONESA ⑤

Rua Hilário de Gouveia 116, tel. 21/2547-7378
HOURS: Tues.-Fri. 6 P.M.-midnight, Sat.-Sun. noon-midnight

A Polonesa has had the honor of being Rio's sole Polish restaurant since it opened its doors back in the 1950s. The atmospheric decor hasn't changed much since then—nor has the menu, which features home-cooked favorites such as paprika-flecked goulash and robust beef, chicken, and (in a concession to local taste buds) shrimp stroganoffs, which easily feed two. When it's hot out, the chilled borscht goes down nicely. On cooler days, the beer soup will warm you up. For dessert, it's a toss-up between the apple tart or the cloud-like chocolate soufflé.

SEAFOOD

MARIUS CRUSTÁCEOS ⑤⑤⑤

Av. Atlântica 290, tel. 21/2104-9002, www.marius.com.br
HOURS: Daily noon-midnight

With cobalt blue tiles, ceiling frescoes of Technicolor coral, and enough nautical relics to rival Disneyland's Pirates of the Caribbean, Marius is certainly not subtle about its seafood. The display of raw oysters, brilliant red lobsters, gigantic shrimp, and even spiky sea urchins—delivered fresh daily from the cool Atlantic waters of southern Brazil—will get you in the mood for the extravaganza to come, in which the saltwater delicacies are grilled or prepared in myriad manners ranging from Bahian *moquecas* to salads, carpaccios, sushi, and sashimi. The excellent quality and service justify the steep prices and also account for the large number of well-heeled gringos who frequent the place.

O CARANGUEJO ⑤

Rua Barata Ribeiro 771, tel. 21/2235-1249, www.restauranteocaranguejo.com.br
HOURS: Daily 8 A.M.-2 A.M.

This unpretentious seafood *boteco* is a fine place to kick back with an icy beer and pig out on fresh fish and seafood purchased daily from the Mercado São José in Niterói. If you're in the mood for a Neptune-worthy banquet, go all out and order the *sínfonia do mar,* an extravaganza featuring shrimp, lobster, octopus, squid, and fish eggs served with broccoli rice that easily feeds three or four people. A more modest but equally tasty choice is the *badejo,* served in a shrimp sauce with mashed potatoes. For a snack, try the *empadas* filled with shrimp and Portuguese olives or the breaded crab claws with tartar sauce.

SPANISH
SHIRLEY ⑤⑤

Rua Gustavo Sampaio 610, Loja A, tel. 21/2542-1003
HOURS: Daily 11 A.M.-1 A.M.

Located on a shady street in Leme, this modest neighborhood haunt has been serving up tasty and generous portions of Spanish seafood dishes such as paella and *zarzuela* since 1952. More original is the house specialty: giant shrimp stuffed with creamy *catupiry* cheese and served with rice and currants. Despite the small interior, the decor has a modishly retro edge. The waiters are very affable. Take note: Try to avoid coming during peak weekend hours when the kitchen gets harried and, as a result, the food isn't always up to par.

Ipanema   Map 5

Ipanema has an incredible diversity of eating options. In keeping with the personality of the *bairro,* there are scads of laid-back bars, cafés, pizzerias, and restaurants with tables overlooking the streets or spilling out onto the sidewalks so diners can check out the constant people parade. Even the more sophisticated restaurants—and there are quite a few, including many serving fine international fare—have a relaxed casual vibe. Meanwhile, the healthy living ethos is reflected in the number of vegetarian and *natural* restaurants, many of which operate on a per-kilo basis.

ASIAN
OPIUM ⑤⑤

Rua Farme de Amoedo 34, tel. 21/3687-2010, www.ipanemaplaza.com.br
HOURS: Sun.-Thurs. 6:30-11 A.M. and 12:30 P.M.-midnight, Fri.-Sat. 6:30-11 A.M. and 12:30 P.M.-1 A.M.

Riding the crest of Rio's Asian culinary wave, this sleek restaurant attempts to embrace the entire continent by mining Chinese, Japanese, Thai, Vietnamese, and Indian culinary traditions—for the most part, with a certain success. The menu juggles tried-and-true standards such as wonton soup and Peking duck along with interpretive fare such as tuna steak seared in a crust of shaved coconut with slivered almonds in teriyaki sauce. The wide veranda looking out onto Ipanema's gayest street, Farme de Amoedo, is highly coveted by those

© MICHAEL SOMMERS

RESTAURANTS

Opium is riding the city's new wave of Asian eateries.

who want to check out the action (and get checked out themselves). At night, candlelight and wild orchids turn the atmosphere decidedly romantic.

BISTROS AND LIGHT FARE
ALESSANDRO E FREDERICO CAFÉ $
Rua Gárcia D'Ávila 134, Loja D, tel. 21/2521-0828,
www.alessandroefrederico.com.br
HOURS: Daily 9 A.M.-2 A.M.

One of the more nicely priced choices for lunch or dinner in the sizzling heart of Ipanema, this laid-back yet always lively eatery has an amazing choice of items for a snack or light meal, including soups, salads, carpaccios, omelettes, paninis, pastas, and basic but well-executed hot entrées such grilled steaks. Made on the premises, the freshly baked bread is pretty scrumptious—to sample some, order a sandwich or stop by in the morning for a copious breakfast. Nab a table on the veranda, which is ideal for people-watching.

GULA GULA $
Rua Henrique Dumont 57, tel. 21/2259-3084,
www.gulagula.com.br
HOURS: Sun.-Thurs. noon-midnight,
Fri.-Sat. noon-1 A.M.

Gula Gula (*gula* means gluttony) is considered by many famished locals-on-the-run to be one of the best, least expensive, and typically Carioca eateries in town. The laid-back, casual vibe and simple, no-nonsense but appetizing quiches, salads, pastas, and grilled meats have proved to be a winning formula, spawning 12 restaurants throughout the Centro and Zona Sul. The most attractive is this Ipanema location, which is situated in a two-story house replete with art deco furnishings.

BRAZILIAN
BRASILEIRINHO $
Rua Jangadeiros 10, Loja A, tel. 21/2513-5184,
www.cozinhatipica.com.br
HOURS: Daily noon-midnight

Walking through the door of this rustic *boteco*

GETTING JUICED

Travelers to Brazil are usually blown away by the diversity of fresh fruit juices available throughout the country. You can get juice all over Rio, in *lanchonetes*, bars, and especially in *bares de suco* (juice bars), which are usually festooned with cornucopias of fresh fruit waiting to be pulverized in front of your eyes. Juice bars are most plentiful in urban beach neighborhoods where they are staples of health-obsessed, body-baring Brazilians. In Rio's Zona Sul neighborhoods of Copacabana, Ipanema, and Leblon they are omnipresent. Aside from run-of-the-mill tropical fruits such as papaya, mango, guava, and *abacaxi* (pineapple), you'll often find exotic fruits of the Northeast (*siriguela, umbu*, and *cajá*) and the Amazon (*bacuri, cupuaçu*, and the super-healthy *açaí*). Even vitamin-packed vegetables such as *cenoura* (carrot) and *beterraba* (beet) are blender worthy.

Fresh-squeezed orange juice (*suco de laranja*), which you'll find everywhere (Brazil is the world's number-one producer and exporter of OJ), is the only juice served pure and unadulterated. Other fruits are mixed with water (filtered), milk (called a *vitamina*), or orange juice. Sugar (*açúcar*) is added, as is ice (*gelo*). If you want your juice *sem gelo* and *sem açúcar*, ask for it *natural*. You can often mix one or more fruits; hard-core juice bars offer a menu of juice cocktails for whatever ails you. Energizers usually feature *guaraná* powder or

.eite	3,80 5,90	Frutas c/ Granola	4,20	6,
veia	3,80 5,90	Frutas c/ Proteinato de Cálcio	5,30	7,
ston	3,80 5,90	Morango c/ Leite	3,80	5,

fruit on display at a juice bar

syrup, açai, and brilliant green magnesium-rich chlorophyll; anti-stress drinks add *suco de maracujá*, a natural sedative (which Brazilians give to hyperactive children).

is like entering a rural home in Minas Gerais. As its name implies, Brasileirinho features uncomplicated home-cooked comfort food from all over Brazil. Representing the Northeast are *carne de sol* (sun-dried beef) and *baião-de-dois* (*feijão* mixed with melted *coalho*, a tangy white cheese). Pungent pork sausages from Goiás make an appearance, as do tender chunks of filet mignon, appreciated all over Brazil but particularly in the South. There is even a delicious *feijoada*. The main focus is the succulent regional fare of Minas Gerais, which includes classic dishes such as *carne seca com abóbora* (dried beef with pumpkin) and *tutu à mineira*

(a hearty stew of pork and pureed beans). Most of the *cachaças* are Mineiro as well, including the oak-aged Vendaval, as is the velvety *doce de leite*, a highly addictive dessert made of caramelized milk.

◖ CASA DA FEIJOADA ❸❸

Rua Prudente de Moraes 10, tel. 21/2247-2776, www.cozinhatipica.com.br
HOURS: Daily noon-midnight

Although Rio's most traditional dish—*feijoada*—is characteristically eaten on Saturday, for years Casa da Feijoada has been serving up a mouthwatering version for those

© MICHAEL SOMMERS

who get cravings on any day of the week. Since gringos flock to the place in droves, the house breaks with convention by letting customers select their own pieces of meat (thus allowing the more squeamish to avoid ears, tails, and feet). Along with the classic accompaniments of braised *couve* (kale), *torresmos* (pork rinds), fried *aipim* (manioc), and *farofa*, the somewhat steep all-you-can-eat price of R$47 includes *caldo de feijão*, a *caipirinha*, and homemade desserts. For those who aren't in a bean-ish frame of mind, there are other classic Brazilian options.

CAFÉS AND SNACKS
ARMAZÉM DO CAFÉ §
Rua Maria Quitéria 77, tel. 21/2522-5039, www.armazemdocafe.com.br
HOURS: Mon.-Fri. 8 A.M.-9 P.M., Sat. 8 A.M.-6 P.M.
This chain of gourmet cafés currently has eight locations around Rio, including four in Ipanema. Since Brazil is the land of coffee, Armazém, which takes its beans quite seriously, is a great place to learn about and savor different homegrown blends (which have been baptized with appropriately melodic names). Fans of ultra-mellow blends will dig the Samba from Bahia, while hard-core revelers in robustness will appreciate the Rumba. Cariocas themselves tend to favor Frevo, made with organic beans from the state of Pernambuco. For noshing, there are sandwiches as well as sweet and savory pastries. Java paraphernalia such as coffee pots, espresso makers, mugs, and, of course, coffee table books, is also sold.

BAZZAR §
Rua Visconde de Pirajá 572, tel. 21/2249-4977, www.livrariadatravessa.com.br
HOURS: Tues.-Sat. 10 A.M.-midnight, Sun.-Mon. noon-midnight
Located on the mezzanine of Ipanema's Livraria da Travessa, there's nothing at all bookish about Bazzar, a sleekly urbane café that serves breakfast, creative sandwiches, and bistro-style meals such as filet mignon with fig sauce and grilled vegetables or spaghettini in pesto made from fresh mint, basil, and caramelized walnuts, along with desserts, coffee, and drinks. Usually filled with

© MICHAEL SOMMERS

Inside Livraria da Travessa, Bazzar offers sustenance for bookstore browsers.

RESTAURANTS

attractive readers and browsers of all ages, it is an appealing place to hang out any time of the day.

☾ MIL FRUTAS CAFÉ $

Rua Gárcia D'Ávila 134, tel. 21/2521-1384, www.milfrutas.com.br
HOURS: Mon.-Fri. 10:30 A.M.-12:30 A.M., Sat.-Sun. 9:30 A.M.-1:30 A.M.

In the late 1980s, journalist Renata Saboya began feeling nostalgic for the exotic fruits of her youth in Northeastern Brazil. She promptly abandoned her writing career and began making all-natural gourmet sorbets from the exotic likes of *açai, bacuri, cupuaçu, jabuticaba, mangaba,* and *pitanga.* The results—icy bursts of pure distilled flavor—were an immediate success. Since then several Mil Frutas have opened around town, and though there are not yet *mil* (a thousand) flavors, there are close to 200, including the decidedly non-fruity white chocolate with *pimenta,* absinthe, and jasmine.

Mil Frutas Café is renowned for its sublime *sorvete* (sorbet).

Although you may balk at paying R$7 for a single scoop, the taste sensation is definitely worth it. Unlike the other Mil Frutas outposts, this laid-back Ipanema café also serves snacks and light meals.

POLIS SUCOS $

Rua Maria Quitéria 70, Loja A, tel. 21/2547-2518
HOURS: Mon.-Thurs. 7 A.M.-midnight, Fri.-Sat. 7 A.M.-2 A.M.

One of the Zona Sul's pioneering juice bars, Polis has the guts to only use fresh fruit that is in season for its juices. Year-round, the biggest bestsellers are *morango* (strawberry), mango, and the harder to come by *fruto de conde* (star fruit). Vitamin-packed cocktails are also popular, particularly the scandalous magenta mélange of *cenoura* (carrot), *beterraba* (beet), and *laranja* (orange) juice. However, if you're feeling creative, you can custom-order a mixture featuring as many different pulps as you want (you'll be charged for the most expensive). The benches are handy if you decide you want to munch on a sandwich as well.

CHURRASCARIAS

ESPLANADA GRILL $$$

Rua Barão da Torre 600, tel. 21/2512-2970, www.esplanadagrill.com.br
HOURS: Mon.-Thurs. noon-4 P.M. and 7 P.M.-midnight, Fri.-Sat. noon-1 A.M., Sun. noon-midnight

This venerable *churrascaria* has been around since 1989 and is one of Ipanema's least trendy dining spots. The decor is pretty passé, but the clientele of moneyed Cariocas and tourists couldn't care less. They have their eyes on the prize, which happens to be some of the most succulent cuts of beef this side of the Pampas, served with panache and accompanied by a tremendous array of fixings. The mouthwatering *picanha* (rump steak) and *bife ancho* (entrecote) from Argentina are the most lusted-after cuts. Not far behind is the New Zealand lamb prepared under various guises, including savory sausage as well as boneless shoulder grilled in rock salt. Prices are a bit steep, but the quality is unbeatable.

© MICHAEL SOMMERS

RESTAURANTS

Zazá Bistrô Tropical is both romantic and relaxing.

VIA SETE 💲
Rua Garcia D'Ávila 125, tel. 21/2221-8020,
www.viasete.com.br
HOURS: Sun.-Wed. noon-midnight, Sat. noon-1 A.M.

A great option for a casual and healthy meal, Via Sete specializes in fresh, attractively presented dishes such as colorful organic salads, wraps, and veggie burgers, as well as grilled meats, fish, and seafood served with an enormous choice of garnishes. Although the cheery interior is very pleasant, the large veranda is the ideal place to linger over a "frozen": a local version of a smoothie made from pure unadulterated frozen fruit pulp (served with or without alcohol) or to indulge in the legendary grilled and flambéed bananas topped with cinnamon ice cream and walnuts. There's a second location in Centro at Rua Sete de Setembro 43 (tel. 21/2221-1820).

CONTEMPORARY
GALANI 💲💲💲
Av. Vieira Souto, tel. 21/2541-4477,
www.caesar-park.com
HOURS: Daily 6 A.M.-midnight

Talk about a room with a view. This old-fashioned elegant yet casual penthouse restaurant is located on the 23rd floor of the Caesar Park Hotel, which just happens to be the highest vantage point in all of Ipanema. As a result, it seems as if both Arpoador and the Morro de Dois Irmãos are right in your face—provoking a sensation that the word breathtaking doesn't even begin to describe. Although three square meals are served daily, the most sought-after are the famous Saturday-afternoon *feijoada* and the decadent Sunday brunch spread featuring blinis, fresh seafood, sushi, sashimi, and an artful array of fabulous desserts.

ZAZÁ BISTRÔ TROPICAL 💲💲💲
Rua Joana Angélica 40, tel. 21/2247-9101,
www.zazabistro.com.br
HOURS: Sun.-Thurs. 7:30 P.M.-12:30 A.M.,
Fri.-Sat. 7:30 P.M.-1:30 A.M.

At this funky hippie-chic eatery tropicality—Asian, African, and American—rules. Typical main dishes on the inventive organic menu include lamb *shishbarak* served on truffles and Arabian ravioli with yogurt mint sauce and almonds. The colorfully whimsical decor—red velvet flowers hanging from the ceiling, silk pillows scattered around the floor, and lots of candlelight—is conducive to both romance and relaxation. Customers are encouraged to take off their shoes and sprawl for a while.

ITALIAN
FORNERIA $
Rua Aníbal de Mendonça 112, tel. 21/2540-8045
HOURS: Sun.-Thurs. noon-1 A.M., Fri.-Sat. noon-1:30 A.M.

The Carioca outlet of this acclaimed São Paulo eatery is a stylish but utterly laid-back bistro designed by ballyhooed contemporary architect Isay Weinfeld. It's beloved by Rio's casual youth, who flock in droves to feast on low-key but high-quality Italian fare. Sandwiches—such as brie, asparagus, and prosciutto in fluffy bread made from pizza dough—are pretty fab, as are the pastas, risottos, and salads prepared in an open kitchen, all of which are well matched with wines from the cellar. During the week there is also a nicely priced three-course lunch menu. Complementing the food is a musical menu—customers choose tunes and a DJ fulfills their orders.

GERO $$$
Rua Aníbal Mendonça 157, tel. 21/2239-8158, www.fasano.com.br/gerorio
HOURS: Mon.-Fri. noon-4 P.M. and 7 P.M.-1 A.M., Sat. noon-2 A.M., Sun. noon-midnight

São Paulo hotelier and restaurateur extraordinaire Rogério Fasano is also the man behind the Carioca version of Gero, considered to be one of the top Italian restaurants in the city. The simple decor—skylights, blond wood floors, and exposed brick walls—belies the fact that even Rio's rich and trendy sometimes find themselves on the waiting list to dine here. Avoid the crush and high prices and come for a weekday three-course R$70 lunch, with delicious Italian classics such as an impeccable mozzarella-stuffed ravioli, as well as the more refined likes of quail stuffed with foie gras and saffron risotto. The service is notable for being both affable and flawless.

MARGUTTA $$$
Rua Henrique Dumont 62, tel. 21/2259-3887, www.margutta.com.br
HOURS: Mon.-Fri. 6 P.M.-1 A.M., Sat. noon-1 A.M., Sun. noon-midnight

Owned and operated by chef Paolo Neroni and his charming wife Conceição, this classic Italian mainstay focuses on unpretentious Mediterranean fare, specifically fish and seafood, which is prepared with delicate sophistication. Standouts include the porgy baked in rock salt with spicy potatoes and grilled endive, which melts in your mouth, as well as a knockout seafood penne. Although the clientele tends to be chic and trendy, the decor is understated, verging on staid. A branch in Centro, open for lunch only, is located at Rua Graça Aranha 1.

OSTERIA DELL'ANGOLO $$
Rua Paul Redfern 40, tel. 21/2259-3148, www.osteriadellangolo.com.br
HOURS: Mon.-Fri. noon-4 P.M. and 6 P.M.-2 A.M., Sat.-Sun. noon-2 A.M.

Politicians, artists, and musicians (among them blue-eyed Chico Buarque, who is a faithful regular) are devotees of this invitingly warm and unpretentious corner restaurant that specializes in robust Northern Italian cuisine. Start off with the justifiably famous antipasti of 15 items, including eggplant parmigiana, polenta with roquefort, and grilled zucchini slices, before plunging into the *primi piatti*, the mouthwatering risottos that are the house forte. Among the most celebrated is the creamy langoustine risotto with asparagus. Also recommended are the fish baked in rock salt and the lamb with rosemary sauce. For dessert, the strawberry tiramisu doused with cassis liqueur is an inspired variation on the classic.

JAPANESE
MINIMOK $$
Rua Vinicius de Moraes 121, Loja C, tel. 21/2523-7026, www.moksushi.com.br
HOURS: Sun.-Thurs. noon-midnight, Fri.-Sat. noon-1 A.M.

Talented young chef Henrique Verdan presides

over this laid-back little Japanese eatery that entices with its clean lines, gleaming natural wood, and soothing palate as well as its inventive menu. Creations such as colored rice with shrimp, squid, and fish served in a crunchy bird's nest, and semi-grilled salmon embellished with dried shrimp *farofa* (manioc flour) and doused in thai vinaigrette, complement the ubiquitous sushi, sashimi, tempura, and *temaki*. For dessert, the ice cream tempura provides an unusual taste sensation. A second Minimok is located in Leblon on Rua Dias Ferreira 116, Loja D (tel. 21/2511-1476).

TEN KAI ❸❸❸
Rua Prudente de Moraes 1810, tel. 21/2540-5100, www.tenkai.com.br
HOURS: Mon.-Fri. 7 P.M.-1 A.M., Sat. 1 P.M.-1 A.M., Sun. 1 P.M.-midnight

Ten Kai is Japanese for "sky and sea," but it is the life aquatic that is given priority at this handsome multifloor restaurant. The elegant decor mingles contemporary materials such as raw steel and concrete with traditional Japanese touches such as slender paper lanterns and tatami mats. Guaranteed to float your boat is outstandingly prepared sushi that combine ingredients such as squid with sea urchin and salmon *brulé* with salmon eggs. The eel sushi is truly exquisite, as is the octopus sashimi in a citrus-sake sauce. The ingredients, many of which are imported from Japan, are of outstanding quality.

PER-KILO BUFFET
DELÍRIO TROPICAL ❸
Rua Gárcia D'Ávila 48, tel. 21/3208-2977, www.deliriotropical.com.br
HOURS: Mon.-Sat. 9 A.M.-10 P.M., Sun. 9 A.M.-9 P.M.

A mere block from Ipanema beach, this relaxed per-kilo joint is a great place for a healthy meal after soaking up the sun. Choose from an array of colorful and unusual salads along with hot daily specials, then take a seat in the upstairs dining area, tropically accessorized with hanging ferns and Tarzanic vines. The glass walls afford a tree house–like view of the comings and goings of beach bums below.

PIZZA
STRAVAGANZE ❸❸
Rua Maria Quitéria 132, tel. 21/2523-2391, www.duducamargo.com.br
HOURS: Sun.-Thurs. 6 P.M.-1 A.M., Fri.-Sat. 6 P.M.-2 A.M.

Stravaganze is at the forefront of Rio's current penchant for "pizza boutiques" that, rebelling against the rustic trattoria aesthetic of yore, marry sleek and sophisticated ambience with gourmet toppings (and upscale prices). The lofty well-lit dining areas are enticing, particularly upstairs where a lovely veranda flaunts views of the treetops. More importantly, the pizzas don't disappoint. Toppings are generous and range from the traditional but perfectly executed *margherita* to more daring concoctions such as goat cheese, figs, and prosciutto drizzled with balsamic vinegar and honey. Those dining solo will appreciate the friendly communal table.

SEAFOOD
AZUL MARINHO ❸❸
Av. Francisco Bhering, tel. 21/3813-4228, www.cozinhatipica.com.br
HOURS: Mon.-Sat. noon-midnight, Sun. noon-11 P.M.

The setting at Azul Marinho—facing the surfer's mecca of Praia do Arpoador—couldn't be more ideal for enjoying a typically Brazilian meal of fish and seafood. The house specialty is the *moqueca,* a fragrant stew made of fish, lobster, shrimp, or crab (the choice is yours), but you can easily while away an afternoon nibbling on raw oysters, *casquinhas de siri* (a salad of shredded crab served in its shell), or the addictive *camarões caipira,* shrimp wrapped in melted tangy *coalho* cheese and bacon and drizzled with honey. While the dining room itself, located within the Hotel Arpoador Inn, verges on tacky (the furnishings and sculptures made from dead tree trunks are somewhat sinister), the outdoor tables are *o máximo* (slang for "the ultimate"), especially at sunset. Service can be slow, but with surroundings such as these you won't be in a hurry.

RESTAURANTS

FASANO AL MARE ⑤⑤⑤

Av. Vieira Souto 80, tel. 21/3202-4000,
www.fasano.com.br
HOURS: Daily 6:30-10:30 A.M., noon-4 P.M.,
and 7 P.M.-1 A.M.

It's a Carioca cliché that only tourists eat at Rio's usually lackluster seaside restaurants, but when the Starck-designed Fasano hotel opened in 2007, Rio's rich and hungry were forced to make an exception. This enchanting restaurant is all about the ocean, with an inspired maritime decor that includes polished sea shells and lamps of translucent Murano glass. The menu offers seafood delights prepared by Luca Gozzani, a three-star Michelin chef imported from Italy. As a starter, the delicate scallops in an asparagus caviar cream set the tone for entrées such as lobster ravioli in a cherry-tomato sauce and shrimp risotto with Sicilian lime. During the week, the executive lunch menu (with an appetizer, main course, and dessert) allows you to indulge without maxing out your credit card.

SATYRICON ⑤⑤⑤

Rua Barão da Torre 192, tel. 21/2521-0627,
www.satyricon.com.br
HOURS: Mon.-Sat. noon-1 A.M., Sun. noon-midnight

Serious seafood lovers will feel as if they've died and gone to Neptune's garden the minute they set foot inside this posh restaurant and are greeted by aquariums filled with lobsters, langoustines, scallops, and glistening arrays of oysters and myriad fish displayed like jewels on crushed ice. The treasures at Rio's temple of haute maritime cuisine don't come cheap, but the Mediterranean-influenced dishes that emerge from the kitchen are fit for a monarch (Madonna dined here she was in town). Start with the Trimare, featuring carpaccio of tuna, salmon, and porgy, and then sample the delicious fish baked in rock salt or the mixed crustacean platter accompanied with a butter sauce and lime risotto.

VEGETARIAN

FONTES ⑤

Rua Visconde de Pirajá 605, Lojas D-F,
tel. 21/2512-5900,
www.fontesipanema.com.br
HOURS: Mon.-Sat. 11 A.M.-10 P.M., Sun. noon-8 P.M.

Hidden away inside the galleria Estação Ipanema, this tiny vegetarian restaurant has been serving tasty health food to Zona Sul residents with slim waists and even slimmer finances for over 20 years. The narrow menu changes daily and rotates weekly, but always features a range of soups, salads, soufflés, and vegetarian dishes such as vegetable tempura, tofu stroganoff, and stuffed mushrooms. Noncarnivores who feel excluded from eating the traditional meat-laden Carioca *feijoada* should drop by on Saturday or Sunday for a vegetarian version swimming with smoked tofu, soya, diced pumpkin, and vegetarian sausage, accompanied by brown rice and nonalcoholic ginger *caipirinhas*.

LÍQUIDO ⑤

Rua Barão da Torre 398-A, tel. 21/2267-6519,
www.liquidosucos.com.br
HOURS: Daily 9 A.M.-11 P.M.

Gazing out onto the perennially vibrant Praça Nossa Senhora da Paz, this airy, laid-back establishment captures the Zona Sul ethos to the hilt. The silhouette-enhancing offerings are both healthy and sophisticated. The *dosas*, an Indian version of a crepe with fillings such as curried chicken, guava chutney, and grilled tuna sprinkled with cashew slivers, are all the rage. Wash down your meal with fresh fruit juice, Nepalese organic tea, or a smoothie (the Lemon Drops, made with green tea ice cream, honey, and lime juice is particularly refreshing). Although more caloric, the carrot muffin topped with chocolate sauce is tough to resist—minimize your guilt by reminding yourself it's made with rice flour.

Leblon
Map 6

RESTAURANTS

For serious foodies, Leblon is very appetizing terrain. Perhaps no other *bairro* concentrates so many gourmet pickings. Many of the city's most reputed chefs have staked out their claim here, often in stylish yet intimate eateries whose small size translates into long lines or advance reservations. And yet, Leblon's gourmet reputation spreads across the board, extending to delis where you can get fabulous sandwiches and lavish breakfasts, cafés whose windows are glutted with mouthwatering pastries, and down-to-earth *botequins* (neighborhood bars that serve up some of the best bar grub in town). Even the juice bars are considered among the best in town.

BISTROS AND LIGHT FARE
GARCIA & RODRIGUES 💲💲
Av. Ataulfo de Paiva 1251, tel. 21/3206-4100, www.garciaerodrigues.com.br
HOURS: Sun.-Mon. 8 A.M.-midnight, Tues.-Fri. 8 A.M.-12:30 A.M., Sat. 8 A.M.-1 A.M.
A major touchstone on Leblon's gourmet circuit, Garcia & Rodrigues is owned and operated by French transplant Christopher Liddy (a graduate of Paris's École Lenôtre), who brings Gallic flair and flavors to the culinary complex that houses a café, *boulangerie,* deli, and bistro. The latter is where French expats and chic Cariocas alike congregate to trade gossip over somewhat pricy plates of oxtail *gâteau* with creamy white polenta and grilled bass bathed in celeriac cream. The more informal café is livelier (not to mention cheaper) and is a pleasant place to indulge in sandwiches, salads, and mouthwatering patisseries. In a neighborhood that takes its breakfast spreads seriously, many claim the weekend buffet served by Garcia & Rodrigues to be the best of the bunch.

BRAZILIAN
ARATACA 💲
Rua Gilberto Cardoso, Loja 4, tel. 21/2512-6249,

www.portaldacobal.com.br/arataca.htm
HOURS: Tues. 9 A.M.-8 P.M., Wed.-Sat. 9 A.M.-9 P.M., Sun. 9 A.M.-5:30 P.M.
Amidst the lively collection of bars and restaurants in Cobal do Leblon, the most original of them all is this *boteco* specializing in delicacies from the Brazilian North and Northeast. From Alagoas, *concha de sururu* is a thick chowder made with a mollusk famed for its aphrodisiac properties. An Amazonian staple guaranteed to whet your imagination as well as your appetite is *caldo de piranha* (piranha soup). More filling sustenance includes *carne de sol* (sun-dried beef), a staple of the Northeastern Sertão, and *bobó de camarão,* a thick Bahian stew of shrimp and pureed manioc. The desserts featuring ambrosial Amazonian fruits such as *cupuaçu* and *bacuri* are to die for—the *pavê de sorvete de cupuaçu,* a loose version of a frozen trifle, is particularly inspired. On Wednesday nights and Sundays live music is performed.

DEGRAU 💲💲
Av. Ataulfo de Paiva 517, tel. 21/2259-3648, www.restaurantedegrau.com.br
HOURS: Daily 11 A.M.-2 A.M.
For close to 60 years now, Degrau has been a favorite neighborhood pit stop for residents on their way to and from the beach. (Don't be surprised to see clients walk through the door still dripping with ocean water.) Showing up shirtless is also no problem (provided you're male)—the restaurant will lend you one. The beef, shrimp, and cheese *pastéis* (deep-fried turnovers) are immensely popular, but those in search of a real meal can rely on fish dishes such as *bacalhau* slathered in garlic and olive oil along with copious portions of hearty, home-cooked favorites such as *feijoada, rabada* (oxtail stew), and *dobradinha* (a version of cassoulet made of tripe, sausage, and white beans).

SUPERMARKETS

In Rio, the supermarkets really are super – particularly in the health-conscious Zona Sul neighborhoods such as Ipanema and Leblon – so if you're looking for cheap and healthy eats, head to the nearest *supermercado*. **Zona Sul** has been around for close to half a century and is a great place to pick up picnic fare, including wine. Cariocas in the know (including top chef Roberta Sudbrack) swear by their fine-crust takeout pizzas (rumored to be some of the best slices in the city). You'll find locations all over town (thought not all have pizzerias); for specific addresses and opening hours check out www.zonasul.com.br. **Horti-Fruti** is another chain that specializes in an astounding variety of fresh fruits and vegetables, most of them organic and dirt cheap. The godfather of them is, of course, in Leblon, on the corner of Rua Dias Ferreira and Rua Professor Azevedo Marques. Here you'll find pre-packaged fruit and vegetables salads as well as a juice bar serving fresh juices and *água de coco*.

CAFÉS AND SNACKS

AQUIM ❸❸

Av. Ataulfo de Paiva 1240, Loja B, tel. 21/2512-4670, www.aquimgastronomia.com.br
HOURS: Mon.-Fri. 10 A.M.-midnight, Sat.-Sun. 9 A.M.-midnight

Hailing from a family of serious gourmets, chef Samantha Aquim studied at the famous Lenôtre cooking school in Paris, where her specialty was the art of chocolate making. Her mouthwatering concoctions (made of high-concentration cocoa) can be purchased at the nearby boutique at Avenida Ataulfo de Paiva 1321 or savored at the sumptuous Aquim café, whose eggplant-hued calfskin banquettes are partitioned by bronze-dipped tree branches and offset by mocha-colored walls. It's not just about the chocolate; other desserts are equally sublime—the Sicilian lime torte with chocolate splinters is especially delicious. The

breakfast, lunch, and dinner menus change seasonally and propose surprising (and posh) variations on simple themes such as a not-so-humble grilled cheese sandwich made with truffle butter.

BB LANCHES ❸

Rua Aristides Espinola 64, tel. 21/2541-4477
HOURS: Sun.-Thurs. 8:30 A.M.-3 A.M., Fri.-Sat. 8:30 A.M.-5 A.M.

In a city where juice bars rule, BB Lanches reigns supreme. For one thing, there's the reassuring fact that at 2 A.M. you can always count on getting your *açai* fix. The bewildering array of fruits used here are pulverized in a blender along with ice and freshly squeezed orange juice, milk, or chlorophyll (a fabulously trendy green antioxidant). More complex fruit *misturas* are also offered, including the perenially popular *açai* with strawberry and the vitamin C–packed bomb of orange, lime, and acerola juices sweetened with honey. To munch on, there is an endless array of sandwiches. The cheeseburgers really hit the spot on the way home from a night of carousing.

BIBI SUCOS ❸

Av. Ataulfo de Paiva 591, tel. 21/2259-4298, www.bibisucos.com.br
HOURS: Sun.-Thurs. 8 A.M.-1 A.M., Fri.-Sat. 8 A.M.-2 A.M.

Rivalling BB Lanches for the city's best and most beloved *bar de suco*, Bibi is another juicy institution with over close to 60 varieties of fruit on the menu. Sample them straight or in unusually refreshing combinations such as watermelon with ginger or *água de coco* and fig. Once your thirst is quenched, assemble your own healthy sandwich. The house favorite is the smoked turkey breast with creamy Mineiro cheese and chopped egg white. The place is particularly popular with Rio's jiu-jitsu crowd, whose tackling of the heaping portions of *açai* fortified with honey, tapioca, or rice flakes is a martial art in itself.

CAFÉ SEVERINO ❸

Rua Dias Ferreira 417, tel. 21/2259-9398, www.livrariaargumento.com.br

© MICHAEL SOMMERS

Talho Capixaba is one of the best gourmet delis in Leblon.

HOURS: Mon.-Sat. 9 A.M.-midnight, Sun. 10 A.M.-midnight

Tucked away in the back of the Livraria Argumento's stacks of books and CDs, this cozy little café serves all the usual suspects—cakes, tortes, brownies, and cappuccinos—with considerable panache, along with sandwiches, salads, waffles, crepes (the brie with almonds and honey goes down especially nice), and a smattering of light entrées such as beef carpaccio and pumpkin ravioli. Sunday morning's brunch-like *café-da-manhã* (served until 1 P.M.) is a charming affair, as are the afternoon teas for two featuring mini sandwiches, biscuits, and a highly addictive orange cake.

KURT ❸

Rua General Urquiza 117, Loja B, tel. 21/2294-0599, www.confeitariakurt.com.br

HOURS: Mon.-Fri. 8 A.M.-7 P.M., Sat. 8 A.M.-5 P.M.

Celebrated for concocting the most divine pastries in town, Rio's oldest pastry shop opened in the 1940s when Kurt Deichmann fled to Rio from Nazi Germany, armed with recipes for French mousses, Austrian and Hungarian tortes, and other sweet delights. The crowds go particularly wild for the *picada de abelha* (bee sting): a torte overflowing with vanilla cream and topped with a coating of honey, walnuts, and crunchy caramel. Also irresistible is the *torta de damasco*, a fluffy apricot torte covered with tart apricot jelly and chantilly and filled with a layer of almond praline. Since this is body-conscious Leblon, there are sugarless diet tortes as well.

TALHO CAPIXABA ❸

Av. Ataulfa de Paiva 1022, Loja A-B, tel. 21/2512-8750, www.talhocapixaba.com.br

HOURS: Mon.-Sat. 7 A.M.-10 P.M., Sun. 8 A.M.-9 P.M.

Talho Capixaba began its life as a neighborhood butcher shop in the 1950s. Over the years it kept expanding, adding a delicatessen, wine cellar, cheese shop, and bakery. This jack-of-all-trades approach explains how this emporium came to be *the* place to go for the best sandwiches in town. The best part is that you get to design them yourself. Start by choosing from more than 40 types of bread, and then begin piling on the sliced meats, cheeses, spreads, pâtés, terrines, jellies, chutneys, sliced veggies, and leafy greens (price is calculated according to weight). Wolf them down at the crowded deli counter or have them wrapped up to go. The fabulous breakfasts have a cult following—especially on weekends when tables and chairs are set up on the sidewalk.

CHURRASCARIAS
GIUSEPPE GRILL ⑤⑤
Av. Bartolomeu Mitre 370, tel. 21/2249-3055

HOURS: Mon.-Thurs. noon-4 P.M. and 7 P.M.-midnight, Fri.-Sat. noon-1 A.M., Sun. 11 A.M.-11 P.M.

For years, this traditional *churrascaria* was the carefully guarded secret of meat-loving business execs who worked in Centro (the original restaurant, at Rua da Quitanda 49, is only open for weekday lunch). But when a more upscale version opened in Leblon in 2007, the rest of the city suddenly discovered the succulent joys of some of the finest cuts of beef this side of the pampas. All meats—there's also chicken and fish—are slowly grilled, roasted, or barbecued over charcoal and served with *caseiro* (home-cooking) style garnishes such as cream of spinach, potato soufflé, and *farofa* with raisins. A special prix fixe menu offers an entrée, main course, and dessert for R$49. The impressive wine cellar boasts over 450 labels.

CONTEMPORARY
CARLOTA ⑤⑤⑤
Rua Dias Ferreira 64, Lojas B-C, tel. 21/2540-6821, www.carlota.com.br

HOURS: Mon.-Fri. 7:30 P.M.-midnight, Sat. 1-5 P.M. and 7:30 P.M.-12:30 A.M., Sun. 1-11 P.M.

One of Brazil's most lauded chefs, Carla Pernambuco is known for her unusual multicultural combinations of flavors and textures. Recent forays into Iberian culinary traditions yielded specialties such as crunchy shrimp with smoked ham risotto and *bacalhau* (cod) ravioli in a truffled mascarpone sauce, but be prepared to expect the unexpected (including the odd dish that doesn't live up to the hype). Among her legendary desserts is a guava soufflé bathed in a creamy sauce of Catupiry cheese. Due to the compact size of this intimate Leblon bistro—dominated by soothing whites, natural woods, and a charming gaggle of porcelain chickens—reservations are recommended.

ZUKA ⑤⑤⑤
Rua Dias Ferreira 233, Loja B, tel. 21/3205-7154, www.zuka.com.br

HOURS: Mon. 7 P.M.-1 A.M., Tues.-Fri. noon-4 P.M. and 7 P.M.-1 A.M., Sat. 1 P.M.-1 A.M., Sun. 1 P.M.-midnight

Self-taught Ludmila Soeira is one of Brazil's most exciting young contemporary chefs. Among her culinary fetishes is an old-fashioned

Koni Store is Rio's latest healthy fast food phenomenon.

charcoal grill featured inside this soothing oasis, which is cloaked in neutral shades and natural materials. Every hot dish passes over the grill's flames in some manner: from the Zuka na Pedra, a shareable appetizer of grilled potatoes, tomatoes, shitake mushrooms, and palm hearts served with a variety of dipping sauces, to entrées such as the *filé negro* (black steak), in which filet mignon is marinated in a dark mixture of soy sauce, squid ink, and garlic. The reasonably priced executive lunch menu offered from Tuesday to Sunday allows small spenders the opportunity to enjoy a truly memorable eating experience.

JAPANESE
KONI STORE ❸

Av. Ataulfo de Paiva 1174, tel. 21/3344-4859, www.konistore.com.br
HOURS: Mon.-Wed. 11 A.M.-3 A.M., Thurs.-Sat. 11 A.M.-5 A.M., Sun. 11 A.M.-midnight

Cariocas seemingly can't get enough of *konis*— "cone"-shaped sheets of *nori* (seaweed) filled with sticky rice, raw fish, and extras such as wasabi peas and fried leeks. With a roll costing between R$7 and R$12, this über-nutritious fast food has become the rage amidst Rio's health-conscious youth. It hasn't hurt that the menu was created by Nao Hara, one of Rio's top Japanese chefs. Since opening in 2006, this first Leblon store has spawned a dozen more throughout the city. It's often packed, and nobody lingers long; while the fluorescent tangerine color scheme functions as a visual beacon, it was also chosen because its inherent irritant properties ensure high turnover (seating is scarce).

SUSHI LEBLON ❸❸

Rua Dias Ferreira 256, tel. 21/2512-7830
HOURS: Mon.-Fri. noon-4 P.M. and 7 P.M.-1:30 A.M., Sat. noon-1:30 A.M., Sun. 1:30 P.M.-midnight

The sushimen at this favorite Leblon eatery are actually from the Northeastern coastal state of Ceará, a region with a strong fishing tradition. Once they acquired Japanese preparation techniques, there was no stopping them, and this sophisticated address has attracted a loyal

Fellini's per-kilo buffet is decidedly gourmet.

following. Both visually striking and appetizing, the sushi always includes startling innovations such as eel sushi with quail's eggs and truffle oil. Non-sushi fare is equally creative: Try the sea urchin ceviche seasoned with ginger, *pimenta*, and Sicilian limes.

PER-KILO BUFFETS
FELLINI ❸

Rua General Urquiza 101, tel. 21/2511-3600, www.fellini.com.br
HOURS: Daily 11:30 A.M.-midnight

In the heart of Leblon, Fellini offers one of Rio's most extensive and refined per-kilo self-service buffets. There's no need to splurge at a five-star restaurant when you can savor the likes of foie gras ravioli, honey-lacquered duck, lobster, escargots, and even caviar for a price only slightly higher than your average per-kilo joint. Aside from more mundane (but no less delicious) options, there are dishes for vegetarians and diabetics. The dessert table is a world unto itself. On weekends, avoid prime time or you'll have to stand in line for some time.

RÁSCAL ❸
Av. Afrânio de Melo Franco 290, Loja 406,
Shopping Leblon, tel. 21/3138-8503,
www.rascal.com.br
HOURS: Mon. noon-3:30 P.M. and 7-11 P.M.,
Sat. noon-midnight, Sun. noon-11 P.M.

São Paulo's favorite self-service chain has set up shop in Rio, and for those who frequent the Zona Sul's most swanky shopping mall the arrival is heaven-sent. The outstanding buffet of salads, freshly baked bread, antipasti, and hot and cold dishes has something for everyone, from delicious thin-crust pizza and spaghetti bolognesa to more sophisticated entrées such as salmon in a sesame crust and Moroccan couscous. There is even an impressively large wine cellar. Although it's not the cheapest kilo place in town, the variety and quality combined with the attractive dining area make this a great choice. A second outlet is located in Botafogo's Shopping Rio Sul (Rua Lauro Müller 116, tel. 21/3873-0339), and more are reportedly on the way.

PIZZA
PIZZARIA GUANABARA ❸
Rua Ataulfo de Paiva 1228, tel. 21/22294-0797,
www.pizzariaguanabara.com.br
HOURS: Daily 9 A.M.-7 A.M.

A far (and refreshingly welcome) cry from the slender-crusted goat cheese–topped pies served at many of Rio's trendy pizza temples, those served up at this decades-old bar and pizza parlor stick to old-fashioned basics such as pepperoni and mozzarella and thick, doughy crusts—which isn't to say that Guanabara doesn't have its fans. It has legions of them, many of whom drop by at all hours of the night for a slice and a *saideira* (last call). At the retro counter or the breezy sidewalk tables, the atmosphere is so convivial that customers inevitably end up staying for a (long) while.

PORTUGUESE
ANTIQUARIUS ❸❸❸
Rua Aristides Espinola 19, tel. 21/2294-1049,
www.antiquarius.com.br

HOURS: Mon.-Sat. noon-2 A.M., Sun. noon-midnight

When Antiquarius opened in 1977, Brazilians were amazed to discover that Portuguese cuisine went far beyond its signature specialty of *bacalhau* (salted cod). While this elegant eatery offers up myriad versions of this classic, neophytes should try the simplest version, roasted in the finest olive oil with onions, garlic, and olives. Diners can also sample lesser-known regional delicacies such as duck risotto with olives and sausage and lobster with lemon rice and emerald-colored kale. Unlike at other expensive gourmet restaurants, the portions here are extremely hearty. Polished antique furnishings, fresh flowers, and fine English porcelain, along with impeccable service, round out this memorable experience.

THAI
SAWASDEE ❸❸❸
Rua Dias Ferreira 571, Loja A, tel. 21/2511-0057,
www.sawasdee.com.br
HOURS: Mon-Thurs. 7 P.M.-midnight, Fri. 7 P.M.-2 A.M.,
Sat. 1 P.M.-2 A.M., Sun. 1-10 P.M.

After 10 years of having to haul themselves off to Búzios (such a penance) to savor the exotic Thai-influenced creations dreamed up by chef Marcos Sodré, Carioca foodies were overjoyed when, in 2008, Sodré and his son Thiago opened a second location in Leblon. Amidst a clean minimalist setting, devotees and neophytes alike can enjoy contemporary dishes that rely on the trademark experimental fusions of sweet and sour or mild and spicy and yield specialties such as grilled grouper with jasmine risotto bathed in a tangy passion-fruit curry sauce. Although it's less fiery than authentic Thai food, peppers make frequent appearances; they're responsible for the extra kick provided by the delicious house *mojitos*.

VEGETARIAN
❰ CELEIRO ❸❸
Rua Dias Ferreira 199, tel. 21/2274-7843,
www.celeiroculinaria.com.br
HOURS: Mon.-Sat. 10 A.M.-6 P.M.

For Leblon's body-conscious residents, this classic vegetarian restaurant and health-food store is a veritable institution. It all started in the early 1980s when two cake-baking sisters, Lúcia and Bia Herz, discovered they couldn't keep up with demand for the carrot cake they sold at a beach *barraca*. Teaming up with their mother, Rosa, they opened their own restaurant where, aside from healthy baked goods, they began concocting salads using organic products from local farms. Today, they offer more than 50 fantastic salads, served by weight, along with soups, snacks, and desserts. One of the priciest per-kilo joints in town, it has such a following that it is routinely swamped with figure-conscious celebs and even hard-core carnivores. Expect to line up.

UNIVERSO ORGÂNICO 🟢
Rua Conde da Bernadotte 26, Lojas 105-106,
tel. 21/3874-0186, www.universoorganico.com
HOURS: Mon. 8 A.M.-7 P.M., Tues.-Sat. 8 A.M.-9:30 P.M., Sun. 11 A.M.-8:30 P.M.

A graduate of New York's Natural Gourmet Institute, chef Tiana Rodrigues is one of Brazil's raw food pioneers. Her Leblon headquarters contains an organic market, a juice bar, and a small restaurant serving up all-natural food—none of which are cooked at temperatures higher than 40°C (104°F) in order to preserve the vitamins and enzymes. To entice the unconverted, Rodrigues takes pains to emphasize the colors, textures, and flavors of her ingredients. The resulting variety is impressive and embraces salads, soups, quiches, and pizzas as well as mushroom burgers and zucchini-eggplant lasagna. To maximize the health quotient, order a *suco de luz do sol* (sunlight juice), a bio-energy tonic whose ingredients—fruits, vegetables, wheat germ, and flax—possess antioxidant and detox properties.

VEGETARIANO SOCIAL CLUBE 🟢
Rua Conde de Bernadote 26, Loja L,
tel. 21/2294-5200, www.vegetarianosocialclube.com.br
HOURS: Mon.-Sat. noon-midnight, Sun. noon-6 P.M.

The small and wittily christened Vegetariano Social Clube came into being when a group of health-conscious pals from Leblon decided to do something about the lack of hard-core vegan restaurants in the hood—instead of griping, they opened one of their own. Choose from buffet or à la carte options, which include pizzas and tofulettes (eggless omelettes). While the selection is narrow, recipes are creative, as evidenced by the stroganoff made with shimeji mushrooms and palm hearts. To drink, there are lots of organic juices and even *caipirinhas* made with organic *cachaça* or sake. Saturday's tofu *feijoadas* have a huge veggie following.

RESTAURANTS

Gávea, Lagoa, and Jardim Botânico   Map 7

This area is largely residential, but if you happen to be in the neighborhood you'll find this trio of pleasant upscale *bairros* has a lot going for it culinarily, especially in view of the striking natural surroundings that embrace Corcovado and the Lagoa Rodrigo de Freitas. Gávea's perennial hot spot is the vibrant Praça Santos Dumont, whose lively bars also serve good traditional meals. The Lagoa boasts its *quiosques,* where you can gorge on everything from Arab to Amazonian food. As for Jardim Botânico, a handful of its gourmet restaurants, such as Roberta Sudbrack and Olympe, are gastronomic references that are truly worth a trip in themselves.

CAFÉS AND SNACKS
ESCOLA DO PÃO 🟢🟢
Rua General Garzon 10, tel. 21/2294-0027,
www.escoladopao.com.br
HOURS: Mon. 9 A.M.-3 P.M., Tues.-Sat. 9 A.M.-midnight, Sun. 9 A.M.-1 P.M.

Growing up in an Italian immigrant community in Rio Grande do Sul, every Sunday Clécia Casagrande joined the women to make bread. As an adult, unable to get the ritual, scent, or taste of fresh-baked loaves out of her mind, she purchased the former four-story abode of Brazilian writer José Lins de Rego and set about resurrecting her family's traditions at this lovely café-bistro, which has become a beloved neighborhood fixture. The breads are truly fabulous, as are the cakes, biscuits, and pastries, and are best savored at high tea or during the lavish weekend breakfast (R$55 per person) that features provençal sandwiches, sesame-banana bruschetta, and a dangerously addictive *creme de mamão* (papaya cream).

CHINESE
MR. LAM ⑤⑤⑤
Rua Maria Angélica 21, tel. 21/2286-6661, www.mrlam.com.br
HOURS: Mon.-Fri. 7 A.M.-midnight, Sat. 7 A.M.-1:30 A.M., Sun. 1-11:30 P.M.

Rio's most fab Chinese restaurant is the fruit of the union between business tycoon Eike Batista (Rio's version of Donald Trump) and Sik Chung Lam, who used to head the kitchen at New York's famous Mr. Chow. Consequently, the decor is an opulent paean to Asiatica with gorgeous dragon frescoes, 360-degree photos of the Great Wall of China, and a terra-cotta replica of a 3,000-year-old Xi'an warrior, along with a massive table supported by the one-ton motor salvaged from the Lamborghini with which Batista won the Brazilian Offshore Championship in 1990. For the most part, the food is as impressive as the surroundings. The appetizers, including delicate dim sum, are particularly inventive; the entrées can be less so.

CONTEMPORARY
DA GRAÇA ⑤⑤
Rua Pacheco Leão 780, tel. 21/2249-5484
HOURS: Tues-Thurs. noon-2 A.M., Fri.-Sat. noon-3 A.M.

Drowning in Brazilian kitsch—painted saints and icons galore; walls papered in a patchwork of tropical patterns, paper blossoms dangling from the ceiling—this restaurant-bar's trippy decor ensures the perpetual hipness of the crowd. Instead of big entrées, the menu traffics in tapa-sized portions of Asian-influenced dishes such as ginger rice balls served with spicy fruit chutney and salmon sushi rolled

in tapioca. Mix and match according to your whim, but be warned that the price can add up—if you're really starving perhaps it'd be best to satisfy your hunger pangs elsewhere.

〔 ROBERTA SUDBRACK ⑤⑤⑤
Av. Lineu de Paula Machado 916, tel. 21/3847-0139, www.robertasudbrack.com.br
HOURS: Tues.-Thurs. 7:30-midnight, Fri. noon-3 P.M. and 8:30 P.M.-close, Sat. 8:30 P.M.-close

Considered one of Brazil's most inventive contemporary chefs, Roberta Sudbrack composes culinary creations that are a feast for the senses. Self-taught, she went from operating a hot dog stand in Brasília to becoming presidential chef during the tenure of Fernando Henrique Cardoso. Her casually tasteful Jardim Botânico restaurant features two floors; the upstairs is dominated by a single long 18-person dining table where strangers can bond over innovative concoctions such as langoustine with pistachio milk and roasted pork with potato chantilly. In order to take advantage of the freshest ingredients, the menu changes daily.

FRENCH
OLYMPE ⑤⑤⑤
Rua Custódio Serrão 62, tel. 21/2539-4542, www.claudetroisgros.com.br
HOURS: Mon.-Thurs. and Sat. 7:30 P.M.-12:30 A.M., Fri. noon-4 P.M. and 7:30 P.M.-12:30 A.M.

One of Brazil's most stellar chefs, Claude Troisgros migrated from Paris to Rio 25 years ago and started a (culinary) revolution by marrying sophisticated French cooking techniques with the unusual textures, flavors, and colorful fresh produce distinctive to Brazil. The restaurant's decor is both as unpretentious and refined as the menus themselves (Troisgros offers several). The Especialidades menu features classic creations such as quail stuffed with *farofa*, raisins, and pearl onions, bathed in a sauce of *jabuticabas*, while the Criatividade menu showcases the chef's current experiments, such as grilled Amazonian fish in a creamy sorrel sauce with asparagus. Truly adventurous souls can splurge on the R$168 Confiance menu, a four-dish tasting feast that Troisgros dreams up daily according to the ingredients at hand.

66 BISTRÔ 💲💲
Av. Alexandre Ferreira 66, tel. 21/2266-0838, www.66bistro.com.br
HOURS: Tues.-Sun. noon-4 P.M. and 7:30 P.M.-12:30 A.M.

Foodies eager to sample Troisgros's culinary wizardry, but without the deep pockets necessary for Olympe, needn't despair—recently Troisgros opened the more affordable 66 Bistrô. With his son, Thomas, in charge of the kitchen, this charming Parisian-style bistro is already *the* place to lunch—apparently not even celebrities can resist a weekday "executive" menu whose buffet of antipasti, salads and several main dishes costs a mere R$28 (R$34 if you succumb to the desserts). Evenings and weekends, the menu is à la carte. A favorite house specialty is the chicken roasted in Dijon mustard.

ITALIAN
QUADRIFOGLIO 💲💲💲
Rua J. J. Seabra 19, tel. 21/2294-1433
HOURS: Mon.-Sat. 12:30-3:30 P.M. and 7:30 P.M.-midnight, Sun. 12:30-5 P.M.

Over the years, the Northern Italian–inspired creations prepared by Lombard chef Silvana Bianchini have been raved about and emulated by professional and amateur gourmets alike. The warm goat cheese salad with heart of *pupunha* (an Amazonian palm); ravioli stuffed with pears, gorgonzola, and crushed almonds; and pistachio-scallop risotto are some of the most famous signature dishes enjoyed by a faithful and somewhat mature clientele who feel right at home amidst the formal yet comfortable surroundings.

PIZZA
BRÁZ 💲💲
Rua Maria Angélica 129, tel. 21/2535-0687, www.casabraz.com.br
HOURS: Sun.-Thurs. 6:30 P.M.-12:30 A.M., Fri.-Sat. 6:30 P.M.-1:30 A.M.

With the opening of Bráz, 2007 became known as the year that São Paulo pizza (deemed the best in Brazil) finally invaded Rio. Topped with the freshest ingredients, these fine-crust pizzas—touted as "paintings you can eat"—taste as great as they look. The house specialty, the *caprese,* comes adorned with artisanal buffalo mozzarella, tomatoes, giant basil leaves, and white-olive pesto. Decorative highlights include wooden armoires rescued from an ancient pharmacy as well as the surreal apparition of two Cristo Redentor statues—the real one perched atop Corcovado and its reflection in a giant mirror.

PORTUGUESE
BACALHAU DO REI 💲💲
Rua Marquês do São Vicente, 11-A, tel. 21/2294-0027, www.bacalhaudorei.com.br
HOURS: Mon.-Fri. 8:30 A.M.-1 A.M., Sun. 9 A.M.-10 P.M.

Fans of *bacalhau* really will feel like *reis* (kings) at this decades-old Portuguese haunt. Despite a recent upgrade that's robbed it of some of its earthy *boteco*-style flavor, the crowds keep packing in to savor salted cod in all its myriad forms: baked, fried, grilled, in salads, and most irresistibly, as deep-fried *bolinhos* whose seasoning, crispiness, and crunch (completely bereft of grease) is dangerously close to perfection—in fact, it's worth dropping by just for a portion and an icy Original beer.

Barra da Tijuca and Recreio Map 8

There's not much going on gastronomically in these suburban-style beach *bairros* of the Zona Oeste—certainly there's no compelling reason to trek out here for a meal. There's no shortage of eating options in Barra, but the most interesting options are located within *shoppings* and are usually outposts of reputed restaurants in Centro or Zona Sul that opened a Barra branch so that the area's nouveau riche can keep up with the Joneses. If you have a car, the bucolic districts of Vargem Grande and Barra de Guaratiba, past Recreio, have some wonderfully secluded gourmet restaurants, engulfed in tropical vegetation, that are favorite weekend lunch spots for Cariocas intent on getting away from it all.

CHURRASCARIAS
ANTIQUARIUS GRILL ⑤⑤⑤
Av. das Américas 4666, Loja 160,
tel. 21/2431-9331,
www.antiquariusgrill.com.br
HOURS: Sun.-Thurs. noon-midnight,
Sat.-Sun. noon-2 A.M.

If you're out in Barra's *shopping* territory and have the urge for a fine-dining experience far from the food courts, Antiquarius Grill is the ticket. It's strategically located between the behemoths BarraShopping and New York City Center, but this refined yet somewhat soulless spin-off of Leblon's cherished temple to Portuguese gastronomy lacks the Old World charm (and service) of the original Antiquarius, as well as the traditional focus on regional specialties. The restaurant's highlights are fine cuts of beef from Argentina and Uruguay, seared to high-tech perfection by infrared rays. The prime rib and sirloin steaks are particularly mouthwatering. Unchanged is the fantastic array of Portuguese desserts, tantalizingly displayed at a buffet table near the entrance.

CONTEMPORARY
QUINTA ⑤⑤⑤
Rua Luciano Gallet 150, Vargem Grande,
tel. 21/2428-1396, www.quinta.net
HOURS: Fri. 1-5 P.M., Sat.-Sun. 1-7 P.M.

It's hard to dream up a more Arcadian eating experience than the one preferred by this bucolic country house lost in a forest of tropical foliage and fruit trees where chattering *mico estrelas* (star monkeys) provide the soundtrack. Nature's bounty supplies many of the fresh ingredients used in imaginative dishes such as wild duck with seasonal fruit chutney, caramelized sweet potatoes, and grilled vegetables. Various menus allow you to eat as much or as little as you want. Far from Rio's crowds, this is Sunday in the country at its best.

PIZZA
FIAMETTA ⑤⑤
Av. das Américas 7777, Loja 303, tel. 21/2438-7500,
www.fiammetta.com.br
HOURS: Daily noon-1 A.M.

There are several branches of this favorite pizzeria around town (including in Botafogo's Shopping Rio Plaza), but this one on the 3rd floor of the Rio Design Center boasts the captivating bonus of a veranda gazing towards the Pedra da Gávea. The pizzas are scrumptious, with crusts that are light, crisp, and airy and hold a varied ensemble of toppings. At lunch, a reasonably priced all-you-can-eat buffet includes antipasti, salads, and pastas.

SEAFOOD
476 ⑤⑤
Rua Barros Alarcão 476, Pedra da Guaratiba,
tel. 21/2417-1716, www.restaurante476.com.br
HOURS: Wed.-Sun. 11 A.M.-7 P.M.

Despite the distance from downtown, on weekends Cariocas (with cars) have no compunction about making the trek to this charmingly renovated yet utterly rustic fisherman's cottage set amidst the lush Atlantic forest. While gazing out to sea diners can feast on fresh fish and seafood, prepared according to recipes that run the gamut from Bahian *moquecas* to Indian curries. The wine list is interesting and the homemade desserts—such as coconut ice cream topped with tangerine coulis and coconut shavings—are pretty sublime.

Greater Rio de Janeiro   Map 9

Considering the distance of these *bairros* from the Centro and Zona Sul, there's no motivation to travel to them expressly for a meal. But should you happen to be checking out neighborhood sights there are several good options that will keep you from going hungry.

BRAZILIAN
QUINTA DA BOA VISTA $$
Parque da Quinta da Boa Vista, tel. 21/2589-6551, www.restaurantequintadaboavista.com.br
HOURS: Daily 11 A.M.–6 P.M.
This decades-old restaurant occupies the chapel of the imperial residence. The former priest's quarters now lodge the kitchen, and the ground-level basement—where the emperor used to while the nights away in the company of his favorite slaves—has been converted into pleasant dining rooms furnished with antiques and oil paintings and views of the surrounding park. The menu is a compelling mishmash of traditional hearty fare. Among the coveted daily specials are *rabada* (oxtail stew) served with watercress and polenta, roasted *cabrito* (kid), and *coelho* (rabbit).

PORTUGUESE
ADEGÃO PORTUGUÊS $$$
Campo de São Cristovão 212, tel. 21/2580-7288, www.adegaoportugues.com.br
HOURS: Mon.-Sat. 11 A.M.–11 A.M., Sun. noon–8 P.M.
Over the decades, this rustic Portuguese restaurant across the street from the Feira de São Cristovão has received rave reviews from VIPS ranging from Juscelino Kubitshek to Lula. Most diners go straight for the outstanding and seemingly endless choices of *bacalhau* (including flawless *bolinhos* to start things off), but meatier fare such as pork and lamb, roasted and bathed in garlic, onions, and saffron, is always tasty. Portions are generous and edible accessories such as potatoes, broccoli, and the finest of olive oils are memorable in their own right.

RESTAURANTS

NIGHTLIFE

As laid-back and relaxing as Rio can be by day, at night it becomes a buzzing hive of activity. As soon as happy hour rolls around, Rio's traditional casual bars—*botequins*—are flooded with Cariocas downing ice-cold *chopes* (draft beer) and trading quips and *fofocas* (gossip). Some tuck in here for the night; for others these neighborhood bars are merely warm-up zones.

Rio is one of the most musical cities you'll ever encounter, and there is no shortage of bars, clubs, dance halls, and open-air venues featuring live performances of Brazil's myriad musical styles. Since Cariocas rarely listen to music without succumbing to the urge to move their bodies, most of these places feature dancing as well. For those who prefer a more globalized beat, the city has its share of nightclubs and discos, although they are much blander and mimetic than one might expect (in terms of contemporary sounds, São Paulo definitely has the advantage).

Although much of Centro shuts down after happy hour, for some years now the traditional bohemian *bairro* of Lapa has been reclaimed by new bohos who flock to hear samba, *chorinho, forró,* and other home-grown melodies. Meanwhile the swankier watering holes and nightspots of the Zona Sul offer more internationally urban brands of fun, albeit with a decidedly bossa nova twist.

Whether you feel like listening to music, dancing, or both, the options are limitless. Aside from bars, clubs, and concert venues, there are always live performances—whether organized or improvised—taking place in *praças,* parks, and on the beach. When you're in

© MICHAEL SOMMERS

HIGHLIGHTS

LOOK FOR  TO FIND RECOMMENDED NIGHTLIFE.

◖ Best Places to Hear Live Samba: There are so many great places to hear samba in Rio that the act of narrowing it down is cruel. To savor an authentic samba scene, check out **Centro Cultural Carioca,** which occupies a turn-of-the-20th-century dance hall in Centro. Lapa is a samba hotbed, and despite the fact that it is routinely swamped with tourists, **Rio Scenarium** boasts top performers and a fabulous setting inside a three-story antiques store (pages 124 and 126).

◖ Best All-Around Entertainment: **Lapa 40°** is more than Lapa's hottest new *boîte du jour;* the four-story house is a veritable entertainment complex equipped with a bar, dance hall, stage for live shows, cyber café, smoking room, whiskey bar, dart boards, and 30 billiards tables (page 125).

◖ Best Dance Club: Lounge 69 is more than just Ipanema's sexiest dance club. A combination of Rio's best sound system and a mesmerizing light show attracts big-name DJs as well as those intent on dancing the night away (page 131).

◖ Best Venue for Star-Gazing: Eternally fashionable **00** attracts star-gazers of all types. There are those hoping to catch sight of celebrities, and those who want to take in the 6,500 heavenly bodies projected on the ceiling at the planetarium next door. There are also those who, when not grooving to tunes, drinking in the lounge, or eating at the cool contemporary restaurant, just want to retire to the garden and gaze up at the galaxy (page 131).

◖ Most Atmospheric Neighborhood *Boteco:* Perched on a tranquil corner of Santa Teresa, **Armazém São Thiago** underwent a transformation from old-fashioned corner store to cool neighborhood bar without missing a beat, or losing the early-20th-century fixtures and furnishings that make it so utterly charming (page 133).

◖ Most Romantic Atmosphere: Located in the Hotel Marina All-Suites, **Bar d'Hotel** possesses a stylish decor and a tantalizing cocktail menu, but best of all is the view that just won't quit, courtesy of the enormous windows that gaze out over the beaches of Ipanema and Leblon (page 134).

◖ Best Beach Bar: A classic Carioca *botequim* dating back to the 1930s, **Bar Urca** has a privileged location that allows you to savor food and drinks while using the nearby sea wall overlooking Baía de Guanabara as your own personal bar counter (page 135).

◖ Best Beer: In a beer-loving town where Brahma *chope* holds sway over the draft beer culture, **Devassa** became a phenomenon by creating its own delicious line of microbrews and naming each beer type after a classic Brazilian female biotype (page 137).

◖ Best Outdoor Lounge: With its wood furniture, cocktails made with Amazonian fruits, and torch-lit tropical foliage, **Palaphita Kitch** is the most captivating of the kiosk bars dotting the shores of Lagoa Rodrigo de Freitas (page 141).

◖ Most Unpretentious Gay Bar: Buraco da Lacraia offers three floors of fun that range from drag shows and videoke competitions to pool tables and good old-fashioned dark rooms (page 142).

NIGHTLIFE

the interior of Armazém São Thiago

© MICHAEL SOMMERS

town, pick up a copy of *Veja Rio* (a supplement of *Veja* magazine—you can also check listings online at www.vejario.com.br) or rifle through the arts sections of the two main dailies, *O Globo* and *Jornal do Brasil*. At many bars and clubs, you can pick up *Vai Rolar* (www.vairolar. com.br), a free weekly cultural guide that lists all upcoming musical events.

Live Music

Music is more abundant than sunshine in Rio. Although you can and will hear live music all over town, the greatest concentration of options is in Lapa. If you only have one night in Rio, you would be crazy not to spend it under the Arcos, where jams take place, or at the dozens of atmospheric bars and live-music clubs that occupy turn-of-the-20th-century houses. Lapa is Rio's traditional samba *bairro,* and it is here that you're likely to see the best performances of samba, along with other popular Brazilian forms such as *chorinho, forró,* and MPB. The scene is especially vibrant Thursday to Saturday, when streets are filled with revelers and the beat goes on until dawn; Sunday and Monday are pretty dead.

ALLEGRO BISTRÔ MUSICAL

Rua Barata Ribeiro 502, Loja D, tel. 21/2548-5005, www.modernsound.com.br
HOURS: Mon.-Fri. noon-9 P.M., Sat. noon-8 P.M.
COST: Free
Map 4

Tucked away at the back of what is arguably Rio's best CD store, the tiny stage of this "bistro" has propped up the weight of some of the top names in contemporary MPB (Música Popular Brasileira, or popular Brazilian music), including Lenine, Ana Carolina, and Maria Rita. The atmosphere is intimate and the acoustics are superb. The only drawback is having to arrive early for "big-name" shows (admission tickets are distributed on a first-come, first-served basis). While the music moves you, indulge in creative sandwiches and snacks, such as chick-pea *bolinhos* served with hummus, pita, and pickles. The appropriately named Amigo Allegro, a house cocktail

of vodka, pineapple juice, and mint, will leave you feeling very affable indeed.

BIP BIP

Rua Almirante Gonçalves 50, Loja D, tel. 21/2267-9696
HOURS: Daily 7 P.M.-1 A.M.
COST: R$15-20
Map 4

Bip Bip is a tiny hole-in-the-wall of a *botequim* with two saving graces: its location on a quiet Copa street that allows tables and chairs to be arranged outside, and terrific musical jams by top Carioca samba, *choro,* and bossa nova performers. Sunday's rousing *samba-de-roda* sessions always spill over into the street. Aside from *bolinhos de bacalhau* and salami slices, you won't find much to nosh, but the beer is always chilled. Utterly unpretentious, Bip is a welcome antidote to Copa's touristy oceanfront bars.

CABARET KALESA

Rua Sacadura Cabral 61, tel. 21/2516-8332, www.kalesa.com.br
HOURS: Wed.-Sat. 10 P.M.-5 A.M.
COST: R$10-20
Map 1

Ensconced amidst the dives and whorehouses of the once incredibly seamy port zone, Kalesa was hipper-than-thou in the 1980s and early '90s and was sorely missed when it went out of business. Resurrected in 2005 as part of the growing trend to revive the Saúde area surrounding Praça Mauá, the club has picked up where it left off with an irreverent mix that often includes DJ-spun samba, MPB, and electronica, along with pseudo Carnaval balls and male and female striptease shows. To cool down, aside from cocktails, there are a couple of terraces that offer great views.

CARIOCA DA GEMA

Av. Mem de Sá 79, tel. 21/2221-0043,
www.barcariocadagema.com.br
HOURS: Mon.-Thurs. 6 P.M.-1:30 A.M.,
Fri.-Sat. 8 P.M.-3:30 A.M.
COST: R$15-20
`Map 1`

Inaugurated in 2000, Carioca da Gema was one of the pioneers of Lapa's revival movement and, despite the many acts that have followed, it still remains one of the hood's classic spots to listen to top-quality samba and *choro* performed by big names and rising stars as well as house favorites singer Teresa Cristina and guitarist Paulão Sete Cordas. Performances usually begin at 9 P.M. Although it can get pretty crowded, the ambience has remained warm and down-to-earth. For nibbling, there is a copious menu.

CASA BRASIL MESTIÇO

Av. Mem de Sá 59-61, tel. 21/2509-7418
HOURS: Wed.-Sun. 7 P.M.-4 A.M.
COST: R$10
`Map 1`

Casa Brasil Mestiço is a great place to listen to authentic Brazilian music that you won't hear anywhere else in Lapa, let alone the rest of Rio. Aside from ubiquitous samba and *choro*, you'll be treated to traditional Afro-Brazilian rhythms such as *jongo, afoxé, coco,* and *tambor de crioula* performed on the downstairs stage. Meanwhile, upstairs DJs spin more contemporary, but no less eclectic, tunes. Eats (velvety *caldo de feijão* and manioc fries with grated parmesan) and drinks (Bohemia beer in cans) are simple and cheap, but do the trick. The bar also houses an NGO, operated by part-owner and singer Luciane Menezes, devoted to researching Brazilian popular and folk culture.

CASA DA MÃE JOANA

Rua Gomes Freire 547, tel. 21/2224-4071,
www.casadamaejoana.com.br

BRAZILIAN BEER

Nothing beats the heat like a *cerveja estupidamente gelada,* otherwise known as a "stupidly cold" beer. It's hard to overexaggerate Brazilians' love of beer. *Cerveja* is a day-to-day companion, enjoyed not just at the corner bar but at a meal, on a beach, in the street, at a *festa.* A lot of foreigners used to dark malts and microbrewery ales with nuanced flavors scoff at pale Brazilian beer with its low alcohol content and supposedly weak, watery taste. However, if you're going to be drinking all day (or night) in 40°C (104°F) heat, you'll come to appreciate the lightness of Brazilian beer. Just make sure it is always *bem gelada* (nicely chilled). The idyllic beer is the *véu de noiva,* in which the bottle arrives at your table cloaked in a thin layer of frost that resembles "a bride's veil."

Most bars sell beer in 600-milliliter bottles, but fancier places sell so-called "long necks," similar to those you'll find in North America and Europe. At supermarkets, on beaches, and in the streets, beer is often sold in *latas* (cans). There are various rival national brands (Antarctica, Skol, Nova Schin) and some very good regional ones such as Bohemia (from Petrópolis) and Serramalte (from Rio Grande do Sul). *Chope* is a pale draft – both Brahma and Antarctica have their own versions – with a nice foam that is particularly popular in Rio. Essential bar vocab includes *"mais uma"* ("another beer, please") and *"a saideira"* ("last call").

HOURS: Tues.-Fri. 7 P.M.-2 A.M., Sat. 9 P.M.-3 A.M.
COST: R$10-15
`Map 1`

Originally located in the Zona Norte *bairro* of São Cristovão, Casa da Mãe Joana was responsible for turning Rio's younger generations on to the classic sambas of yore with performances by an ongoing roster of old-school *mestres* such as Monarco and Zé Keti. After closing down the Casa migrated to Lapa in 2006; while the new digs may be spiffier and more secure (with a well-lit entrance and security guards brandishing walkie-talkies), the clientele remains reassuringly untrendy. Inside, the decor verges on tacky—in front of the stage is a fountain with water spewing forth from a lion's mouth—and the dance floor is always writhing with bodies (thankfully, there is a/c) samba-ing away to their heart's content.

◖ CENTRO CULTURAL CARIOCA

Rua do Teatro 37, tel. 21/2252-6468,
www.centroculturalcarioca.com.br
HOURS: Tues.-Wed. 7 P.M.-midnight, Thurs. 7 P.M.-1 A.M., Fri.-Sat. 8 P.M.-2 A.M.
COST: R$10
Map 1

Between the 1930s and '60s, this majestic turn-of-the-20th-century *sobrado* housed the Dancing Eldorado, one of Rio's most famous dance halls, where eager gents received dance cards and then proceeded to spend the night whirling (not always respectable, but very proficient) ladies across the parquet floor. Today, both men and women pay for the privilege of samba-ing the night away to performers such as Mart'nalia and Nilze Carvalho (although old-style *bailes*—balls—are still held on Fridays). Charmingly retro, with original marble tables where you can enjoy delicious *caldos* (soups) and icy beer (in cans), this is one of the best places to get a feel for Rio's samba scene.

CLUBE SANTA LUZIA

Av. Almirante Sílvio de Noronha 300, tel. 21/9864-4111
HOURS: Fri. 9 P.M.-close
COST: R$12 (men), R$10 (women)
Map 1

For authentic samba with a view to boot, check out Friday evenings at the Clube Santa Luzia, where master *sambistas* and their bands perform outdoors (adjacent to the Aeroporto Santos Dumont and behind the MAM). Beer (served in large bottles) is always icy and the atmosphere is convivial, to say the least. In terms of the enchantment factor, it's hard to surpass samba-ing in front of a moonlit Pão de Açúcar and Baía de Guanabara.

DRINK CAFÉ

Av. Borges de Medeiros, Quiosque No. 5, Parque dos Patins, tel. 21/2239-4136,
www.drinkcafe.com.br
HOURS: Mon.-Thurs. 5 P.M.-1 A.M., Fri. 5 P.M.-2:30 A.M., Sat. 11 A.M.-3 A.M., Sun. 10 A.M.-1 A.M.
COST: R$6
Map 7

It's hard to imagine a more mellow evening than one spent at this kiosk, gazing out over the Lagoa Rodrigo de Freitas against a soothing musical backdrop of live (mostly instrumental) jazz, bossa nova, MPB, and *chorinho*. To nibble, there's a delicious antipasto platter with baked garlic, gratinéed eggplant and zucchini, gorgonzola, and lots of toast. Hungrier souls will appreciate the filet mignon grilled on a hot stone with fries or Northeastern grub such as butter-grilled *carne de sol* (sun-dried meat) with peppers and bacon. The drink menu includes an impressive array of fine *cachaças*.

ELITE

Rua Frei Caneca 4, tel. 21/2232-3217
HOURS: Fri. 7 P.M.-close, Sat. 10 P.M.-close, Sun. 6 P.M.-close
COST: R$6 (drink minimum)
Map 1

Among the few remaining traditional dance halls known as *gafieiras* that once flooded Rio's Centro and Lapa, the Elite is one of the most famous. Occupying a charming curving pale-pink colonial building with enormous windows and wrought-iron balconies, the Elite Club (as it was originally known) opened its doors in 1930 and for decades served as a clubhouse for Rio's artist and bohemian set. You can still catch a whiff of yesteryear when you show up and see elegant older gents twirling their ladies around the dance floor. The aura of déjà vu that permeates makes it a favorite shooting location for period films and *novelas*.

ESTRELA DA LAPA

Av. Mem de Sá 69, tel. 21/2509-7602,
www.estreladalapa.com.br
HOURS: Fri. 7 P.M.-close, Sat. 10 P.M.-close,
Sun. 6 P.M.-close
COST: R$15-30
Map 1

More sophisticated and upscale (and consequently also more pricy) than its neighbors, this multilevel club is undeniably charming with its black-and-white checkerboard marble floors, warm wooden fixtures, art nouveau wrought-iron balconies, and romantic lighting. Musical performances (which usually start at 9 P.M.) run the gamut from samba and *choro* to MPB, jazz, and swing. The tone is mellower and more mature than most of Lapa's other offerings and so is the crowd, which tends towards their late thirties and early forties. Things get livelier on weekend nights when DJ's host *festas*.

J CLUB

Praia do Flamengo 340, tel. 21/2251-1278,
www.casajulietadeserpa.com.br
HOURS: Fri.-Sat. 9 P.M.-12:30 A.M.
COST: R$15-30
Map 2

Housed inside the Casa Julieta de Serpa, a 1920s mini-palace converted into a cultural center, this swank retro piano bar is the brainchild of antiques dealer and empresario Carlos Alberto Serpa, whose decorative flair is more than apparent in the Baccarat crystal chandeliers and zebra-upholstered chairs that adorn this sophisticated space. It's a mellow alternative to Rio's more frenzied weekend nightlife offerings; the only energy you'll need to expend is to order a glass of wine or a kir royal before you curl up and listen to the intimate shows of jazz, bossa, and MPB standards, often performed by big Brazilian names.

LAPA 40°

Rua Riachuelo 97, tel. 21/3970-1329,
www.lapa40graus.com.br
HOURS: Daily 6 P.M.-4 A.M.
COST: R$5
Map 1

In Carioca-ese "40°" refers to the temperature (in celsius) that descends upon the city

The swank J Club occupies a 1920s palace in Flamengo.

in the heat of summer. The name is apt: Since it opened in 2007, this vast four-story building has become Lapa's hottest spot. More than a bar or nightclub, Lapa 40° is a revolutionary concept—an entertainment complex outfitted with a bar, ballroom, and stage for live shows as well as a cyber café, a *tabacaria* (for smoking cigars), a *uisqueiria* (for doing whiskey shots), and dart boards. Oh, and if you get bored, there is an entire floor outfitted with 30 pool and billiard tables.

MISTURA FINA
Av. Rainha Elisabeth da Bélgica 769, tel. 21/2523-1703, www.misturafina.com.br
HOURS: Daily noon-close
COST: R$20-60
Map 5

One of Rio's swankiest musical clubs, Mistura Fina moved in 2008 from Lagoa to this renovated space on top of Barril 1800, whose terraces flaunt magnificent views of Ipanema beach. Although its main fare is jazz, this piano bar also hosts a variety of national and international performers that play MPB, blues, and samba performed on an intimate stage with great acoustics. In keeping with the prices and refined ambience, the clientele is older and more upscale. If you feel the urge to nosh, the discreetly romantic restaurant has an extensive menu.

NOVA ESTUDANTINA
Praça Tiradentes 79, tel. 21/2232-1149, www.estudantinamusical.com.br
HOURS: Wed.-Fri. 6 P.M.-1 A.M., Sat. 10 P.M.-3 A.M.
COST: R$10-20
Map 1

Gafieiras, ballrooms where Rio's working classes came to dance the night away, began springing up in Centro during the 1920s. The oldest survivor, Nova Estudantina, dates back to 1928; despite some much-need restoration work, the decor hasn't changed much since then (including the signs forbidding "scandalous" kissing and women dancing together). Aside from live orchestras playing traditional

ballroom ditties on Saturday afternoons, evening repertoires have been updated to samba, *forró,* soul, and rock. The crowd is very mixed, with people of all ages, in a space with room for 1,500 dancing fools, so you certainly won't feel claustrophobic.

RIO SCENARIUM
Rua do Lavradio 20, tel. 21/3147-9005, www.rioscenarium.com.br
HOURS: Tues.-Thurs. 7 P.M.-2 A.M., Fri.-Sat. 7 P.M.-5 A.M.
COST: R$10-25
Map 1

One of the city's most enchanting bars, Rio Scenarium is perpetually packed (often with tourists). If it's lost much of its cachet (lots of gringos trying to samba), it's succeeded in retaining its unique charm. Located on Lapa's antiques row, its three floors are chock-full of antiques (some 10,000 at last count)—you can sit, sprawl, and lounge upon certain pieces while others are merely eye candy (such as the art deco pharmacy on the 2nd floor). On most nights, top names in samba, *choro,* and *forró* perform, inciting the mixed public to take to the dance floor. To beat the crowds, arrive early (i.e., before 8 P.M.), or reserve a table.

SEMENTE
Rua Joaquim Silva 138, tel. 21/9781-2451
HOURS: Sat.-Thurs. 8 P.M.-1 A.M.
COST: R$10-25
Map 1

Semente (which prophetically means seed) was one of the first bars to open at the beginning of Lapa's resurrection as a bohemian hot spot. And despite having closed and reopened its doors several times, it has managed to stay true to its roots by sticking to tried-and-true samba and *choro* performances, leaving trends and mobs to its neighbors (evidenced by the fact that closing time is an obscenely early 1 A.M. and that it doesn't open at all on Friday). Although the ambience is relaxed and intimate, food, drink, and decor are all kept to a minimum—it's all about the music.

TRAPICHE GAMBOA

Rua Sacadura Cabral 155, tel. 21/2516-0868,
www.trapichegamboa.com.br
HOURS: Tues.-Thurs. 6:30 P.M.-1 A.M., Fri.
6:30 P.M.-3:30 A.M., Sat. 8:30 P.M.-3:30 A.M.
COST: R$10-20
Map 1

In 2004, lawyer and samba aficionado Claudia
Melo Alves was a pioneer for opening the doors
of this renovated 19th-century *sobrado* in the
otherwise louche and deserted port zone of
Centro. But when she started offering some
of the best live samba performances in town,
music lovers took notice—as did other risk-
taking entrepreneurs who, feeling that trendy
Lapa had become saturated, slowly began moving into the neighborhood. As a result, Gamboa
and adjacent Saúde have become home to a progressive and hip scene. To quench your thirst,
diss the classic lime *caipirinha* in favor of one
made with fragrant red *pitangas*.

VINICIUS PIANO BAR

Rua Vinicius de Moraes 39, tel. 21/2523-4757,
www.viniciusbar.com.br
HOURS: Daily 9 A.M.-2 A.M.
COST: Shows R$25-38
Map 5

Billing itself as the Temple of Bossa Nova,
this restaurant-bar lures a steady stream of
homegrown bossa nostalgists and tourists
with "The Girl from Ipanema" on their brain.
The interior is a veritable Vinicius shrine, with
portraits and memorabilia galore. From the
2nd-floor piano bar, nightly shows pay musical homage to the beloved poet, composer,
diplomat, and bon vivant. The most frequent
crooner-in-residence is Maria Creuza, who
shared the stage with Vinicius on many occasions. The downstairs restaurant serves a
passable lunch in the afternoons as well as a
large array of drinks (and small selection of
petiscos) in the evening.

Dance Clubs

Many of Rio's clubs promote thematic *festas*
that change nightly. Often they focus on a
certain musical style, feature a guest DJ, or
even cater to a specific crowd (such as gays
and lesbians). To ensure that the spirit (and the
music) is going to move you, you might want
to check out the club websites in advance or
pick up a copy of the weekly *Vai Rolar* (www.
vairolar.com.br), which is distributed free
around town.

BARONNETI

Rua Barão da Torre 354, tel. 21/2247-9100,
www.baronneti.com.br
HOURS: Tues.-Sun. 10:30 P.M.-close
COST: R$20-50 (women), R$40-70 (men)
Map 5

Baronneti is everything you might expect
from one of Ipanema's surprisingly scant
nightclubs: a little swank, a little stark, and a
little pricy (although the cover does include a

Rio's club scene boasts thematic *festas* that
change nightly.

drink) with some sultry lounging spaces and the obligatory sushi bar. Consequently, the crowd is well heeled, well dressed, and well beyond adolescence. The DJs spin hip-hop, house, and funk music on two dance floors.

BUNKER

Rua Raul Pompéia 94, tel. 21/2247-8724, www.bunker94.com.br
HOURS: Thurs.-Sun. 11:30 P.M.-close
COST: R$10-20
Map 4

This classic Copa hot spot reels in a mixed public of international *turistas* and young locals (with a strong gay and lesbian contingent) looking to rock out. All will find what they're after at this tri-level party zone where some of the city's top DJs take to heart their mission to make sure that the music—an eclectic melee of rock, funk, hip-hop, trance, and soul—never stops.

CASA DA MATRIZ

Rua Henrique Novaes 107, tel. 21/2266-1014, www.casadamatriz.com.br
HOURS: Wed.-Mon. 11 P.M.-close

CACHAÇA

What rum is to Cuba, tequila to Mexico, and vodka to Russia, *cachaça* is to Brazil. Distilled from fermented sugarcane juice, to which sugar is then added, *cachaça* packs a wallop – with an alcohol strength between 38 and 48 percent. Whether drunk pure or as the base of the world-famous and highly addictive national cocktail known as the *caipirinha* (*cachaça*, sugar, crushed ice, and lime), Brazilians swear by their *cachaça*. In fact, the average Brazilian imbibes about three gallons (or 12 liters) of the stuff in a given year, which explains current production levels of 1.3 billion liters.

Caipirinhas and other cocktails are usually made with the clear, industrially manufactured varieties – such as Pitú and 51 – that you can buy in any supermarket. Dirt cheap, these are pretty foul-tasting on their own, and if you want to savor *cachaças* on par with the world's finer aged whiskies, you're better off choosing from one of the thousands of artisanal varieties, produced at small mills throughout the country (most famously in Minas Gerais). These are more often golden in hue, with a variety of fragrances and tastes, often depending on the wooden barrels they are aged in, many of which are made from native trees such as almond, brazilwood, and the exotically named *ipê, jequitibá, tibiriça,* and *jatobá.* These *cachaças* are usually sold directly to bars, restaurants, supermarkets, and discerning consumers.

Cachaça began life as a drink imbibed by African slaves who worked on sugarcane plantations. For centuries, *cachaça* was produced almost exclusively for slaves and the lower classes. The Brazilian middle and upper classes viewed *cachaça* as the poor man's poison and instead drank imported wines and other spirits. However, since the late 1990s the fabrication of artisanal and even organic *cachaças* has led to a major boost in its reputation, with aficionados sipping it pure. In 2003, the Brazilian government trademarked the *cachaça* name with the goal of marketing it – at home and abroad – as a fine alcohol. Nonetheless, *cachaça* is nothing if not democratic, and it shows up around the nation under a variety of names, including *pinga* (as in "drop"), *cana* (cane), *aguardente* (burning water), *mardita* (from *maldita,* meaning "the damned one"), *água-que-passarinho-não-bebe* (water that birds don't drink), and *aquela-que-matou-o-guarda* (that which killed the cop). Aside from *caipirinhas,* other popular *cachaça* potions include:

- *batida* – Cachaça, milk, and the pulp of fresh fruit; it's like a sweet milkshake with a kick. It tends to give hangovers. Popular flavors include passion fruit, coconut, and pineapple.

- *bombeirinho* – The Brazilian version of a kir

COST: R$10-25

Map 3

Located in an attractive turn-of-the-20th-century house, Casa da Matriz hosts some of the most happening dance parties in town, courtesy of an eclectic roster of house DJs and a styling, alternative (and, these days, fairly youngish) crowd with a proclivity for contemporary sounds. Monday's *A Maldita* (The Damned) *festas* promise that you'll begin the week feeling trashed. If you need a breather, check out the rotating photo exhibits, test your retro reflexes with a game of Pac-Man or Atari, or simply flake out in the dimly lit lounge with an imported beer.

CASA ROSA

Rua Alice 550, tel. 21/2557-2562, www.casarosa.com.br

HOURS: Fri.-Sat. 10:30 P.M.-close, Sun. 5:30 P.M.-close

COST: R$10-20

Map 2

Casa Rosa is quite literally pink (a shocking one at that), but from the turn of the 20th century to the late 1980s its chromatic association was red: It was the town's most famous

© MICHAEL SOMMERS

improvised Ipanema beach bar

royal is *cachaça* and gooseberry (*groselha*) syrup.

- *capeta* ("demon") – This is a truly diabolical mix of *cachaça* along with cinnamon, red-hued fruit juice (cherry, strawberry, or grape), red wine, vodka, and sugar. It is served in large portions, with dry ice added to enhance fumes.

- *leite de onça* ("jaguar's milk") – This favorite during the Festas Juninas mixes *cachaça* with milk, condensed milk, and cinnamon.

- *quentão* ("hot stuff") – Similar to a sangria, this hot mixture of cheap (sweet) wine and *cachaça*, spiked with ginger, cinnamon, and cloves, is also a popular favorite during the Festas Juninas.

- *rabo-de-galo* ("rooster's tail") – *Cachaça* mixed with red vermouth.

NIGHTLIFE

Casa Rosa, a former bordello, now hosts weekend *festas*.

bordello, frequented by Laranjeiras's resident politicians, magnates, and military officers. Now one of Rio's coolest cultural centers, it holds classes and events during the week in the main house, annex, and courtyard; on weekends the place rocks with live music and dance *festas* such as Friday's Baile Alice and Sunday's famous Feijoada do Projeto Raiz. The place gets packed, but the multitude of ambiences and the good-looking crowd will keep you from losing your patience.

CLUBE DOS DEMOCRÁTICOS
Rua Riachuelo 91, tel. 21/2252-4611,
www.clubedosdemocraticos.com.br
HOURS: Wed.-Sat. 9:30 P.M.-2 A.M.
COST: R$7-15
Map 1

In 1867, three pals with a winning lottery ticket decided to put their fortune to good use by purchasing a palace and turning it into a social club, which became headquarters to one of Rio's most genteel Carnaval societies, the Democráticos. Members were a forward-thinking Republican and abolitionist

bunch (which didn't stop emperor Pedro II from partying here), whose bashes were legendary well into the 1940s when it began to sink into dilapidation. Rescue came about in 2004, when a young historian organized a *baile* that became such a cult hit that dance soirees are now held regularly in the vast ballroom. Music ranges from samba to *choro* and the crowd is young and eager to strut their stuff.

CLUB SIX
Rua das Marrecas 38, tel. 21/2510-3230,
www.clubsix.com.br
HOURS: Fri.-Sat. 11 P.M.-close
COST: R$20-40
Map 1

If, during your wanderings through Lapa, you start to grow weary of samba and *choro* (it happens to the best of us), take refuge at this three-story warehouse-sized club where you can rock out or mellow out to the post-modern likes of trance, drum and bass, hip-hop, and electronica. The decor is an atmospheric fusion of medieval and industrial flourishes that contrasts nicely with the external surroundings. Five bars and a pizzeria ensure you'll neither dehydrate nor starve.

FOSFOBOX

Rua Siqueira Campos 143, 22-A, tel. 21/2548-7498, www.fosfobox.com.br
HOURS: Wed.-Sun. 9:30 P.M.-2 A.M.
COST: R$20-30
Map 4

A relatively recent upstart on Copa's club scene, this underground basement club shares space with an antiques gallery. Depending on your spatial sensibilities, Fosfo's dance floor is either intimate or claustrophobic, but the upstairs Fosfobar is definitely conducive to mellowing out, especially if you opt for a Fosfodrink such as the *fada azul* (blue fairy), which combines lime juice, curaçao, and absinthe. The DJ-spun soundtrack ranges from rock to techno, and the scene is Copa cool with a definite alternative edge.

(LOUNGE 69

Rua Prudente de Moraes 416, tel. 21/2522-0627, www.69lounge.com.br
HOURS: Tues.-Sun. 11 P.M.-close
COST: R$30-60
Map 5

Hard-core clubbers, major celebrities, and big-name DJs have all been lining up to get into this innocuously named and extremely happening boîte since it opened in late 2007. Much of the reason the DJs are clamoring to spin here has to do with the state-of-the-art sound system that propels the soundtracks of the nightly *festas*—house, hip-hop, disco, soul, and electronic; on any given night the menu is varied—but equally hypnotic is the light show conceived by designer Muti Randolph. When your senses feel as if they're going into

overdrive, the upstairs lounge offers a chill-out sanctuary.

MELT

Rua Rita Ludolf 47, tel. 21/2249-9309, www.melt-rio.com.br
HOURS: Wed.-Sun. 9:30 P.M.-2 A.M.
COST: R$10-20
Map 6

Melt is utterly Leblon: sleek, chic, and oh so fashionable, just like the toned and tanned crowd that turns up to work up a glow on the dance floor and sling back cosmos à la Carrie Bradshaw. The inspired musical selection—ranging from bossa and funk to samba-rock and hip-hop—is courtesy of a rotating handful of DJs, but there are some great live bands as well. Creative dishes are served in the classy candlelit downstairs lounge.

(00

Av. Padre Leonel França 240, tel. 21/2540-8041, www.00site.com.br
HOURS: Wed.-Sun. 8:30 A.M.-3:30 A.M.
COST: R$20-50
Map 7

Zero Zero (as it is pronounced) is located inside Rio's planetarium, and the likes of Mick Jagger and Javier Bardem are constantly cropping up amidst the usual bevy of wealthy young Zona Sulistas, models, and TV celebs—but it isn't either type of star-gazing that makes this one of Rio's trendiest nightspots. The space itself is the real attraction: Merging outdoor gardens and a contemporary restaurant with an indoor lounge, bar, and (smallish) dance floor, 00 oozes glammy sophistication. To keep clients on their well-pedicured toes, the tunes are eclectic and vary from house to '80s and '90s memorabilia, with guest DJs taking charge of frequent *festas*.

Bars

After a long hard day at work, or on the beach, or at a soccer game, or...(the list goes on) Brazilians will often suggest to their companions *"vamos tomar uma"* ("let's have one"), by which it's understood that they will go and have a beer (although it's also understood that *"uma"* is a very loose euphemism for many). Bars are ubiquitous in Brazil, but not because everyone's an alcoholic, but because the neighborhood *boteco* functions as a second home where Brazilians eat, gossip, catch up on news, flirt, watch TV, and observe the world going by. The "second home" analogy also explains why Rio's bars are so unanimously laid-back and simple and why they are assiduously frequented from lunchtime until the wee hours. It also explains why there is scant difference, aside from perhaps the prices, between the classic *botecos* of Centro and Lapa and those in Leblon.

Forget about decor—considering the tropical climate, the vast majority of bars are at least partially outdoors and any decorative needs are supplied by the city itself and the constant parade of people. What most Cariocas are concerned with is the temperature of the beer, the crunchiness of the *bolinhos de bacalhau,* and the friendliness of the service. If you want ambience and a decorative scheme go to a hotel bar in Copa, Ipanema, or Leblon. But if you want to soak up Carioca ambience (and beer) head to a *botequim,* the best of which have been around for decades and are still going strong. Despite (and often because of) their simplicity, many of the older ones possess an undeniable charm that will seduce you and make it impossible for you, too, to drink just *"uma."*

ACADEMIA DA CACHAÇA
Rua Conde de Bernadotte 26, Lojas E-G, tel. 21/2239-1542, www.academiadacachaca.com.br
HOURS: Sun.-Thurs. noon-1 A.M., Fri.-Sat. noon-2 A.M.
Map 6
If you're feeling beer weary, head to the official-

sounding "Cachaça Academy" to savor one of the city's most famous *caipirinhas.* With hundreds of bottles of Brazil's national liquor on display (and available for purchase), you might also want to sample some of the finer *pingas* (or "drops"—slang for *cachaça*), which rival the smoothest whiskies. Once you've whetted your appetite, dig in to the famous *feijoada* or try the *escondidinho,* sun-dried beef hidden *(escondido)* beneath a creamy blanket of pureed manioc. The laid-back ambience makes lingering easy.

ADEGA DO TIMÃO
Rua Visconde de Itaboaraí 10, tel. 21/2224-9616
HOURS: Tues.-Sun. 4 P.M.-midnight
Map 1
This charming little bar is decorated with nautical gear and a fancy crystal chandelier thrown in for good measure. Its proximity to the Centro Cultural Banco do Brasil and Centro Cultural dos Correios has made it a beer stop *obligé* for the culture crowd. The tables outside on the cobblestones are a relaxing place to nibble on beef croquettes served with black mustard or a generous portion of calamari.

ADEGA PÉROLA
Rua Siqueira Campos 138, Loja A, tel. 21/2255-9425
HOURS: Mon.-Sat. 10 A.M.-midnight
Map 4
Opened in 1958 across the street from two vanguard theaters of the time, this understated Portuguese-owned *boteco* became the unofficial clubhouse for artists and actors. The long wooden tables and communal benches are still conducive to convivial conversation in the company of an icy *chope* and lip-smacking (if slightly overpriced) *petiscos* such as *bolinhos de bacalhau, polvo à vinagrete* (octopus salad), and the house specialty, a sushi-like roll of marinated sardine known as a *rolmop.*

BOTEQUINS

Rio is legendary throughout Brazil for its *botequins:* informal bars that function as neighborhood headquarters for residents from all walks of life. Whether considered *pé sujo* ("dirty foot") – i.e., a mildly mangy hole-in-the-wall – or *pé limpo* ("clean foot") – somewhat more refined and upscale – the simple *botequim* is first and foremost a democratic enclave where Cariocas get together (usually after work or the beach) to talk about *futebol,* politics, or their sex lives for hours at a time. The drink of choice is ice-cold *chope* (draft), served in traditional glasses that come in three sizes: the *tulipa* ("tulip"), *garotinho* ("little boy"), and the mug-sized *caldeireta* (rarely seen, since Cariocas subscribe to the belief that the larger the glass, the warmer – and more undrinkable – the beer gets). To nibble, there are always plenty of mouthwatering *petiscos* (bar snacks), the most common being *bolinhos de bacalhau* (deep-fried cod fish balls), *carne seca desfiada* (shredded sun-dried beef), and velvety thick *caldo de feijão* (black bean broth), traditionally served with chopped cilantro, *torresmos* (pork rinds), lime, and *pimenta* (hot pepper).

© MICHAEL SOMMERS

caldo de feijão (black bean broth) with an icy *chope* (draft beer)

AMARELINHO

Praça Floriano 55-B, tel. 21/2240-8434, www.amarelinhodacinelandia.com.br
HOURS: Daily 11 A.M.-2 A.M.
Map 1

Both for people-watching and monument-gazing, its hard to beat a table at Cinelândia's oldest *boteco.* Dating back to 1921, the famous outdoor bar is covered in yellow *(amarelo)* tiles and offers views of the Theatro Municipal and Biblioteca Nacional—and hundreds of Cariocas parading back and forth. The *frango a passarinho* (chicken nuggets doused in sautéed garlic) is a happy-hour favorite. More exotic, yet also delicious, is the *codorna* (quail), marinated for three days and stuffed with bacon.

◧ ARMAZÉM SÃO THIAGO

Rua Áurea 26, tel. 21/2232-0822
HOURS: Mon.-Sat. noon-midnight, Sun. noon-8 P.M.
Map 2

Santa Teresa's coolest bar by far was originally a general store that first began selling *secos e molhados* (dry goods and spirits) back in 1919. The *molhados* persevered, and today the dark wood shelves and cabinets are stacked sky-high with bottles and cases of wine and *cachaça.* A wooden fridge, marble-topped tables, deco fixtures dangling from the high ceiling, and jocular waiters round out the retro pleasures. The clientele is made up of spirited locals, who all seem to know each other and sit in groups enjoying pitchers of *chope* and sliced pastrami served with toast and wedges of lime.

Overlooking Praça Floriano, Cinelândia's Amarelinho bar is great for people-watching.

© MICHAEL SOMMERS

BAR BRASIL

Av. Mem de Sá 90, tel. 21/2509-5943

HOURS: Mon.-Tues. 11 A.M.-11 P.M., Wed.-Fri. 11 A.M.-midnight, Sat. 11 A.M.-6 P.M.

Map 1

Like Centro, Lapa has some wonderful old *botequins* that have survived from its heyday—whose walls, if they could talk, would surely have a lot of stories to tell. Having just celebrated its 100th birthday in 2007, Bar Brasil is a neighborhood institution, serving German food such as *eisbein* (pig's cheeks), *kassler* (smoked pork), and sauerkraut—perfect between sips of frothy tap beer, considered by many to be the best *chope* in town. The canvases on the walls are by Chilean artist Selarón, creator of the famous mosaic-covered staircase that leads from Lapa up to Santa Teresa.

◖ BAR D'HOTEL

Av. Delfim Moreira 696, tel. 21/2172-1100, www.marinaallsuites.com.br

HOURS: Daily 6 P.M.-2 A.M.

Map 6

Located on the 2nd floor of the Hotel Marina All-Suites, the always stylish and romantic Bar d'Hotel is decorated in a tasteful mix of modern design and antiques. It's Leblon's best bar with a view, where the windows overlooking Ipanema and Leblon beaches make it a favorite cocktail haunt for Carioca lovebirds (both gay and straight) who can toast each other with valentine-red *caipirubys* (vodka *caipirinhas* made with red fruits). Snacks range from mini lamb burgers with foie gras to delicious Nutela crepes (no sharing allowed, or you'll have to pay extra). If you want a coveted window table, reserve in advance.

BAR DO MINEIRO

Rua Paschoal Carlos Magno 99, tel. 21/2221-9227

HOURS: Tues.-Sat. 11 A.M.-2 A.M., Sun. 11 A.M.-midnight

Map 2

Inspired by the typically rustic bars of Minas Gerais, Bar do Mineiro is a charmingly old-fashioned *botequim*, accessorized with black-and-white photos and miniature wooden *bondes*. Aside from its delicious homemade *pastéis* stuffed with fillings such as *feijão mineiro* (black beans) and *carne seca com abóbora* (sun-dried beef with pumpkin), the bar is noted for its *feijoadas*. While mellow during the week, on weekends it gets quite crowded. To drink there's icy Bohemia and Original beer, or sample a shot of Minas *cachaça* or the killer ginger *batidas*.

BAR LAGOA

Av. Epitácio Pessoa 1674, tel. 21/2523-1135, www.barlagoa.com.br
HOURS: Mon. 6 P.M.-2 A.M., Tues.-Sun. noon-2 A.M.
Map 7

The art deco interior of this beloved *botequim* has changed little since it first opened in 1934. Back then its name was Bar Berlin, but with the outbreak of World War II the owner opted for a strategic name change. The kitchen, however, continues to serve hearty yet simple German fare that goes nicely with an icy *chope*. From the balcony, customers enjoy a privileged view of the Lagoa Rodrigo de Freitas.

BAR LUIZ

Rua da Carioca 39, tel. 21/2262-6900, www.barluiz.com.br
HOURS: Mon.-Sat. 11 A.M.-11 P.M.
Map 1

Founded in 1887, this classic old Carioca *botequim* possesses a German accent and menu, including a famous potato salad with homemade mayo and various grilled sausages and schnitzels. Whatever you choose, it will invariably go nicely with the creamy *chope* on tap. The charmingly retro atmosphere—the current art deco interior dates back to 1927—remains intact.

◖ BAR URCA

Rua Cândido Gaffré 205, tel. 21/2295-8744, www.barurca.com.br
HOURS: Mon.-Sat. 11 A.M.-11 P.M., Sun. 11 A.M.-6:30 P.M.
Map 3

One of Urca's oldest bars happens to be one of the most scenic *botequins* in Rio. Although a renovation has restored the curving 1930s facade and spruced up the interior, the bewitching view over the Baía de Guanabara remains intact. The upstairs dining room functions as

Founded in 1887, Bar Luiz is one of Rio's oldest *botequins*.

a restaurant whose menu emphasizes fish and seafood dishes, but you can also savor *petiscos* such as *caldinhos de frutos do mar* (seafood chowder) and grilled sardines while soaking up the sun out on the sidewalk (many locals bring their own beach chairs). Saturday's traditional *feijoada* attracts a loyal following.

BELMONTE

Praia do Flamengo 300, tel. 21/2552-3349, www.botecobelmonte.com.br
HOURS: Daily 10 A.M.-4 A.M.
Map 2

A Flamengo favorite, Belmonte is a little more refined and *pé limpo* (upscale, literally "clean foot") than your average Carioca *botequim*—which perhaps explains its popularity. It gets so busy in the late afternoons that customers stand and balance their cups on shiny metal barrels of beer. The *empadas*—with a variety of fillings—complement the icy *chope*. Although other locations have opened throughout the city, this original bar, opened in 1952, is the most atmospheric.

NIGHTLIFE

Flamengo's original Belmonte opened in 1952.

BOTECO CASUAL

Rua do Ouvidor 33, tel. 21/2232-0250,
www.casualcheffsantos.com.br
HOURS: Mon.-Fri. noon-11:30 P.M., Sat. noon-5 P.M.
Map 1

Perched on one of the most picturesque (and thankfully traffic-free) corners of Rio's colonial center, this atmospheric bar in a 19th-century mansion lives up to its name. The tables out on the cobblestones are a coveted spot for unwinding after work in the company of a frosty beer and the *petiscos* whipped up by stellar Portuguese chef Joaquim Santos, which have earned him accolades from serious foodies. (Mouthwatering examples include grilled sardines and octopus stuffed with tomatoes and garlic and cooked in a sauce of white wine and cognac.) Meals are also served. Every second Saturday afternoon, live samba is performed.

BRACARENSE

Rua José Linhares 85, tel. 21/2294-3549,
www.bracarense.com.br

HOURS: Mon.-Sat. 7 A.M.-midnight, Sun. 9 A.M.-10 P.M.
Map 6

By day, this tiny neighborhood bar, located on a shady side street, is easy to miss. Come happy hour, however, you might feel as if you've stumbled onto an impromptu street party as locals, on the way home from work or the beach, invade the surrounding sidewalk with tables and animated conversation. The *petiscos* are justly celebrated: The house specialty, *bolinho de aipim com camarão,* is a crisp ball of deep-fried pureed manioc filled with shrimp and creamy Catupiry cheese. The velvety *caldo de feijão,* served with cilantro and pork rinds, is ambrosial.

BRASEIRO DA GÁVEA

Praça Santo Dumont 116, tel. 21/2239-7494,
www.braseirodagavea.com.br
HOURS: Sun.-Thurs. 11 A.M.-1 A.M., Fri.-Sat. 11 A.M.-3 A.M.
Map 7

After years of hazily referring to it as "that bar across from the racetrack," it seems as if everyone not only knows about this classic *boteco,* but ritually descends upon it—particularly on weekends and Monday evenings when the area surrounding the Praça Santos Dumont (known as Baixa Gávea) is transformed into an outdoor street party churning with university students and the back-from-the-beach crowd. Consequently, Braseiro is a great place to *paquerar* (flirt—the waiters have been known to deliver phone numbers to ripe prospects)—but if you actually want to eat something, avoid the lineups and come during the week to feast on the grilled *picanhas* and barbecued *galetos* (chicken) served with broccoli rice and fries.

CAFÉ E BAR PAVÃO AZUL

Rua Hilário de Gouveia 71, Lojas A-B, tel. 21/2236-2381
HOURS: Daily 9 A.M.-midnight
Map 4

Few bars can vaunt a more secure location—right across from a police station—but the main attraction at this smallish but friendly decades-old neighborhood *boteco* is the delicious home cooking that has made faithful

Boteco Casual is one of Centro's happy-hour havens.

regulars out of generations of customers. To accompany your *cerveja*, try the famous *pataniscas de bacalhau*, lightly battered cod fritters. For an all-out meal, it's hard to go wrong with inexpensive fish and seafood dishes such as *arroz de polvo* (octopus rice). The *feijoada* is also recommended.

CERVANTES
Av. Prado Júnior 335-B, tel. 21/2275-6147, www.restaurantecervantes.com.br
HOURS: Tues.-Thurs. noon–4 A.M., Fri.-Sat. noon–6 A.M., Sun. noon–3 A.M.
Map 4

No matter what your tribe, a rite of passage for all serious bohemians is a pre-dawn, post-carousing pit stop at this favorite Copa *botequin*. To kill any late-night hunger pangs (and stave off a hangover), the house specialty is the delicious and impossibly thick sandwiches—most of which feature *abacaxi* (pineapple). Try the Cervantes *especial*—*abacaxi* with filet mignon and pâté—but keep in mind that the classic no-nonsense remedy features roast pork and

should be washed down by a couple more *saideiras* (last calls).

CHAMPANHERIA OVELHA NEGRA
Rua Bambina 120, tel. 21/2226-1054
HOURS: Mon.-Fri. 5:30-11:30 P.M.
Map 3

In the early 2000s, Rio fell prey to a champagne-bar phase. For better or worse many subsequently fizzled out, but the city's original "champagne only" bar—occupying an inviting and handsomely renovated 19th-century house—is still going strong. A welcome alternative to the hegemony of beer-soaked happy hours, Ovelha Negra's menu showcases more than 40 domestic and international brands of bubbly. Don't be intimidated by the price of the Veuve Clicquots; there are plenty of reasonable (national) bottles that will go to your head for only R$30. Accompanying the bubbly are delicious sandwiches and antipasti platters.

◖ DEVASSA
Rua Prudente de Moraes 416, tel. 21/2522-2468, www.devassa.com.br
HOURS: Sun.-Thurs. 11 A.M.-2 A.M., Fri.-Sat. 11 A.M.-3 A.M.
Map 5

Cariocas love their *chope*, but Rio was essentially a monogamous one-brand draft town until Devassa came along to shake it up. This chain of bars (you'll find outlets throughout the Zona Sul) not only had the guts to launch its own microbrewery, but went further and named its various flavors of pilsen after classic Brazilian female biotypes; to wit, you can choose to kick back and relax in the company of a *loira* (blonde), *ruiva* (red head), *negra, mulata,* or *índia* (which, beer-wise, translates into pale ale).

DRINKERIA MALDITA
Rua Voluntários da Pátria 10, tel. 21/2527-2468, www.matrizonline.com.br
HOURS: Tues.-Thurs. 6 P.M.-4 A.M., Fri.-Sat. 6 P.M.-5 A.M., Sun. 8 P.M.-3 A.M.
Map 3

Drinks, drinks, and more drinks—well over 100 to be precise, and that's just on the official cocktail menu. The choices at this comfortably casual bar across from the Espaço Unibanco de Cinema range from classics such as manhattans and cosmos to wilder concoctions such as the grown-up's version of Nestlé Quik—the Nutella ice drink—and the piquant *diablo,* a mixture of hot red peppers floating casually in a potion of tequila, lime, and club soda. If the choices overwhelm, opt for the *bebum confiança,* a sampling of four cocktails selected by the bartender; creative spirits are equally free to design their own drinks.

GAROTA DA URCA

Av. João Luíz Alves 56, Lojas A-B,
tel. 21/2541-5040
HOURS: Sun.-Thurs. noon-2 A.M., Fri.-Sat. noon-3 A.M.
Map 3

Amidst the proliferation of "Garota da . . ." bars throughout Rio's *bairros,* many devotees claim this Urca location, facing Praia da Urca, to be the best. While the predictably icy *chope* and succulent charcoal-grilled *picanha* are trademarks of all the bars, none can lay claim to the stunning views of Baía de Guanabara with the once-glamorous Cassino da Urca (soon to be the European Design Institute) in the foreground. On weekends, the usually tranquil neighborhood bar is stuffed to the gills with non-Urca invaders, lured by Praia da Urca's designation as an "it" point.

GAROTA DE IPANEMA

Rua Vinicius de Moraes 49-A, tel. 21/2523-3837,
www.garotaipanema.com.br
HOURS: Sun.-Thurs. 11 A.M.-2 A.M., Fri.-Sat. 11 A.M.-4 A.M.
Map 5

Yes bossa buffs, this is the famous bar (originally called Bar do Veloso) where Vinicius de Moraes and Tom Jobim were inspired to write "The Girl from Ipanema" after being mutually entranced by said girl (named Helô Pinheiro), who was passing by on her way to the beach. This event alone has made the bar somewhat of a *ponto turístico,* but since this is Ipanema and the *chope* is nice and cold, you could do a lot worse.

GOYA BEIRA

Largo das Neves 13, tel. 21/2232-5751
HOURS: Sun.-Thurs. 5:30 P.M.-midnight, Fri.-Sat.
5:30 P.M.-2 A.M.
Map 2

One of Santa Teresa's most picturesque local drinking holes is this simple but welcoming bar with its arcades and soaring ceilings, facing out onto Largo das Neves and the rumbling *bondes.* Aside from icy beer, try the *cachaças* infused with orange, ginger, and the more unusual watercress. To nibble on, the homemade pizza is quite tasty. French-fry fanatics should try the *aipim frito* (manioc fries) sprinkled with oregano and parmesan.

JOBI

Rua Ataulfo de Paiva 1166-B, tel. 21/2274-0547
HOURS: Daily 8 A.M.-4 A.M.
Map 6

With 50 years under its belt, this classic Carioca *botequim*—the type of place where waiters know the clients' names—is a beloved haunt of artists, journalists, and intellectuals (for this reason, passing pedestrians always shoot surreptitious glances at the outdoor tables in search of celebs). Consistently chosen as one of the city's top bars due to the quality of its *chope* and flavorful *petiscos*—such as *carne seca desfiada* (shredded sun-dried beef), *bolinhos de bacalhau,* and *caldo de feijão*—it often fills up; arrive early if you want a table.

MIRANTE DO LEBLON

Av. Niemeyer at Mirante do Leblon, tel. 21/2530-5801
HOURS: Daily 24 hours
Map 6

If you're walking west along Leblon and come to the end of the beach, don't stop—continue on along Avenida Niemeyer until the lookout point known as Mirante do Leblon. When you catch sight not only of Leblon, but Ipanema and Arpoador in all their panoramic glory, you'll be so staggered that you'll probably need a stabilizing beer. Anticipating such needs are two humble kiosks, Quiosque 1 and Quiosque 2 (also known as Tia Sonia), serving *cerveja em lata* (in cans) and cheap eats such as *bolinhos de bacalhau* and fried fish that perfectly complement the priceless view. At night, a taxi is recommended.

SATURNINO

Rua Saturnino de Brito 50, tel. 21/3874-0064, www.saturnino.com.br
HOURS: Tues.-Thurs. 8 P.M.-2 A.M., Fri.-Sat. 8 P.M.-3 A.M., Sun.-Mon. 8 P.M.-1 A.M.
Map 7

For a drink and a bite, Saturnino is one of posh Jardim Botânico's cooler and more casual options. While the interior is stylishly relaxed, the most coveted tables are outside beneath an enormous fig tree (if it rains, there's a retractable roof). The ridiculously long drink menu boasts over 200 offerings—if you're feeling indecisive go for the mixed *caipivodca* kit, with a sampling of six different *caipis* ranging from pineapple with mint to mango with *pimenta*. Burger connoisseurs will easily succumb to the cheddar-topped *burguer de carne seca,* made with sun-dried beef. Background tunes are suitably lounge-ish.

VILLARINO

Av. Calógeras 6, Loja B, tel. 21/2240-1627, www.villarino.com.br
HOURS: Mon.-Fri. noon-10 P.M.
Map 1

This 1953 delicatessen-bar was a favorite haunt of a mid-century bohemian crowd that

© MICHAEL SOMMERS

Saturnino is a casually stylish Jardim Botânico haunt.

included Tom Jobim and Vinicius de Moraes, who were introduced here for the first time in 1956 and then subsequently used it as their private clubhouse. Today the retro *uisqueria* with its scarlet banquettes and elegant marble tables attracts a suit-and-tie crowd who alternate whiskey shots with bites of delicious prosciutto and brie sandwiches.

Lounges

ATLÂNTICO
Av. Atlântica 3880, tel. 21/2513-2485
HOURS: Daily 7 P.M.-4 A.M.
Map 4

Overlooking the glimmering sands of Copacabana, this bar is that rare anomaly on Copa's beachfront: an intimate lounge so cool that fashionistas have descended in droves. A little spare cash is necessary to pay for the two house specialties: oysters and champagne. If you're inclined to eat a real meal, there are some inventive (and expensive) specials that harmonize nicely with the refreshingly modern setting.

BOSSA LOUNGE
Av. Atlântica 994, tel. 2543-3381,
www.bossaloungerio.com.br
HOURS: Daily 4 P.M.-close
Map 4

Opened in 2009, laid-back Bossa Lounge lives up to the bossa part of its name more than the lounge. Aside from a couple of token benches posing as sofas, don't expect to do lots of slouching or sprawling. Do be prepared to hear lots of classic bossa, performed live nightly, and after 10 P.M. played as contemporary remixes by the resident DJ. Daily happy-hour specials and sidewalk tables overlooking Leme beach harmonize all too well with the cool melodic strains.

CAROLINE CAFÉ
Rua J. J. Seabra 10, tel. 21/2540-0705,
www.carolinecafe.com.br
HOURS: Mon.-Wed. noon-2 A.M., Thurs.-Fri. noon-4 A.M., Sat. 7 P.M.-4 A.M.
Map 7

Both cosmopolitan and relaxed (if a little preppy), Caroline Café is one of those rare places that, despite having been around for years, has never gone out of fashion. Sporting

Atlântico is one of Copacabana's coolest beachfront hot spots.

© MICHAEL SOMMERS

Caroline Café has a friendly, sophisticated pub atmosphere.

two floors and a romantic terrace, it has various ambiences to choose from, including a lounge with DJ-spun tunes and a pub-style bar whose tables are lit by candlelight. The imported beers are a big draw, as are the delicious burgers and fries.

LONDRA

Av. Vieira Souto 80, tel. 21/3202-4000,
www.fasano.com.br
HOURS: Mon.-Wed. 7 P.M.-1 A.M., Thurs.-Sat.
7 P.M.-2:30 A.M.

Map 5

If you can't afford to splurge on a room or even a meal at Rio's über-chic Starck-designed Hotel Fasano, the next best thing is a cocktail in its suavely clubby bar-lounge. Within minutes of this hotel's 2007 opening, the bar had been anointed as *the* place to see and be seen in the Zona Sul. In fact, don't be surprised if you run into Elton John or Madonna (both of whom had post-show wrap parties here). Trendiness

aside, the warm brick walls, inviting leather sofas, elegant service, and a mean apple martini will have you mellow in no time.

◖ PALAPHITA KITCH

Av. Epitácio Pessoa, Quiosqe 20, Parque do Cantagalo, tel. 21/2227-0837, www.palaphitakitch.com.br
HOURS: Daily 6 P.M.-3 A.M.

Map 7

With its laid-back environs and stunning views of Corcovado and Lagoa Rodrigo de Freitas, the Lagoa area has become quite a scene at its many kiosk bars, but by far the most imaginative and seductive of them all is Palaphita Kitch. Here, Zona Sul cool meets the Amazon rainforest, with lounge furniture made from reforested wood and plenty of lush foliage as a decorative flourish. At night the place is lit up by torches. As soothing music lulls you, sip on exotic fruit drinks and feast on appetizers made with Amazonian ingredients such as wild passion fruit, *açai,* and *jacaré* (cayman).

Gay and Lesbian

A BOFETADA
Rua Farme de Amoedo 87-A, tel. 21/2227-1675
HOURS: Sun.-Thurs. 8 A.M.-2 A.M., Fri.-Sat. 8 A.M.-4 A.M.
Map 5

Although the name (*a bofetada* means "the slap") conjures up Joan Crawford–esque drama, the bar itself is an innocuous, laid-back, and friendly place that has become a favorite roosting point for a mixed GLS (gay, lesbian, and sympathizers) crowd on their way to and from the beach and other neighborhood bars and clubs. The best thing about this venue is that it offers a prime vantage point for checking out the action along Ipanema's gayest thoroughfare.

BURACO DA LACRAIA
Rua André Cavalcanti 58, tel. 21/2221-1984,
www.buracodalacraia.com
HOURS: Fri.-Sat. 11 P.M.-close
COST: R$18-23
Map 2

Hilariously kitschy and deliciously untrendy, this three-story gay club offers all sorts of amusement from drag shows and videoke contests to billiards tables, electronic games, and even dark rooms for the more erotically inclined. As a (big) extra bonus, the entrance fee includes all-you-can-drink beer. From time to time, fourth-rate pop stars from decades gone by make live appearances to the delight of adoring fans.

CABARET CASANOVA
Rua Mem de Sá 25, tel. 21/2221-6555,
www.cabaretcasanova.vai.la/
HOURS: Fri.-Sat. 10 P.M.-2 A.M., Sun. 8 P.M.-1 A.M.
COST: R$5-12
Map 1

Rio's oldest gay bar, dating back to 1939, attracts a refreshingly non-trendy (downwardly mobile) crowd who cheer on good old-fashioned drag queens. The house star is Meime dos Brilhos, a local legend who has been

flamboyantly strutting her stuff for 35 years. Aside from the sequined ladies the decor is pretty unglam, with a dim, cellar-like dance area where DJs spin dance music. There is also a small atmospheric back terrace that is conducive to romance.

CINE IDEAL
Rua da Carioca 62, tel. 21/2221-1984,
www.cineideal.com.br
HOURS: Fri.-Sat. 11:30 P.M.-close
COST: R$12-18
Map 1

Another alternative to the Zona Sul's upscale muscle-boy scene are the wild parties held at Centro's Cine Ideal every weekend. Occupying an ingeniously renovated belle epoque building that was formerly one of Rio's largest and most glamorous cinemas, this massive disco is a current hot spot featuring various bars and a fabulous open-air rooftop lounge. In terms of tunes, house rules. A big lure is that the cover charge includes all-you-can drink beer.

DAMA DE FERRO
Rua de Vinicius de Moraes 288, tel. 21/2247-2330,
www.damadeferro.com.br
HOURS: Wed.-Sat. 11 P.M.-close
COST: R$15
Map 5

Presided over by artist Adriana Lima, the Dama de Ferro (Iron Lady) is a funky lounge–disco–art gallery that attracts a diverse crowd of GLS (gay, lesbian, and sympathizers) and *alternativos*. Lima designed the inspired furnishings (for sale) in the industrial-chic downstairs lounge, while upstairs an impressive roster of international DJs makes sure everyone's taken care of on the musical front. The bathrooms, which open right onto the dance floor, are tiny galleries unto themselves. To say the menu is unusual is an understatement, but after you've danced up a storm perhaps chicken sorbet with warm tomato topping will prove refreshing.

GAY RIO

© MICHAEL SOMMERS

The strip of Ipanema beach stretching from Posto 8 to Posto 9 is Rio's unofficial gay headquarters.

With its reputation as the Marvelous City, one would expect Rio to have more of a gay scene. While the vibe is gay friendly, there is not really a gay neighborhood to speak of, and fewer specifically gay and lesbian venues than there are in São Paulo (actually, lesbian venues are pretty nonexistent). Instead, GLS (a Brazilian slang term for *gay, lesbica, e simpatisante* – i.e., gay friendly) spaces rule, with gays, lesbians, and heteros mixing socially.

The closest thing Rio has to a gay hood is a high-profile strip of Ipanema beach stretching from Posto 8 to Posto 9. If you're walking along Avenida Vieira Souto, you'll see beach *barracas* flying rainbow flags and the toned outlines of well-oiled muscles. The street perpendicular to the beach, **Rua Farme de Amoedo,** also attracts a gay crowd. In Copaca-

bana, a tiny gay area has taken root in front of the ultra-glam Copacabana Palace, where two *quiosques,* **Rainbow** and **Quiosque 35,** cater to a mature and bearish crowd (particularly on the weekends).

In terms of nightlife, aside from the bars and clubs listed in this book, there is a lively circuit party scene. For dates, locales, and other info, check out the following websites: **B.I.T.C.H.** (www.bitch.com.br), **R:Evolution** (www.revolutionparty.com.br), and **Moo** (www.moo.com.br).

For more info about Rio's gay scene, check out www.riogaylife.com. You can also get in touch with **Rio G Travel Services** (Rua Prudente de Morais 167-C, tel. 21/3813-0003, www.riog.com.br). Among other services, they guide night tours of Rio's "in" spots.

GALERIA CAFÉ
Rua Teixeira de Melo 31, tel. 21/2523-8250,
www.galeriacafe.com.br
HOURS: Wed.-Sat. 10:30 P.M.-close, Sun. 8:30 P.M.-close
COST: R$12-18
Map 5

While some view Galeria Café as intimate, others find it unbearably cramped (and somewhat generic). No matter—a surprisingly eclectic group of thirtysomethings religiously lines up in the street to vie for the chance to get up close and personal at the nightly *festas*. As "Galeria" denotes, frequent exhibits by local artists are held here, which are easier to view during the day (the space functions as a café Wed.-Sat. 9 A.M.-1 P.M.). On Sunday, the sartorially curious swing by between 11 A.M. and 8 P.M. to browse through young designers' creations sold at the Galeria Bazar.

LA CUEVA
Rua Miguel Lemos 51, tel. 21/2176-0469,
www.boatelacueva.com
HOURS: Daily 6 P.M.-close
COST: R$20-30
Map 4

This granddaddy of Carioca gay clubs first opened its doors in 1964, and it is one of Adonis-oriented Rio's few gay havens where mature men can hang loose with each other and younger admirers. Its underground reputation is translated quite literally by the subterranean decor that replicates a vast *cueva* (cave), replete with private little grottoes for intimacy. House DJ Beto keeps everyone on their toes with dance, house, and a campy mix of cheesy 1980s anthems (i.e., Laura Branigan) and homegrown beats. Nightly parties draw an alternative crowd intent on partying 'til their hair gets messy.

LA GIRL
Rua Raul Pompéia 102, tel. 21/2513-4993,
www.lagirl.com.br
HOURS: Daily 11 P.M.-close
COST: R$10-15, free before midnight
Map 4

The media-savvy Frenchman Gilles Lascar's gay empire includes La Girl, which can sadly claim the title of the Zona Sul's only exclusively lesbian club. Smaller and less manic than its alter ego (brother club Le Boy downstairs), this sophisticated club—with its glittery fuchsia color scheme, heavily mirrored lounge, and go-go girls—attracts a rather glam following of girls (including lots of *gringas* and even a few boys) who just wanna have fun.

LE BOY
Rua Raul Pompéia 102, tel. 21/2513-4993,
www.leboy.com.br
HOURS: Tues.-Sun. 11 P.M.-close
COST: R$10-15, free before midnight
Map 4

Gilles Lascar's main club, this notorious temple of gaydom has an international profile that attracts a big mix of homegrown and visiting gay men (including celebs such as Carioca convert Calvin Klein). Aside from dancing galore, this enormous club (the ceiling is as high as a four-story building) offers debauchery in the form of go-go boys and a *quarto escuro* (dark room). To get into shape for the night's activities, the adjacent fitness "annex" features a gym, sauna, relaxation room, and "erotic" performances in the gym's showers by male strippers. Arrive early, or be prepared to line up.

THE WEEK
Rua Sacadura Cabral 150, tel. 21/2253-1020,
www.theweek.com.br
HOURS: Sat. midnight-close
COST: R$35-60
Map 1

With Rio's mania for importing successful Paulistano bars and restaurants to the Cidade Maravilhosa, it was only a matter of time before Sampa's biggest and most brazen gay disco opened up a Carioca outpost in the up-and-coming port zone of Saúde. While smaller than its mother club, The Week is hardly intimate, as its mammoth dance floor, lounge, outdoor swimming pool, VIP areas, and quintet of bars attest (the bathrooms are so big that they end up hosting mini *festas*). Despite the inflated prices, the Saturday-only policy guarantees that the place is always packed.

ARTS AND LEISURE

Rio has a diverse and sophisticated cultural scene. Historically, as the seat of the Brazilian empire and capital of its first republic, the city has always been a flourishing artistic center where foreign and national influences and erudite and popular forms of artistic expression have coexisted.

Music is the art form most obviously linked to Rio, and there is no denying that the city boasts one of the richest musical traditions and most vibrant contemporary music scenes on the planet. Samba is everywhere, but so are bossa nova, MPB, *chorinho,* hip-hop, and funk. Artists as influential and diverse as Heitor Villa-Lobos, Carmen Miranda, Tom Jobim, Cartola, Chico Buarque, and Seu Jorge are names that easily roll off one's tongue and whose musical identities are linked with the

city, its cultural legacy, and its constant innovations. In few other cities is music woven into the thread of daily life in such an essential way. As a result, you can see high-quality live performances by national and international artists in venues as prestigious as the opulent turn-of-the-20th-century Theatro Municipal, as state-of-the-art as the 21st-century Citibank Hall, as intimate as a bookstore or bar, or as relaxed as Copacabana beach.

Unbeknownst to many foreigners, Rio is also a hothouse for other forms of artistic expression. The city has a thriving contemporary theater and dance scene. It also possesses cinemas galore, including some wonderful independent and art-house theaters (all movies are screened in their *versão original,* with Portuguese subtitles). Rio's remarkable galleries

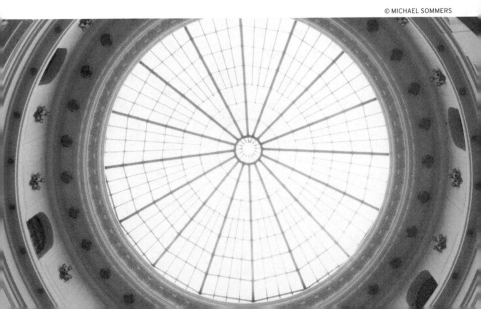

HIGHLIGHTS   LOOK FOR ◖ TO FIND RECOMMENDED ARTS AND ACTIVITIES.

◖ **Best Cultural Center:** The magnificent neoclassical palace is a worthy sight in itself, but the former headquarters of Brazil's national bank – **Centro Cultural Banco do Brasil** – is also rich in cultural events. You'll find the best in art, theater, dance, and music here for prices that won't break the bank (page 152).

◖ **Best Modernist Cultural Oasis:** The temporary exhibits held at the **Instituto Moreira Salles (IMS)** are usually engaging, and the permanent collection of historic photos of Rio quite interesting. But regardless of what's on exhibit, the real attraction of this private cultural center tucked away in Gávea's lush hills is the space itself: a streamlined modernist mansion surrounded by gardens landscaped by Burle Marx (page 153).

◖ **Most Eclectic Musical Menu:** Housed in an atmospheric turn-of-the-20th-century Lapa warehouse, **Teatro Odisséia** hosts a roster of high-quality performances of traditional and vanguard Brazilian music that is so diverse, not even the faithful know what to expect (page 155).

◖ **Best Surviving Deco Movie Palace:** The sole survivor from Cinelândia's days of cinematic glory, the handsomely renovated **Cine Odeon BR** mixes retro glamour with cutting-edge screenings, events, and movie marathons (page 156).

◖ **Best *Festa*:** The fame of Rio's **Carnaval** precedes it. This fabulous five-day celebration is extravagant, exuberant, and extremely multifaceted. Aside from the samba school parades, check out the multitude of balls, shows, and *festas* (organized and improvised) that takes place in streets, squares, and clubs all over the city (page 158).

◖ **Next Best Thing to Sprouting Wings:** If you wonder why hang gliding is Rio's most popular individual sport after surfing, you'll understand why after throwing yourself off the Parque da Tijuca's Pedra Bonita, gliding over the city and sea, and landing (in time for a *caipirinha*) on São Conrado's beautiful Praia do Pepino. **Just Fly** and **Super Fly** both offer amazing hang-gliding adventures (pages 164 and 165).

◖ **Best Insider City Tour:** Be a Local hooks up foreign visitors with English-speaking locals to check out *favelas*, funk parties, soccer games, and samba school rehearsals, opening the door to aspects of Carioca life that you would never experience on your own (page 166).

◖ **Best Betting Event:** Even if your horse never comes in, there's no way you'll come away a loser after spending a day or night at the races held at Gávea's elegant **Jóquei Club** (page 169).

◖ **Most Dramatic Sporting Ritual:** Aside from the thrill of seeing Brazil's top *futebol* players butt heads in the flesh, taking in a game at the world-famous **Maracanã** stadium offers large-scale theatrics as fans cheer, sob, chant, drum, implore saints, curse coaches, and explode with joy (page 171).

Carnaval masks for sale

do an admirable job of focusing on specific themes, moments, and artists, as well as showcasing contemporary and up-and-coming figures through a constantly changing roster of temporary exhibitions involving all forms of visual media.

Cariocas may be famed for their proficiency at the art of relaxation, but they are also extremely sporty, a hardly surprising fact considering Rio's tropical climate and the abundance of spectacular natural surroundings. The most obvious draw is the city's beaches, which offer myriad activities on the sand and in the sea. But there is also the Lagoa Rodrigo de Freitas, a vast leisure area endowed with multiple sports facilities, as well as all those famous mountains (Pão de Açúcar, Corcovado, Pedra da Gávea) that provide opportunities for climbing and hang gliding. The city also boasts many parks, among them the Parque Nacional da Tijuca, an urban oasis of native Atlantic forest, that's a perfect destination for a bike ride, a hike, or merely a picnic at the foot of a waterfall. Finally, even those who don't play soccer will never forget watching a *futebol* game on Brazilian turf, particularly if they happen to be seated in the world's most famous stadium, Maracanã, where fans' quasi-religious fervor is a spectacle in itself.

The Arts

Rio boasts an impressive and dynamic arts scene with a multitude of events held at venues that are often quite striking due to their architecture, their natural surroundings, or a combination of both. Rio's museums are covered in the *Sights* chapter, while this chapter focuses on private art galleries and cultural centers. One of the best things about the city's cultural life is the mushrooming number of public and private cultural centers, whose offerings are extremely diverse. Aside from hosting art exhibits, they also have stages and/or theaters where you can see musical, dance, and theatrical performances. A few even have cinemas. Many offerings are free, while others charge minimal cover fees. And almost all of these cultural centers feature charming bars, cafés, and restaurants where you can have a snack or a drink and hang out for a while.

For information (in Portuguese) about what's going on, check out the arts sections of the two daily papers, *Jornal do Brasil* and *O Globo,* or purchase *Veja Rio,* which comes with *Veja* magazine and offers comprehensive listings of everything going on in the city. For upcoming events in English as well as Portuguese, log on to www.riodejaneiro-turismo.com.br. Tickets (which are generally quite affordable) can be purchased directly at theaters and concert spaces.

GALLERIES
A GENTIL CARIOCA
Rua Gonçalves Ledo 17, tel. 21/2222-1651, www.agentilcarioca.com.br
HOURS: Tues.-Fri. noon-7 P.M., Sat. noon-5 P.M.
Map 1

Operated by artists Laura Lima, Márcio Botner, and Ernesto Neto, this small alternative gallery is located in the heart of the traditional Judeo-Arab (and increasingly Chinese) Saara district. The provocative, cutting-edge exhibitions held here by up-and-coming Brazilian artists are about more than art, they're about community, and the gallery itself plays its part with projects that range from having artists paint neighborhood frescoes to creating "educational" T-shirts.

ARTE EM DOBRO
Rua Dias Ferreira 417/205, tel. 21/2259-1952, www.arteemdobro.com.br
HOURS: Mon.-Fri. 10 A.M.-6 P.M.
Map 6

A relative newcomer to Rio's gallery scene, Arte em Dobro's glistening white cube (above

ARTS AND LEISURE

148 ARTS AND LEISURE

the Argumento bookstore) serves as an ideal backdrop to the eclectic contemporary works displayed here. The owners (who have been friends since childhood) take care to embrace all generations of artists and aren't afraid to wander far from the dominant Rio–São Paulo grid in search of regional talents. Their firm belief that would-be collectors shouldn't be deprived of owning art due to not having millions of dollars to spend ensures the presence of works most people could actually contemplate buying.

ESTÚDIO GUANABARA
Rua Visconde de Pirajá 82, tel. 21/2521-0197, www.estudioguanabara.com.br
HOURS: Mon.-Fri. 1-7 P.M.
Map 5

This basement gallery specializes in abstract Brazilian art—paintings, drawings, and sculptures—of the 1950s and '60s and, if the works truly smite you, offers consulting services for those interested in building their own private collection. Among the gallery's 400 pieces are signature works by Aluísio Carvão, Rubem Ludolf, Ubi Bava, Ivan Serpa, and Iberê Camargo.

GALERIA ANNA MARIA NIEMEYER
Rua Marquês de São Vicente 52/205, Shopping da Gávea, tel. 21/2239-9144, www.annamarianiemaeyer.com.br
HOURS: Mon.-Sat. 10 A.M.-10 P.M.
Map 7

From the depths of Shopping da Gávea, Anna Maria Niemeyer operates one of Rio's most traditional galleries of contemporary art. Daughter of legendary architect Oscar Niemeyer—and cocreator of the space-age Museu de Arte Contemporânea (MAC), designed by her father, in Niterói—Niemeyer represents and exhibits an impressive roster of Brazilian talents including Ricardo Ventura, Victor Arruda, Monica Sartori, Jorge Duarte, Victor Salgado, and (of course) her famous dad. She's opened a second space nearby at Praça Santos Dumont 140, Loja A, tel. 21/2140-8155 (Mon.–Fri. noon–9 P.M., Sat.–Sun. 1–5 P.M.).

GALERIA DE ARTE IPANEMA
Rua Anibal de Mendonça 38, tel. 21/2512-8832, www.galeria-ipanema.com
HOURS: Mon.-Fri. 10 A.M.-7 P.M., Sat. 10 A.M.-2 P.M.
Map 5

Specializing in major names in Brazilian art, this venerable gallery was originally located in the Copacabana Palace before moving to a handsome whitewashed house in the heart of Ipanema. One of the oldest galleries in the country (it was founded in 1965), it has had plenty of time to amass one of the city's most impressive collections, featuring modern and contemporary figures such as Candido Portinari, José Pancetti, Alfredo Volpi, Cícero Dias, Alberto Guignard, Tomie Ohtake, Iberê Camargo, Antonio Bandeira, and Djanira.

GALERIA MOVIMENTO
Av. Atlântica 4240, Loja 211, Shopping Cassino Atlântico, tel. 21/2267-5989, www.galeriamovimento.com
HOURS: Mon.-Sat. 10 A.M.-7 P.M.
Map 4

Launched in 2007, Movimento is the first gallery in the country to specialize in Brazilian graffiti art. The founders' mission is to valorize this oft-dissed art form by taking graffiti out of the streets and *favelas* and getting it onto the walls of museums, galleries, and collectors' living rooms.

While in the Shopping Cassino Atlântico, fans of more conventional 20th-century artistic *movimentos* should check out two venerable galleries devoted to the works of major Brazilian modernists: **Arte 21** (Loja 123, tel. 21/2227-7280) and **Athena Galeria Arte** (Loja 120, tel. 21/2227-7280), both of whose walls are littered with canvases by heavyweights such as Di Cavalcanti, Alberto Guignard, Lasar Segall, José Pancetti, and Candido Portinari.

GALERIA PAULO FERNANDES
Rua do Rosário 38, tel. 21/2233-1537, www.galeriapaulofernandes.com.br
HOURS: Tues.-Sun. noon-6 P.M.
Map 1

Right behind the Centro Cultural Banco do

© MICHAEL SOMMERS

Laura Marsiaj Arte Contemporânea

Brasil, Paulo Fernandes represents some of Brazil's best-known contemporary artists, including Antonio Dias, Cildo Meireles, Miguel Rio Branco, Rubens Gerchman, Waltercio Caldas, and Tunga. With a prime location amidst Centro's slew of cultural centers, the exhibits at this tiny exposed-brick gallery are always worth checking out. Also worth visiting is the LGC Arte Contemporânea gallery next door.

LAURA MARSIAJ ARTE CONTEMPORÂNEA

Rua Teixeira de Mello 31-C, tel. 21/2513-2074, www.lauramarsiaj.com.br

HOURS: Tues.-Fri. 10 A.M.-7 P.M., Sat. noon-6 P.M.

Map 5

Conveniently located in the heart of Ipanema, this well-appointed and relatively new gallery on the block has already left an indelible impression on the city's art scene. Laura Marsiaj represents an important number of contemporary Brazilian artists, including Eduardo Sued, Antonio Dias, Lygia Clark, Waltercio Caldas, Anna Bella Geiger, and Mira Schendel, and is also a fervent champion of up-and-coming talent such as recent newcomers Felipe Barbosa,

Lenora de Barros, Deise Xavier, and Marcos Chaves.

LURIXS ARTE CONTEMPORÂNEA

Rua Paulo Barreto 77, tel. 21/2541-4935

HOURS: Mon.-Fri. 2-7 P.M.

Map 3

The owner of this Botafogo gallery, Ricardo Rego, has an eye for vanguard Brazilian art and is always on the lookout for emerging home-grown talents who aren't afraid to take risks. Among the artists whose works you'll find here are Hélio Oiticica, Geraldo de Barros, Afonso Tostes, José Bechara, and Luciano Figueiredo. Exhibition viewing takes place only on weekdays 2–7 P.M. Potential buyers can visit the gallery by appointment only Tuesday–Friday 2–7 P.M. and Saturday 4:30–8 P.M.

MARCIA BARROZO DO AMARAL GALERIA DE ARTE

Av. Atlântica 4240, Loja 129, Shopping Cassino Atlântico, tel. 21/2267-3747, www.marciabarrozodoamaral.com.br

HOURS: Mon.-Fri. 10 A.M.-6 P.M., Sat. noon-6 P.M.

Map 4

When Marcia Barrozo first opened her gallery

ARTS AND LEISURE

in 1974, she specialized exclusively in engravings. Over the years, however, her expertise and curiosity expanded, as did her collection of art, which now includes over 2,000 paintings, sculptures, and artists' objects created by contemporary Brazilian artists such as Anna Letycia, Eduardo Sued, Iole de Freitas, Antonio Dias, Artur Luíz Piza, and Tunga. Those who are fond of constructivist and geometric art will find much to admire, as will fans of prints and etchings.

MERCEDES VIEGAS ARTE CONTEMPORÂNEA
Rua João Borges 86, tel. 21/2294-4305, www.mercedesviegas.com.br
HOURS: Mon.-Fri. 2-7 P.M., Sat. 4-8 P.M.
Map 7

Occupying a spacious, light-filled modernist house with a small green garden, this very pleasant gallery operated by former museologist Mercedes Viegas makes a compelling showcase for paintings, drawings, photos, and objets d'art by contemporary Brazilian artists. Among the handful of names represented are vanguard Brazilian artists such as Anna Maria Maiolino, Angelo Venosa, and Ivens Machado.

PEQUENA GALERIA 18
Av. Atlântica 1782, Loja F, tel. 21/2549-3897, www.pequenagaleria18.com.br
HOURS: Mon.-Fri. 11 A.M.-7 P.M.
Map 4

Housed in the Edifício Chopin, a handsome landmark building next to the Copacabana Palace, this truly small gallery also happens to be Rio's first devoted exclusively to photography. According to the photo-philic gallerist Mario Cohen, most people aren't aware that Brazilian photography is as significant as its music. If in doubt, just cast an eye on Cohen's discerning and eclectic collection of shutterbugs such as Pierre Verger, Cesar Barreto, Walter Firmo, Otto Stupakoff, and João de Orleans e Bragança. Before exiting the building, take a peek down the hall at **Galeria Tempo** (Loja E, tel. 21/2255-4586, www.galeriatempo.com.br), a space devoted to exhibiting

as well as archiving, restoring, and preserving images. Prints as well as videos and other digital art forms are often on display.

PINAKOTHEKE CULTURAL
Rua São Clemente 300, tel. 21/2537-7566, www.pinakotheke.com.br
HOURS: Mon.-Fri. 10 A.M.-7 P.M., Sat. noon-4 P.M.
Map 3

Aside from organizing other Brazilian museums' collections, curating their exhibits, and publishing lush catalogues and art books, the Pinakotheke Cultural's headquarters, in a gracious old mansion on sweeping Rua São Clemente, often hosts top-notch exhibitions devoted to major Brazilian modernists (many culled from its permanent collection) such as Antonio Bandeira, Bruno Giorgi, Di Cavalcanti, Alberto Guignard, José Pancetti, Lasar Segall, and Lygia Clark.

SILVIA CINTRA GALERIA DE ARTE
Rua Teixeira de Melo 53, Loja D, tel. 21/2521-0426, www.silviacintra.com.br
HOURS: Mon.-Fri. 10 A.M.-7 P.M., Sat. noon-4 P.M.
Map 5

Considered one of the best gallerists in town, Silvia Cintra represents a bevy of Brazilian contemporary artists including Daniel Senise, Luiz Ernesto, Nelson Leirner, Amílcar de Castro, and photographer Miguel Rio Branco. In an annex Cintra's daughter, Juliana, operates Box 4, which exhibits works by up-and-coming artists. Stay tuned: Both mother and daughter will move to larger digs in a four-story house in Gávea sometime in late 2009 or early 2010.

CULTURAL CENTERS
CAIXA CULTURAL
Av. Almirante Barroso 25, tel. 21/2240-7055, www.caixa.com.br/caixacultural
HOURS: Tues.-Sun. 10 A.M.-10 P.M.
Map 1

Occupying the ground floor and mezzanine of the gleaming high-rise headquarters of the nationally owned Caixa Econômica Federal bank, at any given moment the Caixa Cultural plays host to several intriguing art exhibits, many dealing with interesting Brazilian themes. A pair of film-screening rooms and a small amphitheater reserved for plays and concerts round out the offerings. Events are free or cost next to nothing. The vast café (with free Wi-Fi), furnished with equally vast white leather sofas, is ideal for relaxing while gazing out the picture windows at Largo da Carioca.

CASA DE ARTE E CULTURA JULIETA DE SERPA

Praia do Flamengo 340, tel. 21/2251-1278, www.casajulietadeserpa.com.br

HOURS: Daily 9 A.M.-7 P.M.

Map 2

Only in Rio would a romantic (and wealthy) young man by the name of Demócrito Seabra consider building a miniature Louis XVI–style palace on the edge of Praia do Flamengo as a present for his beloved wife. The year was 1920 and Rio's elites were still swayed by the influence of things Parisian. Decked out with imported European swag, the *palacete* hosted the crème-de-la-crème of Carioca society and

remained in the family until 2000, when it was saved from demolition by antiques dealer and empresario Carlos Alberto Serpa, who transformed it into a jaw-droppingly opulent cultural-gastronomic center. Its Versailles-worthy salons now play host to exhibits and artistic events and also house the classy **J Club** piano bar and an elegant French restaurant, **Blason,** along with a *campagnard*-style bistro, a posh tea salon, and a garden café.

CASA FRANÇA-BRASIL

Rua Visconde de Itaboraí 78, tel. 21/2253-5366, www.fcfb.rj.gov.br

HOURS: Tues.-Sun. 10 A.M.-8 P.M.

Map 1

Completed in 1820, Rio's first neoclassical construction was designed by French architect Auguste Grandjean de Montigny. As part of the French Artistic Mission, Montigny was one of a fleet of French artists invited to Brazil as part of an imperial desire to modernize (i.e., Europeanize) Rio by imposing some order on the excesses of Brazilian baroque. Originally,

facade of the Casa de Arte e Cultura Julieta de Serpa

this elegant building with trompe l'oeil Doric columns and a soaring central cupola operated as a stock exchange and, later, as Rio's main customs building. In its present incarnation as the Casa França-Brasil it serves as a venue for compact but generally thought-provoking art exhibits. In keeping with its French connection, you'll also encounter a tiny cinema screening French (and indie) flicks, a cool little boutique, and a charming French bistro, **Bistrô da Casa,** where you can get a mean *salade Niçoise* or *steak frites.*

CENTRO CULTURAL ARTE SESC

Rua Marquês de Abrantes 99, tel. 21/3138-1343, www.sescrio.org.br
HOURS: Tues.-Wed. noon–6 P.M., Thurs.-Sat. noon–8 P.M., Sun. 11 A.M.–5 P.M.
Map 2

Just across the street from the Flamengo Metrô, this cultural center is housed in a splendid early-20th-century domed mansion that bears a certain resemblance to a heavily frosted wedding cake. It was constructed by Fred Figner, a Czech tycoon who also happened to own Brazil's first phonograph recording company, Casa de Edison, and its record label, Odeon. Aside from a large auditorium where concerts are held, a quintet of spacious salons play host to temporary small-scale art exhibitions of varying (or sometimes little) interest.

◖ CENTRO CULTURAL BANCO DO BRASIL

Rua Primeiro de Março 66, tel. 21/3808-2000, www.bb.com.br/cultura
HOURS: Tues.-Sun. noon–8 P.M.
Map 1

If only all bank buildings could look and behave like this one. Built at the turn of the 20th century, this magnificent edifice is the former headquarters of Brazil's national bank (which explains the convenient presence of ATMs in the foyer). That Banco do Brasil is also a major patron of the arts means that most major (national and international) art exhibits that pass through Rio inevitably stop here; you'll also

find an excellent program of contemporary theater, dance, and music, along with film and video screenings—all of which cost very little (or nothing at all). With a **Livraria da Travessa** selling books and CDs, a café, and a regal tea salon, the CCBB is also a favorite meeting and hanging-out point. Cultural offerings aside, the building itself is a must-see.

CENTRO CULTURAL DA JUSTIÇA

Av. Rio Branco 241, tel. 21/3212-2550, www.ccjf.trf2.gov.br
HOURS: Tues.-Sun. noon–7 P.M.
Map 1

Built in the early 20th century in an eclectic style that was in vogue at the time, this grand building housed Brazil's Supreme Court from 1909 to 1960, and then various justice ministries before being transformed into a cultural center. Apart from a library and an auditorium where classical concerts are held, two floors of palatial salons host excellent photography exhibits (usually of a historical nature). The building itself has some wonderful features including a majestic central staircase of Carrera marble adorned with twirling art nouveau wrought-iron banisters and a slew of gothic-style stained-glass windows. A small café serves snacks and lunch.

CENTRO CULTURAL DOS CORREIOS

Rua Visconde de Itaboraí 20, tel. 21/2253-1580, www.correios.com.br
HOURS: Tues.-Sun. 10 A.M.–7 P.M.
Map 1

Just across from the Centro Cultural Banco do Brasil, the Centro Cultural dos Correios was formerly the headquarters of Rio's postal service (there is still a small post office should you have the urge to send a postcard). Completed in 1922, the building's vast salons host top-notch art exhibits of local and national artists. An ancient wrought-iron elevator shuttles you between the three floors. For coffee or snacks, there is a great café overlooking the adjacent Praça dos Correios, where live musical performances frequently take place.

CENTRO DE ARTE HÉLIO OITICICA

Rua Luís de Camões 68, tel. 21/2232-4213
HOURS: Mon.-Fri. noon-8 P.M., Sat.-Sun. 11 A.M.-5 P.M.
Map 1

The site of Rio's former conservatory, this imposing neoclassical building pays homage to one of Brazil's most avant-garde and influential contemporary artists: Hélio Oiticica (1937–1980). Born into a Carioca family of leftist intellectuals (among other things, his father was a math teacher, an experimental photographer, and an entomologist), Oiticica grew up surrounded by radical ideas. In his short life, he produced an important body of work ranging from early Mondrian-like abstract compositions exploring space and color to transgressive "anti-art" sculptural objects and "habitable paintings." The most famous of these were *parangolés:* immense tent-like capes designed to be worn while swaying to samba rhythms. Aside from a permanent collection that leans towards earlier works, the center also organizes some temporary exhibits.

ESPAÇO CULTURAL MAURICE VALANSI

Rua Martins Ferreira 48, tel. 21/2527-4044
HOURS: Mon.-Fri. noon-3 P.M. and 7 P.M.-midnight, Sat. 7 P.M.-midnight
Map 3

This charming house owned by architect Ricardo Valansi (and named in honor of his father, Maurice, who left a mark on Carioca culture as a founder of a number of Rio's original movie theaters) manages to unite a bookstore, café, gallery space, and, most intriguing of all, a Museu da Cadeira (featuring 200 chairs) all in one very compact space. If you're in the neighborhood it's worth popping in, but it's more worth your while to make the trip on a Wednesday, Thursday, or Saturday evening, for the intimate performances of jazz and bossa nova.

ESPAÇO RIO CARIOCA

Rua das Laranjeiras 307, tel. 21/2225-7332, www.espacoriocarioca.com.br
HOURS: Mon. 5-10 P.M., Tues.-Thurs. and Sun.

noon-10 P.M., Fri.-Sat. noon-11 P.M.
Map 2

Rio's most charming new cultural center (inaugurated at the end of 2007) occupies part of a rare surviving 19th-century multiresidential complex of six houses, the Casas Casadas, built in the 1880s (and saved from demolition in the 1990s). The beautifully renovated space features a large book and CD store specializing in hard-to-find, independently produced Brazilian music, and a small stage (with great acoustics) where MPB, jazz, and *chorinho* shows take place (Wed.–Sat.). Overlooking the proceedings from the 2nd floor is the Bistrô Rio Carioca, its orange walls decorated in ingenious flatware sculptures, where you'll find creative sandwiches and salads and light meals with a Franco-Italian bent. Downstairs, a small café also offers free wireless Internet access. A two-screen movie theater is in the works.

INSTITUTO MOREIRA SALLES (IMS)

Rua Marquês de São Vicente 476, tel. 21/3284-7400, www.ims.com.br
HOURS: Tues.-Sun. 1-8 P.M.
Map 7

Halfway up a steep hill dotted with villas, the IMS is among the city's most striking privately owned cultural centers. In 1951, the prominent Moreira Salles family (owners of Unibanco, one of the country's major banks) commissioned architect Olavo Redig de Campos to build this house—an example of Brazilian modernism at its most streamlined and alluring, with the added bonus of gardens designed by Burle Marx. The Moreira Salles family have always had a strong commitment to the arts (Walter Salles Jr.—the director of the films *Central Station* and *The Motorcycle Diaries*—is a member of the clan) and part of their important collection of historical photographs (many depicting 19th- and 20th-century Rio) can be viewed along with interesting temporary exhibitions. Other attractions include a cinema, a boutique, and an inviting café that serves a lavish (though extravagantly priced) afternoon tea.

ARTS AND LEISURE

OI FUTURO

Rua Dois de Dezembro 63, tel. 21/3131-3060,
www.oifuturo.org.br
HOURS: Tues.-Sun. 11 A.M.-8 P.M.
Map 2

Operated by the Oi telephone operator, this cutting-edge cultural center takes the future seriously—as evidenced by the revamped exterior of a 1918 phone company building and high-tech aesthetics and workings of the interior. Eight levels offer ample space for contemporary art exhibits—many of which try to incorporate technology—along with concerts and dance performances. The fact that Oi runs the show accounts for the wireless access (on wireless laptops) in the cyber café as well as a museum devoted to the history of the phone in Brazil (you can even leaf through old phone books printed by the now-defunct Companhia Telefônica Brasileira). On the top floor, a cool contemporary café (with chairs once used by telephone operators in the 1920s), **Conexão Sabor,** serves snacks and light meals and offers high-resolution views of the Baía de Guanabara.

THEATER AND CONCERT VENUES

CANECÃO

Av. Venceslau Brás 215, tel. 21/2105-2000,
www.canecao.com.br
Map 3

Upon releasing new CDs, Brazil's major artists inevitably kick off their national tours at this giant supper club, located next to Shopping Rio Sul. Since it first opened as a giant beer hall in 1967, it has morphed into Rio's most legendary concert hall; its stage, the site of anthological shows, has been graced by all the icons of MPB. Despite endless renovations, it's a little worn around the edges, stage visibility is not always the best (try for seats in Setor A and the *balcão nobre*), and the food is only so-so. But the nostalgia-soaked atmosphere is something to behold.

CIRCO VOADOR

Rua dos Arcos, tel. 21/2533-5873,
www.circovoador.com.br
HOURS: Tues.-Fri. 7 P.M.-close, Sat.-Sun. 8 P.M.-close
Map 1

Located beneath the Arcos da Lapa, the gigantic canvas dome that shelters the Circo Voador (Flying Circus) has been one of the city's most vanguard outdoor musical venues since the 1980s, when Rio's alternative artists and musicians desperately seeking a space of their own literally pitched their tent here. Seminal Brazilian rock bands such as Barão Vermelho, Blitz, and Legião Urbana all got their starts here. Since then, the Circo has been a right of passage for musicians, dancers, and theater troupes. The space itself, consisting of a stage, dance floor, and bar, is basic (though impressively state-of-the-art following a renovation), but the atmosphere is always fun and lively.

CITIBANK HALL

Av. Ayrton Senna 3000, Shopping Via Parque,
tel. 21/2156-7300, www.citibankhall.com.br
Map 8

Formerly known as Claro Hall, Rio's biggest concert hall is gigantic and state of the art, safely ensconced within a shopping mall in Barra da Tijuca. It's a trek to get there, but you may be seduced by a particular attraction: With seating for 8,000, it hosts many large-scale, big-name national and international musical, theatrical, and dance events (although you can probably skip the Brazilian versions of Broadway musicals).

FUNDIÇÃO PROGRESSO

Rua dos Arcos 24, tel. 21/2220-5070,
www.fundicao.org
HOURS: Daily 10 A.M.-10 P.M.
Map 1

National rock stars, local alternative bands, and theatrical groups are regular performers at this wonderful old iron foundry (*fundição*) next to the Circo Voador, outfitted with a stage, dance floor, and bleacher-style seating area with room for 5,000. During Carnaval, a crush of revelers take part in the rehearsals headed by Monobloco, one of Rio's most popular *blocos,* led by musician Pedro Luís and his band, A Parede. Aside from offering workshops and courses on everything from capoeira to circus acrobatics, the Fundição is also the home of the Intrépida Trupe, a radically innovative performance group that combines dance, theater, and circus. On Saturday nights, it hosts rollicking GLS (gay, lesbian, and sympathizers) *festas.*

SALA CECÍLIA MEIRELES
Rua da Lapa 47, tel. 21/2224-4291, www.salaceciliameireles.com.br
Map 1

This elegant cream-colored building dating from 1896 was a grand hotel and an even grander cinema before being transformed into a music hall named after Brazilian poet Cecília Meireles. With a refined ambience and boasting excellent acoustics, it is one of the best places in town to take in a classical music performance. Bossa nova, jazz, and *chorinho* are also frequently performed.

TEATRO CARLOS GOMES
Praça Tiradentes, tel. 21/2232-8701
Map 1

Overlooking Praça Tiradentes, this theater, named for the renowned 19th-century Paulistano composer Carlos Gomes, originally dates back to the 1870s. Some of the greatest names in Brazilian theater have walked its stage, which was twice destroyed by fire. By the 1980s, the theater had fallen into disrepair and was purchased by the City of Rio. Major restoration has brought luster back to the grand marble staircase and art deco lobbies, and today some of Rio's most vanguard works of dance and theater are performed here.

TEATRO JOÃO CAETANO
Praça Tiradentes, tel. 21/2221-1223
Map 1

One of the oldest theaters in all of Brazil, the Teatro Real de São João, as it was christened

upon its 1810 inauguration, also suffered through various fires, the last of which, in 1923, was so devastating that a whole new building was constructed, with some magnificent panels by painter Di Cavalcanti based on the theme of Carnaval. Today, some of the most interesting theatrical, musical, and dance performances in Rio are staged here. Meanwhile every Wednesday at noon, the project Sambando e Chorando presents top samba and *choro* musicians for the low price of R$1.

TEATRO ODISSÉIA
Av. Mem de Sá 66, tel. 21/2224-6367, www.teatroodisseia.com.br
HOURS: Tues.-Sat. 9 P.M.-close
Map 1

At one of Rio's most eclectic music venues, even die-hard fans never know what to expect (which is why they're so faithful): Talented performers of traditional regional music such as *baião, forró, coco,* and *maracatu* rub shoulders with alternative rockers and new-generation

© MICHAEL SOMMERS

ARTS AND LEISURE

Teatro Odisséia hosts a diverse array of musical performances.

Carnaval *blocos*. The renovated turn-of-the-20th-century warehouse, with its rugged stone walls and exposed beams, is large enough to contain 600 people and multiple ambiences (and sound levels) including a stage, dance floor, and bar, a mezzanine with tables for dining and conversation, and, on the 2nd floor, a gallery and performance space with a terrace facing the Arcos da Lapa.

TEATRO RIVAL

Rua Álvaro Alvim 33, tel. 21/2240-4469, www.rivalbr.com.br
Map 1

Tucked away on a narrow alley behind Praça Floriano, this classy little deco supper club has been around for 75 years and is one of the few survivors of Cinelândia's glamorous heyday. Looking spiffier than it has for a while after an overhaul, the Rival is a great place to catch some of the top, as well as up-and-coming, names in MPB perform in an intimate setting. Aside from cocktails, the café sells a wide range of CDs featuring classic Brazilian performers (otherwise difficult to find), many of whom once performed at the Rival.

THEATRO MUNICIPAL

Praça Floriano, tel. 21/2299-1677, www.theatromunicipal.rj.gov.br
Map 1

Celebrating 100 years in 2009, Rio's landmark Theatro Municipal has seen some of the biggest national and international names in music, dance, opera, and theater perform upon its stage surrounded by the most ornate of trappings. Aside from hosting visiting attractions, the Theatro has its own renowned symphony orchestra, opera company, and ballet troupe. No matter what is on, a night at the Theatro is truly an event (designer gowns and tuxes aren't necessary, but leave the shorts and flip-flops in your hotel room). Ticket prices aren't prohibitive (R$20–70), but if you're really on a budget take advantage of the lunchtime *meio-dia* (noon) opera series and the Sunday-morning (11 A.M.) concerts for R$1.

VIVO RIO

Av. Infante Dom Henrique 85, tel. 21/2169-6600, www.vivorio.com.br
Map 1

Located in the Parque do Flamengo, this mega–show space inaugurated in 2006 was built following the original plans drawn up 50 years earlier by Affonso Eduardo Reddy. The facade is modernist, but the interior is resolutely 21st century with a modular stage that can be transformed to accommodate intimate acoustic shows or megaextravaganzas (there's standing room for up to 5,000). The roster of big names that have performed here ranges from national icons such as Gilberto Gil, Maria Betânia, and Marcelo D2 to international crowd-pleasers such as Julio Iglesias and Liza Minnelli. While the location is great, prices (often over R$100 for good seats) can be a little steep.

CINEMA

CINE ODEON BR

Praça Mahatma Gandhi 5, tel. 21/2240-1093
Map 1

Although scads of glamorous movie palaces once blossomed around Cinelândia, the sole survivor is this handsomely restored deco gem from 1926, which takes the seventh art very seriously. Aside from screening (usually indie and national) films on its humongous screen, it hosts a terrific variety of events ranging from star-studded premiers and Rio's annual film festival to the Cachaça Cinema Clube where, every Wednesday, screenings of short features are followed by *pinga* tastings, and the GLBT Cineclube, a Friday-night happening in which gay- and lesbian-themed shorts segue into an all-night dance-a-thon in the lobby.

CINE SANTA TERESA

Rua Paschoal Carlos Magno 136, tel. 21/2507-6841, www.cinesanta.com.br
Map 2

Fondly referred to in the hood as Cine Santa, this tiny cinema was willed into existence by Fernanda Oliveira, a young actress who thought it was time that Rio's most artistic *bairro* had a movie theater of its own. After an

Cinelândia's Cine Odeon BR

initially nomadic existence, it found a permanent home in a building shared with a local police station. Despite its size (only 46 seats), the programming is very diverse and ranges from afternoon matinees for kids to national, foreign, and art films.

ESPAÇO MUSEU DA REPÚBLICA
Rua do Catete 153, tel. 21/2558-6350
Map 2

Although the theater itself is pretty petite, this is one of the cheaper places to see indie and commercial films that have otherwise departed from major screens. The big bonus, however, is the atmospheric location inside of the Palácio do Catete, which allows lingering over an espresso and plate of *pães de queijo* at the small café that looks out towards the Parque do Catete.

ESPAÇO UNIBANCO DE CINEMA
Rua Voluntários da Pátria 35, tel. 21/2226-1986,
www.cinemaunibanco.com.br
Map 3

Operated by Unibanco, one of Brazil's largest banks, this cozy complex with a trio of theaters, charming café, and bookstore has long been a major hangout for fervent cinephiles in search of non-commercial fare shown on screens larger than those of a TV. Imagine their rapture, when, in 2005, an even bigger cinema opened only blocks away. More gleaming and high tech, the **Unibanco Arteplex** (Rua Voluntários da Pátria 336, tel. 21/2259-8750) juggles (intelligent) mainstream flicks with alternative films on its six giant screens.

ESTAÇÃO BOTAFOGO
Rua Voluntários da Pátria 88, tel. 21/2226-1988,
www.estacaovirtual.com.br
Map 3

Across the street from the Espaço Unibanco, Estação Botafogo is one of Rio's oldest alternative cinemas, dating back to 1980. Like its neighbor, it screens a wide array of art and international films in three theaters and film and video festivals, both large and small, are often hosted here. Aside from a bookstore and a DVD-rental shop, its café, operated by the gourmet chain Ateliê Culinário, serves delicious snacks and pastries.

ESTAÇÃO LAURA ALVIM
Av. Vieira Souto 176, tel. 21/2267-4307,
www.estacaovirtual.com.br
Map 5

Imagine going to the movies right at one of the world's most famous beaches. If you aren't allergic to small screens and cramped quarters (at regular movie prices), then check out the offerings of indie and wanna-be-indie commercial films screened at this charming cultural center facing the sands of Ipanema. On days when rain spoils your tanning session, this place is a godsend.

ROXY
Av. Nossa Senhora de Copacabana 945-A,
tel. 21/3221-9292, www.severianoribeiro.com.br
Map 4

It's hard to go wrong with a name like Roxy. The sole surviving cinema of Copa's age of glam, this deco theater inaugurated in 1938

ARTS AND LEISURE

has it all: a sweeping staircase, plush lobby, and three big theaters sporting screens worthy of Panavision, where Hollywood blockbusters continue to be projected in all their spectacular glory. Although popcorn is sold inside, the salted or caramel corn made by the *pipoqueiros* (popcorn men) outside is cheaper, fresher, and crunchier.

Festivals and Events

There is always something going on in Rio, but the biggest, most popular, and most characteristically Carioca extravaganzas are, without a doubt, Réveillon and Carnaval.

JANUARY
DIA DE SÃO SEBASTIÃO
Various venues

According to legend, January 20 marks the day that, inspired by the apparition of Saint Sebastian brandishing a sword, Portuguese and Indian forces succeeded in vanquishing French occupiers from Rio. Since the day was already Dia de São Sebastião, it subsequently became the official birthday of the city known as São Sebastião do Rio de Janeiro. Today, Cariocas proudly commemorate their hometown's birthday with the usual syncretic mixture of celebrations that mingle Portuguese traditions with Afro-Brazilian rituals (Saint Sebastian is associated with Oxossi, the *orixá*, or divinity, known as the King of the Forests) and are carried out in churches, *terreiros*, and in the streets, marked by the vivid presence of the color red (associated with both the saint and the *orixá*). The main event is the procession of the saint's statue (brought from Portugal in 1565 by the city's founder, Estácio da Sá) from the Igreja de São Sebastião dos Capuchinos (Rua Haddock Lobo 266), in the Zona Norte *bairro* of Tijuca, to the Catedral Metropolitana, in Centro, where it is swathed in ornate robes and blessed by Rio's archbishop.

FEBRUARY-APRIL
C CARNAVAL
Sambódromo, Rua Marquês de Sapucaí (Praça Onze), Cidade Nova, www.rio-carnival.net
Surely, no other event on the planet involves such eager anticipation and unbridled hedonism, not to mention the hangovers (both physical and emotional), as Carnaval in Rio. To experience the city's five-day (Fri.–Tues.) *festa* in all its butt-swaying, ear-blasting, eye-popping, mind-blowing glory, make sure to book your accommodations *far* in advance. Although the main event, receiving all the media coverage, is the spectacular *desfile* (parade) of Rio's traditional samba schools through the Sambódromo, alternative festivities are rampant. Thousands flock to the municipal bash held outside the Sambódromo at Terreirão do Samba, as well as Cinelândia's popular *baile* (for 60,000) and the alternative Rio Folia held beneath the Arcos da Lapa. There are also the more spontaneous, but no less ritualistic, street parades and subsequent parties organized by neighborhood *bandas* and *blocos* that take place in *bairros* throughout the city, featuring crazy costumes and lots of revelry. Also legendary are the traditional (and highly titillating) Carnaval balls held at nightclubs and swank hotels throughout the city, where costumes tend toward the elaborate but customs are sinful, to say the least.

PÁSCOA
Arcos da Lapa
Map 1

Depending on the year, the long Easter weekend occurs in March or April. For most Cariocas, Páscoa signifies a nice long weekend to escape to the beach, while for kids, it means being showered with (hollow) chocolate eggs (beginning in January, the Brazilian chocolate industry kicks into high gear and you can see the fruits of their labor dangling from supermarket ceilings throughout the country).

escolas de samba at the Sambódromo

While Rio lacks the Easter pageantry that takes place in towns such as Ouro Preto, fans of the crucifixion story can witness a performance of the Passion of Christ staged beneath the Arcos da Lapa on Good Friday.

MAY-AUGUST
FESTA DE NOSSA SENHORA DA GLÓRIA DO OUTEIRO

Praça Nossa Senhora da Glória, tel. 21/2225-2869

`Map 2`

Every August 15, to mark the Dia de Assunção (Day of Ascension), which in Brazil is a national holiday, the faithful—together with fans of religious pageantry—gather at the historic church atop the Morro da Glória for a mass, in which the church is beautifully illuminated and decorated. Afterwards, a procession descends the hill to the Largo da Glória, where more-profane street festivities take place.

FESTAS JUNINAS

Various venues

June is an important month in the Brazilian interior and Northeastern states due to a trio of popular *festas* devoted to three beloved saints: Antônio, Pedro, and João, which are known collectively as the Festas Juninas. In honor of this powerful triumvirate, fruit liqueurs flow, corn and peanuts are roasted over open fires, fireworks explode, and everyone swings to the strains of *forró*. São Pedro, patron saint of rain, is especially important in the parched Northeastern Sertão, and Santo Antônio, patron saint of marriage, is assiduously courted by singles of both sexes on the prowl for a mate. However, the one who inspires the most hoopla is São João (St. John the Baptist), whose birthday and feast day falls on June 24, which coincides with summer solstice in the Northern Hemisphere and the winter solstice in South America. Although the holidays are not native to Rio, Northeastern immigrants commemorate these *festas* (in watered-down versions) in areas such as the Feira de São Cristovão.

SEPTEMBER-DECEMBER
FESTA DA PENHA

Igreja da Nossa Senhora da Penha, Largo da Penha 19, Penha

`Map 9`

The only glimpse most tourists get of the

ARTS AND LEISURE

CARNAVAL PRACTICALITIES

Although Carnaval is all about leaving your inhibitions in your hotel room and taking your skimpily clad, sequined id out into the street, there are some practical considerations that can enhance your enjoyment and ensure your safety. Two good sources for tickets and general information about Carnaval are the **Rio Carnival Guide** (www.rio-carnival.net) and **Riotur** (www.riodejaneiro-turismo.com.br). Riotur distributes a free and very useful *Guia do Rio (Rio Guide)* that gives detailed information about all Carnaval events (including neighborhood *blocos* and balls) in both English and Portuguese.

THE SAMBÓDROMO

Getting inexpensive tickets to the samba school *desfile* (parade) at the Sambódromo is a tricky affair since most of them are sold long before the event itself (they usually go on sale in January). Lineups are enormous and savvy scalpers and travel agents often snatch up the best seats. The municipal tourist secretariat, Riotur, sells (expensive at R$500) tickets for seats in private boxes for tourists, which are much more comfortable than the regular bleachers. Tickets for other sections range R$10-290. Try to sit in the central sections, which offer the best views and the most animation. You can also purchase tickets online at www.rio-carnival.net, or in person at Rio travel agencies (who usually charge a commission). If you find yourself without tickets at the last minute, you can head straight for the Sambódromo and look around for scalpers (who will also be looking around for you). If you're willing to miss the first couple of schools and arrive fashionably late (like most Cariocas), you can usually get some good bargains.

The Sambódromo is divided into 19 *setores* (sectors). Numbers 1-7 and 9, 11, and 13 are all reserved for the public and have seating that ranges from bleachers to boxes. In terms of visibility, 3, 5, and 7 are the best.

Although you can get to the Sambódromo by bus, these are usually packed, rowdy, and full of pickpockets. You're much better off taking a taxi or the Metrô (which runs 24 hours during Carnaval) to Praça Onze (if you're seated in an even-numbered sector) or Central (for an odd-numbered sector). Although the Metrô is also crowded, it's surreal to see the many *passistas* walking along the subway platforms in full regalia. Remember to leave all valuables and ID (carry a photocopy) in your hotel.

hilltop Igreja da Penha in the Zona Norte *bairro* of Penha is from afar as they shuttle to and from the airport. Originally built in 1635 by a Portuguese captain as thanks for saintly intervention in a deadly snake attack, the church is one of Rio's most important. The 365 steps leading to its threshold are often taken by the faithful as "payments" to Nossa Senhora for wishes fulfilled (there is also an elevator). *Festas* in honor of the saint have been held here since the 18th century, every weekend throughout October and into the first weekend of November. Originally Portuguese in nature, by the early 20th century the *festas* had turned into lively samba sessions where great composers of the day—Donga, Pixinguinha,

Sinhã—tested new ditties for the following year's Carnaval. Today, the celebration is one of Rio's biggest and most rambunctious, attracting the faithful and the festive. Considering the sketchy security of Penha, however, it's best to go with a local, a group, or by taxi.

FESTIVAL INTERNACIONAL DE CINEMA
Various venues, www.festivaldorio.com.br
For two weeks in late September and early October, Rio hosts a top-notch international film festival, the Festival do Rio, which always features an engaging array of movies from all over the planet. The selections occupy cinemas throughout the city, and screens are erected on Copacabana beach for your viewing pleasure.

CARNAVAL BALLS

Many of Rio's clubs and hotels host Carnaval *bailes*. The most famous and fabulous event (costumes or formal wear required) is the **Magic Ball** held at the Copacabana Palace (Av. Atlântica 1702, tel. 21/2445-8790) on Saturday night – tickets cost around R$1,500. Tickets to most other balls, however, are in a much more affordable range of R$30–50. The **Scala** (Av. Afrânio de Melo Franco 292, tel. 21/2239-4448) holds legendary balls every night during Carnaval, as does **Le Boy** (Rua Raul Pompéia 102, tel. 21/2513-4993).

SAMBA SCHOOLS

If you want to not just watch, but actually be *in* the samba school parade, contact the *escola de sambas* (most have websites) either in advance or as soon as you arrive to purchase the costume of your choice (which, on average, cost around R$500-600). If you're not in town for the big event, it's worthwhile visiting the schools' neighborhood headquarters to watch a rehearsal. Since many are located in the sometimes-sketchy Zona Norte, it's recommended you go with a Carioca or take a tour with an outfit such as **Be a Local.** For more information about *escolas de samba* and

ensaios (rehearsals), contact the **Liga das Escolas de Samba** (tel. 21/3213-5151, www.liesa.globo.com) or contact the schools directly:

- **Beija Flor** (Praçinha Wallace Paes Leme 1025, Nilópolis, tel. 21/2791-2866, www.beija-flor.com.br)

- **Grande Rio** (Rua Almirante Barroso 5-6, Duque de Caxias, tel. 21/2771-2331, www.academicosdogranderio.com.br)

- **Império Serrano** (Av. Ministro Edgar Romero 114, Madureira, tel. 21/2489-8722, www.imperioserrano.com)

- **Mangueira** (Rua Visconde de Niterói 1072, Mangueira, tel. 21/3872-6878, www.mangueira.com.br)

- **Portela** (Rua Clara Nunes 81, Madureira, tel. 21/2489-6440, www.gre-portela.com.br)

- **Salgueiro** (Rua Silva Teles 104, Andaraí, tel. 21/2253-7608, www.salgueiro.com.br)

- **Unidos da Tijuca** (Clube dos Portuários, Rua Francisco Bicalho 47, Cidade Nova, tel. 21/2516-4053, www.unidosdatijuca.com.br)

Bring a *kanga* and a few icy beers, and pray that everyone turns off their cell phones.

PARADA DE ORGULHO GAY

Av. Atlântica (Posto 6), tel. 21/2222-7286, www.arco-iris.org.br
Map 4

Although quite a bit smaller than São Paulo's extravaganza (which is one of the biggest Gay Pride parades on the planet), Rio's Parada de Orgulho Gay, held in October or June, puts a quintessentially Carioca spin on the festivities with lots of *sunga*-clad muscle boys, bikini-clad drag queens, and a Carnaval-esque flavor. The parade is organized by Rio's reigning gay activist group, Arco-Iris.

RÉVEILLON

Copacabana Beach
Map 4

Ringing in the New Year on Copacabana Beach is one of the most magical and mystical New Year experiences…at least in the Western Hemisphere. Rio's Réveillon is second only to Carnaval in terms of pure spectacle. As night falls, millions of people clad in white begin congregating on the beach of Copacabana. The white symbolizes the purity of the new year, and is also the color associated with Iemanjá, an immensely popular Afro-Brazilian religious deity (*orixá*) whose title is Queen of the Seas. As legend has it, Iemanjá is a vain woman who loves beautiful things. Accordingly revelers

ARTS AND LEISURE

CARNAVAL – OUT OF SEASON

If you can't get to Rio for Carnaval, you can still experience an authentic slice of the action by taking part in the *ensaios* (rehearsals) by Rio's various *escolas de samba*. These are generally held every weekend beginning in August or September. Aside from getting a behind-the-scenes glimpse at the makings of a successful *desfile*, you'll get to soak up some authentic neighborhood atmosphere while listening to terrific samba. Since most schools are located in the Zona Norte, sometimes close to *favelas*, you're best off taking a tour or a taxi. Among the most traditional samba schools, **Mangueira** and **Salgueiro** are the most popular with tourists due to their more sophisticated infrastructure and proximity to Centro.

As Carnaval approaches, the *escolas de samba* hold dress rehearsals at the Sambódromo that are open to the public. You can also catch them at the **Cidade de Samba,** a vast complex created out of Rio's abandoned dockside warehouses. Here the *grupo especial escolas* have ample space to store materials, sew costumes, build allegorical floats (a process that you can observe from a metallic catwalk if you're in town between November and the days leading up to Carnaval), and display their talents to the public weekly on Thursday nights. In addition to the Thursday night performances, the *sambistas* also give small shows for tourists who visit the complex on other days of the week.

Finally, in the month before Carnaval, even neighborhood *blocos* and *bandas* start taking it to the streets. *Ensaios* are often (very conveniently) held in front of traditional *bairro* bars, which serve as an informal clubhouse and ensure a steady supply of *cerveja*.

arrive at the beach bearing her favorite gifts: roses, perfumes, jewelry, and champagne. At the stroke of midnight, they wade into the ocean and toss their offerings into the dark Atlantic. If Iemanjá accepts their gifts, they are ensured a happy year. If the waves sweep them back to shore, better luck next time.

Midnight also signals the start of a gigantic fireworks display (touted as the world's biggest) as well as a series of open-air live-music shows that take place at stages erected at various points along the beach. Then it's dancing and drinking the night away under the stars until morning, when everyone rings in the first day of the year (and rinses off the night's excesses) with a dip in the ocean.

TIM FESTIVAL RIO

Marina da Glória, www.timfestival.com.br
Map 2

One of the biggest and best music festivals in Latin America is organized by cell-phone provider Tim. During several days in late October, an eclectic collection of international and Brazilian talent—from jazz legends and pop stars to proponents of New Rave and Bossa Mod—descend upon the multiple stages erected at Glória's marina, satiating music fans' hunger for a glimpse of artists and bands that rarely venture south of the Equator, such as Kanye West, the Kings of Leon, and the Strokes. Big names sell out way in advance, so purchase tickets ahead of time.

Recreation

In a sense, the city of Rio de Janeiro is one big playground. Whether you want to work out or chill out, there are endless options no matter where in the city you happen to be. The beaches, of course, offer plenty of R&R as well as every kind of sand and water sport imaginable (although practitioners of radical sports will find the most options on the longer and less-urbanized Zona Oeste beaches of Barra and Recreio). More central *bairros* such as Glória, Catete, Flamengo, Botafogo, Urca, and Cosme Velho offer easy access to scalable peaks such as Pão de Açúcar and Corcovado and lie within close proximity to the oceanfront Parque do Flamengo. Although the calm waters of the Baía de Guanabara aren't very swimmable, those who choose to navigate them by boat, yacht, or even kayak are in for a visual treat. Of course, gleaming sands and azure waters practically define the Zona Sul beach *bairros* of Copacabana, Ipanema, and Leblon, but the trio also have easy access to the Lagoa Rodrigo de Freitas. Gávea and Jardim Botânico are also near the lake, and their lack of beaches is easily compensated for by proximity to spectacular peaks such as Morro dos Dois Irmãos and Pedra da Gávea, and the immense Parque Nacional da Tijuca. The upshot is that no matter how much languor or adventure you may be craving at any given moment, you're never more than five minutes away from satiating your desire.

CLIMBING

There are those who are perfectly content to contemplate natural wonders such as Pão de Açúcar, Corcovado, and Pedra Bonita, and others who, once they've set eyes upon them, won't rest until they are actually scaling them. Rio is a climber's heaven, not just on account of the fantastic scenery but because with its estimated 1,000 or so routes it is considered the city with the most climbing options on the planet.

CENTRO DE ESCALADA LIMITE VERTICAL
Rua Bambina 141, tel. 21/2246-9059, www.celimitevertical.com
Map 3

Centro de Escalada offers a wide variety of climbs and hikes (and combinations of both activities) around Rio with English-speaking guides. Rates vary depending on the location and difficulty of the climb, but a four-hour climb up Pão de Açúcar costs R$80.

COMPANHIA DA ESCALADA
Rua Valparaiso 81, Apt. 401, tel. 21/2567-7105, www.companhiadaescalada.com.br
Map 9

Created in 1995 by Flavio Daflon, the Companhia da Escalada is a school that offers courses for rock climbers of all levels as well as outings throughout Rio. The most popular excursion is the one that scales Morro da Urca, where many classes are held, but you can also set your sights (and your cleats) on neighboring Pão de Açúcar as well as Corcovado, Pedra da Gávea, and Pico da Tijuca. With advance reservations, you can strike out on any day of the week for R$100–160 per person. Guides speak English and Spanish as well as Portuguese.

CYCLING

Nobody in their right mind would ever consider cycling amidst Rio's lunatic traffic, but in spite of—and probably because of—this the city boasts an impressive 140 kilometers (87 mi) of *ciclovias* (cycling trails) that allow you to pedal along the oceanfront all the way from Barra da Tijuca to the Marina da Glória, as well as around the Lagoa Rodrigo de Freitas, where you can rent bikes at either Parque dos Patins or Parque do Cantagalo. If you're staying in the Zona Sul, you can take advantage of the fact that Consuelo (tel. 21/2287-7616), located at Copacabana's Posto 4, picks up and delivers

cycling through Parque do Flamengo

rental bikes to your hotel for a cost of R$10 an hour (with a two-hour minimum) or R$40 for the entire day (rental fees include delivery).

BIKE & LAZER
Rua Visconde de Pirajá 135-B, tel. 21/2521-2686, www.bikelazer.com.br
Map 5

Aside from fitness and camping gear, this specialty bike store sells all sorts of bikes (mountain, speed, kid's bikes) and rents them as well, for R$15 an hour or R$60 for an entire day. A second location can be found in Laranjeiras near Largo do Machado (Rua da Laranjeiras 58, tel. 21/2285-7941).

SPECIAL BIKE
Rua Barata Ribeiro 458-D, tel. 21/2547-9551, www.specialbikebotafogo.com.br
Map 4

Rio's largest bike store—also with branches in Ipanema (Rua Teixeira de Melo 53, Lojas J–K, tel. 21/2513-3951) and Jardim Botânico (Rua Jardim Botânico 719, Loja 2, tel. 21/2239-9700)—organizes various free group outings for local cycling enthusiasts. Night owls will dig the nocturnal excursions through Ipanema and Leblon, while mountain bikers can challenge their leg muscles during Saturday jaunts up the hilly roads of Santa Teresa and Corcovado. Should you want to take to the streets solo, you can rent a bike for R$15 an hour and R$35 for the day.

HANG GLIDING
The popularity of hang gliding in Rio—second only to surfing—is unsurprising considering the spectacular surroundings involved. The classic (and most breathtaking) trip is to jump off Pedra Bonita (in the Parque Nacional da Tijuca) and glide down to the Praia do Pepino in São Conrado. No experience is necessary; just a shot of recklessness.

JUST FLY
Rua Barão da Torre 177 (inside the Karisma Hostel), tel. 21/2268-0565, www.justfly.com.br
Map 5

A former agricultural engineer, Paulo Celani started out researching planting techniques for vegetable seeds before deciding his life was too earthbound. The antidote was to become a pilot—first of commercial jets, then of hang gliders. He has logged over 6,000 tandem hang gliding missions with tourists ranging in age from 8 to 80. Flights last around 15 minutes and cost R$200, which includes transportation to and from your hotel.

🅲 SUPER FLY

Estrada das Canoas 722/109, São Conrado, tel. 21/3322-2286, www.riosuperfly.com.br
`Map 9`

Between them, Ruy Marra and his team of highly trained pilots make over 2,000 tandem hang gliding and paragliding flights a year. Superfly takes the act of gliding very neuroscientifically; by evaluating factors such as pulse rate, breathing, and facial contractions, and emotional reactions before and after a flight, they have got the "biopsychological" aspect of this adventure down to a T. What all this means is that they know how to make first-timers, in particular, feel at ease. Flights cost R$210 (which includes an *água de coco* at the end of the ride). There's an additional charge for extras such as digital in-flight photos of your descent and a filmed interview upon landing (both courtesy of the pilot).

HIKING AND ADVENTURE OUTINGS

Rio possesses an enormous number of options for hiking and climbing within and around the city. While a few trails such as those in the Floresta da Tijuca can be undertaken solo, for reasons of security and to avoid getting lost, it's recommended to go with an organized group. Apart from being more informative, it's an excellent way to meet people.

CENTRO EXCURSIONISTA DO RIO DE JANEIRO

Av. Rio Branco 277, tel. 21/2220-3548, www.cerj.org.br
`Map 1`

This local hiking and climbing club organizes regular outings for members and non-members

PEDALING GOES PUBLIC

In early 2009, inspired by cycling-friendly cities such as Amsterdam and Paris, Rio jumped on the bike bandwagon with an initiative known as **Pedala Rio.** For a fee, you can pick up a bike at various terminals throughout the city and, after pedaling to your heart's content, deposit it at another terminal. By the end of 2009 there are expected to be over 40 of these bike terminals scattered throughout Centro and Zona Sul.

The bikes themselves have 15 speeds, are adjustable, and, to dissuade thieves, the parts are all soldered to the frame. The only drawback is the bureaucracy involved. To actually get your hands on one, you have to register at www.mobilicidade.com.br. With a credit card, you choose whether you want to rent for a day (R$10), a month, or a year (R$300). Not only do you have to pay the fee up front, but you also have to leave a deposit of R$260-320. Making things even more complicated for tourists is that when you go to pick up the bike at a terminal, you need a cell phone to call and activate the electronic lock. Sertell, the company that won the consignment to operate the service, claims this is so cyclists won't have to walk around with cash or credit cards, which could leave them vulnerable to muggings.

alike. They hold weekly meetings, and you can visit their website to see the list of upcoming excursions. Courses in climbing are also offered for beginners, but they take place over a three-month period.

RIO HIKING

Rua Coelho Neto 402, tel. 21/2552-9204, www.riohiking.com.br
`Map 2`

Rio Hiking is a highly recommended mother-son outfit operated by friendly English-speaking Denise Werneck and

Gabriel Baroin. They specialize in hiking excursions around the city that cater to various levels of difficulty. The six-hour hike (R$150 pp) to Pedra da Gávea combines strenuous hiking with dips in waterfalls and the ocean, but shorter, easier, and equally enticing options abound as well as more-adventurous outings including rappeling, climbing, cycling, trekking, kayaking, and scuba diving.

TRILHARTE ECOTURISMO

Rua Almirante Tamandaré 77, tel. 21/2245-5626, www.trilharte.com.br

Map 2

Trilharte offers many interesting eco-trips—all of which are slanted towards adventurers with cameras. Photographic safaris to a wide range of photogenic destinations also involve hiking, horseback riding, climbing, and rafting—the only drawback is that tours are in Portuguese. Trip prices vary depending on the length and the activities involved. They range from R$35 for a light hike up the Pão de Açúcar to R$180 (including lunch) for a full-day guided excursion into the Mata Atlântica.

TRILHAS DO RIO

Rua Francisco Sales 645, tel. 21/2425-8441, www.trilhasdorio.com.br

Map 8

Trilhas do Rio's expert guides are highly knowledgeable about Rio's natural surroundings and are committed to sustainable tourism. They lead hiking as well as biking, horseback riding, climbing, and trekking tours both in and around the city. All outings come in easy, medium, and advanced versions; there is even a yoga tour. A four-hour hike up Pão de Açúcar costs R$130, while a six-hour hike up and around Pedra da Gávea is R$160. Other half- and full-day adventure sports excursions range R$130–250.

CITY TOURS

An increasing number of organized tours allow you to explore Rio's diverse neighborhoods and natural attractions and to experience different aspects of Carioca life and culture.

█ BE A LOCAL

tel. 21/9643-0366, www.bealocal.com.br

Be a Local matches foreign visitors with English-speaking locals in an attempt to show them aspects of Carioca life—a funk party in a Rio *favela*, a soccer game at Maracanã—that they could otherwise never experience. Rates vary depending on the activity; for example, a half-day trip to a *favela* with a *motoboy* costs R$65.

CARLOS ROQUETTE

tel. 21/9911-3829, www.culturalrio.com.br

Carlos Roquette is a former judge with an art history degree and a command of English (and French) who has been leading historic and cultural tours of Rio for over 25 years. Aside from the dozens that already exist—ranging from the conventional (Baroque Rio, Belle Epoque Rio, and Art Deco Rio) to the more unusual (Esoteric Rio, Lesbian Rio, People Watching, and Historic Barbershops)—Roquette can also custom-design tours for individuals and groups of all sizes. Customized private tours average around R$50 per hour (discounts are available based on the number of people on the tour or the length of the tour).

FAVELA TOUR

tel. 21/3322-2727, www.favelatour.com.br

Favela Tour was a pioneer in Rio's currently burgeoning *favela* tourism. The controversial concept was the brainchild of operator Marcelo Armstrong. Born and raised in Rio, Armstrong speaks fluent English and offers perceptive and insightful commentary as he leads groups on walking tours of the *favelas* of Rocinha and Vila Canoas (part of the rate charged is donated to community projects). A four-hour tour including transport to and from your hotel costs R$70.

HELISIGHT

tel. 21/2511-2141 or 21/2542-7895, www.helisight.com.br

Perhaps the most spectacularly scenic tour

you could ever take in Rio is by helicopter. Helisight offers various breathtaking forays into Rio's blue skies, lasting between 6 and 60 minutes (with prices ranging from a hefty R$150 to a stratospheric R$875 and with a required minimum of three people).

IKA PORAN

tel. 21/3852-2916, www.ikoporan.org

Ika Poran runs tours to cultural and social development projects located within Rio's poorer communities and *favelas* in an attempt to show foreigners that social problems have solutions. Visitors get to interact with residents, and most of the tour fee goes to specific projects. A full-day tour including lunch and transportation costs R$145 per person. A half-day tour costs US$53. Trips are organized through the Triple M travel agency (tel. 21/2224-0202).

JEEP TOUR

Rua João Ricardo 24, São Cristovão,
tel. 21/2108-5800,
www.jeeptour.com.br
Map 9

Although Rio is hardly safari country, the hilly terrain coupled with sometimes bumpy roads makes Jeep-ing around a great way to explore the city—not only do the open roofs assure 360-degree views, but they provide a permanent breeze. The most popular outings are to natural attractions such as the Floresta da Tijuca and Corcovado (R$100–130 per person), but there are also tours of topographically challenging urban neighborhoods such as Santa Teresa and to hilltop *favelas* as well.

PRIVATE TOURS

tel. 21/2232-9710,
www.privatetours.com.br

Carioca Pedro Novak offers various Jeep tours around Rio as well as to historic towns, beaches, and natural attractions throughout Rio de Janeiro state. The highly personalized tours are tailored to groups of up to four people. A four-hour city tour generally costs around R$50–60.

DIVING

One of the best diving spots in Rio itself is amidst the Ilhas Cagarras, a rocky archipelago visible from Ipanema beach where, aside from colorful schools of fish, more advanced divers can inspect 19th-century sunken ships. Recreio dos Bandeirantes and Urca's Praia Vermelha (especially good for night diving) are two other favorite destinations.

DIVE POINT

Av. Ataulfo de Paiva 1174, Loja 4,
tel. 21/2239-5105,
www.divepoint.com.br
Map 6

In addition to lessons for divers of all levels, including beginners, Dive Point organizes diving, underwater fishing, and photography excursions in and around Rio's beaches as well as to underwater paradises further afield such as the Baía de Angra, Arraial do Cabo, and Búzios. An introductory five-hour course including theory and a 30-minute dive costs R$165.

PROJETO MERGULHAR

Estrada do Gabinal 500, tel. 21/2443-8421,
www.projetomergulhar.com.br
Map 8

Projeto Mergulhar offers diving courses for all levels as well as excursions into the deep blue sea around Rio and to spectacular underwater hot spots such as Cabo Frio, Arraial do Cabo, and Angra dos Reis, all located within several hours of the city. If you're eager to get your feet wet, a basic but intensive 30-hour course including theory as well as dives in a pool and then four dives at Cabo Frio costs R$800.

SAILING AND BOATING

Better than gazing at the Baía de Guanabara is to actually get out on its blue waters. From the Marina da Glória, various boat and schooner companies offer tours around the bay as well as excursions up and down the coast to destinations such as Arraial do Cabo, Búzios, and Ilha Grande.

ARTS AND LEISURE

MARLIN YACHT

Av. Infante Dom Henrique, Marina da Glória,
tel. 21/2225-7434, www.marlinyacht.com.br
`Map 2`

Marlin offers a variety of boat excursions around the Baía de Guanabara, including jaunts to Ilha de Paquetá, trips to the historic fortresses of both Rio and Niterói, and, for the romantically inclined, a two-hour sunset schooner jaunt that departs daily at 3 P.M. and costs R$50 per person. It also offers sailing clinics, sailboat rentals, and diving and snorkeling outings.

SAVEIRO'S TOUR

Av. Infante Dom Henrique, Marina da Glória,
tel. 21/2225-6064, www.saveiros.com.br
`Map 2`

Saveiro's Tour rents out all types of seaworthy vessels as well as water skis. Those interested in a mini cruise can charter a posh yacht to go up and down the coast to deserted beaches and islands along the Costa do Sol and the Costa Verde. A two-hour tour around the Baía de Guanabara costs R$30 per person.

SURFING

Rio is a surfers' haven, luring wave junkies from around the world to ride breaks that reach heights of 2–3 meters (6–10 ft). The fun begins at Arpoador, continues (depending on the season) at São Conrado, and gets really serious at Barra da Tijuca, particularly at a 1-kilometer-long (0.5-mi) stretch in the middle known as Barra Meio (located approximately at Av. Sernambetiba 3000). Recreio is also a big mecca, particularly at the westernmost end known as Praia da Macumba, which segues into the lovely wild beaches of Prainha and Grumari, both of which are *surfista* nirvanas.

To get around town, the city ingeniously operates a special **Surf Bus** (tel. 21/2539-7555, www.surfbus.com.br) equipped to deal with boards and dripping bodies. Departing from Largo do Machado in Botafogo, it travels all the way down the coast from Copacabana to Prainha. Departure times are 7 A.M., 10 A.M., 1 P.M., and 4 P.M. Despite the fact that it's

equipped with air-conditioning, a minibar, and a 29-inch TV that screens surfing DVDs, the cost is only R$3.

To buy or rent surf equipment, check out the stores at **Galeria River** in Arpoador (Rua Francisco Otaviano 67). **Hot Coast** (Loja 12, tel. 021/2287-9388) rents various styles of boards for R$40 a day.

ESCOLA DE SURF RICO DE SOUZA

Av. Sernambetiba, tel. 21/2438-1821,
www.ricosurf.globo.com
`Map 8`

If you want to hone your technique, Escola de Surf Rico de Souza offers daily lessons at its headquarters (in front of Posto 4 at Barra) and at Prainha. The school has lots of information about surfing conditions, events, and equipment rental. Private lessons (including equipment) cost R$60 per person for one hour.

ESCOLINHA DE SURF PAULINHO DOLABELLA

Av. Vieira Souto, tel. 21/2259-2320,
www.escolinhadesurfipanema.com
`Map 5`

With a prime location just across the street from the Caesar Palace, Paulo Dolabella has been teaching the art of surf to students as young as three for over 20 years. Regular two-hour classes are usually scheduled on Tuesday and Thursday at 8 A.M. and 3 P.M., but you can call and reserve a private lesson at any time for R$30 an hour. Dolabella also rents long boards, short boards, fun boards (some of which he makes himself), and rubber suits.

KITESURFING, WINDSURFING, WAKEBOARDING, AND WATERSKIING

K-08 KITESURF CLUB

Av. do Pepê, Quiosque 8, tel. 21/2494-4869,
www.k08.com.br
`Map 8`

Francisco "Frajola" Ferreira da Silva discovered kitesurfing on a trip to Hawaii in 1999. He instantly became so addicted that upon his return to Rio he opened K-08 to teach the sport, virtually unknown in Brazil, to fans of other radical sports. Kitesurfing isn't the safest sport on the planet, but it is one of the most thrilling. Frajola takes no risks with his students, but he allows you to experience the unique sensation of simultaneously flying through the air and skimming over the sea. The cost for an hour-long lesson is R$190.

RIO WAKE CENTER
Lagoa Rodrigo de Freitas, tel. 21/2239-6976, www.riowakecenter.com.br
Map 7

A variation on waterskiing, wakeboarding combines a great workout with the refreshing sensation of a serious hydromassage. At the Rio Wake Center, former wakeboard and waterski champ Marcos "Marquinhos" Figueiredo offers individual lessons for aquatic daredevils of all levels who are interested in wakeboarding and wakeskating as well as plain old-fashioned waterskiing for traditionalists. Lessons (R$160 for an hour, which can be split between more than one person) take place on the Lagoa (the meeting point is near Rua Garcia D'Ávila).

RIO WIND SURF
Av. Sernambetiba, Quiosque 7, tel. 21/9893-6475, www.riowind.com.br
Map 8

Rio Wind Surf will teach you everything you need to know about windsurfing, no matter what your level of experience. In fact, it guarantees that at the end of your first hour on the board, you'll already be able to do basic maneuvers on your own. Both individual and group courses take place on Praia da Barra and nearby Lagoa Marapendi. Lessons for children over eight years old are also available.

SPECTATOR SPORTS
Horseracing
☕ JÓQUEI CLUB
Praça Santos Dumont 131, tel. 21/2259-1596
HOURS: Daily 8 A.M.–5 P.M.; races Mon. 6–11 P.M., Fri. 4–10 P.M., Sat.–Sun. 2–8 P.M.
Map 7

If you've ever dreamed about a day (or night) at the races, then you should head to Rio's Jockey Club, also known as the Hipódromo da Gávea. You've likely never seen a racetrack with

© MICHAEL SOMMERS

the exterior of Gávea's Jóquei Club

FUTEBOL IN RIO

It's hardly a secret that soccer (known in Portuguese as *futebol*) is not just Brazil's national sport, but a passion that borders on the fervently religious. It was introduced by a Brazilian-born man by the name of Charles Miller, who in 1894 returned from higher studies in England toting a soccer ball and equipment. The first soccer games played in São Paulo proved enormously popular, and *futebol* swept through the country like wildfire. Today, Brazil is the only country in the world to have won five World Cups (1958, 1962, 1970, 1994, and 2002), and during World Cup games the entire country shuts down to cheer on the Seleção Brasileira (or to scream advice to the coach or players). While Brazilians are ferocious in their support of their teams, they are equally fierce at criticizing any botched play or strategy;

consequently the range of emotions witnessed in any stadium or around any TV set is impressive. You're as likely to witness big macho guys hugging and kissing each other for joy after a victory as you are to see them sobbing tragically following a defeat. In Brazil, *jogadores de futebol* rank as the country's reigning celebrities, despite the fact that many of them spend most of the year overseas, playing for top European teams. Aside from seeing people watching *futebol* (a year-round pastime since there is no "season") everywhere you go, you'll also encounter Brazilians (mostly males) playing *futebol*. From the floodlit sands of Copacabana to the dilapidated streets of an urban *favela*, soccer is ubiquitous. Often, players are barefoot and the goalposts are rolled-up T-shirts – but the passion is always the same.

a soccer game on Praia de Botafogo

© MICHAEL SOMMERS

such stupendous surroundings—the Cristo Redentor hovers directly above the bleachers. Built in 1926, the rather grand complex was featured in the 1946 Hitchcock film *Notorious,* in which Cary Grant (as a U.S. government agent) and Ingrid Bergman (as a former Nazi spy) took some time out from espionage and romance to bet on the horses. Even if you don't want to gamble (race days are Monday, Friday, Saturday, and Sunday), the club itself is a fun place to grab a drink (no shorts allowed). If you prefer shopping to racing, come on the weekend for the **Babilônia Feira Hype** (every other Sat.–Sun. 2–10 P.M., R$5).

Soccer

Brazil's favorite sport is also Rio's, and you'll see everyone from female tykes to *favela* kids to beer-bellied seniors dribbling, passing, shooting, and scoring, particularly on the beaches. However, if you want to see the real deal, head to the largest and most famous *futebol* stadium in the world: Maracanã.

◖ MARACANÃ

Rua Profesor Eurico Rabelo, tel. 21/2566-7800, www.suderj.rj.gov.br

Map 9

Built in 1950 to host the World Cup, Maracanã seats close to 90,000 people. Even if soccer itself leaves you cold, it's worth taking in a game for the sheer theatrics of the crowd as they toot whistles, beat drums, unfurl gigantic banners, and wield smoke bombs in team colors. When things aren't going well, fans shed tears, implore saints, and hurl death threats (as well as cups of urine—for this reason, you might want to consider seats in the lower levels, which are sheltered by a protective canopy). However, when victory rears its head, it's like a collective mini Carnaval.

Rio's four biggest and most traditional teams are Flamengo, Fluminense, Botafogo, and Vasco da Gama. Each has its die-hard followers, but the most toxic rivalry of all is the legendary Flamengo-Fluminense ("Fla-Flu") matchup. Games are played throughout the

week and throughout the year. When going to a game, avoid rabid fans on the bus and take the Metrô or a taxi. During the day, Maracanã is open for guided tours (daily 9 A.M.–5 P.M., 8–11 A.M. on game days, R$14).

GYMS AND HEALTH CLUBS

Cariocas take their gyms very, very seriously. Working out at an *academia* is a sacred and very democratic rite indulged in by all Cariocas, regardless of social or economic factors. Whether they're pumping homemade scrap-metal weights or hailing the statue of Cristo Redentor as they assume the lotus position, the end result of a toned and healthy body is the same. Most upscale hotels have fitness rooms of their own, but if you want to sample Rio's fitness culture for yourself, many Zona Sul gyms have reasonably priced daily or weekly memberships.

A! BODY TECH

Rua General Urquiza 102, tel. 21/2529-8898, www.bodytech.com.br

Map 6

A! Body Tech is a mega–fitness chain with top-of-the-line gyms in practically every *bairro* (and several in Ipanema alone). It possesses state-of-the-art equipment, countless classes, and an assortment of cool outdoor activities such as night bike rides and trekking on Prainha beach. The swanky six-floor Leblon branch offers the bonus of a rooftop spa with a pool, sundeck, massage area, sauna, whirlpool, and bar. The day fee is R$100.

ESTAÇÃO DO CORPO

Av. Borges de Medeiros 1426, tel. 21/2108-3903, www.estacaodocorpo.com.br

Map 7

One of the most postcard-perfect gyms you can imagine, Estação do Corpo gazes out over the Lagoa Rodrigo de Freitas and takes advantage of its fabulous setting by offering lots of outdoor facilities, including two swimming pools and a restaurant (for working your digestive muscles). The day fee is R$60.

NIRVANA
Praça Santos Dumont 31, Jóquei Club,
tel. 21/2187-0100, www.enirvana.com.br
Map 7

Adhering to the philosophy that health is more than just a toned body, Nirvana brings together activities guaranteed to promote your physical, mental, spiritual, and even gastronomical well-being. In addition to yoga, pilates, tai chi chuan, capoeira, and bio-gymnastics, there is also a spa where you can indulge in a massage or holistic treatments, and an organic restaurant (open to the public) where you can eat to your heart's content without worrying about toxins or calories. Located inside an elegant pavilion that belongs to the Jóquei Club, the space itself is very attractive.

SAMBA CLASSES

Ah, to be able to samba like a Brazilian! It's a common longing for foreigners who arrive in Brazil and are stunned by locals' virtuosity in dancing the national dance. They make it look so natural, and easy, until you try to imitate them and the crowd around you shares those conspiratorial knowing smiles…"gringo." Truth be told, most gringos will never truly get the hang of it, but there's certainly no harm, and lots of fun to be gained, in trying. Although most Brazilians boast that they are born knowing how to samba (and, indeed, many a frustrated gringo has rationalized that there must be some genetic factor involved), in the months leading up to Carnaval many Rio dance halls and *academias* are filled with women (as well as some men and gringos) looking to perfect their moves and increase their stamina. Many gyms, including A! Body Tech, begin offering samba classes as early as October. Meanwhile, there are several dance schools and cultural centers that offer samba and other dance classes year-round.

CASA DE DANÇA CARLINHOS DE JESUS
Rua Álvaro Ramos 11, tel. 21/2541-6186,
www.carlinhosdejesus.com.br
Map 3

One of Rio's most renowned dancers and choreographers, Carlinhos de Jesus has taught many of Brazil's leading showbiz personalities how to dance. Although he made his name in *dança de salão* (ballroom dancing), at his Botafogo academy you can also learn other specifically Brazilian rhythms such as samba, *forró,* and *maxixe.* Both group and individual classes are available, usually for R$30; check the website for schedules. And if you're around during Carnaval, drop by for rehearsals of the Casa's own famously irreverent *bloco,* Dois Prá La Dois Prá Ca, which takes to the streets on Saturday of Carnaval.

CENTRO CULTURAL CARIOCA
Rua do Teatro 37, tel. 21/2252-5751,
www.centroculturalcarioca.com.br
Map 1

Located in one of Rio's most legendary turn-of-the-20th-century dance halls, Centro Cultural Carioca is still one of Rio's best authentic samba scenes. If you want to bone up on your technique before gyrating the night away in front of hard-core *sambistas,* sign up for samba, zouk (the new millenium's *lambada*), or ballroom lessons. The website lists all upcoming classes, which are usually held Monday–Thursday at 8 P.M. A private lesson lasting one hour costs R$70; discounts are available for multiple lessons.

CAPOEIRA

This uniquely Brazilian activity—a graceful but vigorous mix of dance and martial art—has become a popular sport throughout Brazil. In fact, as you wander through the city's parks, it's not at all uncommon to see two men (or women) swinging, kicking, and sparring with each other, within a *roda* (circle) of other *capoeiristas* who sing and clap to the accompaniment of drums, tambourines, and the twang of a *berimbau*—a traditional one-string instrument, essentially a long piece of wood with a metal wire running along it, whose hypnotic sound is caused by the wire's reverberations.

African slaves originally brought the *berimbau*—and capoeira—to Bahia. On plantations, fights sometimes broke out between slaves from different tribes. To avoid being severely punished by plantation owners for fighting, the slaves added music and song to the fights and refined the movements so that, when masters suddenly appeared, the air kicks and lunges resembled a dance—which became capoeira.

Capoeiristas are so agile they never touch their opponents. Aside from a variety of kicks and lunges, movements include crouches, rolls, spins, and cartwheels. Only a "player's" feet, hands, and head can ever touch the ground. The goal is to develop and demonstrate strength, flexibility, and artistry. If you'd like to see *capoeiristas* in action, head to one of the city's Academias de Capoeira, traditional schools where you can observe classes free of charge or join in and pay the class fee.

CASA ROSA

Rua Alice 550, tel. 21/2557-2562, www.casarosa.com.br
Map 2

This very cool—and pink—neighborhood cultural center offers a number of activities during the week, among them samba and capoeira classes. The latter are held on Tuesdays and Thursdays at 8 P.M. and cost R$30. You can also book private lessons (R$50 pp) with one of the *mestres,* providing there are two of you.

GALPÃO DAS ARTES

Av. Padre Leonel França, tel. 21/2249-2286
Map 7

Located in front of the Planetário, the Galpão das Artes Hélio G. Pelligrino offers capoeira classes taught by some of the city's most esteemed *mestres.* Classes are held on all weeknights at 7 P.M. Monthly fees range R$80–100, but the *mestres* are very friendly and flexible and will negotiate a fee for a shorter duration. Since the Galpão is well known in capoeira communities around the world, a lot of foreigners show up to take classes. All levels of experience are welcome.

SHOPS

Like any big, cosmopolitan city, Rio is a great place for shopping, with a wide variety of temptations for most tastes and budgets. However, there are some items you'll find here that you'd be hard pressed to find elsewhere. Fans of Brazilian music can pick up traditional percussion instruments or treat themselves to DVDs, CDs, and vinyl by both contemporary and classic artists. Antiques junkies can spend happy hours combing markets and stores in search of cheap tropical kitsch or rare treasures. And those seeking to spice up their wardrobe will be seduced by the alluring array of beach and casual wear dreamed up by creative local designers. Indeed, with respect to clothing as well as furniture and decorative objects, Rio possesses a unique contemporary art and design scene that draws upon and caters to the city's ethos and lifestyle. Due to a belated recognition of the great richness of Brazil's *artesanato popular,* you'll also find a growing number of boutiques specializing in traditional folk art culled from all over the country.

Shopping in Rio is a fun experience—especially during the major clearance sale seasons—the end of summer (Feb.–Mar.) and winter (Aug.–Sept.)—when stores announce major *liquidações* (sales). Outside of shopping malls *(shoppings),* which can get very packed, stores are rarely crowded. Sales staff are generally welcoming (in more upscale boutiques you'll be offered mineral water and espresso) and aggressiveness and/or snootiness is very rare.

Ipanema is grand shopping central, with throngs of fashionable boutiques hidden away in *galerias* along the main drag of Rua Visconde

HIGHLIGHTS

LOOK FOR  TO FIND RECOMMENDED SHOPS.

◖ Most Unique Accessories: Gilson Martins is inspired to create accessories out of rubber, plastic, and other industrial castaways. Much of his collection cleverly riffs on Carioca icons (i.e., Pão de Açúcar-shaped purses), which makes for great gifts (page 176).

◖ Best Eco-Jewels: Using polished seeds from exotic Amazonian trees as her prime material, Manaus native **Maria Oiticica** creates unusual bio-jewelry that is as striking as it is sustainable (page 177).

◖ Best Antiques: Although Lapa's Rua Lavradio is known as Antiques Row, it's Copa's **Shopping dos Antiquários** that has all the great finds – distributed amidst the 70 antiques and second-hand stores of this appealingly retro 1960s mall (page 179).

◖ Best Brazilian Folk Art: Hidden away on a tranquil Laranjeiras street, **Pé de Boi** boasts an unusually wide selection of expertly crafted Brazilian folk art – sculptures, toys, trinkets, and myriad objects – culled primarily from Minas Gerais, the Northeast, and the Amazon (page 181).

◖ Best Bookstore: Ipanema's **Livraria da Travessa** has everything a discriminating foreign bookworm could ask for: shelves of English-language books and international mags, a terrific array of CDs and coffee-table books, extended hours, and a cool contemporary bistro (page 183).

◖ Best Beachwear: The flagship store of hot Carioca beachwear brand Osklen, **Brazilian Soul** is as artfully laid-back and carelessly sophisticated as its impeccably designed casual apparel – which suits the Ipanema lifestyle to a tee (page 185).

◖ Best Tropical Beauty Potions: All the sweet-smelling lotions, soaps, bath salts, and scents sold at **Ms. Divine** are created by a Carioca chemist who studies the rejuvenating and beautifying properties of Brazil's native fruits and flowers (page 191).

◖ Best Music Store: For both new releases and obscure lost treasures, all musical paths lead to **Modern Sound**, a Copacabana megastore with a helpful staff, great café, and a stage that hosts live music events (page 195).

◖ Best Flip-Flops: Ousadia sells only the crème-de-la-crème of flip-flops – Havaianas – in a mind-boggling number of styles, and at prices that will encourage you to buy more than one pair (page 196).

◖ Chicest Shopping Mall: Cariocas love their *shoppings;* while newcomer Shopping Leblon is pretty fancy, **São Conrado Fashion Mall** continues to rule the roost (page 197).

© MICHAEL SOMMERS

Check out Pé de Boi for the best Brazilian folk art in Rio.

de Pirajá or lining leafy side streets. Centro, Lapa, Santa Teresa, Copacabana, Leblon, and Gávea also have their share of interesting little shops—some traditional purveyors that have been around for decades, others cutting-edge ateliers run by artists and artisans. More relaxing than stressful, shopping in Rio involves pleasant strolls combined with the adventure of happening upon interesting nooks and corners that you might not otherwise encounter.

Accessories and Jewelry

ANTONIO BERNARDO

Rua Gárcia D'Ávila 121, tel. 21/2512-7204, www.antoniobernardo.com.br
HOURS: Mon.-Fri. 10 A.M.-8 P.M., Sat. 10 A.M.-4 P.M.
Map 5

Antonio Bernardo is a goldsmith, artist, and orchid lover (he maintains the Jardim Botânico's *orquidário* as a private donor) who designs beautifully wrought contemporary jewelry with great attentiveness to color, form, and texture. His modern pieces, many of yellow, red, and white gold, are nicely showcased at this flagship store whose fluid lines echo those of the jewels themselves. Don't forget to check the upstairs gallery, Espaço AB.

◖ GILSON MARTINS

Rua Visconde de Pirajá 462, tel. 21/2227-6178, www.gilsonmartins.com.br
HOURS: Mon.-Sat. 10 A.M.-8 P.M.
Map 5

As a young art student, Gilson Martins decided to patch a hole in his knapsack with a strip of canvas torn from a beach chair. The improvisation not only fixed his bag, but paved the way for a future as a designer of bags made from throwaway flotsam such as plastic, rubber, and the foam insulation from the roof of his VW bug. The ingenious models in comic-book colors are as scuptural as they are functional. Much of the collection, which includes jewelry, design pieces, and accessories, riffs creatively on Carioca icons (some are shaped as Pão de Açúcar and the Cristo Redentor, for example), making them ideal for gifts or souvenirs. Don't leave without checking out the gallery space in back that displays artwork that references Rio and Brazil.

GLORINHA PARANAGUÁ

Rua Visconde de Pirajá 365, tel. 21/2267-4295, www.glorinhaparanagua.com.br
HOURS: Mon.-Fri. 8:30 A.M.-7 P.M., Sat. 9:30 A.M.-2 P.M.
Map 5

A diplomat's wife, Glorinha Paranaguá spent years traveling the world before returning to Rio and launching her own handbag empire. Her time outside Brazil instilled the designer with an acute appreciation of her homeland's rich natural bounty, reflected in the materials she employs—straw, bamboo, and wood—as well as the artisanal forms and techniques she draws upon. The final high-quality products,

exterior of Gilson Martins

however, are sophisticated enough to turn heads on 5th Avenue or the Faubourg St. Honoré.

H. STERN

Rua Visconde de Pirajá 490, tel. 21/2274-3447, www.hstern.com.br
HOURS: Mon.-Fri. 10 A.M.-6 P.M., Sat. 9 A.M.-3 P.M.
Map 5

H. Stern is Rio's equivalent of Tiffany's. And if you haven't already heard of Brazil's most famous miner and maker of jewels, you will: Their PR team sends flyers to basically every hotel in Rio, offering to pick you up, take you to the Ipanema headquarters for an interesting tour of their ateliers (featuring a fabulous collection of more than 1,200 tourmalines), and bring you back home again (hopefully with a small bag full of pricy rocks). Specialists in Brazil's dazzling array of precious and semiprecious stones, H. Stern's jewelers create some very innovative contemporary designs as well as more classic, conservative bling.

◖ MARIA OITICICA

Rua Afrânio de Melo Franco 290, Shopping Leblon, Loja 112-B, tel. 21/2508-6083, www.mariaoiticica.com.br
HOURS: Mon.-Sat. 10 A.M.-10 P.M., Sun. 3-9 P.M.
Map 6

When Maria Oiticica was growing up in Amazonas's capital, Manaus, exotic seeds from exotically named trees such as *tucumã*, *morototó*, *buriti*, and *babaçu* were ubiquitous. However, it was only as an adult that she hit upon the idea of stringing said seeds together into a necklace for a friend—and the result was such a hit that Oiticica went into the biobijou business. Aside from seeds, Oiticica also incorporates tree bark, plant fibers, leather, and fish scales, as well as traditional indigenous techniques, in her eco-jewels and accessories that are as elegant as they are sustainable.

MONICA PONDÉ

Rua Visconde de Pirajá 365, Loja 4, tel. 21/2522-2193, www.monicaponde.com.br

© MICHAEL SOMMERS

H. Stern's Ipanema flagship store

HOURS: Mon.-Sat. 10 A.M.-10 P.M., Sun. 3-9 P.M.
Map 5

Monica Pondé came to jewelry via architecture, which explains much about her creations: pared-down, elegant pieces that are all about constant experimentation with form, texture, and materials. The latter in particular really sets her works apart and is the reason so many Brazilian designers consult with her when launching accessory lines. Pondé delights in mixing precious metals with substances such as semiprecious stones, crystals, and found wooden objects (often uncovered from demolition sites). The results are original and disarmingly elegant. Look for a second boutique (Av. Ataulfo Paiva 270, tel. 21/2512-6889)in Shopping Rio Design Leblon.

PARCERIA CARIOCA

Rua Jardim Botânico 728, tel. 21/2259-1437, www.parceriacarioca.com.br
HOURS: Mon.-Fri. 10 A.M.-7 P.M., Sat. 10 A.M.-2 P.M.
Map 7

Parceria is Portuguese for partnership, and alludes to how owner-designer Flávia Torres came to open this store. It was the result of an artistic collaboration with a group of under-privileged girls from a Rio *favela* whom, under her guidance, created a line of woven bracelets that became so in demand that the store became a necessity. Since then, further collaborations with other cooperatives, organizations, and NGOs throughout the country have followed. The pieces, which run the gamut from *artesanato* and accessories to T-shirts and totes emblazoned with Rio iconography, are utterly original and innovative. This shop is highly recommended for those in search of anti-touristic gifts and souvenirs.

SOBRAL JOIAS
Rua Visconde de Pirajá 550, Loja 113,
tel. 21/2274-7162,
www.rsobral.com.br
HOURS: Mon.-Fri. 9 A.M.-6 P.M., Sat. 9 A.M.-3 P.M.
Map 5

At first glance, Roberto Sobral's jewelry—brightly colored with the shiny gleam of jelly beans—appears much more edible than wearable; your first urge might be to bite into one of the chunky rings or bangles—until you realize that they're made out of polyester resin. Sobral first discovered resin back in the 1970s, when he was selling homemade hippie jewels on the beach and ran into some Argentinian competitors hawking wares made out of this shimmering translucent substance. Having seen the light, Sobral spent the next decades creating a small resin empire of jewels, and more recently "poetic objects" that range from key chains, boxes, and (truly gorgeous) toilet seats to sculptures of Carioca icons such as Pão de Açúcar and Cristo Redentor. Travelers in search of last-minute gifts can take advantage of his boutiques at both of Rio's airports.

Antiques

As the imperial and republican capital of Brazil, Rio had a lot of luxury going for it, not to mention scores of aristocratic families used to high living—until their luck or money ran out and they needed to hock their goods. Consequently, there are some interesting knickknacks floating around if you have the eye and patience to find them.

ATELIÊ E MOVELARIA BELMONTE
Rua do Lavradio 34, tel. 21/2507-6873,
www.lucianocavalcanti.arq.br
HOURS: Mon.-Fri. 9 A.M.-6 P.M., Sat. 10 A.M.-2 P.M.
Map 1

In 2001, architect-decorator Luciano Cavalcanti de Albuquerque converted this secular mansion into a combination atelier and boutique selling exclusive restored Brazilian furniture and design objects. Named in honor of his great-great grandmother, the Countess of Belmonte (a title she earned for tutoring Dom Pedro II in his youth), this wonderful space now includes

a café-restaurant and art gallery as well as a showroom where you can pick up treasures that range from Persian carpets to a restored Oscar Niemeyer chair.

FEIRA DE ANTIGUIDADES DE PRAÇA XV
Praça XV de Novembro
HOURS: Sat. 7 A.M.-3 P.M.
Map 1

One of Rio's most traditional and picturesque markets, Praça XV's antiques fair is great fun for trollers who love the thrill of the hunt and have the patience (and humor) to comb through lots of interesting (and junky) flotsam and jetsam in search of a treasure. In general, the earlier you come, the better the pickings.

FEIRA DO RIO ANTIGO
Rua do Lavradio, tel. 21/2224-6693
HOURS: first Sat. of month 10 A.M.-7 P.M.
Map 1

Even if you're not a big antiques junkie, you

© MICHAEL SOMMERS

antiques along Rua do Lavradio

won't want to miss this once-monthly street fair during which all the stores and dealers along Rua do Lavradio's antiques row set up shop in the street alongside independent exhibitors. Aside from the bewitching array of furniture, art, decorative objects, and rare books on display, just soaking up the novel scene (Lapa by day!) is entertaining: Tables and chairs fill the streets and free music and dance performances take place, but just milling around and people-watching is a great diversion in itself.

MERCADO MODERNO

Rua do Lavradio 130, tel. 21/2508-6083, www.mercadomodernobrasil.com.br
HOURS: Mon.-Fri. 9 A.M.-6 P.M., Sat. 9 A.M.-3 P.M.
Map 1

One of the best places in the city to find mid-century furnishings and decorative objects—with a strong emphasis on local designers such as Sérgio Rodrigues, Joaquim Tenreiro, Zanine, and Ricardo Fasanello—this sizeable emporium is also a treasure trove of swinging '60s and '70s vintage gear (there is a great collection of lamps and electronic gadgets). If you come by late in the afternoon, stick around until the evening when the furniture is dragged out of the way to make room for intimate jazz and bossa nova shows.

☾ SHOPPING DOS ANTIQUÁRIOS

Rua Siqueira Campos 143, tel. 21/2255-3461
HOURS: Mon.-Sat. 10 A.M.-7 P.M.
Map 4

Built in the 1960s, Rio's first *shopping* (whose official name is Shopping Cidade de Copacabana) is slightly beat up and weirdly futuristic, but its three floors crammed with over 70 antiques stores sell everything from colonial furniture, baroque sacred art, and antique dolls to deco dishware and Bakelite jewelry. Make sure to check out Machado Antiguidades (Loja 114), with over 4,000 19th-century antiques; Retrô (Loja 159) for art deco; Grafos (Lojas 1–2) for Brazilian designer originals; Onze Dinheiros (Lojas 144–146) for imperial swag; and Hully Gully (Lojas 102 and 139), with a mixture of Brazilian modernism and kitsch objects. Aside from the serious stuff, there are some fun junk stores with surprising treasures.

Arts and Crafts

Neither Rio de Janeiro nor the surrounding state has much to boast in terms of folk art or traditional crafts. However, if you won't be traveling to other parts of Brazil, there are a few recommended boutiques where you can pick up some authentic artifacts and objets d'art.

ARTÍNDIA

Rua das Palmeiras 55, tel. 21/2286-8899, www.museodoindio.org.br
HOURS: Tues.-Fri. 9 A.M.-5:30 P.M., Sat.-Sun. 1-5 P.M.
Map 3

For indigenous art and artifacts, there's nowhere better than this boutique adjacent to the Museu do Índio. It carries an enticing variety of items made by various Brazilian Indian groups, ranging from seed jewelry, baskets, and ceramic vessels to toys, weapons, and musical instruments. Prices are quite reasonable and proceeds are reverted to the indigenous communities who produced the items.

BRASIL & CIA

Rua Maria Quitéria 27, tel. 21/2267-4603, www.brasilecia.com.br
HOURS: Mon.-Fri. 10 A.M.-7 P.M., Sat. 10 A.M.-4 P.M.
Map 5

Brasil & Cia works with a hand-picked group of talented artists from all over the country who create decorative objects that, while steeped in regional traditions, also bear the individual mark of their creators. The materials used are as varied as ceramic, wood, sisal, fabric, papier-mâché, gourds and *capim dourado* (golden straw, derived from the fragile stem of an Amazonian flower). The results are colorful, multi-textured, and impossible to resist.

GETÚLIO DAMADO

Rua Leopoldo Fróis, near No. 15, tel. 21/2531-9066
HOURS: Daily 9 A.M.-6 P.M.
Map 2

For years, local Santa Teresa artist Getúlio

Damado earned a modest living by repairing local residents' pots and pans. As he worked, his constant companion was the sound of the *bondes* clattering up and down the hill from Centro. Unable to get the *bondes* out of his

CHORAR: THE BRAZILIAN ART OF BARGAINING

In Brazil, bargaining is more than just haggling for a good price, it is a lively social ritual. Once you get the hang of it, you will likely enjoy yourself so much that subsequent trips to the impersonal aisles of supermarkets and department stores will seem downright dull. The best way to bargain with someone is to *chorar* (cry). This doesn't mean you have to literally burst into tears (although this technique actually works wonders), but you do have to haggle down the cost of an object based on some operatic tale of woe that will convince the seller that you have suffered immensely and are thus deserving of a discount. For instance, when you arrive at an airport and are confronted with the inflated prices a cab driver is charging for a ride into town, you do the following: complain about how many delays you faced, lament that your luggage was lost, curse the fact that security tore through your bags, etc. Based on your acting chops, you'll be able to knock 5-10 percent off the fare. While a greater command of Portuguese makes for highly effective *chorando*, exaggerated facial gestures, hand-wringing, and sign language can do wonders. Although the person you're bargaining with will do his or her share of "crying," too, once you get your discount, you'll find that you're actually both satisfied — due to the sheer satisfaction of having had a good "cry."

mind, in his spare time Damado began fashioning colorful miniatures made out of scrap wood and metal, which subsequently became so popular that the artist was able to open up his own atelier (resembling, of course, a lifesized *bonde*). In this picturesque studio, the "master of recycling" uses everything from bottle tops to discarded cell phones to create inspired dolls, furniture, and myriad decorative objects that make ideal gifts for kids and adults alike.

Pé de Boi has a terrific selection of Brazilian folk art.

LA VEREDA
Av. Almirante Alexandrino 428, tel. 21/2507-0317
HOURS: Mon.-Sat. 10 A.M.-8 P.M., Sun. 10:30 A.M.-8 P.M.
Map 2

Near Largo do Guimarães, this tiny shop is a favorite tourist haunt for good reason: It brings together an idiosyncratic and carefully chosen selection of regional art and artifacts from all over Brazil, ranging from ceramics, wood carvings, and brightly hued handwoven cotton hammocks to rarer and more unusual finds such as delicate silver jewelry and vintage photographs of Rio dating back to the 1920s.

O SOL
Rua Corcovado 213, tel. 21/2294-5099,
www.artesanato-sol.com.br
HOURS: Mon.-Fri. 9 A.M.-6 P.M., Sat. 9 A.M.-1 P.M.
Map 7

Founded in 1965, O Sol is an NGO whose mission is to develop and support artisans throughout Brazil by helping them to preserve traditions and market their creations. This boutique has a wide selection of handmade objects that are often as practical as they are pretty. The choice includes ceramic vessels, mats woven from jute and cotton, lamps made of *açaí* palm, and delicately hand-embroidered place mats, towels, and tablecloths.

◖ PÉ DE BOI
Rua Ipiranga 55, tel. 21/2285-4395,
www.pedeboi.com.br
HOURS: Mon.-Fri. 9 A.M.-7 P.M., Sat. 9 A.M.-1 P.M.
Map 2

Tucked away on an atmospheric residential street of turn-of-the-20th-century houses, this spacious shop sells a carefully chosen array of Brazilian folk art—sculptures, toys, trinkets, and myriad objects—culled primarily from Minas Gerais, the Northeast, and the Amazon. Highlights include the eerily expressive ceramic dolls from Minas's Vale do Jequitinhonha; geometrically patterned pottery from Pará's Ilha de Marajó; and the splendidly embroidered pieces made for Maranhão's Bumba-Meu-Boi festivities. Friendly proprietor Ana Maria Chindler is very knowledgeable about the pieces and about *arte popular* in general.

Books and Magazines

Like most places in Rio, *livrarias* aren't just for reading or browsing, but for seeing and being seen. This explains why they fill up on weekends and at night (many are open until midnight) with real and pretend intellectuals who spill into the delightful cafés and bistros that coexist with the stacks of books and magazines. Aside from author readings, many offer intimate live musical performances of jazz, samba, *chorinho,* and bossa nova—all of which only enhance the romance factor. The best *livrarias* are in Ipanema and Leblon, where in addition to a wide assortment of English-language books and media you'll be seduced by the excellent array of art and coffee-table books. These are also great places to buy maps and guidebooks.

A CENA MUDA
Rua Visconde de Pirajá at Rua Jangadeiros, tel. 21/2287-8072
HOURS: Mon.-Fri. 10 A.M.-7 P.M., Sat. 10 A.M.-5 P.M.
Map 5

Whatever your profession, if you seek inspiration from leafing through old magazines you'll find a major muse in A Cena Muda. This large walk-in *banca de revistas* specializes in mags that date all the way back to the 19th century, along with comic books and *fotonovelas* (a deliriously kitschy cross between a comic book and a frothy soap opera). The majority are Brazilian, but even if you can't read the text the images speak volumes.

ARGUMENTO
Rua Dias Ferreira 417, tel. 21/2239-5294, www.mercadomodernobrasil.com.br
HOURS: Mon.-Fri. 9 A.M.-6 P.M., Sat. 9 A.M.-3 P.M.
Map 6

This cozy neighborhood *livraria* functions as a second home for many Leblon residents who drop by as if casually popping in to visit an old friend to check out new arrivals, flip through magazines, or trade gossip over a *cafezinho* at

the beckoning Café Severino. When it first opened in the mid-1970s, it was one of the few bookstores in town that dared to carry books written by "prohibited" Brazilian authors such as Miguel Arrães, Dias Gomes, Fernando Henrique Cardoso, and Chico Buarque, whose works were banned by the military dictatorship. Today, with branches in Barra Shopping and Copacabana, it continues to play an important role in the city's literary life with readings, signings, and other events.

BARATOS DA RIBEIRO
Rua Barata Ribeiro 345, Loja D, tel. 21/2549-3850, www.baratosdaribeiro.com.br
HOURS: Mon.-Sat. 9 A.M.-11 P.M.
Map 4

Imbued with a cool neighborhood vibe, Rio's largest and most inviting *sebo,* or second-hand bookstore, is about a lot more than just used books. Although you'll no doubt stumble upon many literary treasures, you can also spend hours rummaging through comics, CDs, vinyl (including hard-to-find bossa nova and samba pearls and small indie labels), and films on video and DVD. On the weekends, there are often free shows featuring alternative bands.

BECO DAS VIRTUDES
Av. Ataulfo de Paiva 1174, Loja 3, tel. 21/2249-9525
HOURS: Mon.-Fri. 10 A.M.-1 P.M. and 3-7 P.M., Sat. 10 A.M.-3 P.M.
Map 6

Hidden at the back of a rather nondescript *galeria,* amidst a bike-repair shop and tattoo parlors, this tiny but charming combination gallery and second-hand bookstore sells contemporary artworks by local artists as well as new, imported, rare, and used books devoted to art, architecture, design, and cinema.

LETRAS E EXPRESSÕES
Rua Visconde de Pirajá 276, tel. 21/2521-6110, www.letraseexpressoes.com.br

HOURS: Mon.-Thurs. 8 A.M.-midnight, Fri.-Sat.
8 A.M.-2 A.M., Sun. 8 A.M.-midnight

Map 5

In the heart of Ipanema, the main branch of this bookstore is a favorite hangout for intellos and insomniacs, who end up staying up even later after ordering reportedly the best cappuccino in the city at its Café Ubaldo. The collection of international magazines is enormous here and you can buy all types of fancy cigars (including Cuban) at its tobacco shop.

(LIVRARIA DA TRAVESSA

Rua Visconde de Pirajá 572, tel. 21/3205-9002,
www.livrariadatravessa.com.br
HOURS: Mon.-Sat. 9 A.M.-midnight, Sun.

11 A.M.-midnight

Map 5

Livraria da Travessa is one of those cool, good-looking bookstores that sometimes show up in movies; the ones where people bump into each while browsing, go upstairs for a coffee, and fall hopelessly in love. This main Ipanema branch—you'll find others in Leblon, Barra Shopping, and Centro—is the largest and most handsome of the lot, with an extensive collection of books about Rio (some in English), as well as lots of CDs and DVDs. Its sleek mezzanine bistro, Bazaar, has delicious things to nibble on.

LIVRARIA LEONARDO DA VINCI

Av. Rio Branco 185, tel. 21/2533-2237,
www.leonardodavinci.com.br
HOURS: Mon.-Fri. 9 A.M.-7 P.M., Sat. 9 A.M.-1 P.M.

Map 1

The landmark 1952 modernist Edifício

© MICHAEL SOMMERS

Livraria da Travessa

Marquês do Herval is irreverently known by Cariocas as Tem Nego Bebo Aí(There's a Drunken Black Man There) due to the fact that the dark building's original window's slanting parapets made the entire edifice look as if it were in a constant state of drunken weaving. This bookstore location hidden away in the basement is as old as the building itself and has long been a favorite browsing ground for Rio's intellectuals and academics, who spend hours perusing both national and international reading fodder. A second smaller store is located in the Museu de Arte Moderna.

SHOPS

Cachaça, Cigars, and Wine

CHARUTARIA LOLLÔ
Av. Nossa Senhora de Copacabana 683,
tel. 21/2235-0625
HOURS: Daily 7 A.M.–midnight
Map 4

A proud and beloved relic of Copa's heyday, Lollô has been the place to go for a smoke and a *cafezinho* since it first opened in 1952. While it's a pleasure to savor both on the spot, you can also do like Tom Jobim, who strolled by every Sunday to buy a box of his favorite cigars, and make your purchases to go. Aside from a wide choice of tobacco, cigars, and pipes, you'll find classic smoking accessories such as lighters, ashtrays, decks of cards, domino sets, and key chains with dangling Carioca icons.

ESCH CAFÉ
Rua Dias Ferreira 78, tel. 21/2512-5651,
www.esch.com.br
HOURS: Daily noon–1:30 A.M.
Map 6

Esch Café is the private clubhouse that most cigar aficionados only dream of. It's decked out like a dusky New Orleans–style café, where jazz wafts through the background while waiters in Panama hats offer food, drinks, and an aromatic array of the finest Cuban cigars—which you can have to stay or to take away. Americans in particular will be thrilled at the relative cheapness, not to mention legality, of brands such as Cohiba, Monte Cristo, and Partagas (just remember to take the bands off before going through U.S. Customs). If you're in Centro, check out the branch at Rua do Rosário 107 (tel. 21/2507-5866).

GARAPA DOIDA
Rua Carlos Goís 234, Loja F, tel. 21/2274-8186
HOURS: Mon.–Fri. 11 A.M.–8 P.M., Sat. 11 A.M.–5 P.M.
Map 6

Rio's first and only store devoted exclusively to *cachaça,* Garapa Doida reunites over 150 brands of *pinga* from all over Brazil, all of which have been certified by government institutions and approved by connoisseurs (clients are also encouraged to sample the wares). Among the rarest labels is Senador, from Minas Gerais, which is aged for 18 years in barrels made of native *garapa* wood. Complimenting the bottled offerings are shot glasses and other accessories, and a collection of *cachaça*-themed books.

LIDADOR
Rua Barata Ribeiro 505, tel. 21/2549-0091,
www.lidador.com.br
HOURS: Mon.–Fri. 9 A.M.–7:30 P.M., Sat. 9 A.M.–1 P.M.
Map 4

This old-fashioned food and wine emporium has been around for over 80 years and has various branches around the city, including this one in Copacabana that has a small bar. The selection of wine and liquors is intoxicating; you'll find some nicely priced vintages from neighboring Argentina and Chile as well as some decent local wines, although if you want to buy Brazilian you're better off investing in one of the better *cachaças*. The original Centro location (Rua da Assembleia 65, tel. 21/2533-4988) has changed little from 1924 and features a charmingly retro bar where you can sample the wares.

Carioca Fashion

Rio fashion is all about beachwear—it's a great place to buy a cutting-edge bikini or *sunga* (male version of a bikini), guaranteed to transform you into the queen or king of the pool back home. Men can indulge in surf wear and some summery street wear (jeans and T-shirts), but otherwise Carioca designers cater more to the fairer sex, in general with clingy, sexy lines and designs in bright colors and featuring interesting details that show off the body's natural attributes to great advantage (it helps if you have the body of a top model or a volleyball player). Women will find lots of great shoes—the higher the heel, the better—while both sexes will delight in the variety of funky flip-flips available.

Most of the boutiques listed here have at least one outlet located in one of the larger Zona Sul *shoppings* such as Rio Sul, Shopping Leblon, Shopping Gávea, São Conrado Fashion Mall, and Barra Shopping. If *shoppings* leaving you feeling cold (a literal possibility, considering the way they blast the air-conditioning), take your "buysies" to Ipanema, whose tree-lined streets are stuffed with boutiques selling the latest creations from Brazilian and Carioca designers and where an increasing number of flagship stores and concept boutiques have been opening. The largest concentration of stores can be found on Rua Barão da Torre, Rua Gárcia D'Ávila, Rua Anibal de Mendonça, and Rua Visconde de Pirajá, where many *galerias* (similar to micro malls) offer hidden treasures that you'd never guess existed. Two of the biggest and most posh are **Galeria Forum Ipanema** (Rua Visconde de Pirajá 351, tel. 21/2523-2140, www.forumipanema.com.br) and **Galeria Ipanema 2000** (Rua Visconde de Pirajá 547, tel. 21/2512-4224, www.ipanema2000.com.br).

ALESSA

Rua Nascimento Silva 399, tel. 21/2287-9939, www.alessa.com.br
HOURS: Mon.-Fri. 10 A.M.-7 P.M., Sat. 10 A.M.-3 P.M.
Map 5

There's nothing subtle about Alessa Migani's fashions. That the designer used to work in advertising is telling, as is her view of the human body as a vehicle of constant exhibition enhanced by clothing that is meant to provoke and seduce. Alessa's irreverence reveals itself in her use of unorthodox fabrics such as tablecloths and baby diapers, and her fusion of Brazilian artisanal traditions with elegant cuts and styling. The resulting pieces make a serious fashion statement while being stark raving fun.

AÜSLANDER

Av. Afrânio de Melo Franco 290, Shopping Leblon, tel. 21/2512-8458, www.auslander.com.br
HOURS: Mon.-Sat. 10 A.M.-10 P.M., Sun. 3-9 P.M.
Map 6

Aüslander is German for foreigner, but since this label's launch in 2004 it's mostly been cool Cariocas who migrate en masse to this funky little shop, ready to pounce on the latest arrival of the exclusive T-shirts (editions are pretty limited) that are as beloved for their form-accentuating cuts as they are for the creative panache of their graphics. To acquire a vintage flavor, many are subjected to a special treatment that leaves them with the softness and slight fadedness of that favorite tee that's been washed and worn a hundred times. The pickings are better for men than for women.

◖ BRAZILIAN SOUL

Rua Maria Quitéria 85, tel. 21/2227-2930, www.osklen.com.br
HOURS: Mon.-Fri. 9 A.M.-8 P.M., Sat. 9 A.M.-6 P.M., Sun. 11 A.M.-5 P.M.
Map 5

You've rarely seen beachwear as jaw-droppingly sleek, cool, and pricy as that bearing the label Osklen. Designer Oskar Metsavaht makes high art out of lowly surfing and cargo shorts, flip-flops, and sneaks, creating casual wear that is sophisticated without losing its slouchy, insouciant edge. Several *shoppings* boast Osklen boutiques, but this concept store, just off the beach

BIKINIS AND *SUNGAS*

It's hardly surprising that in a country blessed with 7,400 kilometers (4,600 miles) of beaches, bikinis and *sungas* have the status of a uniform. Fact: More beachwear is manufactured and consumed in Brazil than any other country on the planet. While all Brazilians take their beachwear seriously, Cariocas have it down to a fine art. The beaches of the Zona Sul serve as open-air runways upon which bronzed bodies display the latest tendencies, which are then avidly copied throughout the fashion world. Over the years, the Carioca bikini has definitely gone through various metamorphoses, including the famously skimpy *tanga* that emerged in the '60s, the even skimpier *fio-dental* (dental floss) model – the name says it all – that created scandals in the '70s, and, more recently, models such as the *asa-delta* ("hang glider") and *tomara-que-caia* ("hope it falls"), whose wishful designation alludes to a strapless top. Today's bikinis are a particularly diverse bunch, made with the most sophisticated high-tech materials that ensure stretchability and resistance. In terms of looks, they run the gamut from primitive crochet models that are ideal for a deserted island to embroidered, beaded, and sequined numbers that wouldn't be out of place on a red carpet (Cher, take note).

The male version of a bikini is known as a *sunga*. While back in the 1980s *sungas* resembled Speedos, those days are gone; in recent years, to differentiate them from the micro models worn by women, they have grown to resemble flattering and very masculine briefs, often called *sungãos*. Like bikinis, *sungas* cater to all crowds: You'll find basic, no-nonsense sporty models as well as wild patterns and exuberant colors.

Rio is the ideal place to invest in swimwear, since most of the major brands are Carioca. **Blue Man** (www.blueman.com.br), **Lenny** (www.lenny.com.br), **Bumbum** (www .bumbum.com.br), **Salinas** (www.salinass-wimwear.com), and **Rosa Chá** (www.rosa-cha.com.br) are all labels whose eternally fashionable *sungas* and bikinis are sold at eponymous boutiques around town as well as in most *shoppings*. Catering to younger women, Salinas and Bumbum styles are showy, daring, and revealing, while Lenny and Rosa Chá's stylish designs are geared towards a more discreet, older, and upscale female clientele. Blue Man has the widest, not to mention wildest, array of masculine gear, with daring cuts and Brazilian motifs. In Ipanema, Blue Man, Lenny, and Bumbum have stores in Forum Ipanema, while Salinas is in Galeria Ipanema 2000. Rosa Chá is at the São Conrado Fashion Mall.

© MICHAEL SOMMERS

bikini at Blue Man

in a big white house that also hosts exhibits and cultural events, admirably shows off both men's and women's lines to their best advantage.

CONTEMPORÂNEO

Rua Visconde de Pirajá 437, tel. 21/2287-6204, www.contemporaneabrasil.com.br
HOURS: Mon.–Sat. 10 A.M.–8 P.M.
Map 5

This spacious upstairs boutique (which includes plenty of cushy chairs where impatient mates can cool their heels) has a terrific range of mostly women's fashions designed by leading Brazilian designers such as Alexandre Herchcovitch, Reinaldo Lourenço, Ronald Fraga, Glória Coelho, Fause Hauten, and Huis Clos. Although the prices can be steep, savvy bargainers willing to buy multiple items and pay in cash can finagle some interesting discounts.

DONA COISA

Rua Lopes Quintas 153, tel. 21/2249-2336, www.donacoisa.com.br
HOURS: Mon.–Fri. 9 A.M.–6 P.M., Sat. 9 A.M.–3 P.M.
Map 7

Dona Coisa is no misnomer; this lovely house, located in a Montmartre-esque section of Jardim Botânico rife with artists' ateliers, is crammed with infinitely appetizing *coisas* (things) that run the gamut from *artesanato*, housewares, and coffee-table books to handbags, jewelry, stationery, and chocolates. Then there are the clothes—a handpicked selection of top Brazilian designers, chosen for women who want to relax in style, whether at home or on the town. Don't leave without having a bite at the mezzanine café, operated by celebrated contemporary chef Roberta Sudbrack.

FARM

Rua Visconde de Pirajá 365, Lojas C–D, tel. 21/2508-6083, www.farmrio.com.br
HOURS: Mon.–Fri. 9 A.M.–6 P.M., Sat. 9 A.M.–3 P.M.
Map 5

If you want to leave Rio looking like a well-dressed clone of a Zona Sul *garota,* head to Farm, whose clothes are made for clients whose life consists of endless summer days and nights

Osklen is a leading name in stylish Carioca beachwear.

on Ipanema beach. Light and breezy skirts and dresses stamped in brightly colorful prints share hanger space with a wide assortment of jeans designed for curves and comfort. Although there are several branches at *shoppings* throughout the city, this flagship is a novelty with its organic forms, natural light, internal garden, and fitting rooms sporting soundtracks.

FOCH

Rua Visconde de Pirajá 365-B, Loja 10, tel. 21/2521-1172, www.foch.com.br
HOURS: Mon.–Fri. 10 A.M.–8 P.M., Sat. 10 A.M.–4 P.M.
Map 5

This well-tailored and coolly casual São Paulo clothing line has a loyal following among gym dandies of the gay persuasion. The street wear and work-out duds are slick, but what really stokes loyal customers' fire are the very fashionable and form-fitting *cuecas* (briefs) that are sort of the Brazilian equivalent of what CKs were in the early 1990s. It's definitely worth picking up a pair or two for yourself and/or the man back home who's welded to his Hanes.

SHOPS

GALERIA RIVER
Rua Francisco Otaviano 67, tel. 21/2522-1967,
www.galeriariver.com.br
HOURS: Mon.-Sat. 9 A.M.-8 P.M.
Map 5

The surf's always up at Galeria River, an alternative enclave whose tiny but well-stocked stores are devoted entirely to the art, lifestyle, and fashion of radical sports and lifestyles. Most of the clients are teen and twentysomething Adonises who strut around this micro mall as if they just stepped off Arpoador beach (many did). Aside from surf gear and surf wear, this is a great place to get a surfer's haircut or a tattoo (or three), or to energize yourself with a super-healthy *vitamina*, chock-full of fruit juices and medicinal herbs.

ISABEL CAPETO
Rua Dias Ferreira 45-B, tel. 21/2540-5232,
www.isabelcapeto.com.br
HOURS: Mon.-Fri. 10 A.M.-8 P.M., Sat. 10 A.M.-6 P.M.
Map 6

One of Brazil's foremost fashion talents, Capeto offers designs that are so singular that if you see a woman ambling down the street in one, her name will immediately pop into your mind. Ultra-romantic without being coy or sentimental, each piece is handmade and has features such as delicate embroidery, flared skirts, visible stitching, and a rich mixture of colors. Some are downright extravagant, as are the prices, although they're more affordable in Leblon than in Barney's New York or Collette in Paris. The accessories are something wild.

LIGA RETRÔ
Rua Visconde de Pirajá 303, Loja 1204,
tel. 21/3202-1057, www.ligaretro.com
HOURS: Mon.-Fri. 10 A.M.-7 P.M., Sat. 10 A.M.-2 P.M.
Map 5

Obsessive soccer fans beware! Not content with merely memorizing all the World Cup statistics since the beginning of time, an equally obsessive Carioca named Leonard Klarnet decided to turn his passion into profits by fashioning flawless replicas of original jerseys worn by legendary players of the past. Due to a special stonewashing technique that gives the shirts a timeworn sheen, they look as if they were ripped from the players' torsos and preserved in mothballs for a few decades. It's hard to keep score of the selection: the 1974 Dutch team, the 1982 Italian team, the 1952 Brazilian team—you'll find shirts from all these countries and years, and even some retro soccer balls as well.

MARIA BONITA
Rua Vinicius de Moraes 149, tel. 21/2523-4093,
www.mariabonita.com.br
HOURS: Mon.-Fri. 9 A.M.-8 P.M., Sat. 9 A.M.-4 P.M.
Map 5

"Pretty Mary" has been on the Carioca fashion scene for well over 30 years. The label's longevity can be attributed to its sophisticated, timeless designs that, despite a marked contemporary edge, never seem to go out of style. The collection is quite complete and ranges from evening gowns to pajamas, as well as accessories including shoes, bags, and jewelry. A spin-off sportswear line, Maria Bonita Extra (Rua Anibal de Mendonça 135, Lojas C–D, tel. 21/2540-5354, www.mariabonitaextra.com.br), offers a more playful, youthful take on the original without forsaking elegance.

RESERVA
Rua Maria Quitéria 77, Loja F, tel. 21/2247-5980,
www.reserva.com.br
HOURS: Mon.-Fri. 9 A.M.-8 P.M., Sat. 10 A.M.-6 P.M.,
Sun. noon-6 P.M.
Map 5

This menswear line was born in 2004 when, during a workout, three friends noted that almost all the other guys at the gym seemed to be wearing the same shorts. Just for fun, they decided to play around with designs for a line of beach shorts. Before they knew it, they had an entire clothing line and a clubby Ipanema boutique named after their favorite beach, Reserva (located between Barra and Recreio). While there are plenty of sporty pieces—often branded with iconic Carioca references such

© MICHAEL SOMMERS

Maria Bonita is a classic Carioca women's clothing label.

as *chope*, samba, and *favelas*—guys after more classically dressy shirts and trousers will also find plenty of options.

SEMENTEIRA
Rua Visconde de Pirajá 414, Loja 212,
tel. 21/2508-6083, www.sementeira.com.br
HOURS: Mon.-Fri. 9 A.M.-6 P.M., Sat. 9 A.M.-3 P.M.
Map 5

Peace, harmony, 100-percent organic fibers, and a mild mint fragrance reign at this boutique specializing in creative yoga and meditation gear for both men and women. That the sherbet-hued sweats, tees, shorts, and leggings are also worn by those who still confuse Vinyasa with a fiery type of Indian curry is evidence of their comfort and casual stylishness. Check out the newest branch in Shopping Gávea, whose environmentally correct curvilinear furnishings are made entirely of sustainably harvested *pupunha* palm and bamboo.

TOTEM
Rua Visconde de Pirajá 547, Loja F,
tel. 21/2540-0061,
www.totemnet.com.br
HOURS: Mon.-Fri. 10 A.M.-8 P.M.,
Sat. 10 A.M.-6 P.M.
Map 5

Although floral prints (the bigger and more colorful the better) are likely to appear on its cotton shorts, shifts, shirts, and skirts, Totem's sophisticated beachwear for young Cariocas of both sexes is not for wallflowers. Perennially hippie chic, the colors tend to scream and the prints are so bold that they could easily start a war with the rest of your wardrobe. If you can pull them off, Totem's clothes are expertly cut and great fun to wear. Aside from these adjoining men's and women's Ipanema boutiques (where you'll also find Totem Kids), there are various branches in most of the city's *shoppings*.

VERVE

Rua Gárica D'Ávila 149, tel. 21/3202-2680,
www.verve.com.br
HOURS: Mon.-Fri. 10 A.M.-7 P.M., Sat. 10 A.M.-3 P.M.
Map 5

Once Rio starts working its romantic spell on you (or if you merely can't stand the heat and humidity), you might feel the urge to slip into a little something more comfortable. Operated by a trio of Carioca pals who understand that women want comfort as much as va-va-voom in their lingerie, this pretty shop sells slips, nightgowns, bras, and panties that are all very well fitted and feature geometric and floral patterns that are more playful than fancy. A big relief for foreign shoppers is that the bra sizing adheres to international standards used in Europe and North America.

VIRZI

Rua Nascimento Silva 309,
tel. 21/2267-1625,
www.virzi.com.br
HOURS: Mon.-Fri. 10 A.M.-7 P.M., Sat. 10 A.M.-2 P.M.
Map 5

One of the few Brazilian designers that is accomplished at creating haute couture pieces, Marcella Virzi is a classicist whose clothing happily transcends scenes and seasons. However, in Virzi's case sophistication doesn't mean staidness. A woman has to have a certain confidence to pull off these bold yet sensual designs, many of which feature tattoo-like embroidery and semiprecious stones and Swarovski crystals. Virzi has also introduced a more casual sportswear line of shorts, T-shirts, minis, and accessories.

Health and Beauty

CARE BODY & SOUL

Rua Barão de Jaguaripe 289, tel. 21/3813-0560,
www.crystalcare.com.br
Map 5

Both men and women are welcome at this urban oasis that offers a panoply of beauty and body treatments, ranging from hair care, waxing, and depilation to facials and full-body massages. Much of the pampering—including manicures, pedicures, and reflexology—takes place in a Zen garden beneath a jasmine tree. There's even a tanning salon for those who hit a rainy spell and don't want to leave town without a serious tan. A second Care Body & Soul is located in the Copacabana Palace (Av. Atlântica 1702, tel. 21/2255-0912).

CLUB CAPELLI

Av. Ataulfo de Paiva 270, 2nd fl., Rio Design Leblon,
tel. 21/2511-2588, www.clubcapelli.com.br
Map 6

To combat the wear and tear caused by necessary exposure to sun and saltwater, fashionable Cariocas take their locks for a tune-up at this sleek hair spa. Aside from cuts and coloring,

you can get replenishing treatments with products as varied as chocolate and orchids while zoning out in front of your own private plasma TV. Manicures, pedicures, eyebrow-shaping, massages, and even thalassotherapy treatments are available.

GRANADO

Rua General Artigas 470, Loja A, tel. 21/3231-6759,
www.granado.com.br
HOURS: Mon.-Sat. 10 A.M.-7 P.M., Sun. noon-6 P.M.
Map 6

When this pharmacy first opened back in 1870, customers as VIP as emperor Dom Pedro II were among those who purchased the potions and powders sold in the glass vials that are still on display in the wonderfully retro shops in Centro and here in Leblon. Aside from high-quality remedies and cosmetics, Granado was a pioneer in the fabrication of 100-percent-natural soaps made from the pure essences of Brazilian herbs, fruits, and flowers. You can still purchase these and other century-old formulas along with newer but no less natural lines, including ones for babies and even pets.

◑ MS. DIVINE

Rua Visconde de Itaboraí 6, tel. 21/2223-3785,
www.msdivine.com.br
HOURS: Mon.-Fri. 9 A.M.-7 P.M., Sat. 9 A.M.-1 P.M.
Map 1

Facing the back of the Centro Cultural Banco do Brasil, this innovative cosmetics boutique and *parfumerie* is owned and operated by a Carioca chemist who decided to apply his scientific learnings to the art of beauty. Experimenting with Brazilian fruits and plants renowned for their nourishing and rejuvenating properties, he has developed a line of sweet-smelling lotions, soaps, bath salts, and scents that make great gifts. If you're armed with *maracujá* (passion fruit) moisturizer or *cupuaçu* shower gel, the long winters of the Northern Hemisphere won't seem quite so cold and harsh.

Home Furnishings and Design Objects

ATELIÊ ALICE FELZENSZWALB

Rua Lopes Quintas 732, tel. 21/2512-5034
HOURS: Mon. 9 A.M.-10 P.M., Tues.-Fri. 9 A.M.-5 P.M., Sat. 10 A.M.-noon
Map 7

Like Santa Teresa, Jardim Botânico is home to many houses that are used by artists as ateliers. One of them is the open studio of Alice Felzenswalb, a master ceramicist who holds classes here throughout the week. Although you're likely to unknowingly eat upon Felzenszwalb's simple yet elegantly crafted plates and bowls at a handful of Rio's funkier restaurants, you can fully admire their forms and finishes at the atelier, where dishware as well as lamps, vases, and other objects are for sale.

CDLH CANDELÁRIA BAZAR

Rua Conceição 11, tel. 21/2507-4294
HOURS: Mon.-Fri. 8 A.M.-6 P.M., Sat. 8 A.M.-2 P.M.
Map 1

Hidden amidst the souk-like atmosphere of Saara, this tiny store will thrill those with excess white space on their refrigerators. The entire place is filled with bins and bins of magnets that are artisanally produced using materials ranging from plastic and paper to plaster. By far the coolest (and most souvenir-worthy) are tropical items such as bananas, mangos, palm trees, and parrots, but those with an iota of Pop sensibility will fall hard for the miniature brand-name bottles of beer and *cachaça,* as well as *guaraná* and boxes of Brazilian food products and laundry detergent. There are also all the necessary ingredients for those who want to go into the magnet business themselves. Oh yes, and everything is dirt cheap.

DAQUI

Av. Ataulfo de Paiva 1174, Loja F, tel. 21/2508-6083, www.daquidobrasil.com.br
HOURS: Mon.-Fri. 10 A.M.-8 P.M., Sat. 10 A.M.-6 P.M.
Map 6

This boutique may be small in size, but lack of space doesn't hamper the happy cohabitation of artwork, design objects, housewares, jewelry, furniture, toys, and fashion—all created by some of the most interesting contemporary Brazilian artists and designers. Many pieces are one-of-a-kind or limited editions and there are always new surprises arriving. Prices are very reasonable. If you're in one of those "I don't know what I'm looking for" moods, there's a very good chance you'll find it here.

MENDES EMBALAGENS DE VIDRO

Rua do Senado 67, tel. 21/2252-9025
HOURS: Mon.-Fri. 9 A.M.-6 P.M., Sat. 9 A.M.-3 P.M.
Map 1

This idiosyncratic store sells all manner of glass objects, from chemists' beakers, pharmacists' vials, and industrial jars and bottles to vases similar to those your great Aunt Edith might have shown off on her dining-room sideboard. Inexpensive and original, transparent or tinted, none of the glassware here has to fulfill its intended use—with a little imagination, these

SHOPS

make unusual gifts and/or inspired decorative accessories.

NOVO DESENHO

Av. Infante Dom Henrique 85, Museu de Arte Moderna (MAM), tel. 21/2524-2290,
www.novodesenho.com.br
HOURS: Mon.-Fri. noon-6 P.M., Sat.-Sun. noon-7 P.M.
Map 1

Design devotees are in for a treat when they begin browsing through the wares for sale at MAM's design store. In the mood for a Lina Bo Bardi table? How about a "Spirit" fan by Guto Índio da Costa? Or a soap dish by Zanini de Zanine? This airy boutique showcases the best of modern and contemporary Brazilian design with lamps, clocks, housewares, office accessories, and creative toys by stellar figures such as the Campana brothers, Sérgio Rodrigues, Ricardo Fasanello, and Maurício Klabin. You'll also find collaborative works made by traditional folk artists in conjunction with designers in an effort to create sustainable artistic communities throughout various regions of Brazil.

O-21 MÓVEIS CARIOCA

Rua Paul Redfern 55, tel. 21/2249-5506,
www.021moveiscariocas.com.br
HOURS: Mon.-Fri. 9 A.M.-7 P.M., Sat. 10 A.M.-5 P.M.
Map 5

This funky little gallery of a store is owned and operated by Zanini de Zanine and Márcio Lewkowicz, who, along with a handful of other vanguard Brazilian designers, dream up many of the exclusive furniture and accessories exhibited here. Their goal is to carry pieces that correspond to a quintessentially Carioca style of living. Count on being seduced by organic forms and the use of precious (but sustainably harvested) native woods. While you may not get away with taking home a coffee table, smaller items such as stools, lamps, vases, magazine racks, and laptop trays are all fair game.

Markets

BABILÔNIA FEIRA HYPE

Praça Santos Dumont 131, Jóquei Club,
www.babiloniahype.com.br
HOURS: Sat.-Sun. 2-10 P.M. (every other weekend)
COST: R$5
Map 7

This large combination flea and fashion market usually lives up to the hype. Held on alternate weekends at the Jóquei Clube, you'll find an interesting assortment of clothing, jewelry, and design pieces by up-and-coming Rio designers. Most of the items are geared toward a beach-y lifestyle, and the stock skews heavily in favor of young females. However, in addition to browsing the market you can take advantage of the various food stalls and have lunch while watching the horse races.

COBAL DO HUMAITÁ

Rua Voluntários da Pátria 448, tel. 21/2537-0186,
www.portaldacobal.com.br
HOURS: Market Mon.-Sat. 8 A.M.-7 P.M.,
Sun. 8 A.M.-1 P.M.; bars and restaurants daily 1 P.M.-4 A.M.
Map 3

By day this colorful European-style covered market is filled with locals on the prowl for fresh fish, fruits, and vegetables. In the afternoon, the simple bars and restaurants begin filling up with the lunch crowd, which then segues into the happy-hour crowd, which then keeps going until almost dawn. At night, from the outside tables, the illuminated statue of Cristo Redentor nearby appears to float magically in the air.

SAARA BAZAAR

For a change of pace – and price – head to the Centro's cluster of pedestrian-only cobble-stoned streets known as Saara (Portuguese for Sahara, www.saararario.com.br). The name is not accidental; it conjures up the bazaar-like atmosphere of bustling shops (many owned by Lebanese and Syrian immigrants) where working-class Cariocas head for bargains. Along with discount clothing, all types of materials for making Carnaval costumes are sold: from ribbons, spangles, and sequins to gaudy kitsch worthy of Carmen Miranda. Pop into **Casa Turuna** (Rua Senhor dos Passos 122/124, tel. 21/2509-3908), one of the largest and most fun of these shops, which has been around since 1915. Saara is a great place to pick up dirt-cheap Carioca souvenirs (there are lots of R$1.99 stores), and you'll enjoy simply wandering around and soaking up the colorful and rambunctious atmosphere. The most interesting streets include Rua da Alfândega, Rua Buenos Aires, Rua Senhor dos Passos, and Rua das Andradas. The closest Metrô stops are Uruguaiana and Presidente Vargas.

© MICHAEL SOMMERS

Carnaval gear for sale at the Saara bazaar

COBAL DO LEBLON

Rua Gilberto Cardoso, tel. 21/2540-0604, www.portaldacobal.com.br
HOURS: Market daily 8 A.M.-6 P.M.; bars and restaurants daily 9 A.M.-2 A.M.
Map 6

The Leblon outpost of the original Humaitá market is equally vibrant, although its Leblon location means the edible offerings tend to be more elaborate, with stands selling fresh artisanal pasta, cheeses, and other imported delicacies. This is a fine place to pick up picnic fare, but it's equally tempting to stick around and soak up the atmosphere at the handful of restaurants and bars.

FEIRA HIPPIE

Praça General Osório, www.feirahippieipanema.com
HOURS: Sun. 9 A.M.-7 P.M.
Map 5

In the early '70s, a scattering of long-haired artist types began selling their objects, jewelry, and wares in this large Ipanema square. Over the years, the hair grew shorter and the wares grew increasingly numerous. Today's "Hippie Fair" possesses a lively rummage-sale atmosphere. Although the location attracts an awful lot of tourists (and pickpockets), the market itself is overrated.

Music

BISCOITO FINO

Rua Lauro Müller 116, Shopping Rio Sul,
tel. 21/2279-3605,
www.biscoitofino.com.br
HOURS: Mon.-Sat. 10 A.M.-10 P.M., Sun. 3-9 P.M.
Map 3

This indie record label was created in 2002 by businesswoman Kati de Almeida Braga and singer-composer Olivia Hime with the mission of producing intelligent and innovative MPB (*biscoito fino*—fine cookie—is a Brazilian expression meaning high quality). Biscoito Fino embraces promising vanguard artists as well as consecrated legends who are weary of corporate labels, and is also involved in uncovering lost relics from Brazil's musical past (including some amazing *choro* recordings). It also launched Biscoitinho, specializing in popular Brazilian music for children. You can also find Biscoito Fino kiosks in Rio Design Leblon, Shopping Gávea, and Barra Shopping.

BOSSA NOVA & CIA

Rua Duvivier 37, tel. 21/2295-5096,
www.bossanovaecompanhia.com.br
HOURS: Mon.-Fri. 9 A.M.-6 P.M., Sat. 9 A.M.-3 P.M.
Map 4

Strategically (and symbolically) located in the Beco das Garrafas (Alley of Bottles), an infamous 1950s and '60s haunt where the founding figures of bossa nova congregated to chat, drink, and make music until the wee hours (much to the ire of the neighbors, who routinely tossed bottles down at them), this music store–gallery is actually more appropriate for fans of samba. Aside from a great collection of samba CDs, you can pick up books about Brazilian music, and even a tambourine-like *pandeiro* to beat upon.

guitars for sale on Rua da Carioca

© MICHAEL SOMMERS

CASA OLIVEIRA

Rua da Carioca 70, tel. 21/2508-8539
HOURS: Mon.-Fri. 9 A.M.-7 P.M., Sat. 9 A.M.-1 P.M.

Map 1

Rua Carioca has no shortage of music stores that sell typical Brazilian instruments. One of the most traditional of them, Casa Oliveira is a great place to pick up any number of string instruments (from Bahia's twangy single-stringed *berimbau* to the ukelele-like *cavaquinho*) and drums, rattles, or other percussion instruments—to start your own micro samba school or to pound on when your longing for Rio starts to overwhelm you.

MARACATU BRASIL

Rua Ipiranga 49, tel. 21/2557-4754,
www.maracatubrasil.com.br
HOURS: Mon.-Fri. noon-8 P.M.

Map 2

Occupying a house on a quiet street in Laranjeiras, Maracatu Brasil combines a music school and recording studio with a great array of traditional handcrafted and modern Brazilian percussion instruments that can be rented as well as purchased both new and used. The staff is friendly and very knowledgeable. When you drop in, check to see who's performing in the small courtyard out back; talented percussionists often give happy-hour shows. And if you're interested in learning to play drums in a samba *bloco* or drums in a *maracatu band,* sign up for lessons taught by top-notch musicians.

◖ MODERN SOUND

Rua Barata Ribeiro 502, tel. 21/2548-5005,
www.modernsound.com.br
HOURS: Mon.-Fri. 9 A.M.-9 P.M., Sat. 9 A.M.-8 P.M.

Map 4

Many *livrarias* have good CD sections devoted to Brazilian music, but if you're a serious aficionado, equally seduced by golden oldies and the latest trends, all roads lead to Modern Sound. In existence since 1966, this

facade of Toca de Vinicius

megastore has an amazing variety of CDs and very friendly, helpful staff. In the evenings, its Allegro Bistro Musical hosts great shows featuring an eclectic diversity of performers from all over Brazil.

TOCA DE VINICIUS

Rua Vinicius de Moraes 129, tel. 21/2247-5227,
www.tocadevinicius.com.br
HOURS: Daily 9 A.M.-8 P.M.

Map 5

Bossa nova fans should head to the Espaço Cultural Toca de Vinicius, a CD store–shrine to the poet, diplomat, and beloved Carioca composer who penned *A Garota da Ipanema* on this very street along with Tom Jobim. Aside from personal mementoes and original music by Vinicius, this is a good place to pick up bossa nova, *chorinha*, samba, and MPB CDs and vinyl. On Sundays, there are frequently free shows out front—often with a piano on the sidewalk.

SHOPS

Shoes

CONSTANÇA BASTO

Av. Afrânio de Melo Franco 290, Shopping Leblon,
tel. 21/2511-8801, www.constancabasto.com

HOURS: Mon.-Sat. 10 A.M.-10 P.M., Sun. 3.-9 P.M.

Map 6

Nicole Kidman, Cameron Diaz, and Charlize
Theron are just some of the Hollywood starlets
to have slipped their feet into the sophisticated
shoes designed by Carioca Constança Basto.
Sparing no expense, Basto uses the finest materials—satin, snakeskin, alligator leather—to
create footwear that is light and luxurious, classic and comfortable. For those who won't be
attending the Oscars this year, the recently
launched Peach (with outlets at *shoppings* such
as Rio Sul) is a more daring, casual line aimed
at girls who want to have fun with unusual patterns and textures and semiprecious stones.

JELLY

Rua Visconde de Pirajá 529, tel. 21/3813-9328,
www.jellyweb.com.br

HOURS: Mon.-Fri. 9 A.M.-7 P.M., Sat. 9 A.M.-2 P.M.

Map 5

© MICHAEL SOMMERS

Back in the days when Americans were wearing
"jelly shoes," Brazilians were wedging their feet
into Melissas, the original "jelly" invented in
Brazil in 1979. After 30 years on the market,
these humble plastic shoes have been revamped
beyond recognition—see for yourself at this
tutti-frutti-colored, bubble gum–scented shoe
temple that sells cutting-edge versions of this
surprisingly flexible and comfortable classic,
reimagined by design gurus such as Alexandre
Herchcovitch, the Campana brothers, and
Karim Rashid. Complementing the footwear
is an equally Pop line of fun accessories such as
purses, bags, key chains, and jewelry.

◖ OUSADIA

Rua Farme de Amoedo 76, tel. 21/2267-7395,
www.ousadiario.com.br

HOURS: Mon.-Fri. 9 A.M.-8 P.M., Sat. 9 A.M.-6 P.M.

Map 5

Ousadia means dare, as in nobody in their

right mind would dare to leave Brazil empty-
handed (or -footed), having failed to pick up
a pair (or five) of highly coveted and authentic Havaiana flip-flops. Being Brazil's
first exclusive Havaiana boutique not only
means that this store has every single model
under the sun ("traditional" and "trend" to
"slim" and "surf" lines), but ensures prices
are lower than elsewhere. Moreover, if you're
not satisfied with the hundreds of styles on
display, you can ask to have them customized, with the application of studs, rhine-
stones, beads, and other baubles right before
your eyes.

SOLLAS

Av. Henrique Dumont 68, Loja C, tel. 21/2511-5239,
www.sollas.com.br

HOURS: Mon.-Fri. 9 A.M.-8 P.M., Sat. 9 A.M.-6 P.M.

Map 5

Sole mates (and siblings) Carla and Bruno
Gugliemetti grew up helping out at their

father's shoe store before going into business for themselves. Carla designs stylishly alternative footwear such as suede ballet slippers and satin-covered platforms for women, while

Bruno recently began dabbling in cool leather sandals for men. Both place a priority on comfort as well as good looks, and, to boot, the prices are quite affordable.

Shopping Malls

Rio's *shoppings* are more than just malls: They are (blissfully air-conditioned) microcosms where Cariocas can shop 'til they drop, and also wander around, gossip, flirt, read, eat, drink, check out a movie or play, and even go skating. Depending on the neighborhood, the clientele, shops, and ambience vary vastly.

BARRA SHOPPING
Av. das Américas 4666, tel. 21/4003-4131, www.barrashopping.com.br
Map 8

Suburban Barra has no shortage of *shoppings*. In fact, it's famous for them. However, the most overwhelmingly gargantuan of them all is this monstrosity with over 500 stores, tons of fast fooderies, a cineplex—not to mention an indoor amusement park suggestively dubbed The Hot Zone and the most "modern" bowling alley in all of Latin America. If by chance you work your way through the entire mall, take comfort in the fact that only one parking lot away is the equally massive New York City Center (Av. das Américas 5000, tel. 21/2432-4980, www.nycc.com.br).

BOTAFOGO PRAIA SHOPPING
Praia de Botafogo 400, tel. 21/3171-9880, www.botafogopraia.shopping.com.br
HOURS: Mon.-Sat. 10 A.M.-10 P.M., Sun. 3-9 P.M.
Map 3

This centrally located but rather claustrophobic *shopping* (its narrowness translates into lots of escalator-riding) has lots of middle-of-the-road boutiques and eating options, which while short on interesting designers offer lots of decent basics that don't require any splurging. For entertainment, there's a big cineplex and, from the top floor, a terrific in-your-face view

of Praia do Flamengo with Pão de Açúcar hovering in the background—make sure you have a camera on you.

RIO DESIGN LEBLON
Av. Ataulfo de Paiva 270, tel. 21/2224-0697, www.riodesignleblon.com.br
HOURS: Mon.-Sat. 10 A.M.-10 P.M., Sun. 3-9 P.M.
Map 6

In spite of its sleek trappings, this compact three-story *shopping* has an almost homey feel. Indeed, originally the majority of its stores specialized in swanky designer furniture and home accessories. These days, however, the majority have switched to clothing by Brazilian designers, which, in most cases, you'll also find elsewhere. What's nice about this *shopping* is having coffee or pastries amidst the glitz of Leblon. If you have a laptop, head for the relaxation lounge, where, ensconced in a leather armchair, you can plug in and surf to your heart's content.

🄲 SÃO CONRADO FASHION MALL
Estrada da Gávea 899, tel. 21/2111-4444, www.scfashionmall.com.br
HOURS: Mon.-Sat. 10 A.M.-10 P.M., Sun. 3-9 P.M.
Map 9

Until its title was threatened (and perhaps usurped) by the opening of Shopping Leblon, this smallish mall, which pleasantly integrates lots of tropical foliage and skylights into its design, was deemed Rio's most chic. Due to its size, location, and clientele, it's still pretty exclusive (if a little empty). The boutiques are all "*feshun*" (Carioca speak for "fashion," i.e., tasteful and pricy). Don't miss master silversmith José Carlos Guerreiro's bold and fashionable jewelry and accessories at **Guerreiro** (Loja

Shopping da Gávea

114, tel. 21/2111-4444, www.guerreiro.com, Mon.–Sat. 10 A.M.–10 P.M., Sun. 3–9 P.M.). Most of the food court offerings follow suit. For tasteful French food, mix with Rio's high-rolling fashionistas at **Club Chocolate** (Loja 202, tel. 21/3322-1223, www.clubechocolate.com.br, Mon.–Sat. 10 A.M.–10 P.M., Sun. 1–9 P.M.), an exclusive café/boutique with views of the golf course. For entertainment, there's a small cineplex.

SHOPPING DA GÁVEA

Rua Marquês de São Vicente 52, tel. 21/2294-1096, www.shoppingdagavea.com.br
HOURS: Mon.-Sat. 10 A.M.-10 P.M., Sun. 3-9 P.M.
Map 7

This dim and somewhat confusingly organized mall is an odd one. Despite its Zona Sul location, it's neither posh nor especially attractive—which, oddly enough, is kind of refreshing. More a neighborhood hangout than a hyper shop-'til-you-drop experience, this *shopping* has a good range of boutiques (a few you won't find elsewhere) and some very good food options. The presence of traditional theaters and art galleries lends it airs of a cultural center and tones down the level of rampant consumerism.

SHOPPING LEBLON

Av. Afrânio Melo Franco 290, tel. 21/3138-8000, www.shoppingleblon.com.br
HOURS: Mon.-Sat. 10 A.M.-10 P.M., Sun. 3-9 P.M.
Map 6

Giving São Conrado Fashion Mall a serious run for its *reais,* Shopping Leblon opened its glittering doors at the end of 2006 and has quickly become *the* place to shop in the Zona Sul. Befitting its Leblon address, it's a beautiful place for beautiful consumers, although you might OD watching so many perfect specimens indulge in spending sprees. There are 200 stylish stores, a cineplex, and a cultural center, and the food court boasts stunning views of Lagoa Rodrigo de Freitas and Corcovado.

SHOPPING RIO SUL

Rua Lauro Müller 116, tel. 21/3527-7200, www.riosul.com.br
HOURS: Mon.-Sat. 10 A.M.-10 P.M., Sun. 3-9 P.M.
Map 3

One of the oldest—dating back to 1980—and most popular of Rio's *shoppings,* Rio Sul benefits from its convenient location in Botafogo, close to the tunnel entrance to Copacabana, which means that every single bus under the

interior of Shopping Leblon

sun passes right in front of its doors. In 2007, it emerged from a much-needed makeover looking considerably more refreshed. Its 400 stores embrace a wide mix of products and prices and there's no shortage of places to eat.

VERTICAL SHOPPING

Rua Sete de Setembro 48, tel. 21/2224-0697, www.verticalshopping.com.br
HOURS: Mon.-Fri. 9 A.M.-8 P.M.
Map 1

From the sidewalk, you'd never guess that inside this nondescript 1950s skyscraper lurks Rio's only "vertical mall." Spread out amidst 13 floors, you'll find over 30 boutiques carrying low- to mid-end local fashions (for the most part for women) and accessories, most of which are very reasonably priced. A definite bonus is that instead of wearing out your flip-flops on those mosaic walkways, you get to zoom up and down the air-conditioned elevator. Oh, and there's also food—ranging from gourmet cookies to sushi.

HOTELS

Rio is one of the world's most beautiful cities—and Brazil's number-one tourist destination—so hotels feel entitled to charge a lot for the (undisputed) pleasure of staying in the Cidade Maravilhosa. Until recently, the choices were underwhelming. Centro offers few options and is unsafe at night. The well-located—albeit beachless—neighborhoods of Botafogo, Flamengo, Catete, and Glória offer an assortment of affordable, but rarely inspiring, options, often geared towards business travelers.

Of course, the main tourist draws are the beaches of Copacabana and Ipanema, and this is where you'll find scads of hotels catering to international tourists. Copacabana, the most traditional tourist magnet, has the most options, many of which line the spectacular beachfront of Avenida Atlântica. With the exception of the legendary Copacabana Palace, many of Copa's hotels are mammoth overpriced chains, which (aside from the high-end luxury hotels) offer fairly standard rooms in various states of decay. Happily, in the last couple of years this has begun to change; an increasing number have received well-overdue renovations and a few classic hotels from Copa's 1950s heyday (some of which are owned by the Othon chain) have been treated to makeovers.

More chic than its neighbor, Ipanema used to offer accommodations veering between luxury beachfront hotels and mediocre two-stars charging four-star prices for the privilege of having a pied-à-terre in this coveted neighborhood. This too has begun to shift thanks to some conscientious upgrading as well as the opening of several appealing and nicely priced

HIGHLIGHTS

LOOK FOR 【 TO FIND RECOMMENDED HOTELS.

【 **Most Creative Ambience: Solar de Santa** is owned by one of the founders of Cirque du Soleil, so it's no wonder that it hums with creative energy. Located in the artists' *bairro* of Santa Teresa, this renovated 19th-century mansion has rooms decorated with works by local artists and surrounded by gardens that are conducive to meditation (page 207).

【 **Unique Bed-and-Breakfast:** Built by a British artist and former war correspondent, the labyrinthine ensemble of curvaceous white concrete buildings at **The Maze Inn** exists in perfect harmony with the surrounding mountains and *favela* of Tavares Bastos. The informal rooftop bar – where jazz concerts and barbecues take place – boasts breathtaking views of Pão de Açúcar (page 207).

【 **Best Home Away from Home: Ananab Guesthouse** bills itself as a guesthouse, but soon after you arrive at this charming turn-of-the-20th-century house ensconced on a lush mountain in Laranjeiras you'll feel like one of the household. Friendly owners, dogs, a cat, multiple verandas, communal breakfasts, and a pool with a view of Corcovado all conspire to make you extend your stay (page 208).

【 **Most Exclusive Boutique Hotel: Casa 32** is so exclusive that it only has two apartments – both of which occupy a mid-19th-century neocolonial house on Largo do Boticário, a charming architectural ensemble at the foot of Corcovado that resembles a period movie set. Rooms are vast and exquisitely furnished, and surrounded by lush gardens and a pool from which you can contemplate the hovering statue of Cristo Redentor (page 210).

【 **Best Luxury Hotel:** There are many luxury hotels in Rio, but there is only one **Copacabana Palace.** While the surrounding neighborhood has changed, the gleaming white deco palace hasn't lost a shred of the elegance and glamour that has lured monarchs, millionaires, and movie stars since the 1930s. The Palace offers impeccable service, elegant surroundings, and nonstop pampering...the only rub is the price (page 210).

【 **Best Retro Hotel:** Amidst the high-rise behemoths that line Copa's Avenida Atlântica, the **Dayrell Ouro Verde** is a breath of fresh air. This early 1950s deco hotel is full of charm and personality; rooms maintain their original furnishings and a small but very classy bar overlooks the beach (page 211).

【 **Best Place to Make Friends:** You'll never be lonely at **Stone of a Beach.** Rio's coolest hostel occupies a historic house in Copa with a rooftop pool and deck where weekly barbecues are held. The friendly staff organize group outings and activities that encourage guests to explore the city together (page 214).

【 **Best Design:** What happens when you give French design guru Philippe Starck and a handful of cutting-edge Brazilian designers who really know their native woods the task of dreaming up a boutique hotel on Ipanema beach? The result is the **Fasano Rio,** in which sleek is cool, but never cold, and countless terraces, decks, and windows ensure that you never forget that the only neighbor in sight is the Atlantic Ocean (page 215).

【 **Ipanema's Cheapest and Most Charming Hotel:** Ipanema is Rio's most coveted address, but until **Ipanema Beach House** came along, options were very expensive (and luxurious) or cheap (and mediocre). Occupying a charming art deco villa, this hostel-guesthouse has a pool, a garden, creatively decorated rooms, and nice amenities – all for an unbeatable price (page 216).

【 **Surfer Sanctuary: Rio Surf n Stay** is a beach house-style hostel only steps away from the splendid surfer's paradise of Praia da Macumba. The owners, *surfistas* themselves, offer equipment rental, lessons, and outings (page 220).

bed-and-breakfasts that occupy old houses on leafy residential streets. In fact, the opening of atmospheric and affordable bed-and-breakfasts, as well as exclusive guesthouses in historic houses, is an emerging and very welcome trend that is taking place not only in Ipanema, but in other traditional residential *bairros* such as Santa Teresa, Laranjeiras, and Gávea as well.

As for Leblon, for a long time this tony residential hood's contribution to the tourist hotel segment could be summed up by the pair of luxury beach hotels, the Marina Palace and Marina All-Suites. However, even Leblon seems to be on the verge of change; in 2008, the unthinkable occurred when the *bairro* witnessed the opening of its first-ever hostel!

CHOOSING A HOTEL

Brazilian hotels are quite varied. Although they receive star ratings (from one to five), these ratings are more impressionistic than accurate, and not all hotels have stars. Rooms are generally ranked as standard, superior, and *luxo* (luxury). A standard *apartamento* (hotel room) usually comes with basic amenities such as a *ventilador* (fan) or air-conditioning, a TV, a stocked mini-fridge, and a phone. Depending on the hotel, the *luxo* room can be a mild upgrade from the standard or can include pampering at the level of rock stars and royalty. In Rio, rooms with sea views are highly coveted and can cost up to 50 percent more.

Hotel rates are almost always based on double occupancy, but single travelers can always try bargaining for a lower rate. In fact, everyone should bargain. No self-respecting Brazilian ever pays the rates listed at the reception desk—known as *balcão* (counter) rates. Outside of high season (Christmas–Carnaval and July), many hotels offer significant discounts of up to 50 percent. You can also ask for a *desconto* if you stay in one hotel over several nights. In this guide, most rates for larger hotels do not factor in special Internet or holiday promotions or those obtained via travel agents or websites. Don't let high prices dissuade you: It's possible to live it up in a fantastic luxury hotel for considerably

PRICE KEY

$ Under R$150 per night

$$ R$150-300 per night

$$$ Over R$300 per night

less than it would cost you in North America or Europe.

Advance reservations are recommended throughout high season, and are essential during Réveillon and Carnaval. For confirmation, some hotels may ask for a deposit of 50 percent (for one night) or that you pay one night (if you're staying for several) upfront.

No matter what the price, rates always include *café da manhã,* or breakfast. This can range from a coffee, rolls, ham and cheese, and a piece of fruit to a lavish affair with dozens of freshly baked breads and cakes, eggs, cheeses and pâtés, fruit jellies, yogurts, and freshly squeezed juices.

As in any city, where you choose to stay in Rio depends upon your priorities. For most tourists, proximity to the city's legendary beaches is first and foremost on their minds. If that's indeed the case, you'll want to be in Copacabana, Ipanema, or Leblon, which is where all the action is—both day and night. If money is no object, splurge for a hotel on the beachfront itself: Avenida Atlântica (Copacabana), Avenida Vieira Souto (Ipanema), or Avenida Delfim Moreira (Leblon). Remember to actually book a room with a sea view—which will cost either a little or a lot more, but is definitely worth it. If you're not going to fork out for the sea view, you might as well pick a hotel back from the beach, where you'll usually immediately find much better bargains and a wider range of accommodations.

Beach lovers who are fond of huge all-inclusive beach resorts with tons of amenities and lots of space and security for kids might want to consider checking into options in the spacious yet pseudo-suburban Zona Oeste beach neighborhoods of São Conrado or Barra.

Luxury digs here are usually a little less pricy than in the Zona Sul, but you'll be far removed from the city itself.

Centro's hotels cater largely to a business crowd and vary between big chains (many operated by Windsor) and small old-fashioned but basic hotels. Although rates are cheaper, you'll spend a lot of time (and money) schlepping to and from the beach. Despite its architectural and cultural treasures, Centro is awash in traffic by day and eerily deserted at night and on weekends, making taxis a necessity.

If you're looking to save money, a better bet is finding accommodations in Glória, Catete, Flamengo, or Botafogo. Conveniently located midway between Centro and the beach neighborhoods of the Zona Sul (and well served by Metrô and bus), these *bairros* are untouristy and filled with historic architecture and interesting cultural venues. Here, you'll find many formerly grand hotels that have received modern makeovers (usually leaving only the facade intact), but both luxury and charm are in short supply.

If you're looking for luxury or charm (or both), hilly Santa Teresa has it in spades. Since 2005, a spate of boutique hotels, many owned by Europeans, have opened in beautifully renovated historic mansions. Most feature fewer than six rooms and possess swimming pools, rambling gardens, and verandas galore. Even Santa's bed-and-breakfasts and hostels are charming, as is the bucolic *bairro* itself, which is so removed from Rio's hustle and bustle that, if it weren't for the abundance of panoramic city views, you'd feel as if you were in a tropical mountain village. Santa's seclusion is both its biggest strength and its biggest drawback. If you want to lounge around your hotel or wander the cobblestoned streets, Santa is perfect. Otherwise, you'll be spending a lot on cab fare.

HOTELS

Centro   Map 1

HOTEL BELAS ARTES 𝕊
Av. Visconde do Rio Branco 52, tel. 21/2252-6336, www.hotelbelasartes.com.br
Located in a handsome historic building in the heart of Centro, this well-regarded hotel offers simply furnished but spotless rooms with high ceilings and (in some cases) polished parquet floors—all for an unbeatable price (R$78–94 d). Perks include a cyber café and 24-hour room service (so you don't have to wander the streets of Centro at night).

IBIS CENTRO 𝕊
Rua Silva Jardim 32, Torre 1, tel. 21/35111-8200, www.ibishotel.com
A member of the highly functional and low-budget Ibis chain, this megahotel located in an ugly modern tower close to Praça Tiradentes offers small, tidy, generic rooms with cheap but cheerful blond wood fixtures and your basic modern comforts (although you pay extra for wireless access). An on-site pseudo-Italian cantina serves pizza and pasta and there is 24-hour room service. Staff is friendly and efficient. In terms of value, this Ibis is unbeatable; while regular rates are R$139 d, frequent promotions go as low as R$59.

WINDSOR ASTURIAS 𝕊𝕊𝕊
Rua Senador Dantas 14, tel. 21/2195-1500, www.windsorhoteis.com.br
Operated by the Windsor chain (which owns a handful of hotels in Rio and appears to have a fondness for Centro—the Serrador is next on its soon-to-be-inaugurated list), the Asturias is one of Centro's tonier accommodations options—and with rooms priced at R$255–350 d, it's cheaper than comparable digs in Copa or Ipanema. While modern and comfortable—it's a favorite with business execs—it won't win any style awards. Lack of charm is compensated for by the efficient service and the rooftop pool and terrace featuring stunning views of the city and the Baía de Guanabara. Close by, the Cinelândia Metrô can quickly whisk you to the Zona Sul beaches.

Lapa Map 1

ARCOS RIO PALACE $$

Av. Mem de Sá 117, tel. 21/2242-8116,
www.arcosriopalacehotel.com.br

The formerly down-and-out Arcos Rio Palace is now a safe, clean, and moderately comfortable hotel with amenities such as a swimming pool, sauna, and 24-hour cyber café (so you can Skype when you come home at four in the morning). Aside from the nice price (R$160–175 d), the real bonus is direct access to Lapa's vibrant nightlife.

SAMBA VILLA HOSTEL $

Rua Evaristo da Veiga 147, tel. 21/2232-4607,
www.sambavilla.com

Smack-dab in the midst of party central, the Samba Villa Hostel offers dirt-cheap digs (R$19 pp) for those who can't get enough of Lapa's nightlife. Standard hostel bunks are livened up by brash tropical colors. Welcome amenities include under-the-bed lockers, air-conditioning, and hot water, as well as low lighting so that when drunken dormmates arrive in the wee small hours, they won't wake you by turning on the lights. Sparkling bathrooms, a small but well-equipped kitchen, and high-speed Internet round out the perks. For your entertainment, the hostel has a disco-bar, a pinball machine, and a trio of scenic terraces from which you can get a taste of Lapa's action before diving into it. The Australian owners are very friendly.

Santa Teresa Map 2

CASA AMARELO $$$

Rua Joaquim Murtinho 569, tel. 21/2252-2549,
www.casa-amarelo.com

The facade of Casa Amarelo is truly *amarelo* (yellow); the warmest, richest, most sunshine-y, buttery yellow you can imagine. These adjectives also describe the rest of this beautiful mansion, designed by a French architect in 1904 and then transformed a century later into an enchanting guesthouse by designer Laurent Gelis, owner of Robert le Héros, a French brand of cutting-edge textiles. Each of the five spacious rooms is christened for the richly patterned, organic fabrics designed by Gelis himself and is decorated with a mixture of mid-20th-century antiques and contemporary designs without forsaking comfort (the owner himself refers to each room as individual "poems"). Included in the rate (R$560 d) are breakfast, lunch, airport pick-ups, and much lolling around the pool with an endless supply of fresh fruit juice. There's a three-day minimum—but you'll be sorely pressed not to stay a week.

CASA 579 $$

Rua Dr. Júlio Otoni 579, tel. 21/3235-6480,
www.casa579.com

One of Santa Teresa's best bargains, this welcoming and original hotel-hostel hybrid offers standard doubles along with two larger rooms that can lodge up to four, which range from R$120–170 (bathrooms are shared). Meanwhile, running the length of the entire mansion is a vast chamber that functions as a dorm for 10. Only unlike most other hostel dorms, this one offers individual storage units, night tables, and reading lamps along with spectacular views of Corcovado for the unbeatable price of R$39 per person. The simple yet pleasant decor, awash in bright tropical colors, is decked out with furnishings and artwork made by local artisans, many who live and work in neighboring *favelas*. Indeed, as part of their commitment to the community, the proprietors not only employ local residents, but also recommend neighborhood cab drivers, tour guides, and even language teachers to guests.

CASTELINHO 38 $$

Rua Triunfo 38, tel. 21/2252-2549,
www.castelinho38.com

One of the precious few mid-range accommodation options in the neighborhood, Castelinho
38 occupies a delightfully Hollywood-esque
castle, complete with turrets and towers, built
in the 1860s. Each of the 10 lovely, spacious
rooms (ranging R$130–240 d) is named after
a fruit tree or tropical plant that thrives in the
jungly garden. Wooden floors, lofty ceilings,
and lots of light reign, as does a mild hippie
vibe that explains the multicolored mobiles and
bean bags in the lounge and the Well Being
space where guests can indulge in yoga, pilates,
and "sacred dances."

HOTEL SANTA TERESA $$$

Rua Almirante Alexandrino 660, tel. 21/2222-2755,
www.santateresahotel.com

With 44 sumptuous apartments (R$475–560
d), the Hotel Santa Teresa is the biggest of
Santa's new boutique hotels. The main building itself, considered a heritage site, is a former
ranch house dating back to 1850. Transformed
into the chicest hotel in the *bairro* in the 1920s
when Santa was sizzling, by the '90s it had followed the neighborhood's declining fortunes
and had garnered a reputation as somewhat
of a halfway house for divorcees and loners,
earning it the name Hotel dos Descasados
(Hotel of the Unmarried). Today, restored to
its former glory and then some, the French-
owned and -operated hotel is Rio's only
member of the prestigious Relais & Chateaux
hotel group. The decor traffics in the best of
Brazil—natural fibers, exotic (and reforested)
woods, and carefully chosen artisanal objects
from all around the country along with tropically inspired furnishings by contemporary
Brazilian artists and designers. The ensemble is so seductive that you'll never want to
leave—and, indeed, you don't have to, since
there is a pool, multiple terraces, and a lush
garden filled with fruit trees and tropical foliage, plus a spa, a gourmet restaurant serving "New World" food, and a lounge-bar that
often hosts *cachaça* tastings.

BED-AND-BREAKFAST NETWORK

Cama e Café (Rua Progresso 67, tel.
21/2221-7635, www.camaecafe.com
.br) is a bed-and-breakfast network that
links travelers with residents who offer
accommodations. In Santa Teresa, you
can choose from more than 50 offerings
based on factors such as cost, comfort,
and common interests. Many of the hosts
are artists and liberal professionals, with
at least a smattering of English and an
impressive knowledge of the city. While
budget and break-the-bank options exist,
the majority of offerings are nicely priced
in the R$100–180 range.

HOTELS

MAMA RUÍSA $$$

Rua Santa Cristina 132, tel. 21/2242-1281,
www.mamaruisa.com

Mama Ruísa is just the kind of perfect hideout
that discreet international celebs seek out to get
away from it all (which is why you shouldn't be
surprised if you find yourself sipping *caipirinhas* on a lounge chair next to Rupert Everett).
Hailing from Paris, owner Jean-Michel Ruís
ceaselessly combed antiques stores for items to
create elegant and vaguely retro ambiences for
this gleaming mansion's seven spacious guest
rooms, terraces, and salons. Having succeeded
magnificently, he then added beautifully landscaped gardens punctuated by an inviting blue
pool. The only indication that you're in Rio is
the fabulous city view glimpsed through the
trees. Aside from the usual creature comforts,
spa services (manicures, pedicures, massages)
and chauffeured city tours are available. Rates
hover around R$500 d.

POUSADA CASA ÁUREA $$

Rua Áurea 80, tel. 21/2242-5830,
www.casaaurea.com.br

Tucked away on a quiet little street, this welcoming guesthouse has a friendly extended-family

© MICHAEL SOMMERS

breakfast in the garden at Pousada Casa
Áurea

vibe. Occupying a renovated two-story villa,
rooms (R$110–140 d) are comfy, if a little on
the rustic side. Those upstairs have the better
views and ambience, with original hardwood
floors and high ceilings. For those demanding
more creature comforts, the darker ground-
floor rooms are equipped with air-conditioning and private (as opposed to shared)
bathrooms. Most of the action, however,
takes place in the leafy Big Chill garden and
patio area where, aside from swinging hammocks, there is an open kitchen where you
can prepare meals and a *churrasqueira* where
barbecues take place. Especially popular with
twentysomethings, this is a great place to meet
up and hang out with other travelers.

POUSADA PITANGA $$

Rua Laurinda Santos Lobo 136, tel. 21/2224-0044,
www.pousadapitanga.com.br
This simple but fetching guesthouse is as warm
and friendly as its young French owner, Lydie
(and two cats), who will make you feel right
at home. It's cozy and intimate with just four

rooms (R$140–190 d), each with colorful decor
inspired by tropical fruits (*açai, caju,* lime, and
tamarind). Tranquility reigns (aided by the ab-
sence of any TVs), and for relaxation purposes
there is a small patio area with lounge chairs
and a refreshing pool.

RIO 180° $$$

Rua Dr. Júlio Otoni 254, tel. 21/2205-1247,
www.rio180hotel.com
The 180° refers to the view, which, unsurprisingly, is pretty fabulous…then again so is this
über-sophisticated hotel, the most contemporary and design-y of all of Santa Teresa's rapidly
expanding boutiquedom. Occupying a 1940s
villa, the octet of sumptuous apartments are
divided into three groups on the luxury scale—
"Oh la la," "Cozy," and "Very Chic"—but all
of them, outfitted by leading Brazilian designers, look as if they were ripped from the pages
of *Architectural Digest*. Of course, looks aren't
everything, which is why you get to choose everything from the music you listen to and the
DVDs you watch to the types of feathers in
your pillows and the scent of your shampoo.
Personalized service is taken to extremes: Upon
check-in you'll be gifted with a walkie-talkie
that will ensure your every whim is catered to
by the 24-hour valet service. However, with
the presence of a swimming pool, spa, restaurant, boutique, smoking room, and art gallery, chances are you won't have many unmet
needs.

RIO HOSTEL SANTA TERESA $

Rua Joaquim Murtinho 361, tel. 21/3852-0827,
www.riohostel.com
Despite the bourgeoning boutique hotel
craze, there is still a refuge for financially
challenged tourists in this neighborhood.
This attractive hostel offers tidy, welcoming dorm rooms (R$35 pp) and minimally
decorated double rooms (R$100–120 d) with
magnificent views (you'll need to reserve
in advance) for impossibly low prices. The
lounge and pool areas are a definite bonus,
as is the prime location—along the *bonde*
line—that offers access to Santa Teresa's

charms and Lapa's nocturnal offerings. It's very popular with the international backpacking set.

◖ SOLAR DE SANTA ❸❸❸

Ladeira dos Meirelles 32, tel. 21/2221-2117, www.solardesanta.com.br

Owned by one of the Canadian founders of the world-renowned Cirque du Soleil, this sprawling 19th-century villa is ensconced in a tropical garden that feels miles away from urban chaos (you can actually sleep with the windows open!). Light-flooded rooms (R$190–560 d) are beautifully decorated with works by local artists (many of which can be purchased). It's also possible to rent the entire villa including all 5 bedrooms (with room for up to 13 people) and kitchen facilities for R$2,000–2,500 (ideal for visiting film crews, artists, and groups of friends with great taste). In fact, billing itself as a purveyor of "creative tourism," the hotel offers guests original services such as custom-designed tours of the city (focusing on fashion, architecture, photography, and gastronomy), as well as visits to artists' studios in Santa Teresa.

HOTELS

Glória and Catete

Map 2

BARON GARDEN ❸

Rua Barão de Guaratiba 195, tel. 21/2245-9929, www.barongarden.com

If you check into this unusually located hybrid guesthouse-hostel, you definitely won't run the risk of running into many other tourists. One of Glória's very few accommodations options, this handsome old manor at the top of a steep hill (the arduous climb is compensated by the stunning views) offers only 16 beds divided between private doubles (R$90–110 d) and an eight-bed dorm (R$45 pp). While the trappings are hardly luxe, the house has plenty of character and a homey vibe, which is actively cultivated by the friendly owners. The possibility of rustling up meals in the gleaming tiled kitchen or chilling out in a hammock by the scenic pool adds to the home-away-from-home sensation.

HOTEL IMPERIAL ❸

Rua do Catete 186, tel. 21/2556-5212, www.imperialhotel.com.br

Occupying an impressive old whitewashed building across the street from the Palácio do Catete, this three-story hotel has been modernized to the point of blandness. However, the rooms (R$125–150 d) are spacious and spotless, the location is great (Catete Metrô is just outside), and the prices are very reasonable.

The tiny pool comes in handy if you have the urge to soak your feet. While hardly memorable, this hotel is very practical.

HOTEL RIAZOR ❸

Rua do Catete 160, tel. 21/2225-0121, www.hotelriazor.com.br

The deceptively grand facade of the former Hotel Monte Blanco dates back to the hotel's 1891 origins and is all that remains of any splendor it once possessed. The basic rooms are clean, and vaguely funky if you're in the right mood, but also kind of shabby. Aside from the odd budget-minded foreign tourists, a lot of small-time execs and somewhat down-on-their-luck Brazilians check in and tend to stay awhile. Service is friendly, if somewhat languorous. It's hard to argue with either the location (only a block from the Catete Metrô) or the price (R$70 d).

◖ THE MAZE INN ❸

Rua Tavares Bastos 414, casa 66, tel. 21/2558-5547, www.jazzrio.com

You've never seen an English bed-and-breakfast like the one built by former British war correspondent Bill Nadkarni. His labyrinth-like ensemble of curving white concrete buildings adorned with Gaudí-esque mosaics (and Nadkarni's art work) blends in with the undulating mountains as well as the surrounding *favela* of Tavares Bastos dangling above the streets of Catete (in terms of safety, the only shooting you'll encounter is TV and movie crews). The eight small suites (R$100 d) are light on furnishings but heavy on atmosphere. You'll have difficulty tearing yourself away from the rooftop terrace, where Pão de Açúcar seems close enough to touch—especially when Nadkarni fires up the barbecue and begins making *caipirinhas*. Even if you don't check in, it's worth checking out the monthly jazz performances, which have become a cult event.

SCORIAL RIO ⑤⑤
Rua Bento Lisboa 155, tel. 21/3147-9100, www.scorialriohotel.com.br

From the outside, the Scorial looks like a very shiny shopping center—and once you step inside the beat goes on. The gleaming surfaces are buffed to a high polish and marble, granite, mirrors, and blond wood dominate. If you prize modernity, comfort, and functionality over personality, the Scorial is a great option, particularly since it's just around the corner from Largo do Machado Metrô. With rooms going for R$190–240 d, it's also a great bargain.

Flamengo and Laranjeiras   Map 2

⟨ ANANAB GUESTHOUSE ⑤⑤
Rua Alice 681, tel. 21/2557-6789, www.ananab.com

For a laid-back home-away-from-home experience, you'll do no better than the wonderfully atmospheric turn-of-the-20th-century hilltop guesthouse owned and operated by Carioca-Belgian couple Roberto and Dirk. Along with a menagerie of friendly dogs and a cat, the duo's mission is to make guests feel at home; proof of their success is that many choose to linger in the handful of artistically decorated rooms (R$155–165 d) for weeks and even months. There are copious communal breakfasts and access to a fabulous pool, and staying here allows you to explore one of Rio's most attractive and undiscovered historic *bairros*, Laranjeiras.

living room of the Ananab Guesthouse

© MICHAEL SOMMERS

facade of Hotel Florida

HOTEL FLORIDA $$

Rua Ferreira Viana 81, tel. 21/2195-6800,
www.windsorhoteis.com.br

Owned by the Windsor chain, the Florida is a tried-and-true Flamengo favorite that's very popular with savvy Brazilian execs. Although little remains from its 1940s heyday beyond a splendid facade and the grand pillars in the ball-room-sized restaurant, the Florida has adapted better than many of its brethren to post-modern times with rooms (R$250–310 d) that are spacious, comfortable, and discreetly decorated. The most attractive (and expensive) ones overlook the gardens of the Palácio do Catete. Free Internet service and local calls, a rooftop pool, and the option of breakfast in bed are welcome extras.

HOTEL INGLÊS $

Rua Silveira Martins, tel. 21/2558-3052,
www.hotelingles.com.br

Although the historic coral-colored facade of this small building enchants, inside this small hotel things take a definite turn for the modern. Clean, no-nonsense rooms (R$125 d) are a little sparse, but possess all the basics and lots of space to move around, making this a good choice for anyone who wants some bang for their buck. By far the best are those at the front that look onto the Parque do Catete.

HOTEL REGINA $$

Rua Ferreira Viana 29,
tel. 21/3289-9999,
www.hotelregina.com.br

When it first opened in the mid-1920s, the Regina quickly became the hotel of choice for government diplomats and ministers. Although a few architectural features allude to its history, the Regina is hardly as grand as it once was. However, its decently sized rooms (R$170–260 d) are bright and comfortable and the location, on a small street just half a block from the Parque do Flamengo, is quiet and convenient.

PAYSANDU HOTEL $

Rua Paissandu 23, tel. 21/2558-7270,
www.paysanduhotel.com.br

Yet another once-grand hotel that over time has morphed into a one-star, the Paysandu has succeeding in preserving its deco-era trappings and personality better than many others—mostly in the warm and woody lobby and lounge, although the otherwise simple rooms benefit from high ceilings, moldings, and large wood-shuttered windows (R$128–143 d). Tranquility is assured due to its located on a residential street lined with statuesque imperial palms.

Paysandu Hotel

HOTELS

Botafogo, Cosme Velho, and Urca — Map 3

◖ CASA 32 ⑤
Largo do Boticário 32, tel. 21/2265-0943,
www.boticario32.com.br

If you visit Largo do Boticário, an almost mirage-like ensemble of charming neocolonial villas in the shadow of Corcovado, your first urge will be to declare, "I want to live here!" The good news is that you can. One of the mid-19th-century houses, Casa 32, now operates as a very beautiful and very select boutique hotel. In fact there are only two apartments (R$640–760 d), but each is exquisite; with a mixture of antiques and modern furnishings that is both stylish and idiosyncratic. The rest of the house is equally atmospheric and you'll soon feel at home as you browse the bookshelves, take a swim or sauna, or mix yourself a drink before retiring to the lush gardens to contemplate the Cristo Redentor.

VILA CARIOCA HOSTEL ⑤
Rua Estácio Coimbra 84, tel. 21/2557-6789,
www.vilacarioca.com.br

This friendly family-owned hostel occupies a newly renovated late-1930s villa with a small courtyard garden. Accommodations (R$35 pp, R$90–100 d) are hostel basic, but clean and cheerful, and the proprietors' helpfulness and goodwill go far in helping guests to feel at home. Aside from a small bar and Internet lounge, guests have access to the kitchen. The location, on a secure residential street that's only three minutes from the Botafogo Metrô, is both convenient and refreshingly untouristy.

Copacabana and Leme — Map 4

ASTORIA PALACE ⑤⑤⑤
Av. Atlântica 1866, tel. 21/2545-9550,
www.astoriapalace.com.br

Inaugurated in 2007, the Astoria Palace (not to be confused with the plain old Astoria around the corner on Rua República de Peru, owned by the Atlântica chain) is for guests who like their hotels gleaming and new. You won't find a lot of personality, but all the surfaces shine, everything works, and, considering the prime location, the price is nice. The rooms (R$265–420 d) are well-appointed and comfortable, although the ones facing the ocean have those unbeatable ocean views. The tiny rooftop pool is more conducive to soaking up rays than actually soaking.

CASA DA VALESKA ⑤
Rua Barata Ribeiro 253, tel. 21/2547-6069,
www.casadavaleska.com

Valeska, the proprietor of a charming house on a quiet residential street in Copa, likes to stress that she's neither running a guesthouse nor a bed-and-breakfast, but having people visit with her. Although, of course, she charges guests to stay in the modest but cozily furnished and bright quartet of rooms (R$110–130 d) in her *casa,* you'll quickly be made to feel like one of the household—particularly since you have access to the kitchen, laundry facilities, and broadband (you supply the laptop). If you're curious to live life as a Carioca for a while, this is an excellent option.

◖ COPACABANA PALACE ⑤⑤⑤
Av. Atlântica 1702, tel. 21/2548-7070,
www.copacabanapalace.com.br

One of the most legendary hotels in the world and a national landmark, the Copacabana Palace is as famous as the beach it sits upon. In fact, when this dazzling white wedding cake of a hotel was constructed in 1923, Copacabana was little more than an unspoiled strip of sand surrounded by mountains. A decade later, the Palace played a prominent role in the RKO classic *Flying Down to Rio,* the first film to pair

© MICHAEL SOMMERS

the legendary Copacabana Palace

Fred Astaire and Ginger Rogers. Since then, while the *bairro* around it has grown and decayed, without losing a shred of its elegance the Palace has continued to attract a nonstop cavalcade of international stars, jet-setters, heads of state, and royalty. When not holed up in the luxury of their poshly furnished rooms (R$820–1,230 d), these privileged guests can often be spotted lounging around the Olympic-sized turquoise pool, getting pampered in the spa, playing a few sets on the rooftop tennis court, or dining in one of the two highly reputed restaurants, Cipriani and Pérgula. Should you care to join them, know that the extravagant cost is worth every penny.

☾ DAYRELL OURO VERDE ⑤⑤
Av. Atlântica 1456, tel. 21/2543-4123, www.dayrell.com.br
Oozing with deco charm, the Ouro Verde has been a favorite with discriminating Brazilian travelers since it opened its doors in 1950. Both the public spaces and shockingly affordable private rooms (R$240–280 d) are classy and understated with elegant original furnishings. That some of its luster has faded only adds to its personality. While more expensive rooms at the front overlook the Atlantic, those at the back provide glimpses of Corcovado. The handsomely retro bar on the ground floor, formerly a notorious high-society haunt, has made a glorious comeback since reopening in 2006.

HOTEL SANTA CLARA ⑤⑤
Rua Décio Villares 316, tel. 21/2256-2650, www.hotelsantaclara.com.br
Although it's a whopping five blocks from the beach, those in search of a little piece of mind, and a great deal, will find this location nicely removed from Copa's bustle. More a guesthouse than a hotel, Santa Clara occupies a pretty whitewashed house with blue shutters and polished wooden floors that, despite the spareness of its trappings, is warm and inviting. Try for rooms (R$153–168 d) facing the front, particularly on the top floor, which are the brightest and breeziest and boast little balconies from which you can sometimes glimpse monkeys in the trees.

HOTEL TOLEDO ⑤⑤
Rua Domingos Ferreira 71, tel. 21/2257-1990, www.hoteltoledo.com.br
A quiet and very affordable low-frills alternative to Copa's megachains, the Toledo is located on an attractive leafy street that's safe, central, and only a block from the beach. Rooms (R$165 d) come in various sizes (ask to take a look), but all are clean and fairly pleasant if you don't mind a decorating scheme reminiscent of your elderly aunt's guest room. A definite perk is the top-floor breakfast room with a smashing view of Copacabana beach.

OLINDA OTHON CLASSIC ⑤⑤⑤
Av. Atlântica 2230, tel. 21/2545-9000, www.othon.com.br
Inaugurated in 1949, when Copa's glamour was peaking, the Olinda's classy art deco facade is a welcome contrast amidst a sea of high-rises. Step inside and the flashback continues; awash in Italian marble, Persian carpets, and crystal

HOTELS

HOTELS

HOSTELS

Since 2007, a new generation of hostels has appeared on the scene in Rio. A far cry from the crowded, institutional dorms of yore that catered exclusively to party animals and backpackers (although there are still many of these around), the new emerging crop often occupy renovated houses that boast gardens, pools, rooftop decks, and barbecue areas. In addition to dorms, the majority possess affordable double rooms that are simple but well decorated; even the communal rooms often sport minimal decor. In addition to amenities such as communal kitchens, Internet, and the possibility of renting bikes and surfboards, enlightened management makes efforts to plan activities and outings for guests. Look for these hostels not only in tourist neighborhoods such as Copacabana and Ipanema, but also in Botafogo, Santa Teresa, and even Lapa. An International Youth Hostel Association card isn't necessary, but it gets you discounts of around R$5-10 a night. For a list of hostels, consult the **Federação Brasileira dos Albergues de Juventude** (tel. 21/2531-1085, www.hostel.org.br).

chandeliers, the lobby oozes grandeur. Rooms (R$275–370 d) retain original features such as wood-framed windows, high ceilings, and moldings, but the retro (and admittedly frayed) furnishings have been replaced with a decor that prizes generic sophistication and modern gadgets (flat-screen TVs and broadband access). The deluxe rooms with ocean views are considerably nicer than the "superior" rooms, especially if you snag one with a balcony.

OTHON CALIFORNIA ⑤⑤
Av. Atlântica 2616, tel. 21/2132-1900,
www.othon.com.br
For those Eagles fans who've always dreamed of living it up at the Hotel California, your fantasy can come true when you check into the Othon California. Well, sort of. The original trappings of the once-grand 1940s hotel are on splendid display in the lobby and dining areas, and barely apparent in the comfortable though wearily nondescript rooms (R$210–290 d), some of which could use some freshening up—as could the musty-scented hallways. Nonetheless, this Othon has personality and prices that are quite good for a beachfront location.

PORTINARI DESIGN HOTEL ⑤⑤⑤
Rua Francisco Sá 17, tel. 21/3222-8800,
www.portinaridesignhotel.com.br
When it opened in 2003, the Portinari had the guts to invite a handful of leading Brazilian architects and decorators to design each of the hotel's 11 floors. The overall results are mostly inspired—although there are some misses along with the hits. For this reason, you should check out the photos on the hotel website to select a room whose colors and accessories jive with your personal preferences. Aesthetics aside, all rooms (R$470–620 d) are very well outfitted with amenities ranging from broadband and flat-screen TVs to luxurious towels and sheets and complimentary flip-flops. The fitness center includes a spa with a sauna and whirlpool. The hotel is only half a block from the beach.

ROYAL RIO PALACE ⑤⑤
Rua Duvivier 82, tel. 21/2122-9292,
www.royalrio.com
The closest the Royal gets to regal is its location: The Copacabana Palace is only several blocks away. However, this glittery newish hotel gets points for comfort, quality, and trying hard to be sleek and modern (for the most part, it succeeds admirably). Although hardly oozing in personality, rooms (R$270–320 d) get a lift from small flourishes of color, tawny wood fixtures, and natural light. A definite bonus is the rooftop pool and terrace; from there you can not only see the beach, but you have a mountain in your face.

HOTELS

Sofitel Rio de Janeiro's rooms all have views of Copacabana beach.

SESC COPACABANA $$

Rua Domingos Ferreira 160, tel. 21/2548-1088,
www.sescrio.org.br

Only a block from the beach, the SESC Copacabana is not only one of the best deals in Copa, but you have the bonus of staying in an architectural landmark designed by Oscar Niemeyer. The bargain prices (R$198–250 d) are due to SESC being a type of union for tradespeople that offers cultural, recreational, and vacation facilities for both members and (at higher, but still unbeatable costs) non-members. Rooms are coolly minimalist and those above the 10th floor offer terrific views of Corcovado. Advance reservations are highly recommended.

SOFITEL RIO DE JANEIRO $$$

Av. Atlântica 4240, tel. 21/2525-1232,
www.sofitel.com.br

Amidst Copa's sea of beachfront hotels, the Sofitel is the most serious contender to the Copacabana Palace's title of luxury queen.

What this ultra-modern, somewhat over-priced hotel lacks in terms of charm and pedigree, it tries to make up for with a dazzling array of enticing extras. The swanky rooms (R$900–1,250 d) are outfitted with plasma TVs, extra large and comfortable beds, and balconies from which you can eat breakfast or sip cocktails while staring at the entire length of Copacabana beach (yes, all rooms have sea views). The presence of two strategically positioned rooftop pools means you can catch rays in the morning and the afternoon. Other bonuses include Le Pré Catalan, considered one of Rio's top French restaurants, and a privileged location on the frontier between Copa and Ipanema.

SOUTH AMERICAN COPACABANA $$$

Rua Francisco Sá 90, tel. 21/2227-9161,
www.southamericanhotel.com.br

Squeezed strategically between Copa and Ipanema—a five-minute walk gets you to either beach—the South American is a good deal for a great location. Rooms are large, bright, and airy with lots of light wood to add warmth to what is otherwise a fairly standard decorative scheme; common rooms adhere somewhat to a polished airport-lounge aesthetic. Although there aren't any sea views, many rooms as well as the pool gaze out at another classic Carioca sight: a hilltop *favela* (fear not: the area surrounding the hotel is safe).

STONE OF A BEACH ⊕

Rua Barata Ribeiro 111, tel. 21/3209-0348, www.stoneofabeach.com.br

If you're young in age and spirits, low on bucks, and coming to Rio for the first time, Stone of a Beach is ideal. Opened in 2006 by a young Carioca couple, this hostel occupying a funky old house is not just into providing bunks (R$30–40 pp) but a cool ambience where young voyageurs from all over the world can hang out and discover the city together with the help of the friendly, savvy staff. As such, it does have bunks (as well as private rooms), but also a communal kitchen, a lounge, and a rooftop deck with a small pool where weekly barbecues, capoeira shows, and other events are held. Also on the premises is one of Copa's most happening

© MICHAEL SOMMERS

Stone of a Beach hostel occupies one of Copacabanas's surviving mansions.

bars, Clandestina; aside from the fact that hostel guests don't pay cover, they also get to save on taxi fare.

Ipanema   Map 5

ARPOADOR INN ⊕⊕

Rua Francisco Otaviano 177, tel. 21/2523-0060, www.arpoadorinn.com.br

Location, location, location…the Arpoador Inn is not only the most affordable beachfront hotel in Ipanema, but it is also within spitting distance of Copacabana. Actually, it looks right onto the surfer's mecca of Praia do Arpoador (without the obstruction of any oceanfront *avenidas*). The rooms themselves are functional, but not overly attractive—especially the cheaper standard ones (R$175–230 d), which are a little on the sad side. If you want a sea view, you'll have to pay a lot extra (R$350 d) for it, but the views from sea-side

room balconies of *surfistas* riding the waves and the bracing sensation of Atlantic breeze ruffling your hair are worth it.

CAESAR PARK ⊕⊕⊕

Av. Vieira Souto 460, tel. 21/2525-2525, www.caesarpark-rio.com

This tried-and-true luxury hotel is a favorite of celebrities, dignitaries, and Madonna, none of whom can resist the top-notch service, multiple amenities (including a great health club), and a coveted beachfront location between Postos 9 and 10. Captains of industry swear by its state-of-the-art business center and the executive lunch menu of

© MICHAEL SOMMERS

Arpoador Inn boasts a prime beachfront location.

acclaimed contemporary restaurant Galani, which, on Saturday, serves one of the city's most sought-after *feijoadas* Only deluxe rooms offer views of the beach (regulars range R$820–1,110 d), but once you're out on the sands you'll be duly pampered (with towels, lounge chairs, fresh fruit, and drinks) and protected (by the hotel lifeguards and security staff).

EVEREST PARK HOTEL ⑤⑤

Rua Maria Quitéria 19, tel. 21/2525-2200, www.everest.com.br

Although the name is a mystery (Ipanema is hardly Himalayan), the Everest is a very affordable, well-managed standard hotel that's popular with execs on tight travel budgets— to wit, the somewhat stodgy but large and comfy rooms (R$240–280 d) come with big desks and wireless access. Sealing the deal is the fact that guests have access to facilities at the neighboring and more luxurious (but overpriced) Everest Rio, which happens to possess

a very inviting rooftop swimming pool with stunning views.

◖ FASANO RIO ⑤⑤⑤

Av. Vieira Souto 80, tel. 21/3202-4000, www.fasano.com.br

For his 2007 Carioca debut, Rogério Fasano— who owns some of São Paulo's most celebrated high-class hotels and restaurants—procured the talents of French design guru Philippe Starck, who, with a team of Brazilian artists, sought to conjure up the spell of 1950s Rio with a contemporary twist. Soft curves and unexpected angles abound, while retro furnishings merge with glass, wood, steel, and marble, not to mention the blue Atlantic, which is prominently on display from the fabulous rooftop pool, fitness center, and spa as well as the sumptuous rooms (R$945–1,020 d)—in the deluxe apartments, you can even see the ocean while taking a shower. Both the elegant Al Mare restaurant and the clubby Londra bar have become major hipster hot spots.

HOTELS

the rooftop lounge of the Fasano Rio

© MICHAEL SOMMERS

HOTEL PRAIA IPANEMA $$$

Av. Vieira Souto 706, tel. 21/2141-4949,
www.praiaipanema.com

On Ipanema's frontier with Leblon, this luxury hotel may not be for budget travelers, but those looking for a slice of the high life will find it here without totally maxing out their credit cards. It's easy to succumb to the tastefully minimalist rooms (R$500–540 d), which are swank, glossy, and lit with flattering spotlights. All have private balconies with sea views, which get better the higher you go and culminate by the side of the glorious rooftop pool. The staff is attentive, but for hard-core pampering hit the spa.

🌙 IPANEMA BEACH HOUSE $

Rua Barão da Torre 485, tel. 21/3202-2693,
www.ipanemahouse.com

Operated by two young and super-friendly Cariocas, Carolina and Bruna, this combination hostel-guesthouse is located in a charming old art deco house with tiled verandas, a small garden, and a pool. Backpackers in Rio rarely have it so good. Aside from a massive kitchen there is also a bar, pool table, lounge, and Internet area. Dorm and double rooms (R$45 pp, R$140 d) are simple, but brightly painted walls, throw pillows, and artwork add considerable charm and *alegria*. As a result of the perks and the location, not to mention the price, traveling doctors, artists, and journalists are giving the backpacking crowd a run for their money.

IPANEMA INN $$

Rua Maria Quitéria 27, tel. 21/2523-6093,
www.ipanemainn.com.br

Among Ipanema's scant budget hotels, the unassuming Ipanema Inn is a good-value pick. It has a terrific location only half a block from the beach, yet that half-block difference makes a world of difference in terms of price. Although quarters are tight, the spotless rooms (R$170–250 d), whose spartan aspect is attenuated somewhat with wooden accents, are modern and functional and service is good. If you plan to spend most of your time on the beach, this is a convenient choice.

IPANEMA PLAZA ⬤⬤⬤
Rua Farme de Amoedo 34, tel. 21/3687-2000,
www.ipanemaplazahotel.com
Owned by the Dutch chain Golden Tulip, the Ipanema Plaza is suave with just the right level of sophistication. Its spacious rooms (R$405–550 d) are awash in neutral tones with blond wood furnishings. Really styling—and not much more expensive—are the boutique-worthy master suites on the newly inaugurated Ipanema floor, where trappings include Italian-designed furniture, fine linens, and whirlpool tubs. The rooftop pool and bar offer views of the beach and Corcovado that will mesmerize by day or night. In keeping with its location, the hotel has a notoriously gay-friendly reputation.

IPANEMA SWEET ⬤⬤
Rua Visconde de Pirajá 161, tel. 21/8204-1458,
www.ipanemasweet.com
A nice, not to mention affordable, alternative to staying in a hotel in Ipanema is to rent your very own home away from home in the neighborhood's hub. Residents of this building rent out their fully furnished and equipped one-bedroom apartments for days, weeks, and months at a time. Prices (hovering around R$200–300 d) and decorating schemes (from uninspiring to attractive) vary, but all units have large windows that let in lots of light (and noise if you're stuck on a floor just above busy Rua Visconde de Pirajá). Outdoor pools, a fitness room, and laundry facilities are available for use and are included in price of the room, but if you don't want to wash your dishes or make the bed, maid service is an extra fee.

THE MANGO TREE ⬤
Rua Prudente de Moraes 594, tel. 21/2287-9255,
www.mangotreehostel.com
One of the best of Ipanema's hostels, the Mango Tree offers clean but basic accommodations in a restored 1930s villa only a block from Ipanema's hippest patch of sand, surrounding Posto 9. The spartan aspect of the dorms (R$35–45 pp) and private rooms (R$140–160

d) is enhanced by original parquet floors, high ceilings, and large wood-shuttered windows. The hostel's small size combined with a strict no-noise-after-10-P.M. rule dissuades late-night party animals from checking in. But plenty of socializing goes on in the lovely common spaces, which include a deck hung with hammocks, a barbecue pit, and a garden where the mascot *mangueira* (mango tree) regularly sheds its succulent fruit.

SOL IPANEMA ⬤⬤⬤
Av. Vieira Souto 320, tel. 21/2525-0202,
www.solipanema.com
Since Sol Ipanema became part of the Best Western chain things have been looking up for the tall and slim-standing hotel, whose nondescript but very pleasant common spaces and comfortable apartments (R$450–550 d) are looking more trim and attractive than ever before. Indeed, considering the amenities

THE MEANING OF MOTELS

Motels in Brazil are nothing like the family-friendly variety North Americans are accustomed to. In Brazil, "motels" are where couples go for encounters of an amorous/sexual nature. Many of these are illicit, but often they provide getaways for harried middle-class couples in search of a quickie or teens or twentysomethings who get no privacy at home. Since their primary purpose is to set the stage for an hour or night of passion, motels usually feature delicious kitsch-erotic decor and accessories and staff that are extremely discreet. Depending on the location and/ or the price, motels can be sleazy and dangerous or quite posh with heart-shaped beds and whirlpools, mirrored ceilings, TVs, wet bars, and so on. Aside from being undeniably atmospheric, they are usually pretty inexpensive (rates by the hour and by the night).

and efficiency of the service, the only difficulty you're likely to encounter is deciding whether to spend your time lounging on the beach (the hotel is right across from Posto 9) or around the fabulous rooftop pool and bar. Some rooms are equipped for elderly and disabled guests.

VERMONT HOTEL $$
Rua Visconde de Pirajá 254, tel. 21/3205-5500, www.hotelvermont.com.br

In terms of low price and great location, it's hard to beat the Vermont Hotel, situated on Ipanema's bustling main shopping drag. However, you get what you pay for: Rooms (R$140–185 d) are somewhat cramped and noisy, and the decor is not what one would call uplifting (the color palette revolves around tones of butterscotch). On the positive side, a change of ownership in 2007 has resulted in some much needed upgrades.

YAYA HOTEL $$
Rua Farme de Amoedo 135, tel. 21/3813-3912, www.yaya.com.br

Yaya bills itself as a hotel, but this small bed-and-breakfast has airs of a hostel and occupies a converted house on a residential street. The leafy tranquility is deceptive: You're only a five-minute walk from Ipanema's thriving bar and restaurant scene, not to mention the beach. The eight simple rooms (R$155–180 d) are small and uncluttered. Careful decorative touches and splashes of color add nice warmth, but some guests may balk at having to share bathrooms (of which there are four). The friendly staff make efforts to maintain a relaxed, homey atmosphere where it's easy to unwind.

Leblon   Map 6

LEMON SPIRIT HOSTEL $
Rua Cupertino Durão 56, tel. 21/2294-1853, www.lemonspirit.com

It was a long time coming, but in 2008 swanky Leblon finally received its first budget accommodation option. The good news is that the opening of this clean and well-run hostel, occupying a 1950s house only half a block from the beach, means that you can stay in Leblon for under R$300 a night with air-conditioning(!)—dorms are R$40 per person, while doubles are R$140. Although furnishings are basic and quarters are cramped, the real bad news is the decor—there quite simply isn't any, an omission that's hard to fathom considering its location in a *bairro* with a rep for stylishness.

MARINA ALL-SUITES $$$
Av. Delfim Moreira 696, tel. 21/2172-1100, www.marinaallsuites.com.br

Inaugurated in 1999, Rio's pioneering boutique hotel is still one of its most stylish. The 39 suites (R$695–1,108 d), which range from sizable to massive (and vaunt kitchens, living rooms, and at least partial ocean views) are beautifully decorated; the careful choice of colors, textures, and artifacts are as personalized as the pampering you'll receive from the staff. The result is top-of-the-line comfort that is both refined and home-like, which explains the faithfulness of a classy celeb clientele (Gisele prefers the Diamante suite). Other model types can be seen hanging around the penthouse pool, taking in a film at the in-house movie theater, or downing *caipirinhas* at the enchanting Bar d'Hotel.

MARINA PALACE $$$
Rua Delfim Moreira 630, tel. 21/2172-1000, www.hotelmarina.com.br

Long before the Marina All-Suites reared its impeccably designed head next door, the early-1970s-era Marina Palace (with the same ownership) held sway over Leblon's beach and luxury hotel scene. Much less exclusive than its

© MICHAEL SOMMERS

lobby of Leblon's Ritz Plaza

sibling, this towering high-rise offers a wider range of accommodation options (R$550–700 d). While some units are more attractive than others (the best are the deluxe rooms with full-frontal beach views), a tasteful but somewhat bland neutrality permeates. Service and amenities, however, are top-notch, with a swish fitness center and a (miniscule, but inviting) rooftop pool.

RITZ PLAZA ❸❸❸

Rua Ataulfo de Paiva 1280, tel. 21/2540-4940, www.ritzhotel.com.br

This late-'80s hotel had become a poor excuse for a Ritz, but an inspired overhaul has given it a new lease on style and comfort. Instead of trying for posh, the new and improved Ritz takes minimalism to the max. From the satiny white reception area to the futuristic fitness center, spa, and rooftop pool, monochromes and gleaming surfaces abound but are softened by the extensive use of glossy hardwoods. Rooms are spacious full-fledged apartments with kitchens and balconies. Although you're not on the beach, you can see it from many of the rooms (R$390–430 d), which are an extremely good value considering the level of quality and comfort.

Gávea, Lagoa, and Jardim Botânico   Map 7

GÁVEA TROPICAL BOUTIQUE HOTEL 🟊🟊🟊

Rua Sérgio Porto 85, tel. 21/2274-6015, www.gaveatropical.com

High in the residential hills of swanky Gávea—a trip that involves steep taxi rides and security checks—this intimate boutique hotel is a world away from Rio's hustle and bustle. More exclusive than luxurious, the six airy and appealing suites (R$390–490 d) have private terraces that give you an eyeful of iconic Corcovado and Pão de Açúcar with plenty of tropical forest thrown in. Friendly service, lush grounds, a small pool and sauna, and plenty of hammocks are conducive to relaxation.

LA MAISON 🟊🟊🟊

Rua Sérgio Porto 58, tel. 21/3205-3585, www.lamaisonario.com

For a home-away-from-home experience, French-owned La Maison offers stylish digs in a sprawling villa where a quintet of apartments (R$350–500 d) are decked out according to themes such as Copacabana (black and white motifs conjure up the beach's famous boardwalk) and Recamier (shades of an early-19th-century Parisian salon). The glossy magazine–style decor is dramatic, to say the least. So are the views, which embrace Corcovado and the Lagoa. The oasis-like grounds feature a small pool, a menagerie of exotic birds, and one Bedouin-style tent for lounging. While far from the madding crowds, you'll spend a lot of time taking taxis (though Leblon beach is only a five-minute ride). If you want respite and romance, this is the place.

Barra da Tijuca and Recreio   Map 8

LA SUITE 🟊🟊🟊

Rua Jackson de Figueiroa 501, tel. 21/2484-1962, fxdussol@hotmail.com

La Suite is like something out of a glamorous movie or fashion spread, so it's not surprising to discover that James Bond (Roger Moore version) stayed next door when filming *Moonraker* and that the on-site pet bunny is leftover from a Gisele Bündchen photo shoot. The three-story clifftop mansion overlooking the sea offers seven candy-colored suites (starting at R$700 d), immaculately furnished with antiques and modern art and sporting marble bathrooms that match the room's decor (even in the purple room!). There are fabulous lounges (stocked with iPods and art tomes) and balconies galore, a designer pool (and private beach), and a dining room lit by the only black crystal Philippe Starck chandelier in Latin America. The downside of isolated bliss is dependence on rental cars, taxis, and helicopters (of course, there's a helipad) to get around.

🇨 RIO SURF N STAY 🟊

Rua Raymundo Veras 1140, tel. 21/3418-1133, www.riosurfnstay.com

Serious surfers will feel right at home at this friendly hostel operated by Katrina and Mauro, a Kiwi-Brazilian couple of well-traveled *surfistas*. Schooled in local wave lore, they offer lessons for beginners as well as surf outings, equipment rental, and even special surf packages. Although the hostel is somewhat of a jaunt from Rio proper, you're only two minutes away from one of Rio's best surfing beaches, the beautiful Praia da Macumba, and surrounded by lots of nature. Both dorm and double rooms (R$30–37 pp, R$80–100 d) offer basic beach-house atmosphere and amenities. There's a shared kitchen, and inexpensive home-cooked dinners (and *caipirinhas*) are available upon request.

SHERATON BARRA HOTEL AND SUITES ❸❸❸

Av. Lúcio Costa 3150, tel. 21/3139-8000,
www.sheraton-barra.com

The only compelling reason to stay in Barra is if you want to live it up in this five-star luxury resort, which opened in 2003. While the spacious ultra-modern rooms (R$520–580 d)—all 290 of which face Barra beach—offer plenty of comfort and amenities, the real draw is the incredible diversity of leisure activities. It's impossible to get bored in the presence of squash and tennis courts, two pools, a state-of-the-art fitness center, and a decadent spa set amidst bucolic gardens where all the potions and lotions are made by Occitane. Oh, and there is also the beach, and (if you really run out of things to do) a free shuttle to Barra Shopping, the largest mall in Latin America.

Greater Rio de Janeiro — Map 9

FAVELA RECEPTIVA ❸❸

Estrada da Canoa 610, Vila Canoas,
tel. 21/9848-6737,
www.favelareceptiva.com

Part of the burgeoning *favela* tourism trade, Favela Receptiva offers tourists a still rare chance to shack up with friendly residents of Vila Canoas and Vila da Pedra Bonita, two communities located on terrain that once belonged to the tony São Conrado golf club. Accommodations in family homes are simple but homey (and hardly cheap at R$160–180 d). Of course, the real bonus is a chance to experience life in a *favela,* with activities that include samba lessons and meals at local eateries and bars. Like many of Rio's *favelas,* these two share the bonus of magnificent views.

SHERATON RIO HOTEL AND TOWERS ❸❸❸

Av. Niemeyer 121, tel. 21/2274-1122,
www.sheraton-rio.com

Rio's most "central" luxury resort (only a 10-minute drive from Leblon) is also, in some ways, its most surreal: Guests share the exclusive (and well patrolled) beach of Praia do Vidigal with residents of the hillside *favela* that can be seen from some apartment verandas, along with more usual sea- and pool-scapes. Contrasts aside, the Sheraton is nothing to scoff at. Although the bright, airy rooms (R$760–1,050 d) are spacious and nicely furnished, you don't need to spend much time in them: A bevy of bars and restaurants will vie for your attention along with three large pools, tennis courts, a fitness center, landscaped gardens, and lots of activities for kids.

EXCURSIONS FROM RIO DE JANEIRO

The Cidade Maravilhosa may indeed be marvelous, but it is also a city, and as with any big city, there are times when the crowds and chaos begin to grate and one begins to yearn for an escape to more bucolic pastures. Like many a modern tourist, Brazil's imperial family enjoyed Rio to the hilt, but when they couldn't stand the heat (40 degrees Celsius, anyone?), they literally took to the hills. In fact, emperor Pedro II went so far as to build an ornate pink summer palace (now a fascinating museum) in the mountains. Other members of the court soon followed suit, giving rise to the imperial town of Petrópolis. Only an hour away from Rio—but usually 5–10 degrees cooler—Petrópolis continues to offer refuge to vacationers, who can take advantage of sophisticated amenities while surrounded by majestic scenery. When

nature beckons, the Serra dos Órgãos national park is close by with orchid-laced hiking trails that wind through native Atlantic forest.

Natural attractions are also in abundance along the coasts of Rio de Janeiro state. Some three hours east of the city, along the Costa do Sol, Búzios offer beautiful sandy beaches, with calm pools for snorkeling fans and big waves for surfers. It was actually a bikini-clad Brigitte Bardot who put this fishing village on the map in the 1960s. Since then, its cobblestoned streets have acquired airs of a tropical St. Tropez, and it has become as famed for its jet set–studded gourmet restaurants and pulsing nightclubs as for its pristine *praias*. Those in search of more tranquil options can head south along the Costa Verde, named for the verdant mountains that provide a striking

HIGHLIGHTS

LOOK FOR (TO FIND RECOMMENDED SIGHTS, ACTIVITIES, DINING, AND LODGING.

(**Most Stunning View of Rio:** Oscar Niemeyer's **Museu de Arte Contemporânea (MAC)** is Niterói's most popular attraction. Although the modern building is itself a sight to behold and temporary art exhibits are sometimes engaging, for many the most impressive feature is the spectacular view of Rio across the bay (page 226).

(**Finest Imperial Moment:** Gliding around the polished parquet floors of Petrópolis's **Museu Imperial** is fun enough, but when you get to ogle treasures such as Dom Pedro I's golden scepter and Dom Pedro II's diamond-and-pearl-encrusted crown, the tour of the emperors' summer palace becomes truly unforgettable (page 229).

(**Best Way to Commune with Nature:** Just outside of Petrópolis, the **Parque Nacional da Serra dos Órgãos** offers hiking trails that wander through a lush, mountainous landscape of native Atlantic forest. Numerous streams and waterfalls offer idyllic bathing opportunities (page 232).

(**Best Party Beaches:** If you like your beaches cosmopolitan, picturesque, and filled with parasols and partiers, then you'll enjoy the **beaches in Búzios.** Although each has its own characteristics, the presence of yachts, creperies, topless sunbathing, and placid coves that conjure up the Mediterranean lend a certain *je ne sais quoi* to the proceedings (page 234).

(**Best Island Paradise:** If you like your beaches primitive and unspoiled with lots of tropical foliage and no or few signs of civilization, you'll enjoy the hundred or so **beaches on Ilha Grande.** Although each of the island's beaches has its own personality – ranging from inlets you can see the stars reflected in them to rough waters that are the delight of surfers – all are captivating (page 239).

(**Best Hiking:** Jungle hikes on **Ilha Grande** offer the chance to see a wide variety of orchids and bromeliads as well as creatures, such as monkeys, parrots, and hummingbirds. Easy and challenging trails abound (page 240).

(**Best Colonial Architecture:** Recognized as one of the world's best-preserved ensembles of colonial Portuguese architecture, Paraty's ***centro histórico*** is small but terrifically charming with baroque churches, whitewashed mansions, and cobblestoned streets that are washed clean by the high tides (page 242).

(**Best Aquatic Adventure:** The vicinity of Paraty boasts over 200 idyllic beaches – some on islands, some along coastline so secluded it can only be reached by sea. Explore them by taking one of the **boat excursions** that include stops for sunning as well as snorkeling and diving in the clear waters of the Baía de Paraty (page 245).

© MICHAEL SOMMERS

You'll see plenty of heliconias on a jungle hike on Ilha Grande.

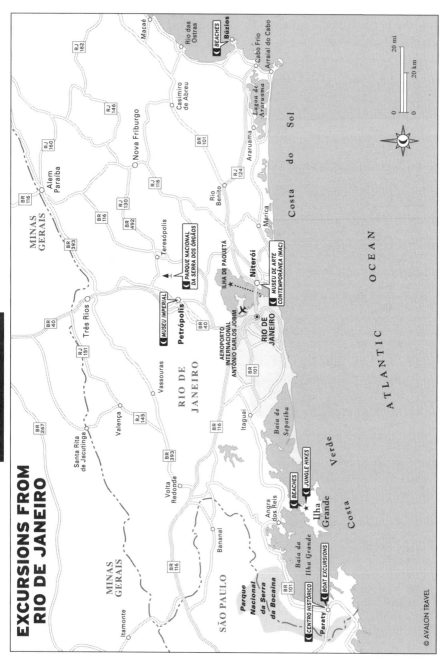

EXCURSIONS

EXCURSIONS FROM RIO DE JANEIRO

backdrop to the unspoiled beaches that stretch down to Rio's frontier with the state of São Paulo. Highlights along this coast include the island paradise of Ilha Grande, located in the bay of Angra dos Reis, and the beautifully preserved colonial town of Paraty.

PLANNING YOUR TIME

Rio de Janeiro state is extremely compact in size. Whether you're headed to the mountains or the sea, most sights are only 3–4 hours away. Some of these destinations—such as Niterói, which is just across Baía de Guanabara and easily reached via bridge or frequent ferry—warrant no more than a full day trip. For others, however, it would be a crime to rush when faced with such intense natural beauty (and such utterly relaxing environs). Only an hour's drive north from Rio, Petrópolis can also be easily visited in an entire day, but you might consider staying overnight in order to explore the surrounding mountains, particularly if you have a car and can drive to out-of-the-way little restaurants and hotels. As for Búzios (three hours from Rio), Ilha Grande, and Paraty (around four hours from Rio, although Ilha Grande can be more depending on boat schedules)—all of which are easily reached by bus or car—it's pretty much impossible to enjoy them without staying at least two or three nights, which will give you adequate time to unwind and explore.

The timing of your excursions will have an impact on the way you experience these destinations. Over long holiday weekends these places will be packed with vacationing Cariocas and Paulistas. During the summer (late December, January, and February), they will be even more packed due to the influx of tourists from further afield. If your prime motivations are to escape Rio's heat and to be exposed to a festive atmosphere with lots of animation and chances to meet new people, then this is a good time to travel. If you don't like crowds, however, you'll risk feeling lost in the crush unless you take great pains to seek out remote sanctuaries. To ensure your place in the sun, advance reservations are often necessary for transportation and accommodations (the prices of which may be 50 percent higher than normal). During the off-season, you'll be treated to peace and tranquility (and cheaper prices)—this can be especially welcome in the case of Búzios, which can get wildly touristy. Despite Rio's tropical climate, winter months of July and August can be a little cool in the mountains (this can be nice due to the abundance of fireplaces and fondue restaurants, but be prepared to dress accordingly) and along the coast as well if a cold front from down Argentine way (which can last two or three days) brings rain, wind, and temperatures of around 15° C (60° F). Indeed, if you're already in Rio, you might want to consider the weather forecast in planning your out-of-town excursion to avoid being stranded in the rain. If you're driving to any of these places, avoid rainy weather (which can turn torrential) as well as Friday and Sunday nights (or the beginning and end of long holidays), when vacationing Cariocas clog the roads and create long traffic lineups. Also avoid driving at night. Finally, keep in mind that visiting either Niterói or Petrópolis on a Monday is a bust since prime attractions such as the Museu de Arte Contemporânea and the Museu Imperial are closed.

Niterói

Only 17 kilometers (10.5 mi) across Baía de Guanabara from Centro, the well-to-do suburb-like city of Niterói makes a great day trip. Aside from its long white-sand beaches, historic fortresses, and space-age Niemeyer buildings—including the iconic *Star Trek*–worthy Museu de Arte Contemporânea (MAC)—you get to view Rio in all its dazzling beauty from the other side of the bay.

SIGHTS
☾ Museu de Arte Contemporânea (MAC)

This contemporary art museum (Mirante da Boa Viagem, tel. 21/2620-4000, www.macniteroi.com.br, Tues.–Sun. 11 A.M.–6 P.M., Sat.–Sun. 1–5 P.M., R$4, free Wed.) is, by far, the most compelling attraction in Niterói. Designed by Oscar Niemeyer and inaugurated in 1996, this fantastic UFO-shaped construction sits upon a slender cylindrical base whose diameter is only 9 meters (30 ft). Since the museum is perched upon an outcrop overlooking the Baía de Guanabara, the 360-degree views are spectacular, often rivaling the museum's hit-and-miss art exhibits. To reach the museum from Niterói's ferry terminal, take a right as you leave the terminal and walk 50 meters (164 ft) to catch the 47B minibus.

The MAC was the first construction of what will eventually constitute the Caminho Niemeyer (Niemeyer Route). Other projects include the curvaceously striking Teatro Popular (completed in mid-2007), the Catedral Metropolitana de Niterói, and the Fundação Oscar Niemeyer, which will house the architect's works and private art collection as well as an art school. When completed, Niterói will be second only to Brasília as a showcase for the vanguard architect's constructions.

Museu de Arte Contemporânea (MAC) in Niterói

Historic Forts

For a taste of history (and more spectacular views), hop the 33 bus (or take a 15-minute cab ride) to Jurujuba to admire the **Fortaleza de Santa Cruz** (Estrada General Eurico Gaspar Dutra, tel. 21/2711-0462, daily 9 A.M.–5 P.M., R$4). Erected in 1555 out of granite and whale oil, this was the first fortress to be built overlooking the Baía de Guanabara. The fortified complex shelters the early-17th-century Capela de Santa Bárbara as well as a sun clock, a prison (where political prisoners were jailed during the military dictatorship), and a firing wall still riddled with bullet holes. Also in Jurujuba, and almost as old, is the **Forte do Rio Branco** (Al. Marechal Pessoa Leal 265, tel. 21/2711-0366, Sat.–Sun. 9 A.M.–4 P.M., R$6), which still sports the cannons used to protect the entrance of the bay from French invaders in 1711. From here, a guided visit leads to two more recent forts: **Forte Imbui,** constructed in the 19th century out of stones and lime made from crushed seashells, and the 18th-century **Forte São Luís,** which was never completed. This ensemble of forts is less architecturally interesting than Fortaleza de Santa Cruz, but once again, you're treated to spectacular views of the bay and Rio as well as the open sea.

BEACHES

The beaches close to Niterói's center are urban, busy, and too polluted for swimming. Niterói's equivalent of Ipanema—sporting its own mosaic promenade with walkers and joggers as well as lots of bars and restaurants—is Icaraí. Facing the Baía de Guanabara, it offers wonderful views of Rio, and watching the sun set behind the recognizable silhouettes of Pão de Açúcar and Corcovado is quite breathtaking. Further along, Charitas is favored by watersports fans and shelters Niemeyer's Estação Hidroviária, where catamarans travel to and from Rio.

Much nicer are the Atlantic beaches easily reached from the ferry terminal by hopping any bus marked Itacoatiara. Among the surprisingly unspoiled *praias* you'll encounter are **Piratininga, Camboinhas, Itaipu,** and the most spectacular of them all, **Itacoatiara** (about 45 minutes from Niterói's center), which is framed by lushly forested hills and whose rough waves attract surfers and their hangers-on. All of these beaches are well equipped with *barracas* where you can feast on fresh fish and seafood.

RESTAURANTS

Niterói has no shortage of eating options, especially along the beaches. For fine Italian fare, the small but stylish **Torninha** (Rua Nóbrega 199, Icaraí, tel. 21/2714-2750. Sun.–Thurs. noon–midnight, Fri.–Sat. noon–1 A.M., R$30–40) is a good choice. The seafood risotto is chock-full of succulent fish, langoustines, octopus, and shrimp with the unusual addition of mascarpone and *grana padano* (popular Italian cheese). Should you want a decent lunch in the center of town, **Caneco Gelado do Mário** (Rua Visconde de Uruguai 288, Loja 5, Centro, tel. 21/2620-6787, Mon.–Fri. 9 A.M.–4 P.M., Sat. 9 A.M.–7 P.M., R$20–30) is a large but appealingly simple *boteco* that's been a favorite local gathering spot for a beer and a home-cooked seafood meal since 1969. The menu has a lot of traditional Portuguese favorites, including *bacalhau*. Finally, don't let its remote location dissuade you from seeking out **Verdejante** (Estrada de São Sebastião, Engenho do Mato Itaipu, tel. 21/3021-2677, www.webduzido.com.br/verdejante/ent.htm, Sat.–Sun. 1–4 P.M., R$35–45). In the charming century-old farm that clings to the lush hills behind Icaraí, every weekend Argentinian artists Maria Pia and Oscar Palácios apply their creativity to the culinary arts—to great effect, since many consider this to be the best vegetarian restaurant in Rio. The hot and cold dishes are sold per kilo and enjoyed in the rambling bucolic garden surrounding the house. Having eaten your fill, take advantage of the forest of swinging hammocks and indulge in a digestive siesta. Due to its cult following, reservations are recommended.

EXCURSIONS

ACCOMMODATIONS

There's really not much reason to stay overnight in Niterói, but should you be so inclined, a good option on the nicest of the beaches is **Itacoatiara Cama e Café** (Rua das Margaridas 364, Itacoatiara, tel. 21/2609-3946, www.itacoacamaecafe.com.br, R$100–180 d), a homey little bed-and-breakfast operated by a well-traveled young couple, Nelson and Roberta. The five comfortable suites, which can sleep up to four people each, sport a warm beach-house vibe with attractive handmade furniture and lots of space and light.

PRACTICALITIES
Information

The municipal tourist office, **Neltour** (tel. 0/800-282-7755, www.niteroiturismo.com.br), has several information kiosks, including one at the ferry terminal and another at the Mirador Boa Viagem, the lookout point adjacent to MAC. Both are open daily 9 A.M.–6 P.M.

Getting There

Although you can take a bus or drive across the Ponte Rio–Niterói, one of the world's longest bridges, the most scenic way to get to Niterói is by taking the ferry that leaves from the Estação das Barcas at Praça XV de Novembro. Boats operated by **Barcas S.A.** (tel. 0/800-704-4113, www.barcas-sa.com.br)—often jammed with commuters during rush hour—leave at 15-to-30-minute intervals between 7:30 A.M. and midnight and at 60-minute intervals between midnight and 6 A.M. Ferry rides cost R$2.30 and take 20 minutes. Quicker and more comfortable, catamarans, also run by **Barcas S.A.,** leave at 15-to-20-minute intervals Monday–Friday 7 A.M.–8:30 P.M. from Praça XV. In Niterói, ferries and catamarans either dock at the Estação Niterói in the center of town or at the Estação Hidroviária at Charitas (only during the week).

Petrópolis

Only an hour's drive north from Rio, the summer getaway of the Brazilian emperor and his family still provides a welcome refuge, offering—aside from imperial trappings—cool respite, fine food, and mountain scenery. Upon his first visit to this idyllic region, Dom Pedro I was so enchanted by the seductive combo of majestic landscapes and moderate temperatures that he drew up plans for a villa. However, it fell to his son Pedro II—who founded Petrópolis (named after his imperialness) in 1843—to actually build his dream house, which (in keeping with the emperor's lofty ambitions) ended up as a full-fledged royal palace. Not wanting to be out of the loop, barons, counts, and marquis came flocking to construct their own elegant mansions. The town's alpine climes also attracted numerous German immigrants, which explains the Bohemian influence present in the architecture as well as the hearty German food and pastries available at local bars and bistros. If you're seeking tranquility, you'll find more of it during the week, since weekends (particularly in the summertime) fill up with a crush of Cariocas. However, avoid Monday, when all the museums are closed and many restaurants take the day off.

Exploring Petrópolis by foot is easy, but if you're feeling lazy, or romantic, or both, you can also hire a horse-drawn carriage, available in front of the Museu Imperial. A tour that takes you to a handful of the major attractions (the driver waits while you visit) costs R$50. A carriage can hold up to six people. Having a car, while not essential, is a bonus since you can easily go zooming off to nearby towns such as Teresópolis and Nova Friburgo and take in a fuller range of natural attractions. Many appealing (and some downright luxurious) lodges are hidden in beautifully remote spots, as are many gourmet restaurants.

SIGHTS

Most of historic Petrópolis lies beyond the somewhat congested commercial center, concentrated in a bucolic cluster of streets lined with 19th-century mansions and laced with tree-shaded canals. Many of the most splendid *casas* are located on the main street of Avenida Koeler.

Casa de Petrópolis

The former home of José Tavares Guerra, nephew of the Barão de Mauá, the Casa de Petrópolis (Rua Ipiranga 716, tel. 24/2231-6197, Thurs.–Tues. 1:30–6:30 P.M., R$5)—also known as the Mansão Tavares Guerra—is a Victorian mansion whose architecture was inspired by Guerra's early years spent living and studying in England. Guided tours are offered of the sumptuous interior with its crystal chandeliers, brocade covered walls, marble fireplaces, and polished jacaranda furniture. The lovely gardens were a favorite strolling spot of Dom Pedro II.

Other Petrópolis palaces of note aren't open for visitation, but their exteriors are worth a look. These include the pretty pink **Palácio Princesa Isabel** (Av. Koeler 42), home of the imperial princess, and the grand **Palácio Rio Negro** (Av. Koeler 255), built by the Barão do Rio Negro, a rich coffee planter. After he sold it, the house became the official summer residence of Brazil's presidents. The **Casa do Barão de Mauá** (Praça da Confluência 3) was home to the Barão de Mauá—one Brazil's most famous entrepreneurs, he founded the Banco do Brasil and was the man behind the construction of the nation's first railroad (linking Rio and Petrópolis).

Casa de Santos Dumont

Brazilians have long snubbed their noses at the Wright Brothers. As far as they're concerned, the first human being to take to the skies in a plane was Alberto Santos Dumont, who in 1906 completed the first non-assisted flight in his plane baptized *14-Bis*. Flying machines aside, Santos Dumont was an avid builder and inventor, and he designed the gracious house known as Casa de Santos Dumont (Rua do Encanto 22, tel. 24/2247-3158, Tues.–Sun. 9:30 A.M.–5 P.M., R$5). Aside from his personal effects, the house displays various other inventions, among them an alcohol-heated shower and a bed that can be transformed into a desk.

Catedral de São Pedro de Alcântara

The imposing French neo-gothic Catedral de São Pedro de Alcântara (Rua São Pedro de Alcântara 60, tel. 24/2242-4300, daily 8 A.M.–6 P.M.), with its 70-meter (230-ft) tower, wasn't completed until 1939. Aside from its somber aura and lovely stained-glass windows—depicting scenes from poems written by the multitalented Dom Pedro II—its main attraction is the marble, bronze, and onyx imperial mausoleum housing the mortal remains of Dom Pedro II, his wife, Dona Teresa Cristina, and their daughter Princesa Isabel.

◖ Museu Imperial

Surrounded by beautifully landscaped gardens, the elegant neoclassical pink edifice that functioned as Dom Pedro II's summer digs now houses the Museu Imperial (Rua da Imperatriz 220, tel. 24/2237-8000, www.museuimperial .com.br, Tues.–Sun. 11 A.M.–6 P.M., R$8). After replacing your shoes with soft-soled slippers, you can glide around the gleaming parquet floors and inspect the myriad regal trappings whose highlights include Dom Pedro I's golden scepter and Dom Pedro II's fairy tale–like crown encrusted with 639 diamonds and 77 pearls. From the ceremonial throne room and the ornate dining room—where the elaborately set table makes you feel as if hungry royals could show up at any minute—to the stables and even the royal commode, the palace gives you a rare day-in-the-life glimpse of an emperor in the tropics. At night (Thurs.–Sat. 8 P.M., R$28), a sound and light show illuminates the palace facade. Even if you don't

EXCURSIONS

BRAZIL'S ENGLIGHTENED EMPEROR

In the 19th century, Brazilian politics was dominated by a singular figure: the emperor Dom Pedro II, whose reign lasted an incredible 58 years. Brazil's last and only native-born emperor, Pedro was born in Rio in 1825, the only son of seven royal siblings. His childhood was quite lonely; before he turned two his mother had passed away, and when Pedro was five his beloved father was forced to return to Portugal – at which point the thin, sickly, and jaundiced little boy became emperor. He spent the next decade preparing for the role he would assume at age 15; Pedro's tutors had him study everything from astronomy and philosophy to fencing and ballroom dancing, with only two hours a day reserved for playtime. It's little wonder that by the age of 11 he was fluent in English and French and could do fractions. He was also trained never to lose his temper or express disappointment, frustration, or even joy in public.

The Brazilian populace was delighted to have a homegrown leader after centuries of colonial rule, and throughout Pedro's adolescence his public appearances (which tormented the shy emperor) were greeted with chants demanding that the young man begin governing immediately instead of his regents. When he finally ascended to the throne in 1840, the crowds in Paço Imperial went wild with joy. A highly educated, tolerant, and progressive man, for the most part, Dom Pedro II presided over a period of relative peace and prosperity. A great believer in education, he founded many schools, universities, and prestigious academic institutes. A patron of the arts, he was also fascinated by science and new technologies. Over the course of his many world travels, he met and subsequently maintained long-standing correspondences with some of the leading minds of his day, including Nietzsche, Lewis Carroll, Jules Verne, Victor Hugo, and Louis Pasteur, whose research he funded long before the French scientist was recognized in his native land. Pedro also traveled to America, where in 1876 he met a man named Alexander Graham Bell demonstrating a new invention called the telephone. Bell left the toy-like gadget with the emperor and then disappeared so he could give him a call. Upon answering the phone, Pedro was so shocked to hear the words "To be or not to be…that is the question" that he shouted, "My God! This thing talks!" Upon his return to Brazil, he installed the nation's first-ever phone line in his Petrópolis palace. Aside from introducing the telephone to his country, the emperor spearheaded the construction of Brazil's first railway (connecting Petrópolis and Rio). An ecological activist before his time, he was also single-handedly responsible for saving the Floresta da Tijuca by ordering that native species be replanted on land that had been devastated by coffee planters.

Pedro II was quite liberal for his day. Under his reign, freedom of the press in Brazil was much greater than during most of the 20th century and he supported the emancipation of slaves (several of his small circle of close friends were black, including his manservant and closest confidant, Rafael, whom upon hearing of Pedro's impending exile in 1889, keeled over and died). However, the empire's dependence on the support of aristocratic landowners (which consequently cost it the support of the rising Republic movement) led Pedro to choose to abolish the "peculiar institution" in increments, over decades, as opposed to in one fell swoop. Regardless, the demise of slavery, which decimated the plantation-owning rural elites, combined with the disastrous Paraguay War of 1870 that turned the army against the emperor as well, paved the way for the republicans to take power in a bloodless coup. Following the declaration of the republic, the ex-emperor and his family set sail for Europe and settled in Paris. Rather unceremoniously installed in a two-star hotel, Pedro spent the last months of his life visiting museums and attending lectures at French institutes and universities. It was riding home from one such lecture in an open carriage that he caught a cold that turned into the pneumonia that killed him on December 5, 1891.

understand the Portuguese narration, the music and setting create a beguiling atmosphere.

Palácio de Cristal

The Palácio de Cristal (Rua Alfredo Pachá, tel. 24/2247-3721, Tues.–Sun. 9 A.M.–5:30 P.M., free) is a striking iron-structured glass palace that was made in France and assembled in Brazil for Princesa Isabel. The princess held fashionable balls and parties here, the most memorable of which occurred in 1888, when she gave out letters of liberation to slaves before signing the signing the Lei Aúrea that officially ended slavery in Brazil. Isabel's husband, the Conde d'Eu, used the palace as a hothouse where he cultivated orchids. In modern times, it is used as a stage for theatrical and musical events.

Palácio Quitandinha

Slightly outside of the center (more easily reached by car or taxi), the Palácio Quitandinha (Av. Joaquim Rola 2, tel. 24/2237-1012, Tues.–Sun. 9 A.M.–5 P.M., R$5) is an impressive if slightly jarring Norman-style palace that was built in the 1940s to house the largest and most glamorous hotel/casino in all of Latin America. While it attracted the likes of Marlene Dietrich, Orson Welles, and Lana Turner, its days as a luxury gaming den were short lived; in 1946 gambling was outlawed in Brazil and the casino was transformed into a posh apartment complex. Today, it functions as an events center. You can explore its surprisingly vibrant interior—the work of famed American decorator and Hollywood set designer Dorothy Draper—who irreverently colored the walls in tones of shocking pink, scarlet, and turquoise reminiscent of a Technicolor movie. Note that the lagoon out front is shaped like Brazil.

RESTAURANTS

Petrópolis has become somewhat of a gourmet destination, but many of the finest restaurants are located far from the city center—along the Estrada União-Indústria that winds from the Centro through the rural districts of Corrêas,

Araras, and Itaipava—requiring a car to get to them. In the center itself, **Rink Marowil** (Praça da Liberdade 27, tel. 24/2243-0743, daily 11 A.M.–4 P.M. and 6–9 P.M., R$15–25) has a nicely priced per-kilo self-service buffet with a wide choice of dishes as well as an à la carte menu at night. Occupying a lovely old house with vaulted ceilings, **Massas Luigi** (Praça da Liberdade 185, tel. 24/2244-4444, www.massaluigi.com.br, daily 11 A.M.–midnight, R$20–30) is a fine place to go for tasty homemade pasta and pizzas—try the canneloni with *carne seca* (sun-dried beef) in a creamy Catupiry cheese sauce. For a light meal or a lavish high tea (complete with croissants and madeleines) in imperial surroundings, the Museu Imperial's **Bistro Petit Palais** (Av. Imperatriz 220, tel. 24/2237-8000, Tues.–Wed. noon–7 P.M., Thurs. noon–8 P.M., Fri.–Sat. noon–midnight, Sun. noon–7 P.M., R$15–25) is a great option. Aside from entrées there are a variety of quiches, salads, and sandwiches available. **Empada Brasil** (Rua Dr. Nelson de Sá Earp 234, tel. 24/2237-7979, www.empadabrasil.com, Mon.–Sat. 9 A.M.–9 P.M., Sun. 9 A.M.–6 P.M.) makes some of the most tasty *empadas* around. Fillings range from heart of palm to leek with crab meat. If you want to venture out of town for an unforgettable meal in an unforgettable setting, one of the closest and most delicious options is the ◖ **Pousada da Alcobaça** (Rua Agostinho Goulão 298, tel. 24/2221-1240, www.pousadaalcobaca.com.br, daily 1:30–10 P.M., R$45–55). Located in the bucolic region of Corrêas (11 km/7 mi from the center of Petrópolis), this beautiful *pousada* occupies an early-20th-century Norman country house surrounded by fragrant herb and vegetable gardens that supply the produce for the excellent breakfasts, lunches, and teas prepared by owner and chef Laura Góes. What Góes doesn't grow or raise herself she purchases from neighbors who do. Specialties include trout in delicate sauces, roast veal and duck, and a highly reputed *feijoada* that is served on Saturdays. Reservations are a must.

EXCURSIONS

RECREATION
Parque Nacional da Serra dos Órgãos

Created in 1939, this national park owes its name to early Portuguese explorers, who thought that its strangely shaped rocky peaks bore an uncanny resemblance to a church pipe organ. Stretching between Petrópolis and Teresópolis, the park comprises 12,000 hectares of exuberant Atlantic forest with waterfalls, hiking trails, and the postcard-worthy **Dedo de Deus** (Finger of God) rising 1,692 meters (5,551 ft) above sea level. Higher, but less dramatic, is the **Pedra do Sino** (Bell Rock, 2,263 m/7,425 ft). There are plenty of other peaks to marvel at and even scale—a fact that has made the park one of Brazil's most popular climbing, trekking, and extreme-sports destinations. From the park's uppermost summits, on a clear day you can see all the way to Rio de Janeiro and the Baía de Guanabara. The park has numerous trails, ranging from easy 30-minute strolls to the very taxing but spectacular three-day, 42-kilometer (26-mi) venture from Petrópolis to Teresópolis. However, since most trails are unmarked, you should hire a guide if you're thinking of doing more than a short hike. Information about guides is available at the park's main entrance and headquarters (Av. Rotariana, tel. 21/2152-1100, www.ibama.gov.br/parnaso, Tues.–Sun. 8 A.M.–5 P.M., entrance R$3 pp, parking R$5 per vehicle), 5 kilometers (3 mi) from the center of Teresópolis on BR-116 leading to Rio. The entrance close to Petrópolis is located 16 kilometers (10 mi) from the center of town on the Estrada União-Indústria. For longer, more strenuous hikes as well as more adventurous excursions such as rappeling and canyoning you can contact **Trekking Petrópolis** (tel. 24/2235-7607, www.rioserra.com.br/trekking). May–October is the best time for trekking, while November to February are more conducive to bathing in the park's many icy streams and waterfalls.

© CHRISTIAN KNEPPER/EMBRATUR

Dedo de Deus (Finger of God) in the Parque Nacional da Serra dos Órgãos

ACCOMMODATIONS

If you choose to stay overnight in Petrópolis, you'll find a handful of basic options in the commercial center, as well as several nice hotels in the older, residential neighborhoods. An even larger number of *pousadas*—often quite posh and set in the midst of gorgeous landscapes—are located in the mountains surrounding town, but you'll need a car to reach them. Take note that from Sunday to Thursday rates can be between 20 and 50 percent lower.

Pousada 14 Bis (Rua Buenos Aires 192, tel. 24/2231-0946, www.pousada14bis.com.br, R$130–180 d), named after Santos Dumont's historic plane, is centrally situated and fetchingly rustic to boot. The lounge pays homage to the homegrown aviator-inventor with a smattering of engaging artifacts related to his life and times. Rooms are cozy and comfortable. Occupying an attractive European-style manor built in 1814, **Pousada Magister** (Rua Monsenhor Bacelar 71, tel. 24/2242-1054,

MATA ATLÂNTICA

When the first Portuguese arrived in Brazil, a dense Atlantic forest, the Mata Atlântica, blanketed the entire coastline from Rio Grande do Norte in the north to Rio Grande do Sul in the extreme south. Stretching west (by an average of 200 kilometers (124 mi) into the interior, this ancient rainforest (far older than the Amazon) measured one million square kilometers (621,000 sq mi). However, five centuries of brazilwood extraction, sugar and coffee plantations, farming, logging, urbanization, and industrialization have taken their toll. Today, only 7 percent of the Mata Atlântica remains, in fragmented but lush patches (notably in southern Bahia, Rio de Janeiro, São Paulo, and Paraná) rife with unique forms of flora and fauna unknown anywhere else in Brazil or the world. Rare mammals that inhabit the forest include the lion tamarin and woolly spider monkey (the Americas' largest primate), while among the precious flora are rare bromeliads, orchids, ferns, and remaining specimens of *pau-brasil*, the wood that lent Brazil its name. Thankfully, much of the remaining forest is now carefully preserved as part of a series of nature reserves and national parks.

www.pousadamagister.com.br, R$180–220 d) is in the midst of all of Petrópolis's historic attractions. The comfortable rooms lack much of a decorative scheme—giving undue attention to the somewhat twee floral bedspreads (rooms are named after flowers)—but all boast soaring ceilings, immense windows, and polished wood floors. A steep uphill walk from the center of town, the **Pousada Monte Imperial** (Rua José de Alencar 27, tel. 24/2237-1664, www.pousadamonteimperial.com.br, R$195–245 d) is worth the physical exertion. With friendly service and small but cozy rooms offering views of the town below, this *pousada* is a lovely rural retreat within spitting distance of Petrópolis proper. Surrounded by mansions that once belonged to barons and counts, **(Hotel Solar do Império** (Av. Koeler 376, tel. 24/2103-3000, www.solardoimperio.com.br, R$430–600 d) will make you feel quite regal. In fact, this ornate 1875 mansion provided refuge for Princesa Isabel while her own *palácio* down the street was undergoing renovation. The stately rooms are decorated with period furniture while offering all modern conveniences. There's a swimming pool and spa, and the hotel's Leopoldina restaurant is a gastronomic reference.

PRACTICALITIES
Information
Petrotur (tel. 0/800-024-1516) operates several kiosks throughout town including at the Rodoviária (daily 8 A.M.–8 P.M.) and at the Praça dos Expedicionários (next to the Museu Imperial, Mon.–Sat. 9 A.M.–6 P.M., Sun. 9 A.M.–5 P.M.). You can also log on to www.petropolis.rj.gov.br, which offers information in both Portuguese and English.

Getting There
From Rio's Rodoviária Novo Rio, **Única** (tel. 21/2263-8792) provides bus service to Petrópolis's spanking-new Rodoviária (tel. 24/2249-9858), which opened at the end of 2005, on the outskirts of town (from there grab a municipal bus or taxi to Centro). Buses leave every 15 minutes between 5:30 A.M. and midnight during the week and between 7 A.M. and 10 P.M. on weekends. The journey takes a little over an hour and costs R$14. By car, Petrópolis is only 65 kilometers (40 mi) from Rio. Take the BR-040, which offers a splendid if hairraising drive through the mountains (beware of rain and crowded weekend rush hours).

EXCURSIONS

Búzios

Búzios is the Gisele Bündchen of Brazilian beach resorts: Both naturally beautiful and sophisticatedly chic, it is internationally renowned and capable of commanding high prices. Before it became Brazil's most perennially stylish beach getaway, Armação de Búzios was a tiny fishing village perched on the tip of a peninsula 190 kilometers (118 mi) east of Rio de Janeiro. All of that changed when, in 1964, sultry French starlet Brigitte Bardot happened upon it with her Brazilian boyfriend of the moment. Aided by the international paparazzi, the bikinied "B. B." singlehandedly put the place on the map. Before long, she had moved on to other boys and other beaches, but idyllic Búzios—the name by which both the village of Armação and the entire peninsula came to be known—quickly become a favorite stop on global jet-setters' paradise party circuit.

The other beach resort that Bardot made famous in the '60s was St. Tropez, and it is interesting to note that both destinations have far more in common than this coincidence. Búzios's narrow cobblestoned streets, yacht-infested waters, cafés and bistros, and softly illuminated landscapes are decidedly Mediterranean—so much so that the endless comparisons to St. Tropez that it garners are not at all far-fetched. Moreover, as the little town has grown, both the permanent population and the tourists who flock here every summer have become increasingly international and moneyed. In the last 20 years designer boutiques, chic restaurants, and posh hotels have mushroomed, and it's often hard to recognize the little fishing village that was. Although the cachet of its Bardot days is long gone, those prepared to fork out big bucks for sophisticated lodgings, food, and nightlife will also gain a very considerable bonus: unlimited access to some of Brazil's most enchanting beaches. And if you time your visit to avoid the hustle and bustle of the summer months, not only will you find a more

pleasantly placid Búzios, but a considerably more affordable one as well.

The peninsula of Búzios has three main settlements. Closest to the mainland on the isthmus is **Manguinhos,** which is the most commercial of the trio. A road paved with hotels leads the way to the charming main village of **Armação.** Most of the chicest boutiques hotels, restaurants, and bars are here, clustered near and along the celebrated main drag of **Rua das Pedras** and its extension, the **Orla Bardot.** A 15-minute walk north along the coast from Armação will bring you to the peninsula's oldest settlement, **Ossos,** with its pretty harbor, yacht club, and sprinkling of hotels.

◖ BEACHES

Visitors to Búzios can either take or leave its cosmopolitan trappings, but no one can resist its beaches. There are close to 30 of them, ranging in size from tiny isolated coves to mile-long sweeps of sand, each flaunting its own distinctive attributes and personality. You can get to most of Búzios's beaches easily by walking, or else by taking a minivan or a taxi. By day, *táxis maritimos,* which hold up to seven people, also regularly ferry passengers from the pier and beach at Armação to the series of bay beaches extending from Tartaruga to João Fernandes. You can also arrange to be picked up again at a specific time. Be warned that at the height of summer, Búzios can get so mobbed by vacationing Cariocas that cars frequently line up to get from one beach to another.

The beaches closest to the northern part of the isthmus at Manguinhos are **Praia de Manguinhos** and **Praia Rasa,** where high winds and low waves attract windsurfers and sailboats as well as families with kids. Going towards Armação, **Praia dos Amores** and **Praia das Virgens** are unspoiled, quite deserted, and framed by lush vegetation. The limpid blue waters of **Praia da Tartaruga** are the warmest on the peninsula and ideal for snorkeling. While the beaches in Armação—**Praia do Canto** and **Praia da Armação**—are pretty to contemplate, with their shores lined with colonial-style buildings and blue waters dotted with boats, they are too polluted for swimming. Picturesque **Praia dos Ossos,** with the 18th-century Igreja de Sant'Ana gazing out over its calm seas, attracts sailors and windsurfers, but also isn't recommended for bathing.

Further north, the pristine beaches of **Azeda** and **Azedinha** are framed by exuberant foliage and famed for their unofficial topless sunbathing. The clear blue waters are good for snorkeling, as are those of neighboring **João Fernandes** and **João Fernandinho.** The beach at João Fernandes is wide and also quite trendy, with numerous beach bars (many run by Argentinians) that serve fresh lobster and seafood. João Fernandinho is smaller and less crowded, with enticing natural pools for bathing. On the easternmost tip of the peninsula are the more isolated beaches of **Praia Brava,** a wide beach whose rough waves attract surfers; **Praia Olho de Boi,** a pretty little beach favored by nudists; and **Praia do Forno,** a tranquil beach with cool but calm waters and natural pools, whose lack of crowds is ensured by its difficult access.

On the southern end of the peninsula, going towards the mainland, **Praia da Ferradura** is more built up, but its calm waters in a sheltered cove are ideal for families with young children as well as fans of sailing and windsurfing. Also pretty, and more isolated, is **Praia da Ferradurinha,** which is good for diving. Closest to the mainland, **Praia de Geribá** is a long sweeping beach that is beautiful but also quite urbanized. It's popular with surfer boys and partying twentysomethings. However, if you feel like being pampered to the hilt, with everything from giant parasols to fancy drinks, this is the place to come. Much more rustic and unspoiled are **Praia dos Tucuns, Praia José Gonçalves,** and **Praia das Caravelas.**

RESTAURANTS

It's impossible to go hungry in Búzios, particularly in Armação, which is home to dozens of sophisticated and highly reputed eateries. One of the town's top restaurants, **Satyricon** (Av. José Bento Ribeiro Dantas 478, Praia da Armação, tel. 22/2623-2691, www.satyricon .com.br, daily 5 P.M.–2 A.M., R$65–80) became so famous after it opened that it spawned a second (equally famous) restaurant in Ipanema. The Búzios original has the advantage of a wide terrace with seductive ocean views, which prove conducive to savoring the freshly caught fish and lobsters (those aquariums aren't just for decoration) prepared with Italian seasonings and flair. Rivaling Satyricon in terms of refinement and price is **Sawasdee** (Av. José Bento Ribeiro Dantas 422, Praia da Armação, tel. 22/2623-4644, www.sawasdee.com.br, Thurs.–Tues. 6 P.M.–close, R$50–65), which specializes in creative Thai-influenced cuisine. Two of the most popular dishes are stir-fried shrimp in oyster sauce with slivers of mango and cashews, and grilled marinated duck in tamarind sauce with sautéed algae.

Cappricciosa (Av. José Bento Ribeiro Dantas 500, Praia da Armação, tel. 22/2623-1595, www.capricciosa.com.br, Sun. and Tues.–Thurs. 5 P.M.–midnight, Fri.–Sat. 6 P.M.–2 A.M., R$25–35) is another successful Búzios gourmet endeavor that proved so popular that Cariocas demanded outlets in Rio as well. You will understand why when you bite into the astonishingly crisp and light pizzas with toppings that range from traditional (bacon, ham, tomato, mushroom, and egg—the restaurant's signature pie) to unlikely (goat cheese, poached pears, orange, and walnuts). **Bananaland** (Rua Manuel Turíbia de Farias 50, Praia de Armação, tel. 22/2623-2666, daily 11 A.M.–midnight, R$12–20) is a self-service per-kilo restaurant that offers one of Armação's most affordable and varied eating options. Meanwhile, if the bronze statue of Brigitte Bardot coupled with Búzios's Mediterranean flavor makes you nostalgic for France, head to **Chez Michou** (Rua das Pedras 90, Praia de Armação, tel. 22/2623-2169, www.chezmichou.com.br, daily 1 P.M.–close, R$12–20), a Búzios institution famous for its mouthwatering crepes.

Although the owner is actually Belgian, the crepes are quite sublime (you can choose from more than 40 sweet and savory fillings). At night, it becomes one of Búzios's major hot spots for tanned twentysomethings. For sweet sustenance of a more tropical variety, head to **Mil Frutas** (Av. José Bento Ribeiro Dantas 362, Praia da Armação, tel. 22/2623-6436), Rio's finest *sorveteria*, where the list of succulent flavors ranges from the most exotic Amazonian fruits to cocktail-worthy concoctions featuring sake and *cachaça*.

Serious beach bums can avoid the congestion of Armação and hop from *barraca* to *barraca* on the peninsula's many beaches. João Fernandes, Brava, Ferradura, and Geribá have lots of idyllic palm-thatched bars that serve up grilled fish and seafood at reasonable prices. At Manguinhos, you can watch the local fishermen haul in the daily catch and then join them at the **Bar dos Pescadores** (Av. José Bento Ribeiro Dantas 85, Box 7, Associação dos Pescadores de Manguinhos, Praia de Manguinhos, tel. 22/2623-7437, daily 10 A.M.–6 P.M., R$20–30). Shaded by a giant almond tree, this appealingly modest hangout serves up inexpensive fish and seafood dishes that are especially good. It's an ideal vantage point for watching the sunset.

NIGHTLIFE

Aside from its beaches, Búzios is famous for its nightlife, most of which is concentrated along Armação's Rua das Pedras and its extension, Avenida José Bento Ribeiro Dantas, also known as the Orla Bardot. Búzios's nocturnal scene sizzles all year round, but during the summer months it boils over. Things don't get going until around 11 P.M. and the partying (which entails a lot of eating, drinking, and checking people out) is so intense that most of the area's hotels serve breakfast until noon and most boutiques don't open their doors until the afternoon. The *creperia* **Chez Michou** is a perennial hot spot, as is **Pátio Havana** (Rua das Pedras 101, tel. 22/2623-2169, www.patiohavana.com.br, daily 6 P.M.–close), a sophisticated place with

various spaces including a wine cellar, whiskey club, bistro, tobacco shop, and a stage that hosts live jazz, blues, and MPB performers. **Anexo** (Av. José Bento Ribeiro Dantas 392, tel. 22/2623-6837, Wed.–Sat. 6 P.M.–close) is a popular lounge-bar-bistro with sofas gazing out towards the sea and a dance floor. Serious dance-aholics can get their fix at **Privilège** (Av. José Bento Ribeiro Dantas 550, tel. 22/2623-0288, www.privilegenet.com.br, daily 8 P.M.–close, cover R$40–70), where a trio of resident DJs serves up an eclectic mix of rhythms to a crowd of international beauties. Having worked up a sweat, you can chill out on the terrace, or at any of the five bars, one of which serves sushi.

RECREATION

For those seeking more than rest and relaxation, Búzios offers an enormous diversity of beach activities and water sports.

Diving

The limpid blue waters off the peninsula offer ideal conditions for diving. **Casamar** (Rua das Pedras 242, Armação, tel. 22/2623-2441, www.casamar.com) organizes daily excursions (including snacks and drinks) for divers of all levels (as well as lessons) to the islands of Âncora and Gravatá, where you can see bright coral and fish, sea turtles, and, if you're lucky, dolphins. A five-hour excursion costs R$150.

Sailing, Windsurfing, and Kitesurfing

The wind conditions at many of Búzios's beaches are excellent for sailing and windsurfing. **Búzios Vela Clube** (Praia de Manguinhos, tel. 22/2623-0508) offers lessons for novices as well as equipment rental for pros. Eight hours of windsurfing and sailing lessons range R$270–300 per person. Equipment rentals cost R$25 (sailboats) and R$50 (windsurf board) per hour. Praia Rasa has become a mecca for aficionados of kitesurfing. **Búzios Kitesurf School** (tel. 22/9956-0668) offers lessons and rents equipment as well. A basic course (8–10 hours) costs R$600.

Boat Excursions

Sampling Búzios's many beaches by a round-trip boat excursion is a delicious option. **Interbúzios** (Rua Manuel Turíbia de Farias 203, tel. 22/2623-6454, www.interbuzios.com .br) offers daily three-hour schooner trips, with various departure times, that stop at 12 beaches and three islands for R$40. More rapid (and reserved) are the daily catamaran excursions offered by **Tour Shop** (Av. José Bento Ribeiro Dantas 550, tel. 22/2623-4733, www.tourshop .com.br), which hit 15 beaches and four islands for R$60 and provide snorkels and masks as well as drinks. Both schooners and catamarans depart from the pier at Praia de Armação.

ACCOMMODATIONS

Where you choose to stay in Búzios depends on your personality (as well as your financial situation). If you want to be near all the action, you'll want to stay in Armação or Geribá. However, if you prize tranquility and seclusion, consider accommodations at the peninsula's other beaches. In terms of price, Búzios is definitely not a bargain, especially in high season, when reservations are a must. However, if you choose to come during the off-season (anytime other than July and December–March) or during the week, you can often take advantage of discounts of up to 30–40 percent. In general, the lower-priced options are small but homey *pousadas* in and around Armação and Ossos.

By far the best deal in Búzios is the **Búzios Central Hostel** (Av. José Bento Ribeiro Dantas 1475, Praia da Armação, tel. 22/2623-2329, www.buzioscentral.com.br, R$126–140 d). The dormitory (R$32–46 pp) and double rooms are cheery, if a little claustrophobic. However the common spaces—a TV room, lush gardens, and a small pool—more than compensate, as does the excellent location close to Rua das Pedras. Bedding and breakfast is extra. Located between Armação and Praia Geribá, **Pousada El Riconcito** (Av. Geribá 142, Praia Geribá, tel. 22/2623-1712, www.buziosonline .com.br/rinconcito, R$180–230 d) offers good value with a Mexican twist. The ensemble of coral-colored bungalows resembles a hacienda,

while the tropically hued rooms conjure up a Frida Kahlo painting. The short distance from the sea is offset by the nicely landscaped gardens. **(C Pousada Janellas do Mar** (Rua Bela Vista 8, Praia João Fernandes, tel. 22/2623-9698, www.pousadajanellasdomar.com.br, R$180–240 d) is an extremely fetching hilltop eco-*pousada* designed and operated by green Gaúcho architect Helena Oestreich. It was constructed entirely from demolition materials—including furniture, doors, and windows (the *ll* in "janellas" isn't misspelled but numerologically inspired)—and painted with artisanal organic paints. Rooms are simple but original, and feature private verandas with sea views. Just off Praia Geribá, **Pousada Casa da Praia** (Rua Papagaio 16, Praia Geribá, tel. 22/2623-6830, www.casadapraia.tur.br, R$190–300 d) is ideal for families and groups. Consisting of several attractive *casas* constructed of (light-colored) brick and surrounded by a pool and gardens, it offers double rooms as well as triples and quadruples and flats, all of which are bright and comfortable.

Casas Brancas Boutique Hotel & Spa (Alto do Humaitá 10, Praia de Armação, tel. 22/2623-1458, www.casasbrancas.com.br, R$560–950 d) has been around since 1973, long before the term "boutique hotel" had ever been uttered. Perhaps for this reason, the cluster of Andalucian-like white hilltop *casas* overlooking Praia de Armação possess none of the contrived sleekness of more contemporary design hotels. The spacious, luminous rooms are soothing refuges featuring lots of whites and natural woods that harmonize with the surroundings. Indeed, health and serenity is the hotel's forte: Yoga classes and various feel-good treatments are offered at the spa, and its delightful terrace restaurant serves up tasty "light" Brazilian-Mediterranean fare. Those in search of all-out luxury will find it in spades at **Pérola** (Av. José Bento Ribeiro Dantas 222, Praia de Armação, tel. 22/2620-8507, www .thepearl.com.br, R$600–780 d), where guests are greeted upon arrival with champagne. Lounging around the pool, you'll be treated to fresh fruit and *refrigerated* towels; when you want to hit the beach, you'll be shuttled to the Espaço Pérola: the hotel's very own sophisticated beach lounge on unspoiled Praia Rasa, where you can stretch out in suspended sofas and drowse off to a soundtrack of rising tides and DJ-spun bossa nova. The hotel's spacious minimalist accommodations come in various sizes. Mezzanine lofts are ideal for families, while couples can get cozy in rooms with their own private garden hot tubs.

PRACTICALITIES
Information
The tourist office (Praça Santos Dumont 111, tel. 22/2633-6200, daily 9 A.M.–10 P.M.) has an information booth in the center of town. A good source of online information is the bilingual website www.buziosonline.com.

Getting There
Búzios is three hours by bus from Rio. There are over a half dozen daily buses operated by **Viação 1001** (tel. 4004-5001 from Rio de Janeiro city, tel. 21/4002-5001 from Rio de Janeiro state, www.autoviacao1001.com.br, R$25–29) that depart from the Rodoviária Novo Rio and arrive at the Búzios Rodoviária (Estrada da Usina, tel. 22/2623-2050), which is only a few minutes' walk from the center of town. By car, after crossing the Rio–Niterói bridge, turn onto BR-101 leading to Rio Bonito. Close to Rio Bonito, turn onto RJ-124 before turning onto RJ-106, which leads to Búzios. The journey is close to 200 kilometers (124 mi) and should take around two hours. Another alternative is to hitch a ride in an air-conditioned minivan. Búzios-based **Malizia Tour** (tel. 22/2623-1226, www.maliziatour.com.br) offers transportation between Rio and Búzios with pickup and deposit at your hotel or the airport for R$50 per person.

Ilha Grande

Stretching south from Rio de Janeiro to the state of São Paulo is one of southern Brazil's most captivating and (for the time being) unspoiled coastlines. Costa Verde is an apt name: Not only do the clear Atlantic waters sparkle in hues of turquoise and jade, but the sugary white-sand beaches are invariably backed by verdant jungle-covered mountains.

The entire coast is beautiful, but the paradise factor kicks into high gear some two hours south of Rio at Angra dos Reis (Bay of the Kings), a magnificent bay dotted with no fewer than 365 islands and over 2,000 beaches. The largest and most enticing island of them all, Ilha Grande boasts more than 100 pristine beaches, many of which—like the stunning *praias* of **Lopes Mendes, Cachadaço, Saco do Céu, Aventureiro,** and **Parnaioca**—are considered among the most drop-dead gorgeous in all of Brazil. A 90-minute boat ride away from the mainland, Ilha Grande's 192 square kilometers (119 square mi) of Atlantic forest are entirely preserved, and no motorized vehicles are allowed on the island. There are, however, abundant walking trails, a wide range of accommodation possibilities, and, of course, beach after beach after beach.

Before becoming one of Brazilians' preferred back-to-Eden retreats from civilization (although, in recent times, foreigners have been outnumbering Cariocas and Paulistas), Ilha Grande went through phases as a pirate hangout and a leper colony. Between 1954 and 1994, it also housed two penitentiaries reserved for some of Brazil's most hardened and violent criminals (some of whom, from time to time, escaped, thus scaring the daylights out of the island's community of fishermen). Although the second prison was demolished in 1994—opening the door to tourism—the not yet overgrown ruins of the original jail still cast a slightly haunting spell.

Ferries and launches from the towns of Angra dos Reis (infamous for sheltering Brazil's most important nuclear reactors, Angra I and Angra II) and Mangaritiba all dock at the main village of **Vila do Abraão**, a picturesque and palmy beachfront settlement clustered around a gleaming white colonial church and backed by mountains. Although there's not much of anything to do here, and the clutter of boats in its small inlet make it unappealing for bathing, Vila Abraão provides the main base for exploration—on foot or by boat—of the island's natural attractions.

◖ BEACHES

You could literally spend weeks exploring all the beaches of Ilha Grande. However, if you're stranded on the island for only a few days, you should focus your worshipful attentions on the crème-de-la-crème. On the east side of the island, to the north of Vila Abraão, **Saco do Céu** is one of the island's most blissful spots. The reference to *céu* (sky or heaven) becomes apparent at night when the moon and stars are literally reflected in the bay's placid waters. The vision is so captivating that nocturnal boat excursions bring tourists to confirm the spectacle for themselves. Meanwhile, south of Vila Abraão lies another pair of idyllic beaches. An hour's walk brings you to **Praia Grande dos Palmas,** a tiny fishing village where rustic bars lie in the shade of a forest of swaying palms. Another 20 minutes away, the palms give way to mangrove at **Praia dos Mangues.** Despite the loveliness of both, most earnest beach pilgrims are loathe to linger when they know that a mere 20-minute walk will bring them to the island's most famously breathtaking beaches located on the island's southern coast: Lopes Mendes and Cachadaço. **Lopes Mendes** is considered by many to be the most stunning of the island's many beaches and one of the most beautiful in Brazil. The contrast between the fine and blindingly white firmly packed sand (walking along its 3-km/2-mi expanse is a delight) and the shimmering bands of emerald and turquoise sea is truly bewitching. If you want to savor it by yourself, head towards the left where you can relax in the shade of an almond tree; to the right is surfer central where

surfistas can rent boards and even take lessons. The immaculate state of Lopes Mendes is guaranteed by its limited access. Boats aren't allowed to dock in its inlet; instead visitors (who don't want to indulge in a 90-minute hike from Vila Abraão) must catch one of three daily boats that shuttle between town and Praia dos Mangues and then follow the trail that leads to Lopes Mendes. **Cachadaço** is also a jewel of a beach—in spite of the fact that it only measures around 15 meters (50 feet). However, the fact that it's hemmed in by boulders and forest (and invisible from the open sea) gives it a wonderful secluded aspect. It's no wonder that it was a favorite pirate refuge. If you're fond of diving, you'll appreciate climbing up the boulders and plunging into the emerald swimming pool below.

A separate trail leads from Vila Abraão to **Praia dos Dois Rios** (a two-hour walk), also on the south coast, whose name refers to the two rivers that bracket each end of the beach. Almost lost amidst the jungle are the vestiges of the Cândido Mendes prison that was destroyed in 1994. This beach is quite enchanting, as is **Praia da Paranaoica,** much further along, where the Rio Parnaioca creates a freshwater lagoon that offers a delicious alternative to saltwater bathing. On the western end of the south coast, **Praia do Aventureiro** has an unspoiled allure courtesy of its location within a nature reserve (although it can be reached on foot and by boat). During periods when the waves swell, it becomes a surfers' paradise.

RESTAURANTS

Unsurprisingly, fresh fish and seafood constitute the main culinary fare on Ilha Grande. Vila Abraão has lots of simple, rustic bar-restaurants to choose from. **Lua e Mar** (Rua da Praia 297, tel. 24/3361-5113, Tues.–Sun. 11 A.M.–11 P.M., R$20–30), with its tables and chairs spread out beneath a giant tree overlooking the beach, is reputed for serving up the island's most succulent fish and seafood *moquecas*. Located in the beachfront *pousada* of the same name, **O Pescador** (Rua da Praia, tel. 24/3361-5113, daily 5–11 P.M., R$30–40) offers tasty dishes

EXCURSIONS

with an Italian influence accompanied by a small but well-chosen wine menu.

RECREATION
Boat Excursions

The best way to discover Ilha Grande's beaches, coves, and grottoes is by boat; many sites are otherwise inaccessible due to the dense and tangled jungle surrounding them. **Sudoeste SW Turismo** (tel. 24/3361-5516, www.sudoestesw.com.br) offers day trips on schooners as well as on motorized launches (for up to 20 people) that can circle the island. Trips usually include visits to seven or eight beaches with stops for snorkeling, diving, basking in the sun, and lunch. The eight-hour trip costs R$70 per person (on a fishing schooner) and R$150 (on a private launch for small groups of up to 10). You can also target individual beaches by hiring a boat at the **Associação dos Barqueiros de Ilha Grande** (tel. 24/3361-5046). Depending on the destination and the number of people traveling, prices can range from R$25–50 per person. Those who want to concentrate specifically on Ilha Grande's spectacular underwater treasures can take advantage of the diving and snorkeling opportunities. **Elite Dive Center** (tel. 24/3361-5501, www.elitedivecenter.com.br) offers lessons, equipment rental, and excursions to the most scenic aquatic spots around the island.

◖ Jungle Hikes

Jungle enthusiasts can tap into their inner Tarzan and Jane by tackling the numerous hiking trails that weave through the spectacularly lush Atlantic forest that carpets the island. The rainforest is home to a variety of wildlife that includes monkeys, parrots, hummingbirds, and (unfortunately) many mosquitoes (for your sanity, repellent is a *must*). Most trails are well signed, but it's best to take a few precautions, such as informing your *pousada* of your route and equipping yourself with water, snacks, and sunscreen. Also carry a flashlight, since night can fall quickly. For serious treks into the interior, such as the five-hour hike across the island to **Praia da Parnaioca** or the three-hour climb up to the summit of **Bico do Papagaio** (Parrot's Beak), it's wise to hire a guide. **Sudoeste SW Turismo** (tel. 24/3361-5516, www.sudoestesw.com.br) organizes day trips (R$150 pp) as well as overnight camping and hiking excursions to these and other destinations for individuals and small groups, led by knowledgeable bilingual guides.

ACCOMMODATIONS

Most accommodations in Ilha Grande are located in or around Vila Abraão, although some more exclusive *pousadas* are hidden away in secluded natural settings. Aside from camping sites (which abound), *pousadas* tend to be fairly simple, although not always that cheap. Less expensive than many beach *pousadas* and more tranquil due to its luxuriant hillside setting, ◖ **Pousada Naturália** (Rua da Praia 149, tel. 24/3361-5198, www.pousadanaturalia.net, R$140–200 d) is an enticing option. Double suites as well as triples and quadruples are handsomely finished with lots of polished natural wood and wide terraces where you can

---

ILHA GIPÓIA

The second-largest island in Angra's bay, Ilha Gipóia is also the most visited. Not only is it just a quick 30-minute boat ride away from Angra's pier, but its waters are ideal for snorkeling and diving and its beaches are spectacular. The most popular, **Praia do Dentista,** is famous for its floating bars, where (stranded on the waves) you can feast on fresh grilled fish, lobster, and even sushi, all of which are delivered by boat. There is even a *sorveteria* that sells ice cream out of a canoe. Those in search of more privacy can take a boat to the deserted beaches of **Juruba** or **Praia do Norte.** If you want to stay on the island, check into the **Pousada Canto do Hibisco** (Praia do Vitorino, tel. 24/9991-6605, www.ilhadagipoia.com.br), which offers six attractive and secluded beach bungalows (R$330-520 d for full board) surrounded by tropical forest.

settle into a hammock and gaze out to sea. Also welcoming is the cozy **Pousada Mara e Claude** (Rua da Praia 333, tel. 24/3361-5922, ilhamara@ilhagrande.org, R$160–200 d). The friendly proprietors, Mara and Claude (a former sausage-maker from the south of France), have decorated the modest rooms with homey touches that will make you feel like a house guest. For complete Edenic isolation with lots of comfort and shades of Zen, it's hard not to succumb to the spell cast by **Sankay Pousada** (Enseada do Bananal, tel. 24/3365-4065, www.pousadasankay.com.br, closed in June), located on the northeastern shore of the island. The only way to get here is by boat (pickup and return from Angra dos Reis is included in the price). A dozen individually decorated chalets (R$270–430 d) for double, triple, or quadruple occupancy (rates include dinner) overlook a very private beach, making this enchanting *pousada* ideal for small groups and families as well as couples. A multilingual library, swimming pool, and sauna complement the natural relaxants offered by waterfalls and a crystalline sea full of brightly colored fish. Reservations are essential.

PRACTICALITIES
Information
Angra's tourist office (Largo do Lapa, tel. 24/3367-7855, daily 8 A.M.–6 P.M.) is conveniently located across the street from the Rodoviária and the pier from where boats and schooners leave. Ilha Grande's tourist office (tel. 24/3361-5508, variable hours) is located close to where the ferries dock. For information about Angra, Ilha Grande, and the surrounding area, www.angra-dos-reis.com is a useful bilingual site. In Portuguese, www.ilhagrande.com.br has lots of information as well as enticing pictures of most of the beaches. There are no vehicles on Ilha Grande, nor any bank machines—make sure you come equipped with cash (although some tonier places accept credit cards).

Getting There
Angra is 160 kilometers (100 mi) south of Rio. **Viação Costa Verde** (tel. 21/2233-3809, www.costaverdetransportes.com.br, R$28) offers hourly bus service between Rio and Angra. The journey takes 2.5–3 hours. If you're driving from Rio, simply follow the BR-101 Rio–Santos highway, but beware of traffic on weekends and holidays.

To reach Ilha Grande by ferry from Mangaratiba takes about 1.25–1.75 hours and from Angra it takes about 1–1.5 hours. **Barcas S.A.** (tel. 24/3365-6426 or 21/4003-3113 in Rio, www.barcas-sa.com.br) offers daily ferry service. Boats depart Angra at 3:30 P.M. during the week and at 1:30 P.M. on weekends, and from the nearby town of Mangatariba daily at 8 A.M. Return boats from Vila Abraão leave daily for Angra at 10:00 A.M. and for Mangatariba at 5:30 P.M. Depending on when you're traveling, the fare ranges from R$6.50 (Mon.–Fri.) to R$14 (Sat.–Sun.). If you miss the ferry, you can wait around for a motorized launch to fill up and leave from Angra's pier (this is more likely to happen quickly during the summer). Both **Escuna Resta** (tel. 24/3361-5667) and **Escuna Água Viva** (tel. 24/3361-5166) operate launch services for R$15 per person.

Paraty

Lying halfway between Rio and São Paulo, set amidst blue ocean and jagged green mountains, Paraty is one of the most charismatic colonial towns you'll ever encounter. Often referred to as a colonial jewel, it's fitting that its origins are linked to the 18th-century gold rush. In the early 1700s, the Portuguese were looking for ways to facilitate the transportation of the extravagant quantities of gold found in neighboring Minas Gerais across the ocean and into their coffers. Traders widened an ancient Guaianá Indian trail that led through the Serra do Mar mountain range and down to the sea; at the end of the route sprouted the tiny port town of Paraty.

Over the next few decades, Paraty grew into a modest yet stately town; its cobblestoned streets filled with single-story whitewashed mansions and austere but elegant churches. However, Paraty remained an isolated spot that was difficult to defend. Increased bandit raids and pirate attacks took their toll and led to the building of a new gold route that linked Minas's gold towns directly with Rio de Janeiro. As a consequence Paraty's importance declined, and over the next two centuries the town, always remote, slowly fell into oblivion. Its faded architecture remained frozen in time, preserved by its very isolation. In fact, until 1954, the only way to reach Paraty was by boat. It wasn't until 1960 that the town was connected to both Rio de Janeiro and São Paulo by the BR-101 (Rio–Santos) highway. Shortly afterward, in 1966, its historical center was declared a national monument. However, it wasn't until the 1970s that Paraty began to attract a small trickle of hippies and artists, who were drawn to its bucolic charm and rich historic legacy. Many settled here and, as a result, the town blossomed into a cosmopolitan place. Artists and entrepreneurs from around the globe transformed its 18th- and 19th-century houses into private homes and ateliers, boutiques, cafés, restaurants, and hotels, which in turn lured a steady stream of weekenders from Rio and São Paulo, as well as international tourists and, more recently, an alternative GLS (gay, lesbian, and sympathizers) crowd.

In the summer, Paraty can get quite busy, but so far it has managed to stave off the mass hysteria and upscale trendiness of other resort towns such as Búzios. During off-season, the town is languorous without being dull, and it is easier to soak up its seductive atmosphere. Urban charms aside, the surrounding region possesses numerous natural attractions. Within close proximity are dozens of gorgeously primitive beaches and deserted islands as well as the majestic Serra do Mar mountain range, riddled with hiking trails and refreshing waterfalls.

SIGHTS
◖ Centro Histórico

Paraty's compact *centro histórico* is considered by UNESCO to be one of the world's most outstanding examples of Portuguese colonial architecture. Although the streets are laid out on a grid plan, the uniformity of the bleached houses coupled with streets' multiple names can make it somewhat of a challenge to find your bearings. The crazily paved streets—constructed by slaves out of large irregular stones known as *pés-de-moleque* ("street kids' feet")—mean that vehicles can't circulate, but also makes getting around treacherous for those with disabilities or sporting high heels. During high tides, the sea actually swallows up some of the streets closest to the port, temporarily transforming them into tropical Venetian canals. While tides and rainwater can leave the streets slippery, they also keep them clean.

The best way to explore Paraty is by wandering around at random. Among the town's most handsome *sobrados* (mansions) is the **Casa de Cultura** (Rua Dona Geralda 177, tel. 24/3371-2325, Wed.–Mon. 10 A.M.–6:30 P.M., R$5). Built in 1758, it hosts cultural events and has a permanent exhibition tracing Paraty's history. Several baroque

cobblestoned street in colonial Paraty

churches are also particularly interesting. The town's oldest church, **Igreja de Santa Rita dos Pardos Libertos** (Largo de Santa Rita, tel. 24/3371-1620, Wed.–Sun. 9 A.M.– noon and 2–5 P.M.), dates from 1722. Built by freed slaves, its interior houses a small collection of religious artifacts. Constructed a few years later, **Igreja Nossa Senhora do Rosário** (Rua do Comércio, Wed.–Sun. 9 A.M.–noon and 1:30–5 P.M.) was built by and for Paraty's slave population. Despite its simplicity, it is the only church in town with gold decoration on its altars (added in the 20th century). Paraty's principal and most grandiose church, **Igreja Matriz de Nossa Senhora de Remédios** (Praça da Matriz, daily 9 A.M.–5 P.M.) was where the bourgeoisie worshipped. Outside on the Praça da Matriz is a small daily crafts market selling local handicrafts. The town's aristocrats held their services in the late-18th-century **Igreja Nossa Senhora das Dores** (Rua Fresca, daily 1–5 P.M.), with a privileged view of the sea (and access to cooling breezes).

Venturing outside the *centro histórico,* take a 15-minute walk past Praia do Pontal to reach the **Forte Defensor Perpétuo** (Tues.–Sun. 9 A.M.–noon and 2–5 P.M., R$1). Crowning the Morro da Vila Velha, this fortress was built in 1703 to prevent Paraty's gold from being hijacked by pirates. Restored in 1822, it houses a small museum with a display of local artisanal objects as well as a store selling handicrafts.

BEACHES

Paraty is rich in beaches: More than 200 can be found along the surrounding coastline and among some 65 islands. Most of the island beaches can be visited by boats leaving from Paraty's Cais de Porto. Those up and down the coastline can be reached by car or bus. Although the town has its own beaches, they aren't that attractive. The closest, **Praia do Pontal,** is a 10-minute walk from the *centro histórico.* While its beach *barraca* scene is lively, swimming isn't recommended. Cleaner and more deserted are **Praia do Forte** and **Praia do Jabaquara.**

Some of the finest and most easily accessible beaches are at **Trindade,** a fishing village and former hippie hangout 25 kilometers (16 mi) south of Paraty along the Rio–Santos highway that can easily be reached by bus. The stunningly wild beaches of **Cepilho** and **Brava** are ideal for surfing, while **Praia do Meio** and **Praia Cachadaço** (which is also good for snorkeling) are prized for their calm waters and natural swimming pools. You can get to Cachadaço by a 20-minute hike through the forest or by boat from Praia do Meio. Trindade's most far-flung beaches—**Praia do Sono** and **Praia dos Antigos**—are gloriously unspoiled. Reaching them entails a two-to-three-hour hike.

Also close by—18 kilometers (11 mi) southwest of Paraty (8 km/5 mi of which are on an unpaved road)—is **Paraty-Mirim,** with a lovely bay and invitingly calm waters—as well as beach *barracas*—that you can reach by municipal bus or by boat. From here, you can catch a boat to the beautiful beaches of **Saco do Mamanguá, Cajaíba,** and **Grande**

da Deserta. This trio of beaches are all backed by lush jungle and boast waterfalls in close proximity.

RESTAURANTS

The majority of Paraty's restaurants—as well as the most expensive—occupy charming *sobrados* in the *centro histórico*. Paraty has attained quite a gastronomic reputation, with many restaurants taking advantage of the abundance of fresh fish and seafood to create innovative fare. *Caiçara* is the name given to local specialties that draw on fish, game, fruits, and vegetables traditionally used by the Costa Verde's indigenous peoples. One of the most popular recipes is a dish called *camarão casadinha* ("married shrimp"). This aptly named treat consists of two jumbo shrimp tied together and fried after being stuffed with a filling of tiny shrimp and *farofa*. You can savor this specialty at **Hiltinho** (Rua Marechal Deodoro 233, tel. 24/3371-1725, daily 10 A.M.–midnight, R$50–60), a traditional eatery famed for its *camarões*, both "married" and in other delicious arrangements.

◖ **Banana da Terra** (Rua Dr. Samuel Costa 198, tel. 24/3371-1725, Wed.–Sun. noon–midnight, R$40–50) serves up *caiçara* fare with a touch of refinement prepared by Ana Bueno, considered one of Brazil's top chefs. True to its name, various varieties of bananas make frequent appearances on the menu—in guises both savory (banana-and-cheese-stuffed squid gratinéed with shrimp) and sweet (warm banana tart with cinnamon ice cream). The colorful interior at **Brik a Brak** (Rua Dr. Samuel Costa 267, tel. 24/3371-1445, daily noon–midnight, R$15–25), with its exposed stone walls displaying vibrant works by local artists, is as creative as the original dishes dreamed up in the kitchen. An abundance of salads, sandwiches, quiches, and appetizers make this an ideal spot for a light bite. Other appealing features are the pretty courtyard garden and live music in the evenings.

The location of **Sabor da Terra** (Av. Roberto Silveira 180, tel. 24/3371-2384, daily 11 A.M.–10 P.M., R$10–20), just outside the *centro*

histórico, may justify the low-wattage decor and equally low prices. However, this per-kilo restaurant earns high marks in terms of the variety, freshness, and tastiness of its buffet offerings, including grilled fish and *churrasco* as well as salads and seafood dishes. Another inexpensive option is **Le Castellet** (Rua Dona Geralda 44, tel. 24/3371-7461, Wed.–Mon. noon–11 P.M., R$12–20). Chef Yves Lapide has outfitted this cozy little creperie with attractive decorative touches from his native Provence, but his real forte is the delicious sweet and savory crepes, along with other French fare such as seafood bouillabaisse and tarte tatin.

Considered one of Brazil's finest restaurants, **Merlin o Mago** (Rua do Comércio 376, tel. 24/3371-2157, www.paraty.com.br/merlin, Thurs.–Tues. 7 P.M.–1 A.M., R$65–80) is owned and operated by German Hado Steinbracher, a former photojournalist and restaurant critic turned immensely creative chef. At his refined and romantic candlelit restaurant, Steinbracher turns out dishes based on French cuisine and laden with strong Asian and Brazilian influences. One of his best-loved dishes is *filé masqué,* in which a filet of *robalo* fish is "masked" in a delicate crepe and bathed in a sauce mixing oranges, saffron, almonds, and caviar.

NIGHTLIFE

Considering its size, Paraty has a vibrant and cosmopolitan nightlife and cultural scene, although most of the action takes place during the summer and on weekends.

Charming bars with live music aren't hard to find in Paraty. **Margarida Café** (Praça do Chafariz, tel. 24/3371-2441, www.margaridacafe.com.br, daily noon–midnight) is an appealingly atmospheric restaurant-bar serving innovative cuisine and pizza and featuring live music every night. **Bar do Lúcio** (Praça da Matriz 3, tel. 24/3371-8663, www.luciocruzz.com.br/bar, daily 6 p.m.–1:30 a.m.) has a mellow bohemian vibe. MPB, jazz, and bossa nova keep things cool, and there are frequent exhibits of works by local artists. **Paraty 33** (Rua da Lapa 357, tel. 24/3371-7311, www.paraty33.com.br, daily noon–close) has a low-key tavern atmosphere and lures a younger, more animated crowd intent on partying the night away.

THEATER

You don't have to understand Portuguese to be enchanted by the plays performed by the Contadores de Estórias at the **Teatro de Bonecos** (Rua Dona Geralda 327, tel. 24/3371-1575, year-round Wed., Fri., and Sat. 9 p.m., R$40). This world-renowned troupe of actors are talented manipulators of a disarmingly lifelike cast of doll-like puppets *(bonecos)* who mutely act out poignant and hilarious dramatic sketches. Leave the kids (under 14) at home, since these puppet shows are for adults only.

FESTIVALS AND EVENTS

Aside from Carnaval, Paraty comes alive in the winter months (May–Aug.) for several popular *festas.* The **Festa do Divino** takes place 40 days after Easter and lasts for two weeks. This colorful religious festival originated in the Portuguese islands of Madeira and the Açores. Religious parades and celebrations are held along with theatrical, dance, and musical performances that take place in the street. During the third weekend in August, *cachaça* lovers from far and wide descend upon the town for the **Festival da Pinga,** at which time the streets are flooded with the local liquor. Not just for bookworms, the **Festa Literária Internacional** (www.flip.org.br), which takes place for five days in August, lures more visitors to Paraty than Carnaval. Aside from readings and debates attended by the likes of Paul Auster, Salman Rushdie, Margaret Atwood, and Ian McEwan, the town comes alive with cultural and culinary happenings.

RECREATION

By sea or by land, there are lots of natural attractions to explore in the area surrounding Paraty.

◖ Boat Excursions

Various schooners offer five-hour trips around Paraty's bay with stops at islands such as Ilha Comprida (known for its diving) as well as otherwise inaccessible beaches such as Praia da Lula and Praia Vermelha. Lunch is included, as are *caipirinhas* (and sometimes rambunctious live music that might grate on those who imagined a more bucolic outing). For more information contact **Paraty Tours** (Av. Roberto Silveira 11, tel. 24/3371-1327, www.paratytours.com.br), which also organizes diving, kayaking, horseback riding, and hiking trips. A five-hour tour costs R$25–30 per person. Individuals and small groups can also charter boats at an hourly rate from the *barqueiros* at Cais de Porto. The hourly rate for a small boat that seats 7–15 people ranges R$30–50.

Trekking

At the **Associação de Guias de Turismo de Parati** (tel. 24/3371-1783), individuals and small groups can hire guides to take them up and down the forested coastline to secluded beaches, with stops for bathing in bays and waterfalls. Another enticing journey is to follow the **Caminho do Ouro,** the route along

COOKING AND OTHER PLEASURES

For an informative – and mouthwatering – introduction to Brazil's regional cuisines, treat yourself to a night of cooking and eating at the **Academia de Cozinha e Outros Prazeres** in Paraty (Rua Dona Geralda 288, tel. 24/3371-6468, R$170). The Academy of Cooking and Other Pleasures is run by Yara Costa Roberts, a professional chef whose fluent English is a result of years she spent in the United States spreading the word about Brazilian cooking. Several nights a week, Yara offers small groups of 10 a chance to learn – hands-on – how to prepare dishes from Bahia, the Amazon, the Cerrado region (in the Central-West of Brazil), and her own home state of Minas Gerais. Once the lesson is over, students get to sit down at Yara's table and dig into the delicious results of their travails.

which gold was transported over the mountains from Minas to Paraty during colonial times. The historical hike along a 2-kilometer (1.2-mi) stretch of irregular cobblestones can be done in the company of a guide from the **Centro de Informações Turísticas Caminho do Ouro** (Estrada Paraty-Cunha, tel. 24/3371-1783, Wed.–Sun. 9 a.m.–noon and 2–5 p.m., R$20). Ascending into the Serra do Mar, you are treated to breathtaking views of Paraty and the ocean.

SHOPS

Paraty is famous for its *cachaças,* produced by traditional alembics in the surrounding region. The varieties available range from "white" and aged to those suffused with honey (great for a sore throat), cinnamon, and numerous herbs, spices, and fruits. One of the most potent brands is Corisco; Paratiana and Maria Izabel are smoother and more discreet. Specialized *cachaça* boutiques—where you can sample the wares, even if you don't want to

purchase—include the **Armazém da Cachaça** (Rua do Comércio, tel. 24/3371-7519) and **Empório da Cachaça** (Rua Dr. Samuel da Costa 22, tel. 24/3371-6329).

ACCOMMODATIONS

Paraty has no shortage of enticing places to stay; the *centro histórico* has numerous *pousadas* housed in colonial mansions, ranging from cozy and affordable to refined and luxurious. In the summer and during holidays (including Carnaval, the Festival da Pinga, and the Festa Literária Internacional) finding a room can be tricky, so make sure to reserve in advance. You might have more luck outside the *centro histórico,* but the charm factor will be less. During off-season, particularly during the week, you can often negotiate rate reductions of up to 30 or 40 percent.

One of the most attractive and affordable hotels in the *centro histórico* is the **Solar do Gerânios** (Praça da Matriz, tel. 24/3371-1550, www.paraty.com.br/geranio, R$100 d). Located in a rambling *sobrado,* it has a homey atmosphere enhanced by the friendly owner and her cats. Rooms are small but spotless and cheery; the best ones have small balconies overlooking the square. **Pousada do Principe** (Av. Roberto Silveira 69, tel. 24/3371-2266, www.pousadadoprincipe.com.br, R$135–179 d) has rooms fit for a *principe* (prince) or *princesa,* but with prices that a plebeian can afford. In fact, this sprawling *pousada* is owned by Dom João de Orleans e Bragança, great-great-grandson of Brazilian emperor Dom Pedro II. It was transformed into a handsome guesthouse by architect-princess Stela Orleans de Bragança. The rooms aren't exactly regal, but they are bright and comfortable with views of a courtyard garden and swimming pool. Common spaces are slightly more palatial and the portraits of the imperial family add an intimate monarchist touch. Lacking in historic character, yet somewhat quaint, **Pousada Flor do Mar** (Rua Fresca 257, tel. 24/3371-1674, wwwpousadaflordomar.com.br, R$100–120 d) offers clean and colorfully painted rooms for a nice price. **Pousada do Ouro** (Rua da Praia 145, tel.

24/3371-2033, www.pousadadeour.com.br, R$230–390 d) is a highly attractive guesthouse with tastefully furnished colonial-style rooms located in a beautiful 18th-century *sobrado* (and a less impressive annex). Small touches—such as vases of wild orchids by the bedside—are abundant. A sauna, fitness room, and pool round out the amenities. Those in search of luxury at affordable prices will find it at ◖ **Pousada da Marquesa** (Rua Dona Geralda 99, tel. 24/3371-1261, www.pousadadamarquesa.com.br, R$300–400 d). Rooms (those in the main house are nicer) are beautifully furnished with local antiques and artwork that capture the refined yet rustic ambience of a tropical colonial home. Verandas and comfortable salons abound and the shady garden boasts a large pool where guests can sprawl on chaise longues veiled by billowy white curtains.

Upon arriving at the **Pousada de Arte Urquijo** (Rua Dona Geralda 79, tel. 24/3371-1362, www.urquijo.com.br, no children under 12, R$290–330 d), guests are invited to remove their shoes and don comfortable Japanese slippers in which they can glide around the polished wood floors of this uniquely renovated 18th-century *sobrado*. Painter-proprietor Luz Urquijo has an artist's eye for detail, reflected in the unusual furnishings, bright, bold canvases on the walls (many by Luz and her daughter), and charming touches such as incense, wafting music, plush towels, and oversized robes. One of Paraty's oldest guesthouses, **Pousada Pardieiro** (Rua do Comércio 74, tel. 24/3371-1370, www.pousadaparideriio.com.br,

no children under 15, R$310–364 d) effortlessly captures the rustic charm and simplicity of Paraty. The cluster of 18th-century houses converted into atmospheric apartments resembles a private colonial village. Rooms are impeccably furnished with antiques and face a pool and tranquil gardens whose trees are filled with monkeys. Service is attentive.

PRACTICALITIES
Information

The Centro de Informações Turísticas (Praça Macedo Sorares, tel. 24/3371-1897, daily 8 A.M.–7 P.M.), located at the entrance to the *centro histórico,* has maps, bus schedules to other beaches, and other information. Two useful bilingual websites with lots of information are www.paraty.com.br and www.paraty.tur.br.

Getting There

Paraty is 236 kilometers (147 mi) south of Rio. **Viação Costa Verde** (tel. 24/3371-1326, www.costaverdetransportes.com.br) and **Normandy** (tel. 24/3371-1277, www.normandy.com.br) offer frequent bus service between Rio's Rodoviária Novo Rio and Paraty. The journey takes around four hours and costs R$36. Paraty's Rodoviária is just a five-minute walk from the *centro histórico.* If you're driving from Rio, simply follow the BR-101 Rio–Santos highway. You can also contact **Paraty Tours** (tel. 24/3371-1327, www.paratytours.com.br), which offers transportation to and from Rio (from your hotel or the airport) for R$125 per person.

BACKGROUND

The Setting

Wedged between blue Atlantic ocean and majestic mountains carpeted in tropical rainforest, Rio's setting is truly magnificent. Although this sprawling city of six million has suffered from urban expansion and over-development, nature, in all its tropical glory, has managed to maintain a strong foothold.

GEOGRAPHY

Occupying an area of 1,182.3 square kilometers (456.5 square mi), the city of Rio de Janeiro occupies a privileged position on the western shores of Brazil's second largest bay, the Baía de Guanabara. As it grew, the city expanded along the (very narrow) alluvial plains hemmed in between the ocean and *morros* (hills) and mountain ranges covered in thick forest. Rio's topography consists of three distinct mountain ranges: Pedra Branca, whose culminating point is the 1,025-meter (3,363-ft) Pico da Pedra Branca, bisects the city from east to west; Gericinó, with its 900-meter (2,953-ft) Pico do Guandu, lies to the north; and covering the center is Tijuca, whose most prominent features are the 1,022-meter (3,353-ft) Pico da Tijuca as well as the landmark Bico do Papagaio, Pedra da Gávea, Dois Irmãos, Corcovado, and Pão de Açúcar, the latter marking the entrance to the bay.

Prevented by the mountains from expanding

© CHRISTIAN KNEPPER/EMBRATUR

inland, the city has stretched out along 197 kilometers (111 mi) of coastline, running from the Baía de Guanabara to the Atlantic Ocean and continuing west to the Baía de Sepetiba, much of which is still surrounded by native *restinga* vegetation. Originally, areas of Rio's low-altitude plains were covered by marshes and lagoons. Over the centuries, urbanization led most to be drained; the Lagoa Rodrigo de Freitas and the Lagoa Marapendi are two notable survivors.

CLIMATE

Rio's climate is officially known as tropical Atlantic. Summer (December–March), when the sun is strongest, is the hottest time of year, with lots of humidity and temperatures as high as 40°C (104°F), although along the open Atlantic trade winds cool things off slightly. Summer is also the rainy season, but brief tropical downpours merely interrupt otherwise sunny weather. Winter (June–September) also gets its share of rain, which migrates up from Argentina in the form of Antarctic cold fronts that last for several days and are accompanied by blustery winds and temperatures that plunge as low as 15°C (59°F). During the rest of the year temperatures are quite moderate, ranging 25–30°C (77–86°F).

EMERALD CITY

One of the adjectives that most often springs to mind when contemplating Rio is "lush," and indeed few cities, let alone of its size, boast so much visible and exuberant greenery. But from a green perspective Rio, true to form, is all about extremes. One one hand, the last 500 years have seen a systematic decimation of the original Mata Atlântica (native Atlantic rainforest) that once covered the region. Over the last century, in particular, population explosion coupled with rampant urbanization has taken its toll. Most recently, the encroachment of *favelas* upon forested *morros* that would appear to defy invasion recently led the state government to float the controversial idea of building one-meter-high (3.3-ft) walls—delicately referred to as "eco-limits"—whose raison

d'être would be to inhibit the spread of *favelas* into protected forest areas.

Yet Rio still vaunts an impressive amount of green space: 72 square meters (236 sq ft) per inhabitant to be perfectly precise, which is six times the amount of shrubbery recommended by the World Health Organization. Paradoxically, throughout its history, as the city grew increasingly urban, it also grew more green. Rio was the first city in Brazil to adopt a sweeping municipal landscaping project. In 1783, the inauguration of Lapa's Passeio Público marked the creation of the first public park in Brazilian territory. Twenty-five years later, recently arrived Portuguese king Dom João VI ordered the construction of the Horto Real (Royal Orchard). Here he planted fruits, vegetables, and spices culled from all over Brazil and the world, which he then hoped to introduce throughout the city. The king's pride and joy were the sky-high slender-trunked imperial palms that he imported from the Caribbean. He coveted them to such a degree that nobody in Brazil could plant them unless they received the cuttings from the king himself. As such, sporting imperial palms in your garden became the ultimate status symbol, proving you had friends in very high places. Later, the Horto Real was transformed into Rio's Jardim Botânico, which today is considered to be one of the most important (as well as lovely) botanical gardens in the world.

The royal family definitely had a green gene. João VI's grandson, Dom Pedro II, was barely into his 30s when he insisted that leading French landscaper Auguste Marie Glaziou come to Rio and perform the same botanical makeover he had given Paris. Glaziou duly got to work designing parks and planting thousands of trees along Rio's grand new avenues and streets. A pioneer, he was the first to include native vegetation (a radical landscaping concept) along with the imported species that were the decorative norm. At the same time, in an environmentally vanguard move, the Brazilian-born emperor also ordered a stop to the expansion of coffee plantations that were leading to the destruction of the native Tijuca forest. Bereft of trees, the mountain streams were drying up and threatening to leave future generations of Cariocas dehydrated. Over the next decade, over 100 native species were replanted amidst the area that eventually became forever safeguarded as the Parque Nacional da Tijuca, whose 3,200 hectares are part of the largest urban forest on the planet.

In the 20th century, Rio was fortunate to have as a native son one of the most talented and celebrated modern landscapers, Roberto Burle Marx. First and foremost a painter, Burle Marx arranged trees, plants, and flowers as if they were integral parts of a harmonious artistic composition. He placed great emphasis on forms, colors, and texture, and was committed to the use of native species—the more local and tropical, the better. Burle Marx's landscaping legacy can be appreciated throughout Rio, but his most iconic contributions were the palm-lined boardwalks of Copacabana (he was the first to systematically plant palms—imported from Bahia—as a decorative element for public spaces) and the vast Parque do Flamengo.

It is believed that if not for these prescient ecological policies of the past 300 years, temperatures would be considerably hotter than they already are; instead of *maravilhosa,* Rio would be insufferable.

Wild orchids grow on the streets of Rio.

FLORA AND FAUNA

Today, Rio's streets are lined with an estimated 800,000 trees. While some such as the *ipê,* with its bright yellow and purple blossoms, are native species, many others—contrary to popular belief—are actually adopted. *Mangueiras* (mango trees), which are so ubiquitous that there is an entire Zona Norte neighborhood, not to mention a champion samba school, named after them, are originally from India. *Amendoeiras* (almond trees), whose thick green leaves provide welcome shade along many of Ipanema's residential streets, are from Malaysia. And the aptly named flamboyants, which routinely erupt into an explosion of fiery red blossoms, hail from Madagascar.

The abundance of fauna provides shelter and sustenance for an impressively diverse array of fauna. Within its municipal boundaries, Rio is home to over 100 species of mammals, close to 500 birds, 50 amphibians, and 30 reptiles. The Floresta da Tijuca is the most densely packed habitat of these creatures. Although the jaguars and giant anteaters that Dom Pedro I used to hunt down as gifts for his mistress the Marquesa dos Santos have long ago vanished, it's not altogether impossible to happen upon traffic-shy creatures such as sloths, squirrels, armadillos, coatis, hedgehogs, *pacas,* and various types of monkeys. Much easier to encounter are jewel-colored birds such as hummingbirds, tanagers, bellbirds, and toucans. Other ecosystems also have their inhabitants. It's not unheard-of to catch sight of capybaras, the world's largest (and strangest-looking) rodents, around the shores of the Lagoa Rodrigo de Freitas and broad-snouted caymans floating along Recreio's Lagoa de Marapendi. Marine turtles are frequent guests on the isolated beaches of Guaratiba (past Praia de Grumari), and it's not uncommon for migrating whales and dolphins to be seen offshore (or even wash up onto Zona Sul beaches).

ENVIRONMENTAL ISSUES

Despite all the attention given to its natural attractions, as Brazil's second largest city and industrial center, Rio is also susceptible to many environmental threats. Pollution from industry and vehicle-exhaust fumes is a major problem, particularly as Brazil's improved economy has resulted in double-digit increases in the purchase of cars in recent years. Water pollution is another major problem. The Baía de Guanabara is continually at the mercy of heavy shipping activities as well as industrial and domestic waste that long ago destroyed the natural mangroves that acted as natural filters. The open Atlantic beaches are cleaner, but after periods of intense rain that clog up the city's ancient drainage system and flood the streets, it's not uncommon for black patches (known as *línguas negras*—black tongues) to appear due to the detritus that streams down from the hillsides. Another chronic problem in many of Rio's *favelas* is lack of adequate water and sewage treatment. There is also the constant threat of human encroachment upon natural ecosystems.

In recent years, progress has been made in addressing some environmental problems. As Brazil has increasingly become a global economic player, in order to compete in world markets manufacturers have had to adopt stringent environmental regulations, including recycling of waste and alternative forms of energy production. Rio's state and municipal governments have also begun to take small steps to integrate—instead of ignore—*favelas,* by attempting to slowly provide the basic services to which all citizens ideally are entitled. Meanwhile growing tourism, particularly ecotourism, has provided a cash incentive for government, businesses, and local populations alike to preserve the environment and look for sustainable means of development. Although many Brazilians are hardly enlightened in terms of littering, the country does boast one of the highest rates of recycling of any nation.

© MICHAEL SOMMERS

birds of paradise in the Floresta da Tijuca

History

The virgin Atlantic rainforests of Rio de Janeiro were inhabited by the Tamoio people when, on January 1, 1502, a Portuguese expedition led by navigator Gaspar de Lemos entered the picturesque bay that the Tamoio called Guanabara ("breast of the sea"). At the time, the Portuguese word *rio* referred to any body of water, be it fresh or salty. Thinking that the bay was the mouth of a river, Lemos baptized it Rio de Janeiro (River of January); despite his mistake, the name stuck. At the time, Rio must have truly resembled Eden with its unspoiled and mesmerizing combination of blue sea, dramatic rocky peaks, and lush jungle.

BRAZILWOOD

It didn't take long for the Portuguese, in search of spoils, to discover that the forests were rife with the same precious timber encountered two years earlier by their kinsman Pedro Alvarez Cabral. Hailed as the "discoverer" of Brazil, Cabral had landed on the southern coast of Bahia in April of 1500 and had claimed the territory in the name of the Portuguese king by planting a great cross on the shores of what today is Porto Seguro. When the expedition returned to Portugal, they had brought samples of a native tree known as *pau brasil*—*pau* means wood and *brasil* is said to be a derivation of *brasa,* a red-hot coal—whose rich, glossy hardwood yielded a deep crimson dye. Overnight, the latter became all the rage in Europe and weaving factories couldn't get enough of this exotic *brasil* wood, whose name soon became shortened to "Brazil."

The Portuguese seemed to have little qualms about the area surrounding the sheltered bay being inhabited. In 1503, they were already plying the Tamoio with trinkets to cut down and harvest brazilwood and had begun building primitive constructions that the perplexed Tamoio people referred to as *cariocas* ("white men's houses"). Nonetheless, over the next decades the main focus of the Portuguese

Crown was the colonization of the Brazilian Northeast, whose rolling hills had proved fertile for the large-scale cultivation of sugarcane. While the Portuguese were busy further north, the colony-hungry French moved in and allied themselves with the Tamoio, who had never been overly fond of the Portuguese. Driven by ambitions of creating a French Antarctica, in 1555 Nicolas Durand de Villegaignon erected a fortress (whose ruins still remain) on the Ilha de Serijipe and began an occupation of Rio. The Portuguese were quick to react and in 1565, after five years of battles, Estácio de Sá and his troops finally routed the French on March 1, 1565, and officially founded, on the beach in front of Pão de Açúcar, the city of São Sebastião do Rio de Janeiro.

INDIGENOUS GROUPS AND AFRICANS

It would be another two years before the French would be expelled from the Baía de Guanabara, allowing the Portuguese to take control of the entire region and of the Tamoio as well. Over the next century, Rio's original inhabitants were enslaved, rounded up and sent to live in Jesuit reservations, or (most frequently) killed in battle. Meanwhile, as a defensive measure against attacks from indigenous groups, foreign invaders, and pirates, the village of São Sebastião do Rio de Janeiro was transferred inland to safer (and, at the time, higher) ground that lay between today's Cinelândia and Praça XV.

By the 17th century, the small fortified town had become Brazil's third major settlement after the colonial capital of Salvador and the northeastern towns of Recife and Olinda. Prompted by the booming sugar-trading industry in these regions, Portuguese settlers in Rio also invested in sugarcane plantations—and in the African slaves necessary for their operation. Over the following decades, Rio became one of the biggest recipients of slaves in the Americas. As a result, by the 18th century the majority

BIRTH OF RIO'S CARNAVAL

The precursors to Rio's Carnaval were the *festas de entrudo*. Beginning in the late 1700s, these street celebrations allowed the masses to challenge the status quo – most famously by hurling flour and *limões de cheiro* ("scented lemons," which were actually wax balls filled with "cheap" perfume) in the streets and at the homes of the ruling elite. By the mid-19th century, Rio's upper classes decided they deserved some fun of their own. Inspired by the masquerade balls of Paris and Venice, they held fancy *bailes* (costume balls). In the tradition of Roman Carnavals of yore, they organized processions featuring carriages that were decorated according to allegorical themes.

Although Rio's lower classes were prohibited from joining in the parades, they watched from the sidelines (and gleefully tossed *limões de cheiro* at the bourgeoisie). Discontented at their exclusion, they also began to form lively *blocos* (groups) and *bandas* (bands) that marched in parades and danced the night away in Rio's streets. Many of these musical groups were organized by Rio's significant black population, who retained a strong African heritage. Featuring groups playing string and woodwind instruments, drummers, and costumed dancers, they were the precursors of Rio's *escolas de samba* (samba schools). Over time, the tensions that existed between Rio's upper and lower classes melted away under the shared heat given off by the increasingly popular *festas*. While the masses adopted the flamboyant costumes and floats of Rio's upper castes, the elites were lured by the multitudes' intoxicating samba rhythms and percussion instruments. The result was a completely original hybrid celebration.

By the turn of the 20th century, music was being written specifically for Carnaval. In the early decades of the 20th century, some of Rio's most talented lyricists and musicians composed tunes that took the city by storm. Carnaval sambas were recorded on vinyl, and when radio came along they were broadcast throughout Brazil. Each *escola de samba* enlisted composers to write words and melodies, which inspired the choreography of an elaborate procession. In 1932, the first Carnaval competition between *escolas de samba* was held and the tradition has remained pretty much unchanged ever since.

---

of the city's inhabitants were of African origin. Despite their servile status, they mingled somewhat freely (and intimately) with their European masters, thus creating a mixed-race society. African religious and cultural customs seeped into the fabric of daily life, and remain strongly present to this day.

THE NEW COLONIAL CAPITAL

In the early 1700s Rio got a boost when gold was discovered in the neighboring state of Minas Gerais; its port subsequently became the taxation and transportation center from which all Brazil's wealth was shipped off to Europe. As a result of its growing strategic importance, the colonial capital was transferred from Salvador to Rio in 1763. But despite its growing political and economic prominence, the city remained a muddy backwater until the early 19th century.

In 1808, Napoleon Bonaparte's army invaded Portugal. Forced into flight, Portugal's king, Dom João VI, sought refuge in Rio—along with some ten thousand nobles, ministers, and royal hangers-on. The tropics agreed so well with the king and his court that even after Napoleon's defeat at Waterloo in 1815, they were loathe to go home. Consequently, the king invented the United Kingdom of Portugal, Brazil, the Algarves, and the Guinea Coast of Africa, and proclaimed Rio de Janeiro as its capital.

SEAT OF EMPIRE

As the new seat of the Portuguese Empire, Rio thrived. The port was opened for commerce

© MICHAEL SOMMERS

colonial architecture in Rio's Centro

with European allies, primarily the English, and as a result many English merchants set up shop in the city, creating a thriving commercial center. Royal patronage favored the development of the sciences and the arts. French influence in the creation of learned institutions and academies as well as in the city's bourgeoning cultural life was very pronounced and led to the creation of a sophisticated and highly educated elite.

In 1822, when João VI was forced to return to Lisbon to settle disputes over the Portuguese throne, he left his only son, Pedro I, in charge. When he wrote to Pedro months later demanding that he too return to Europe, the rebel son not only refused, but went so far as to declare Brazil independent from Portugal on September 7, and to crown himself Brazil's first emperor. (Brazil's second emperor, Dom Pedro II—who reigned for the second half of the 19th century—also came to power after his father was reluctantly returned to Portugal to settle disputes over the throne.) Befitting its status as the nation's new imperial capital, Rio—at least its

well-to-do neighborhoods—received a much-needed overhaul. Grand palaces sprang up and the city's streets were paved and illuminated. In the 1860s, the first *bondes* (trams) were installed. Initially pulled by mules, they were soon modernized when electricity came to town in the 1880s. Even though the wealth from sugar and gold was dwindling—creating a large class of poor, unemployed slaves that migrated to the city's mushrooming slums—new fortunes were being made from the coffee plantations that now covered the surrounding hills.

While Rio was the seat of empire, as the century wore on, it also became a thriving hotbed of two growing national movements: abolitionism and republicanism. Both were debated vigorously in the city's blossoming and increasingly influential press and amongst its vanguard intellectual circles, whose ideals were nourished by European liberalism. As a consequence, in the Paço Imperial in 1888, Princesa Isabel, the daughter of Dom Pedro II, signed the Lei Áurea that finally abolished all slavery in Brazil. A year later, in the Campo de Santana, Marechal Deodoro da Fonseca declared Brazil to be a republic and became its first president.

THE FIRST REPUBLIC AND VARGAS

With the arrival of the 20th century, Rio continued to grow and expand. The center acquired a splendid belle epoque makeover with elegant squares, avenues, theaters, and palaces inspired by Baron Haussmann's Paris. Unfortunately, modernization came at the expense of Rio's colonial past. Entire blocks of monuments and buildings were razed to make way for the grand Avenida Central (today Avenida Rio Branco). Part of this massive overhaul was provoked by the terrible sanitary conditions in which Rio's poor lived—and died; before the "hygienization" of Centro, thousands had succumbed to constant outbreaks of measles, yellow fever, and bubonic plague. Of course, the result of these cleansing renovations was the expulsion of Rio's poor (mostly black) population to the surrounding hillsides.

Palácio do Catete served as the presidential palace until 1960.

In 1892, a tunnel blasted through the mountains opened up access to what would become the world-famous beach *bairro* of Copacabana. By the 1940s, aided in part by the Good Neighborly propaganda of Hollywood films such as *Flying Down to Rio* and anything starring homegrown phenomenon Carmen Miranda, Rio had garnered a reputation as a tropical Paris. Copa's curvaceous deco nightclubs, glamorous casinos, and plush hotels (the most famous being the Copacabana Palace) lured the international jet set. The *bairro* quickly became the epicenter of a modern, liberal, and hedonistic Rio that flourished in spite of the fact that during the 1930s and '40s Brazil was ruled by a dictatorship.

In 1930, political and economic crises provoked by the Great Depression had brought a new president to power: a charismatic politician from Rio Grande do Sul by the name of Getúlio Vargas. In order to effect much-needed reforms to Brazil's economic and social spheres, in 1937 the highly popular and populist Vargas instituted a dictatorship and set about creating an Estado Novo (New State) in which he nationalized and modernized oil, steel, and electricity industries and earned the eternal gratitude of the Brazilian working classes by creating Brazil's first health and social welfare system.

By 1954, when Vargas committed suicide in his bedroom at the Palácio do Catete (having been pressured to step down in 1944, he was voted back into power in 1950), Rio already had the air of the modern city it is today. With the exception of its magnificent churches, the remaining vestiges of colonial Centro had been razed and replaced by high-rise office buildings. The '50s and early '60s saw the building of the Parque do Flamengo, the blasting of more tunnels through Rio's mountains, and the creation of major freeways to ease the traffic that was already suffocating the city. Lured by Rio's vanguard arts and intellectual scene, great minds and talents from all over Brazil flocked to the city's sophisticated new *bairros* of Ipanema and Leblon. Meanwhile, lured by the promise of work, poor migrant workers from the Northeast of Brazil migrated to working-class neighborhoods of the Zona Norte and the growing slums known as *favelas,* whose houses built out of wood and cement blocks gradually covered the lush hillsides.

DICTATORSHIP AND DEMOCRACY

When the nation's capital moved to the newly constructed city of Brasília in 1960, Rio didn't miss a beat (although many politicians vehemently protested trading beach access for the flat, dusty landscapes of the Brazilian Planalto). Nor did it bat much of an eye as the nation's economic power became consolidated in São Paulo in the 1970s and '80s. Of course, during this time Brazil was in the throes of a military dictatorship that began with the overthrow of left-leaning president João Goulart in 1964 and lasted for 21 years. Even during the darkest days of dictatorship, when censorship, repression, and arrests, torture, and exile of political dissidents ran high, Rio's liberal tendencies were never stifled. In 1968, the Passeata dos Cem Mil (March of the Hundred Thousand) saw Cariocas taking to the streets en masse to protest a policeman's public shooting of an innocent student. The following year, a handful of young guerillas kidnapped the American ambassador (the U.S. government had supported the military coup) and demanded the release of 15 political prisoners—the event is the subject of the Oscar-nominated film *O Que É Isso Companheiro? (Four Days in September).* And in 1983 and 1984, Carioca students, workers, labor leaders, artists, and intellectuals joined citizens in other major cities throughout Brazil to demand that the corrupt and unpopular military leaders, who were gradually easing towards free elections, give them their *"direitos já"* ("rights, right now"). Despite crackdowns,

© MICHAEL SOMMERS

a bust of president Getúlio Vargas inside the Palácio Tiradentes

the movement accelerated the return to democracy, which arrived in January 1985 with the election of president Tancredo Neves and the declaration of a new Brazilian republic.

Since then, Rio has continued to thrive even amidst the many problems it faces. Two of the major issues facing the city these days are those that major cities throughout the developing world must grapple with: economic inequality and social exclusion, which are directly linked to the increasing rates of urban violence and the escalating drug wars that pit police against armies of traffickers. And yet through it all, despite it all, Rio continues not only to persevere but to flourish, managing to remain a truly marvelous city with an indomitable spirit and an irresistible beauty.

Government

The Federal Republic of Brazil is a democratic system of government that resembles that of the United States of America. The elected president is both the head of state and the head of the federal government. Brazil's current constitution dates from 1988. Some foreigners mistakenly think that Rio is the capital of Brazil (a privilege it enjoyed for close to 200 years). However, since 1960, the country's federal business has been taken care of within the vast salons and curving chambers of the space-age capital of Brasília, a city designed by Oscar Niemeyer and symbolically located right smack-dab in the middle of the country.

However, Rio *is* the capital of Rio de Janeiro state; the governor's seat is at the Palácio de Laranjeiras while the state assembly occupies the Palácio Tiradentes in Centro. Nearby, overlooking Cinelândia, the Palácio Pedro Ernesto houses Rio's Câmara Municipal, seat of the municipal government. Every four years, Cariocas elect 50 legislators as well as a mayor, known as the *prefeito,* to office. Head of the executive branch, the *prefeito* selects a cabinet of secretaries with ministerial-like powers over key sectors such as public safety, transportation, education, and tourism.

ORGANIZATION

Brazil's national government consists of three branches: the executive, the legislative, and the judiciary. The head of the executive branch is the President of the Republic, who is elected to office by universal suffrage. Voting for all elections in Brazil is done by an extremely high-tech computerized ballot system—error or fraud is almost impossible—while voters who can't read can choose their candidate of choice from among a group of head shots. (To this day, Brazilians are amazed by the infamous system of chads in the United States.) Voting is mandatory for all literate citizens between 18 and 70 years of age. Brazilians who don't vote must present an official justification or pay a (small) fine.

The president chooses a running mate who will be the vice president. Should anything happen to the president, the vice president assumes his or her position for the rest of the four-year term. Once elected to office, the president may appoint his/her own ministers, which he or she can also dismiss at any time. According to the Brazilian constitution, if there is just cause Congress can vote to have the president removed from office through impeachment.

Brazil's legislative power is concentrated in the hands of the National Congress (Congresso), which consists of two houses: The Chamber of Deputies (Câmara dos Deputados) is the lower house and the Senate (Senado) is the upper house. The Chamber of Deputies seats 513 deputies, representing each of the Brazilian states in numbers proportional to their population. Deputies are elected by popular vote for terms of four years. The Senate seats 81 senators—three for each of Brazil's 26 states and three for the Federal District of Brasília. Senators are elected for terms of eight years. Both deputies and senators can run for reelection as many times as they want.

The judiciary is headed by the Federal Supreme Court, which is the highest court in the land. Its main headquarters are in Brasília, but the court's jurisdiction extends throughout the country. Its 11 judges are appointed for life by the president upon approval from a Senate majority; judges in state courts are also appointed for life.

POLITICAL PARTIES

Brazil's party system is fairly chaotic to an outsider. Parties are created and disappear all the time, and candidates easily and opportunistically switch from one to another without any compunction (reforms passed in 2007 have tried to limit this habit). Most often this party switching occurs a few months prior to an election. Both the party names and their more commonly used acronyms are confusing to keep track of, even for Brazilians, and many have no ideological affiliation whatsoever. There are, however, a few main parties whose delegates usually compete for major positions. Presently, after being the country's main opposition party, the traditionally left-wing Partido dos Trabalhadores (Workers' Party), or PT, wields power in the federal government. Other major parties that hover around the center and center-right include the Partido do Movimento Democrático Brasileiro (Brazilian Democractic Movement Party), or PMDB; the Partido da Social Democrácia Brasileira (Brazilian Social Democracy Party), or PSDB; and the Democratas (Democrats) or DEM, which recently changed its name from the Partido Frente Liberal (Liberal Front Party), or PFL. Currently, governing is all about making strategic alliances with members of other parties in order to pass (or defeat) legislation. In general, reaching consensus involves enormous amounts of time and energy (not to mention bribes—in the form of favors or money).

Ironically, in spite of the many scandals and cover-ups, in some ways the operation of the Brazilian Congress is extremely transparent. In theory, any Brazilian (or visiting tourist) can sit in on the daily sessions in the Chamber of Deputies or Senate (you may be amazed at the low attendance, particularly on a Friday). Moreover, Senate debates are broadcast live on a television station known as TV Senado. During major government scandals, this can make for quite dramatic viewing.

JUDICIAL AND PENAL SYSTEMS

Brazilian law is derived from Portuguese civil law. The principal legal document is the National Constitution of 1988, which divides power between federal and state judicial branches. State-level courts preside over all civil and criminal cases (with appeals taken to regional federal courts). The Supreme Court (Supremo Tribunal Federal) makes final, binding decisions on legal matters and is also in charge of interpreting the constitution. Justice, when it is delivered in Brazil, is famously slow. Loopholes are seemingly endless and lawsuits can be delayed by numerous appeals. Often a final ruling can be delayed for years, if not decades.

Justice is definitely not blind in Brazil. The rich, white, and powerful often literally get away with murder, while the poorer you are and the darker your skin tone, the greater your chances of being beaten up, tossed in a crowded cell, and locked away. Crime is a big problem throughout all of Brazil, but the shamelessness with which white-collar crime is committed is staggering. Through fraud, embezzlement, kickbacks, and bribes, billions of dollars in public funds are routinely siphoned away from the people who need it most. Then, as the have-nots resort to ever more violent holdups, kidnappings, and break-ins, Brazil's elite largely wall themselves up in closed condominium complexes with electric fences, cameras, and bodyguards. It's a very vicious, not to mention tragic, cycle, and one of Brazil's greatest challenges. In recent years, some small instances of justice have shaken the complete impunity with which the rich and powerful operate. However, in most cases change is difficult because it's within the interest of many of those in the upper echelons for the status quo to remain the same.

Similarly, by law, penal conditions for criminals who have committed the same crime vary depending on the perp's degree of education. Those without a high school diploma get thrown in overcrowded cells that are reputed for their squalor and violence, while a doctoral degree earns you the privilege of a cleaner, solitary cell or at least one that is shared with two or three other diploma-bearing criminals.

Economy

In terms of natural resources, Brazil has always been incredibly wealthy. Until the 20th century, the economy was based on a series of cycles that exploited a single export commodity: brazilwood in the 16th century; sugarcane in the 16th and 17th centuries; gold, silver, and gemstones in the 18th century; and finally coffee and rubber in the 19th century. Apart from these boom-and-bust cycles, agriculture and cattle-raising were constant activities, but both were mainly limited to local consumption. Industrialization began in the early 20th century, but didn't really kick in until the 1950s, which coincided with the beginnings of Brazil's major automobile, petrochemical, and steel industries.

After a difficult sink-or-swim period that accompanied the opening up of the economy to the world in the mid-1980s, Brazil has enjoyed healthy growth rates of 4 to 5 percent a year. The country now ranks as the world's 10th-largest economy in terms of GDP (according to IMF and World Bank calculations), just behind Canada. Brazil's economy is larger than that of all other South American countries combined and increasingly competitive, high-quality, and innovative Brazilian goods are steadily making their presence felt in international markets. Brazilian industry, which is extremely diversified and well developed, currently accounts for around one-third of the country's GDP. Among Brazil's leading manufacturing industries are the automobile, aircraft, steel, mining, petrochemical, computer, and durable consumer goods sectors. Additionally, the country has a diverse and sophisticated service industry. Financial services are particularly well developed.

As a result of its newfound clout, Brazil is able to go head-to-head with the United States and Europe during global trade talks. Moreover, Brazil has (so far) better survived the recent recessionary tendencies affecting the United States, Europe, and developing countries, which have been rocked by the global economic crisis that began in late

BRAZIL'S ECONOMY IS IMPROVING

Although it seemed to take forever, at long last there is proof that Brazil's riches – both natural and man-made – are finally beginning to be shared by all Brazilians.

Under current president Luiz Inácio "Lula" da Silva's sound economic stewardship, public debt has plummeted, interest rates have decreased, and credit and loans have become much more accessible for working Brazilians. Between 2002 and 2008, the creation of new jobs, higher salaries, and more disposable income for all Brazilians is finally diminishing the gaping abyss that only recently earned Brazil the dubious distinction of having one of the world's biggest discrepancies between rich and poor. Between 2001 and 2006 (according to figures released by Rio's prestigious Getúlio Vargas Foundation), while the top 10 percent of Brazilian wage earners saw their income rise by 7 percent, the earnings of the bottom 10 percent soared by 58 percent. Between 2003 and 2007, minimum wage increased by 36 percent. Moreover, more than 40 million poor Brazilians have benefited from increased social spending via programs such as Bolsa Familia, which provides subsidies to families who incentivize their children to attend school. As a result, a record number of poor and working-class Brazilians are now creeping up into the swelling middle classes.

Despite the ongoing economic crisis in the United States since 2008, which has led to some layoffs and increased unemployment in Brazil, the new socio-economic shift in Brazil has not changed too drastically.

2008. Rich in natural resources and capable of supplying most of its own needs in terms of food, primary resources, energy, and manufactured products, Brazil is extremely self-sufficient. Well prepared to withstand rising imported fuel and food costs that are proving devastating for other countries, the country also boasts a domestic market of 185 million people that have more disposable income to burn than ever before.

As for Rio, as the political, cultural, and commercial capital of Brazil until the middle of the 20th century, the city has always played a major role in the Brazilian economy. To this day, it continues to wield great economic clout. The second-largest industrial center in the country after São Paulo, its most important activities include the production of oil and petroleum products (Rio supplies 80 percent of the nation's oil and gas needs), as well as chemicals, steel and metal products, pharmaceuticals, naval crafts, food, textiles, clothing, and furniture. The two biggest and most lucrative Brazilian companies—Petrobras and Vale—have their headquarters in Rio, as do all the nation's telecommunication companies and Globo, the largest media empire in Latin America. However, more important than manufacturing is Rio's service industry; important sectors include banking and the second-largest stock market in Brazil (the Bolsa de Valores do Rio de Janeiro), along with media, entertainment, and tourism.

ENERGY

Brazil used to import 70 percent of its energy from overseas. However, since 2006 the nation has been capable of meeting all its own energy needs. Brazil is the world's leading supplier of hydroelectricity. To date, more than 90 percent of the country's electricity needs are supplied by enormous hydroelectric dams such as Itaipu in Paraná and Tucuruí in Pará. Brazil has also flirted with nuclear energy with the building of Angra I, Angra II, and the Angra III reactor

(due to be inaugurated in 2014), all of which are located in an otherwise idyllic spot of coastline in the state of Rio de Janeiro.

In late 2007, as rising oil prices sent the planet into panic, Brazil became the envy of many countries when national oil giant Petrobras discovered a vast deepwater reserve off the coast of Rio de Janeiro. The so-called Tupi reserve is estimated to hold up to eight billion barrels of oil and could lead to Brazil becoming the newest member of OPEC. However, it's not as if Brazil is beholden to the increasingly coveted fossil fuel. Following the first oil crisis of 1974, the government's visionary solution was to begin converting sugarcane into ethanol as a cheaper and non-polluting fuel for all vehicles. Today, Brazil is the world's number-one producer of sugarcane alcohol; all Brazilian vehicles are flex-fuel models that run on gas, alcohol, and a mixture of the two.

TOURISM

Since 2000, tourism throughout Brazil has developed enormously, with a major spike in tourists from North America and especially Europe. The increase is largely due to the proliferation of domestic charters and air routes as well as a more sophisticated tourism infrastructure, even in unspoiled destinations far off the beaten path. In 2007, Brazil was the fourth-largest tourist destination in the Americas and the second-largest in Latin America, after Mexico. However, much greater than the growth of international tourism has been the rise in the number of Brazilians themselves who are increasingly able to travel. Due to the country's endless natural attractions, Brazil's major tourism niche is ecotourism, which has the advantage of providing sustainable development. At the moment, the still-growing sector accounts for 4 percent of GDP and, directly and indirectly, accounts for 7 percent of all jobs. Ranked in terms of number of tourists, Rio de Janeiro is Brazil's most-visited city—40 percent of all foreign tourists who come to Brazil are Rio-bound.

People and Culture

DEMOGRAPHICS

According to statistics released in May 2008 by the Brazilian statistics bureau, IBGE, Brazil has a population of more than 186 million people, making it the sixth most-populous country in the world. Until the mid-20th century, Brazil was a largely rural place. However, today more than 70 percent of the population lives in major cities, most of which line the coast. The most populous Brazilian city is São Paulo with 11 million people (according to 2007 IBGE figures), followed by Rio de Janeiro with 6.1 million.

Life expectancy among Brazilians has improved greatly in recent decades. In 2008, the average lifespan of Brazilian women was 76.4 years, while for men it was 68.8 years. Meanwhile, the days of big families are a thing of the past: The average Brazilian woman today bears 1.86 children. Although the official literacy rate of Brazilians over the age of 15 is 89 percent, the concept of "literacy" should be taken with a grain of salt. Included among so-called "literate" Brazilians are many people who can do little more than write numbers and their names, and recognize a few dozen simple words.

ETHNICITY AND RACE

Five centuries of commingling has resulted in a population that is extremely diverse, which explains the endless array of physical types as well as an impressive openness towards biological, cultural, and religious differences. The vast majority of Brazilians are descended from a mixture of indigenous peoples, Africans, and Europeans.

Indigenous Groups

When the Portuguese first arrived in Brazil in 1500, an estimated five million indigenous people, most belonging to the Tupi and Guaraní groups, were inhabiting this vast territory. Today, only about 700,000 (representing 0.4 percent of the total population) of their

descendents remain. According to the results of a recent mitochondrial DNA survey, an estimated 60 million Brazilians can lay claim to at least one Indian ancestor. Brazilians who are descended from both indigenous groups and Europeans are known as *caboclos.*

Africans

Between the early days of colonial Brazil and the abolition of slavery in 1888, it's estimated that more than four million slaves were brought to Brazil from Africa. The majority of them were Bantu peoples from Portugal's African colonies such as Mozambique and Angola, as well as Yoruba from the western-coast nations of Benin and Nigeria. Due to the legacy of slavery as well as migration of poor blacks from the Northeast, Rio has one of the largest black communities in the country.

Overall, only 7 percent of Brazilians (roughly 13 million) consider themselves to be "black." However, according to the 2006 IBGE census, more than 92 million Brazilians can claim to possess some African ancestry. They are often referred to by the traditional appellate *pardo,* meaning colored (*pardo* is actually a beige-caramel color). Due to a tradition of miscegenation (the Portuguese had no compunction about having extramarital relationships with their slaves), most Brazilians are of mixed race, or *mulato* (Brazilians descended from a mixture of Africans and indigenous groups are known as *cafuzos*). However, the varying shades of skin color and the way in which they are perceived and projected among different social milieus is extremely complex and nuanced. The official designation these days is *Afro-Descendente* or *Afro-Brasileiro.* Applicable to anyone with African origins, these terms are based more on cultural identity than skin color. In terms of skin color, Brazilians have come up with hundreds of (often extremely creative) terms to designate themselves (and confound racial categorization). These range from *preto retinto* (repainted black) and *jaboticaba* (a dark purple

RACISM IN BRAZIL

In the early 20th century noted Brazilian anthropologist Gilberto Freyre gave rise to the official myth of Brazil as a paragon of racial harmony whose spontaneous mixture of indigenous groups, Africans, and Europeans stood as a utopic counterpoint to the polarized conflicts that characterized race relations in the United States. To this day, many Brazilians still believe in the myth. Foreigners are inevitably impressed by the easy mingling of people, regardless of color, and of the fact that so many "Afro" elements – samba, capoeira, Carnaval – have become icons of Brazilian-ness, espoused by all Brazilians.

However, dig deep enough and the myth begins to crack. Precisely what makes racism in Brazil so insidious is that, unlike racism in the United States, it isn't in your face – it's thus easier to deny it exists and maintain a status quo in which the whiter you are the more money, education, and opportunities you have. As you travel around Brazil, take note of the politicians, the business leaders, the models and TV stars, the domestic tourists, the kids in private-school uniforms, the people walking around in swanky neighborhoods, eating in upscale restaurants, and staying in hotels and flying on airplanes with you: The vast majority are white. Few tourists will come into contact with Brazilians who live in *favelas*. However, you will notice that the majority of those living on the streets, performing menial jobs or selling wares on the sidewalk, lining up for buses,

or working as doormen, cleaning women, or nannies are inevitably black. If you're a white male and you walk around in Brazil with a black Brazilian female friend, the immediate conclusion is that you're a john and your friend is a prostitute (or else that she's a gold digger and you're rich-husband material). A dark-skinned mother with a lighter-skinned child will often be assumed to be the child's nanny (and be treated as such).

The result of this type of racism isn't hate crimes or white-supremacy groups. But the fact is that white Brazilians overwhelmingly dominate government, business, and the media. (Two notable exceptions are soccer and music, where black Brazilians are revered.) Fortunately, change has finally begun to take root. In 2002, the Brazilian government made it mandatory to teach African and Afro-Brazilian history and culture as part of the universal school curriculum. Federal and state universities recently began implementing quotas in an attempt to redress the fact that only 3 percent of black Brazilians have university degrees. As president, Lula made two notable appointments of Afro-Brazilians. Before stepping down to resume his music career in 2008, Gilberto Gil, the Bahian composer and musician (and former city councilman in Salvador) spent six years as a highly effective Minister of Culture. Lula also nominated another Afro-Brazilian, Edson Santos, to head the newly created Ministry of Racial Equality.

berry-like fruit), both of which refer to darker skin tones, to *jegue quando foge* (donkey when it runs away) and *formiga* (ant), on a somewhat lighter scale. Many of these euphemistic designations have their origin in a subtle yet deeply rooted racism that is still very much alive in Brazil. As a result, darker-skinned Brazilians sometimes try (often subconsciously) to *embranquecer* (to become more white) by choosing a non-black identity for themselves. This phenomenon explains why only 7 percent of Afro-Brazilians refer to themselves as *negro*. Instead, many mixed-race Brazilians refer to

themselves as *mulatos,* or even *mulatos claros* (light-skinned *mulatos*).

Europeans

The first Europeans to set foot in Brazil were the Portuguese, who claimed the territory as their own. The next five centuries saw various waves of immigration; as a result the vast majority of Brazilians can lay claim to some Portuguese ancestry. It wasn't until the mid- to late 19th century that other Europeans began to arrive en masse in Brazil. When slave trafficking was outlawed in 1850, Rio began to receive an influx of European immigrants who arrived to work the coffee plantations and to open businesses in the rapidly expanding city.

RELIGION

Officially, Brazil is the world's largest Catholic country in terms of population. In reality, however, Brazil's great talent for syncretism and diversity has resulted in a country with an amazing number of religions, sects, and communities.

Catholicism

According to the latest IBGE census, around 75 percent of Brazilians identify themselves as Roman Catholic. Despite the strong presence of churches, and endless references to Deus (God), various incarnations of Nossa Senhora (the Virgin), and prayers, promises, and processions offered up to saints, the majority of Brazilians aren't practicing Catholics. While Catholicism is a strong presence in the collective culture, the Catholic church in Brazil has a much less rigid reputation than in other Latin American countries.

Protestantism

Only around 16 percent of Brazilians adhere to some form of Protestantism. However, since the 1990s, an endless number of evangelical and Pentecostal churches have been sprouting like wildfire, particularly in poor rural and suburban neighborhoods where churches such as the immensely popular Igreja Assembleia de Deus (Assembly of God Church) and Igreja Universal do Reino de Deus (Universal Church of the Kingdom of God), and numerous tangents thereof, have taken root, offering succor and solutions to Brazil's poor (often for a price).

Afro-Brazilian Religions

African slaves who were brought to Brazil arrived bereft of everything except their faith. Although the Portuguese strictly banned all such forms of "demon worship," slaves were particularly adept at camouflaging the worship of their deities under the guise of pretending to worship Catholic saints. The consequences of this mingling of religious symbols can be seen today in many religious rituals and celebrations that fuse Catholicism with African and even indigenous religious elements.

The end of slavery did not bring about immediate tolerance for Afro-Brazilians to openly practice purer forms of their faith. Candomblé, Brazil's largest Afro-Brazilian religion, was banned well into the 20th century. Today, less than 1 percent of Brazilians adhere to Candomblé and other popular Afro-Brazilian religions such as Umbanda, which mixes Candomblé practices with spiritualist and indigenous elements and is very popular in Rio. However, in Rio Afro-Brazilian religious elements have entered into mainstream culture. Wide segments of the population participate in *festas* honoring *orixás* (deities) in which *presentes* (gifts) are often offered. In Rio, for instance, you will often find the beaches littered with flowers washed ashore after being offered to the immensely popular *orixá* Iemanjá, goddess of the seas.

Other Faiths

There are numerous spiritualist and esoteric cults practiced throughout Brazil. One of the most popular forms of spiritualism is Kardecism, named after 19th-century spiritualist Allan Kardec. Followers believe in multiple reincarnations and in the idea that the spirits of the dead—who can be communicated with during séances—are present among the living. Spiritualism is so popular that it often works its way into the Globo television network's nightly *novelas.*

Other popular cults draw inspiration from Brazil's indigenous cultures. This is the case with Santo Daime and União da Vegetal, both of which revolve around imbibing a hallucinogenic potion, *ayahuasca,* which Amazonian indigenous groups have used for centuries as a way of achieving transcendental insights. The small but faithful following includes a significant number of middle-class urban dwellers in Rio and other cities.

LANGUAGE

Brazilians speak Portuguese (not Spanish!) and are responsible for the fact that Portuguese is the sixth most-spoken language in the world. Since it crossed the Atlantic from Portugal, Brazilian Portuguese has undergone various modifications. The differences between the Portuguese written and spoken in Portugal and that of Brazil are similar to the differences between American and British English. Brazilian Portuguese is a constantly evolving, dynamic, and very melodic language. Like the country itself, it is a colorful hybrid that has absorbed words and expressions from all the major groups that make up Brazilian society. Early on, Portuguese settlers were quick to incorporate indigenous terms from Tupi and Guaraní languages, in particular terms used to designate the vast compendium of exotica for which no Portuguese words existed. To this day, some names of places (Ipanema, Guanabara) are Tupi-Guaraní, as are names of many foods (*pipoca* is popcorn, *mandioca* is manioc, *abacaxi* is pineapple), animals (*tatu* is an armadillo, a *jacaré* is a cayman, *tucano* is a toucan), and trees (*ipê*, jacaranda). A legacy of slavery is the inclusion of words from African languages (primarily Bantu), ranging from specific terms such as *samba* and *capoeira* to colloquial expressions such as *cafuné* (a caress on the head) and *caçula* (the youngest born). Later on, the arrival of European immigrants in the 19th and 20th centuries introduced new expressions, especially from French—chaise longue, Réveillon (New Year's Eve), the expression *bom apetite,*—and English: *trem* (train), outdoor (billboard), jeans, and email.

Written Portuguese tends to be more formal (although less so than in Portugal), but spoken Portuguese is extremely casual with a fabulous array of slang and idiomatic expressions that vary wildly depending on regions and even city neighborhoods (and which you'll be hard-pressed to understand). Cariocas have a very particular accent (often mimicked by other Brazilians) that tends to be slightly nasal.

THE LONGING THAT IS *SAUDADE*

Saudade is the Portuguese word that has most defied translation. Its origins stem from the Latin term *solitatem,* which means loneliness or solitude. Yet as years have gone by, *saudade* has acquired rich layers of meaning that mingle nostalgia, longing, melancholy, and missing (someone or something). Trying to define the sentiment back in 1912, the English writer A. F. G. Bell wrote: "The famous *saudade* of the Portuguese is a vague and constant desire for something that does not and probably cannot exist, for something other than the present, a turning towards the past or towards the future; not an active discontent or poignant sadness but an indolent dreaming wistfulness." Bell was referring to Portugal, where the term was coined. But of course *saudade* migrated to the New World, where it fit right in with Brazilians' emotionally open natures. Brazilians liberally – and very sincerely – sprinkle their conversations with *"Estava com saudades"* ("I was really missing you") or *"Dá uma saudade!"* ("I really miss this/that"). Unsurprisingly, *saudades* also turn up with great frequency in Brazilian music. In fact, the first bossa nova song ever written was Tom Jobim's "Chega de Saudade." If you listen to the song in Portuguese, you'll get some idea of what *saudade* can mean; the most frequently translated English title, "No More Blue," doesn't even come close.

Art and Architecture

With so much diversity, beauty, and extremities packed into its immense territory, it's no wonder that artistry and creativity run rampant in Rio. Culture, both "high" and "low," but especially *cultura popular,* is seemingly everywhere—from the masterful elaboration of a tall tale at a bar table to the 45-minute choreographed spectacle of enormous floats, dazzling costumes, and thousands of samba-ing singers and dancers vying for the yearly championship title during Carnaval.

MUSIC

Of the various forms of artistic expression, the one that is most particular and reflects the very essence and soul of Rio is its music. From maxixe, *chorinho,* and samba to bossa nova, rock, and rap, Rio's contribution to the world music scene is immeasurable. Meanwhile, in Rio itself, music is inseparable from daily life. It plays a starring role in all types of celebrations, both sacred and profane. There is as much music in the beach vendor's cries as in the samba rhythms teenage boys pound against the metal siding of an urban bus. And it is tattooed into the collective consciousness in such a way that you'll immediately feel as if your education is very lacking. (Cariocas inevitably know *all* the words to *all* the songs, and are not at all timid about singing them for you.)

Music in Rio is also inextricably linked to dance. Many music styles are accompanied by dance steps and it's close to impossible for most Brazilians to stay inert once the music heats up. Needless to say, the effortlessness, grace, flair, and controlled abandon with which the vast majority of Brazilians cut a rug is beyond compare. As a gringo, you'll feel hopelessly inadequate as you stare down at your seemingly two left feet and wonder how on earth they do it.

Influences

The uniqueness and diversity of Brazilian music is a consequence of the country's distinctive mélange of indigenous, African, and European influences. In early colonial days, Jesuit missionaries were already cleverly adapting religious hymns to indigenous tribal music with Tupi lyrics in order to up their chances of converting Brazilian indigenous groups. With the arrival of slaves came percussion instruments—drums, *cuicas,* rattles, and marimbas—that were played during communal jams. Although the Portuguese elite tried to resist these African rhythms on grounds that they incited libidinous dances that were quite immoral, their objections were in vain. These rhythms made their way out of the slaves' quarters and into plantation homes and, from there, spread throughout the country, creeping into popular 19th-century musical styles such as maxixe, a derivative of the European polka, which in Rio's black working-class *bairros* somehow got mixed up with Cuban habanera and Afro-Brazilian *lundu.* In 1914, when the wife of president Hermes da Fonseca gave a party at the Palácio do Catete featuring a performance of *Corta-jaca,* a racy maxixe written by popular Carioca composer Chiquinha Gonzaga (who was not only a *mulata,* but a women to boot), all hell broke loose…at least until the maxixe became the favorite easy-listening music of the rest of the Carioca elite.

Samba

Maxixe was a precursor to Rio's most famous rhythm: samba. It was in early-20th-century Rio, amidst the working-class neighborhoods of liberated black slaves who had migrated to the city from Bahia, that modern samba was born. Officially, samba made its recorded presence known for the first time during Rio's Carnaval of 1917, which featured a ditty called "Pelo Telefone" composed by Donga, a talented young Carioca composer and musician, and from there it took off. The rhythm was so contagious that even Rio's white upper classes were hooked. By the 1930s the combined launch of Brazil's phonographic industry with the spread of national radio allowed

The Afro-Brazilian *xerequê* is often used in samba music.

samba hits to be broadcast throughout the country and quickly soak into the collective consciousness. Meanwhile, with the creation of Rio's first samba school in 1929, samba became inseparable from Carnaval.

The 1930s and '40s were the "golden age" of samba, with composers such as Noel Rosa, Ary Barroso, Lamartine Babo, Cartola, and Ismael Silva penning a string of classics that were popularized by the likes of Carmen Miranda (who, pre-Hollywood, was one of Brazil's preeminent musical stars). There are many different varieties of samba. The classic samba from the '30s and '40s is known as *samba-canção,* in which a slow-tempo samba is belted out by a singer backed by a small band. The more frenetic *samba de enredo* was custom-made for Rio's Carnaval. It involves one or two singers accompanied by a deafening chorus of hundreds of drummers and back-up singers (which, together, constitute a samba school). More recently, in the 1990s, in dance halls and corner bars, swinging *samba pagode* took the genre back to its roots, led by performers such as the

immensely popular and down-to-earth Zeca Pagodinho. Other major samba performers that have marked the genre since the 1970s include Elza Soares, Beth Carvalho, Alcione, Clara Nunes, Paulinho da Viola, Martinho da Vila, and Martinho's daughter, Mart'nália, whose career has taken off in the last few years.

Choro

Choro (which means crying) is another musical style (little known outside Brazil) that developed in Rio at the dawn of the 20th century. Delicate and slightly melancholy, *choro* music is influenced by Argentinian tangos as well as European polkas, mazurkas, and waltzes. During the 1930s, *choro* enjoyed great popularity due to the masterful compositions by a Carioca named Pixinguinha. The classic *choro* trio consists of a flute, *cavaquinho* (a small four-string guitar that resembles a ukelele), and a percussion instrument all played together in a loose manner reminiscent of jazz. Heitor Villa-Lobos, who revolutionized classical music by integrating popular and regional Brazilian forms into his compositions, wrote many *choros* (including some for orchestras). After falling out of favor for decades, traditional *choro* has made a comeback in Rio's bars and clubs.

Bossa Nova

Although poor rural and urban areas alike have proved fertile for the germination of many of Rio's musical styles, one of the genres most famously associated with Rio was the product of an inspired mixture of samba and imported American jazz that grew out of jam sessions held at the swank Zona Sul apartments of Rio's artists and intellectuals during the 1950s. Bossa nova was the name given to the cool, urban modernist style that was essentially a slowing down and breaking up of a classic samba rhythm. The godfather of bossa nova was an eccentric and insanely talented Bahian composer-musician by the name of João Gilberto. Two equally talented men (and famous bon vivants)—the classically trained pianist Antônio Carlos Jobim (aka Tom Jobim) and poet/diplomat Vinicius de Moraes—sat around writing bossa's most famous hits, including "A Garota de Ipanema" ("The Girl from Ipanema"), whose most unforgettable international version was crooned by Astrud Gilberto, João Gilberto's wife at the time. Ironically, Astrud is quite unknown in Brazil, but João's daughter Bebel Gilberto has picked up where her father left off and made an international career of doing slick lounge versions of bossa tunes for the iPod set. Meanwhile, bossa's fresh jazziness allowed "The Girl from Ipanema" to cross over into an immediate jazz standard, which was covered by American artists ranging from Stan Getz and Frank Sinatra to Ella Fitzgerald and Miles Davis. Bossa put Brazilian music on the international map for the first time. But because it was so overplayed, with the years bossa gained an elevator-music aura abroad. However, in Brazil, the repertory of classics such as "Corcovado," "Chega de Saudade," and "Desafinado" have, and continue to be, reverently covered by Brazil's top songstresses, among them Nara Leão and Elis Regina (who both died tragically young), and Gal Costa.

MPB

MPB stands for Música Popular Brasileira (Popular Brazilian Music) and is a rather generic and all-encompassing term that refers to all forms of Brazilian "popular" urban music—folk, pop, rock—created from the 1960s to contemporary times. MPB generally features original songwriting, but can also include revisited classics from the 1930s, '40s, and '50s. Most often songs are interpreted by the composer or by a singer-interpreter, and frequently accompanied by piano or guitar, along with other instruments.

The term MPB was coined in the early '60s as Brazil sought new and modern ways of revisiting its identity amidst the growing oppressiveness of the military dictatorship. Brazilian television, at the time a very new medium, began to broadcast Festivais de Música Popular Brasileira. These live competitions featured up-and-coming singers who performed songs by young composers in the hopes of landing recording contracts; its winners became overnight sensations. The first of these festivals, held in 1965, was won by a tiny yet feisty 20-year-old singer from Rio Grande do Sul by the name of Elis Regina. After moving to Rio, Elis set the standard for MPB. With her rich voice and unbridled emotion she tackled songs by a generation of talented young composers until her untimely death, by a drug overdose, in 1982. One of the young composers whose songs Elis interpreted was a timid blue-eyed Carioca by the name of Chico Buarque, who would go on to become one of Brazil's most prolific and lyrical composers of all time.

Brazilian Rock and Rap

In the late '60s and '70s, Brazilian music went electric and also began incorporating new influences and styles from international (principally American) sources. Afro-Brazilian composers and interpreters such as Jorge Ben and Tim Maia merged samba with black American styles such as funk and soul while

Luiz Melodia created a highly personal oeuvre of samba-tinged ballads. In the '80s, rock came to Rio in a big way. The decade marked the emergence of seminal bands such as Barão Vermelho, Blitz, Kid Abelha, and Os Titãs along with singer-songwiter rockers such as Cazuza, Lobão, Lulu Santos, Fernanda Abreu, and Marina Lima. Since then, Brazilian rock—which generally appeals to a young, urban, white, middle-class crowd—has faded into the musical background somewhat, although Rio has a very strong indie scene.

The 1990s saw the emergence of rap. Like its American urban counterparts, Brazilian rap was born in the *favelas* and featured young black Brazilians who tackled themes of social injustice and violence. A Carioca take on rap is funk, which attracts massive audiences and features lyrics that are so sexually explicit that you don't know whether to be shocked or laugh yourself silly. Among the biggest names in rap are Gabriel O Pensador, MV Bill, and Marcelo D2.

Brazilian Music Today

In recent years there has been a revived interest in traditional music and its preservation. At Lapa's hot spots, young and old Cariocas alike flock to hear legendary *sambistas* of yore (many have been "rediscovered") as well as a new generation of singers intent on interpreting and reinterpreting *choro* and samba standards and forgotten gems. Meanwhile, if no seminal creative figures have emerged on the MPB front that can rival the cultural and musical impact forged by the original talents of the 1960s and '70s, there are quite a few interesting individuals who are carving out their own distinctive paths. Raised in a Rio *favela,* Seu Jorge plays contemporary takes on samba that have earned him international accolades, while classically trained singer-songwriter Marisa Monte continues to carve an eclectic career for herself by mixing her own highly personal MPB songs with covers of classic sambas from the '30s and '40s. Ultimately, what characterizes contemporary Carioca music is a continued willingness towards musical *mestizagem;* the seamless blending of contemporary and international influences with traditional and local sounds to create hybrids—samba-funk, electro-samba, bossa jazz—that are completely unique.

FINE ARTS AND ARCHITECTURE

Foreigners who come to Rio for its natural splendors are often pleasantly surprised to discover that the city is rich in man-made attractions as well. Reflecting its political and cultural importance at various points in history, the city is a treasure trove—albeit not a very harmonious one—of architectural jewels that range in style from baroque, rococo, and neoclassical to art deco and modernist. Meanwhile, from its earliest days Rio has easily seduced artists from near and far, who—bewitched by its light, color, landscapes, and liveliness—certainly never lack for inspiration, even when lacking in funds.

Colonial and Baroque

The earliest known examples of "Brazilian" art were actually paintings of Edenic landscapes done by European artists who were fascinated by the new colony's profusion of exotica. When the Dutch occupied Pernamabuco in the mid-1600s, artists Frans Post and Albert Eckout were assigned to dutifully register the native flora and fauna as well as indigenous inhabitants. Widely reproduced in Europe, their portraits constituted the first images of the American continent painted by artists of some renown. Although less known, colonial Rio also had its landscape painters. A pioneering figure was Leandro Joaquim, a young *mulato* painter known for colorful scenes such as canvases depicting whaling in the Baía de Guanabara. Joaquim was a member of the Escola Fluminense de Pintura, a school of local artists that emerged in the early 1700s around a painter named Ricardo de Pilar. Pilar was a friar—among his best-known works are the panels that adorn the interior of the Mosteiro de São Bento—and his prominence reflects the ties between the church, art, and architecture during colonial times. In fact, Rio's most splendid colonial buildings—and the only ones

CANNIBALISM IN BRAZILIAN MODERN ART

During the Semana de Arte de São Paulo of 1922, Oswald de Andrade, a leading modernist intellectual and playwright, introduced the metaphor of *antropofagia* (cannibalism), which would become a guiding concept in all modern Brazilian art. Andrade's notion was derived from some Brazilian indigenous groups' traditional practice of cannibalism. Contrary to popular belief, Brazil's native peoples didn't eat people to satisfy their hunger pangs. Instead, they recognized that even their staunchest foes possessed gifts they didn't share. The ritual of eating the enemies they captured in skirmishes was a way of absorbing the qualities they most admired in them. Oswald de Andrade proposed that Brazilian artists become cannibals as well, devouring aspects of the European vanguard as well as traditional African and Indian arts, and, after digesting them, making use of them to produce a uniquely Brazilian art that would reflect Brazil itself, with its diversity of colors, peoples, and natural features.

Magnificent churches were built using local materials and decorated in a baroque style whose details, colors, and excessive flourishes were unique in reflecting and incorporating elements from their tropical surroundings. The great figure of Mineiro baroque was a mulatto named Antônio Francisco Lisboa. Known as Aleijadinho (Little Cripple) due to the leprosy that eventually destroyed him, this master builder and sculptor created strikingly expressive works that adorn the churches of Ouro Preto, Congonhas, Tiradentes, and São João del Rei and are considered masterpieces.

Second only to Aleijadinho in talent and output was Rio's Valentim da Fonseca e Silva. Known as Mestre Valentim, this talented mulatto sculptor had a distinctive style that mingled aspects of baroque and rococo with neoclassicism. Apart from the numerous sculptures and carvings he wrought for churches such as the Igreja da Ordem Terceira do Carmo, he was the original designer of the Passeio Público (before it was "French-ified" by landscaper Auguste Glaziou in 1860), where many of his works still stand. Two imposing stone fountains—one which stands in Ipanema's Praça General Osório, the other in Centro's Praça XV—also attest to his talents.

The French Connection

Major political changes in the 19th century had vast repercussions on Brazilian art and architecture. As seat of the Portuguese empire and capital of the newly independent Brazilian nation, Rio became Brazil's undisputed cultural and artistic center. The arrival of Lisbon's royal court in 1808 immediately provoked major transformations as the emperors set to work creating a splendid new capital. In 1816, Dom Pedro I invited a group of leading French artists, known as the Missão Artística Francesa, to Rio in order to transform the city and to instill the precepts and techniques of romanticism and neoclassicism among artists that flocked from all over Brazil to study at the new art academies (among them the prestigious Escola Nacional de Belas Artes), compete for prizes and commissions, and contribute to the beautification

to have partially survived—are ecclesiastical ones. Aside from the Mosteiro de São Bento, examples include the Igreja and Convento do Santo Antônio, the Igreja da Ordem Terceira de São Francisco da Penitência, and the Igreja de Nossa Senhora do Carmo, all of which were built by various religious orders in rigorous adherence to Portuguese styles.

Indeed, between the 16th and 19th centuries artists in Brazil devoured styles that were in vogue in Europe. Although some did so mimetically, others "tropicalized" these styles, imbuing them with a unique "Brazilianness." The most remarkable instance of this tendency occurred with the rise of *barroco mineiro,* which developed in 18th-century Minas Gerais during its massive gold boom.

Artist Candido Portinari's tile panels adorn Palácio Gustavo Capanema, which was designed by Oscar Niemeyer and Lúcio Costa.

of the city. Among the most notable members of the Mission were the painters Nicolas-Antoine Taunay and Jean-Baptiste Debret and the architect Auguste Grandjean de Montigny. Enchanted by Rio's sublime natural features, Taunay set to work capturing the Edenic flora whose vivid detail was shot through with an undercurrent of mysticism. More attracted by Rio's urban landscapes, Debret registered with scientific precision scenes from daily life in the streets, with an emphasis on the great diversity of Rio's human fauna. Together, the works of both artists comprise a precious iconographic archive of 19th-century Rio. Meanwhile, Grandjean de Montigny's legacy was equally important. Although he created few buildings himself, he helped to design many, and he had a lasting influence on the city's love affair with French neoclassicism.

Indeed, with the proclamation of independence in 1822, Brazil not only asserted its political autonomy from Lisbon, but also broke away from Portuguese models of art and architecture that had dominated throughout

colonial times. In terms of painting, romanticism became the rage, with Carioca artists such as Vítor Meireles and Pedro Amérigo portraying national heroes and historic events in epic style. In architecture, the sobriety and elegance of French-inspired neoclassicism and eclecticism held sway. The late 19th and early 20th centuries witnessed the building of grand monuments such as the Biblioteca Nacional, the Museu de Belas Artes, and the Theatro Municipal (inspired by Paris's Opéra Garnier), all of which aspired to conjure up a tropical version of Baron Haussmann's Paris. French influence segued into the early 20th century as well; a flirtation with art nouveau gave way to art deco that characterized the modern new edifices that sprang to aerodynamic life in the 1930s and '40s. Indeed, Rio boasts more examples of art deco than in any other city in the Southern Hemisphere. Some particularly glorious examples are in Copacabana, where the streamlined style was a symbol of the sophistication and glamour of the new beach *bairro*.

© MICHAEL SOMMERS

Brazilian Modernism

It wasn't until the 1920s that Brazilian artists consciously broke with European traditions in the pursuit of art that was typically Brazilian. Led by Oswald and Mário de Andrade, in 1920 the Semana de Arte Moderna de São Paulo created an artistic manifesto and shocked the conservative elite by severing ties with academic, European schools. Brazilian modernists such as Anita Malfatti, Emílio di Cavalcanti, Tarsila do Amaral, Vítor Brecheret, and Lasar Segall were the leading painters and sculptors that emerged from the Semana de Arte Moderna. Espousing a philosophy of national art and culture that revolved around the notion of *antropofagia* (or cannibalism), they created works that, while fed by what was going on in Europe, were also nourished by themes, forms, and subject matter that were distinctly Brazilian. The generation of artists that followed them, including painters Alberto de Veiga Guignard, Candido Portinari, Flávio de Carvalho, Cícero Dias and sculptors Maria Martins, Bruno Giorgi, and Alfredo Ceschiatti, continued to explore the notion of Brazilian modernism.

While each artist followed his or her own individual path, many contributed their talents to adorning public buildings. In Rio, both Di Cavalcanti and Portinari created large panels that can be seen at the Palácio Capanema, the Teatro João Caetano, and the Museu de Arte Moderna. Others actually created the buildings. Two of the most famous modernist architects in Brazil, if not in the world, are Carioca: Lúcio Costa and Oscar Niemeyer. Before going on to design the capital of Brasília, today considered the greatest modernist ensemble in the world, the two cut their teeth in their hometown. Their first collaboration was the Palácio Capanema (formerly occupied by the Minister of Health and Education), which was designed in the late 1930s in consultation with their guru, Le Corbusier, whose ideals of functional, pared-down structures with glossy surfaces and plenty of windows that emphasized natural lighting were ideally suited to Rio's climate. Niemeyer, however, softened the rigid, box-like linearity of the style by adding

Roberto Burle Marx's iconic wave mosaic decorates Copacabana's boardwalk.

© MICHAEL SOMMERS

sweeping curves that reflected the sensuality and natural forms so characteristic of Brazil. Among the many Niemeyer constructions in Rio are the architect's home, the Casa das Canoas, and the flying saucer–esque Museu de Arte Contemporânea in Niterói. Other important contributors to Brazilian modernist architecture include Affonso Eduardo Reidy (who designed Rio's Museu de Arte Moderna) and renowned landscape architect Roberto Burle Marx, whose wave mosaic of black-and-white cobblestones transformed Copacabana's boardwalk into a Carioca icon.

Contemporary Art and Architecture

In Brazil, the 1950s coincided with major experiments in abstract and concrete art. Major Carioca artists of this time included Ivan Serpa, Ferreira Gullar, Franz Weissmann, and Lygia Clark. In the '60s, Clark, along with provocative and crazily talented Hélio Oiticica, began creating vanguard art installations that focused on relationships between objects and the space around them. The iconic example of this period was Oiticica's famous *parangolé*, a capelike work of "wearable art" made famous by the fact that singer-songwriter Caetano Veloso wore one at the height of his late-'60s fame as a charismatic rebel with a cause.

Keeping up with trends in other parts of the world, over the last several decades contemporary Brazilian art has been marked by the successive rise of Pop, installation, performance, video, and digital art. Today, Carioca-based artists such as Daniel Senise, Rubens Gershmam, Beatriz Milhazes, Tunga, Adriana Varejão, Waltercio Caldas, Nelson Lerner, Eduardo Sued, Carlos Vergara, and Sérgio Camargo are all renowned figures and their works are included in leading museums and galleries. Although characterized by more misses than hits, contemporary architecture in Rio has at its best attempted to follow the precepts of *antropofagia*—creating works that bridge cutting-edge universal technology and tendencies with a valorization of local aesthetics and materials.

CINEMA

Rio was born to be in pictures—few cities on earth are quite as photogenic. It's thus unsurprising that, from the beginning, Rio has been at the forefront of Brazilian cinema. In 1897, the nation's first movie theater opened on Centro's Rua do Ouvidor in 1897, and 10 years later the first Brazilian film made with actors, *Os Estranguladores*—dramatizing a sensational murder ripped from the headlines—was produced here.

In the 1920s, Praça Floriano became known as Cinelândia after the elegant downtown square was lined with sumptuous art deco movie palaces that screened all the latest Hollywood flickers. Rio was also the birthplace of the Brazilian film industry. In 1930, pioneering Cinédia studios began producing films such as *Limite* (1931) and *Ganga Bruta* (1933). Other studios followed in its wake. In 1935, Brasil Vita Filmes produced *A Favela dos meus Amores*, which was daring enough to portray daily life in a Carioca *favela*, while Sonofilmes

produced classic musicals such as *Alô Alô Brasil* (1935) and *Alô Alô Carnaval* (1936) starring a young Carmen Miranda, then at the height of her fame as a recording star. In the 1940s, both Atlantida and Vera Cruz also appeared on the scene to produce popular melodramas along with a series of popular romances and burlesque musical comedies known as *chanchadas*, some of which satirized Hollywood fare. During the 1950s, Vera Cruz attempted to attract viewers by emulating Hollywood's tradition of commercial genre films. A massive soundstage was built where the studio could churn out highly popular detective stories and Westerns. Production values were high, but young independent directors chafed at the degree of commercialization and Americanization of the final product.

Dreaming of a *cinema novo* (new cinema), and inspired by Italian neorealism, directors such as Nelson Pereira dos Santos, whose seminal 1955 film *Rio 40 graus* was a stark portrait of Rio's underbelly, took to making low-budget films, many shot on location, which highlighted the stark realities of Brazilian life in expressive black-and-white imagery. If not wildly popular at home, these films were a hit with international critics.

In 1964, the beginning of the military dictatorship caused Cinema Novo to experience a sudden demise. Government hard-liners censored any criticism of Brazil and forced many directors into exile. Instead, in 1969, the government created Embrafilme, a state-run production company whose goal was to develop Brazilian filmmaking. Although censorship, bureaucracy, and favoritism severely limited artistic expression, Embrafilme did provide enough capital to maintain a small industry that funded the production of important films by major directors such as Bruno Barreto's *Dona Flor e Seus Dois Maridos (Dona Flor and Her Two Husbands*, 1976), Cacá Diegues´ *Bye Bye Brasil* (1979), Hector Babenco's *Pixote* (1981), and Nelson Pereira dos Santos´ *Memórias do Cárcere (Memories of Prison*, 1984).

The end of Brazil's military dictatorship also meant the end of Embrafilme and a state-subsidized film industry. By the early 1990s, only three or four Brazilian films a year were being released. Fortunately, things improved under the government of Fernando Henrique Cardoso, with the introduction of new incentive laws whereby private companies that invested in film productions would receive tax breaks. In 1993, Carioca actor-director Carla Camurati's whimsical historical comedy *Carlota Joaquina* (about the Portuguese royal family's picaresque adventures in 19th-century Rio) was a big hit and signaled the beginning of Brazilian cinema's resurrection. Eager to see their lives depicted on-screen, Brazilians flocked to the cinema in record numbers despite the fact that, since the 1970s, more than two-thirds of movie theaters had been closed down (and often converted into evangelical churches), the result of the popularization of television and the increased price of movie tickets. Not only did the number of films produced gradually grow, but the quality was on par with the best of world cinema, and was recognized as such by foreign critics who showered awards on productions such as Bruno Barreto's *O Que É Isso Companheiro? (Four Days in September,* 1998), an Oscar-nominated film that told the gripping true story of the kidnapping of the U.S. ambassador to Brazil by left-leaning guerillas.

Walter Salles, one of Brazil's most important new directors, received two Oscar nominations the following year for *Central do Brasil (Central Station),* the story of a curmudgeonly elderly woman (played by Oscar-nominated Fernanda Montenegro) who makes a living writing letters for illiterate migrants in Rio's Central Station and ends up accompanying a young homeless boy on a search throughout the Northeast to find his father.

Aside from being entertaining, many of these films are loyal to Cinema Novo's mandate of offering critiques of Brazil's many social problems. Indeed, in recent years many films have taken to the urban jungles of Rio to explore issues such as violence and poverty. One of the most accomplished new directors to tackle such themes is Fernando Meirelles. With a background in advertising, Meirelles launched his cinematic career with *Domésticas (Maids,* 2001),

CARMEN MIRANDA

Forget about Hepburn, Hayworth, and Grable. In the mid-1940s, Carmen Miranda was the most highly paid female star in Hollywood. As the Brazilian Bombshell, this tiny Portuguese-born Carioca, who tottered upon foot-high platforms and beneath towering turbans piled high with juicy tropical fruits, proved herself to be much larger than life in a string of Technicolor musical-comedies produced by 20th Century Fox. With her rolling eyes, gyrating hips, and deliriously nonsensical songs, such as "Tico Tico Na Fuba" and "Boom Chica Boom," Carmen took America by storm. She also became the strangest – and perhaps most successful – goodwill ambassador that ever existed between the United States and Brazil. Never before, and never again, would Hollywood – and the world – see a spectacle quite as spectacular as the "Lady in the Tutti Frutti Hat."

which offered a humorous yet realistic glimpse into the lives of the many women who work as maids for wealthy and middle-class Carioca families. His follow-up film, *Cidade de Deus (City of God,* 2002), took both Brazil and the world by storm with its brilliantly acted story of survival amidst the gang warfare typical of a Carioca *favela.* The fragmented editing, hurtling pace, and use of *favela* dwellers as actors was inspired and brought Meirelles (who then went on to direct the English-language film *The Constant Gardener* in 2005), an Oscar nomination for best director.

In 2007, José Padilha—director of the harrowing documentary *Onibus 174 (Bus 174,* 2002), which was based on the 2000 hijacking of a municipal Rio de Janeiro bus in broad daylight and the police's bungling of the rescue of passengers—created another uproar with his controversial fictional feature debut. The film, entitled *Tropa da Elite (Elite Squad),* provided a shocking glimpse at the armed warfare between drug lords and a special squad of Rio's military police created to "protect" *favela* residents. Buzz about the film (based on very true events) was so great that when a prior cut was released via the Internet, an estimated 12 million Brazilians purchased pirated copies in the street, making the film (which later took home the Golden Bear award for best film at the Berlin International Film Festival) one of the most widely watched Brazilian films of all time.

Brazil's burgeoning feature film industry has been accompanied by a renaissance in the production of documentary films. Many delve into social themes, such as Eduardo Coutinho's excellent *Edifício Master* (2002), which offers an intimate glimpse into the lives of 37 families that inhabit a crowded 12-story Copacabana apartment building. An extraordinary number of documentaries pay homage to Rio's musical legends, among them Carmen Miranda in Helena Solberg's *Bananas Is My Business* (1994); Vinicius de Moraes in Miguel Faria Jr.'s *Vinicius* (2005); and Lírio de Ferreira in Hilton Lacerda's *Cartola* (2006).

LITERATURE

Jorge Amado was one of Brazil's most beloved 20th-century writers. His picaresque and colorful novels, inevitably set in his home state of Bahia, are populated by a charismatic (if somewhat caricatural) cast of sensual *mulatas*, fishermen, charming tricksters, and Candomblé priestesses. There is usually a shot of magical realism involved in these highly readable tales. Among his most enduring novels are *Gabriela, Clove, and Cinnamon* and *Dona Flor and Her Two Husbands.*

Mário de Andrade was one of the leading figures of Brazil's modernist movement, and his novel *Macunaíma* (1928) is a Brazilian classic. The title character is a mutant figure from the jungle who begins life as an Indian and then morphs into a black man and a white man. While changing identities, he stars in a variety of comical adventures that integrate all sorts of popular Brazilian myths, folklore, and cultural elements into a highly enjoyable narrative patchwork that is utterly Brazilian.

Machado de Assis is not widely known outside Brazil, but to international literati he has earned a place among the all-time greats. This 19th-century author was extremely vanguard, bringing a modernist sensibility and style, not to mention a rapier wit, to bear upon the lifestyles of the rich and corrupt in fin de siècle Rio. His two most famous novels, *Posthumous Memoirs of Brás Cubas (Memórias Póstumas de Brás Cubas)* and *Quincas Borba*, are both wonderfully imaginative and mordantly funny. His short stories are also quite brilliant; try *The Psychiatrist and Other Stories (O Alienista e Outros Contos).*

Paulo Lins, a well-known photojournalist, grew up in Rio's poor and dangerous Cidade de Deus *favela*, infamous for its violent gangs and brutal drug traffickers. His background supplied the fodder for the gripping novel *Cidade de Deus (City of God)*, which was subsequently made into the highly acclaimed film of the same name by Fernando Meirelles.

Clarice Lispector was one of Brazil's most intelligent and elegantly witty 20th-century writers. Her depth, human insight, and sense of word play are impressively displayed in her numerous short stories, which are meticulously crafted but don't make for light reading. Her most famous and most accessible novel, *The Hour of the Star (A Hora da Estrela)*, is a compact and searing tale of a miserable and homely Northeastern migrant girl's day-to-day trials and tribulations in Rio de Janeiro.

Graciliano Ramos was a novelist from Alagoas who was largely responsible for introducing social realism and regionalism into Brazilian literature in the early 20th century. Written in pared-down prose, his most famous work, *Barren Lives,* portrays the bleak lives of families trying to survive in the hard, arid Sertão of the Northeast.

Moacyr Scliar is one of Brazil's most distinguished contemporary authors. A Jewish doctor from Rio Grande do Sul, he expertly crafts short stories and novels that often touch on the issue of Jewish identity (specifically in Brazil). Apart from his short stories, his best-known novels include *The Centaur and the Garden* and *Max and the Cats.*

ESSENTIALS

Getting There

AIR
Airports

Rio has two airports. International flights and the majority of domestic flights arrive and depart from the **Aeroporto Internacional Tom Jobim** (Av. 20 de Janeiro, Ilha do Governador, tel. 21/3398-4527), also known as Galeão, situated in the Zona Norte, around 20 minutes from Centro and 45–60 minutes from the Zona Sul. Right in Centro, adjacent to the Parque do Flamengo, is Rio's oldest airport, **Aeroporto Santos Dumont** (Praça Senador Salgado Filho, tel. 21/3814-7070), where flights are basically limited to the Rio–São Paulo air shuttle.

Both airports have kiosks for special airport taxis, where you pay your fare in advance based on the distance to your destination, but these are often more expensive than just hailing one of the white radio taxis available at the taxi stands. Two major taxi companies are **Coopertramo** (tel. 21/2560-2022) and **Transcoopass** (tel. 21/2590-6891). Always make sure you use a bona fide taxi company, like the ones listed here or the taxi companies at the airport kiosks. Taxi fare from Galeão is around R$50 to Flamengo, R$60 to Copacabana, and R$80 to Leblon.

From Galeão, the **Real** (tel. 21/2560-7041 or 0800-24-0850) bus company offers regular

executivo service to Rio for R$6. Buses cut through Centro (along Av. Rio Branco) and then stop at Aeroporto Santos Dumont, before continuing along the oceanfront *avenidas* of Flamengo (Av. Beira Mar), Copacabana (Av. Atlântica), Ipanema (Av. Vieira Souto), and Leblon (Av. Delfim Moreira), including stops at all the major hotels along the way. For hotels that are inland, just ask the driver in advance to let you off at the nearest cross street *("Por favor, pode me deixar na Rua . . .?")*. Buses leave the airports daily, at 30-minute intervals, between 5:20 A.M. and 11 P.M. To get to the airport, you can grab the same bus (on the reverse route) or ask your hotel to call you a cab and settle on a fixed rate in advance.

International Flights

Most major airlines service Rio's Aeroporto Tom Jobim. Although many flights are direct, others arrive via São Paulo's Guarulhos airport (a 40-minute flight). From the United States, **American Airlines** (U.S. tel. 800/433-7300, www.aa.com), **Continental** (tel. 800/231-0856, www.continental.com), **Delta** (tel. 800/241-4141, www.delta.com), and **United** (tel. 800/241-6522, www.ual.com) all offer daily flights from major cities including New York, Washington, D.C., Miami, Atlanta, Chicago, Houston, and Los Angeles. **Air Canada** (tel. 888/247-2262, www.aircanada .ca) has direct daily flights from Toronto and **British Airways** (tel. 0/845-702-0212, www .britishairways.com) operates direct flights from London. Currently, **TAM** (tel. 888/2FLY-TAM, www.tam.com.br) is the only Brazilian carrier that offers international service to the United States, Canada, and Europe as well as most other Latin American countries. **Varig** (tel. 800/468-2744, www.varig.com), which used to be Brazil's major national airline before going bankrupt, now only has international service to Argentina, Chile, Colombia, and Venezuela.

If you're planning to travel around to far-flung regions of Brazil, it may make sense for you to buy a **Brazil Airpass,** which can only be purchased abroad (much to the chagrin of Brazilians) along with your international ticket. Currently, TAM offers a pass that allows you four domestic flights to any destination TAM flies to (which is basically everywhere). The pass costs US$529 (if you travel to Brazil on TAM). Otherwise it costs US$699, with an additional US$180 per flight. Various restrictions apply, such as no refunds once you've made your first domestic flight. Rebooking costs US$100.

Due to the rising price of fuel and increased airport taxes, flights are more expensive than they used to be. A round-trip flight (without taxes) for US$700 from New York to Rio is considered a very good deal these days. To shop around for cheap fares, consult www .expedia.com, www.travelocity.com, and www .cheaptickets.com.

In the United States, a very good travel agency (run by friendly English-speaking Brazilians) is the Houston-based **Globotur** (tel. 800/998-5521, www.globotur.com). They consistently come up with great fares for travelers in the United States and Canada. Also recommended is **Brazil Nuts** (tel. 914/593-0266 or 800/553-9959, www.brazilnuts.com). Based in Naples, Florida, they have a highly informed staff and can book flights and hotels as well as customized tours to both major and off-the-beaten-path destinations.

Domestic Flights

There are numerous daily flights available to and from Rio and other major Brazilian cities. Prices between destinations in the Southeast, South, Brasília, and the Northeast are quite reasonable (although they are rising due to increasing fuel costs). Flights to cities in the Amazon such as Manaus and Belém cost quite a bit more.

In recent years numerous domestic airlines have started up, while others have gone out of business. Currently, the major players are **TAM** (tel. 888/2FLY-TAM, www.tam.com.br) and **GOL** (tel. 0/300-115-2121, www.voegol.com .br). To date, **Varig** (tel. 800/468-2744, www .varig.com), which recently went bankrupt and then was repurchased (by GOL), has fewer domestic routes than previously. Two new start-ups that threaten to shake up the market include **Webjet** (tel. 0/300-210-1234, www.webjet.com.br) and **Azul** (tel. 3003-2985, www.voeazul.com.br), owned by New York–based JetBlue. All airlines have websites where you can purchase tickets online. Better yet, you can check out routes, schedules, and promotions. The airlines now offer various fares depending on when you fly, and how far in advance you book. Great promotions (such as paying full fare one way and receiving your return ticket for R$1 for certain routes) are often advertised online. Even if you don't purchase online (with a credit card), you can comparison shop and then take your findings to any local travel agent who can then purchase the ticket for you. For the best fares, it's worthwhile booking as far in advance as possible. Depending on the terms of your ticket, you can usually change your flight or get a refund (within 24 hours), although you might need to pay a fee. Confirm with the airline or travel agency beforehand. Barring delays, flying within Brazil is usually a much less stressful experience than in Europe or North America. You can check in an hour before the flight's departure (although make sure you factor in traffic delays) and security checks are refreshingly free of hassle and humiliation. The carriers themselves are top of the line: clean and comfortable, with gracious cabin staff and (miracle of miracles!) free food and drink.

BOAT

Many international cruise ships to South America make stops along Brazil's Atlantic coast, where Rio is Brazil's biggest port of call (www.portosrio.gov.br). Those traveling by cruise ship will dock downtown, at the terminal located in Centro. Although an entire cruise can be quite pricy, sometimes portions can be purchased at substantial discounts.

BUS

Rio's main bus station, **Rodoviária Novo Rio** (Av. Francisco Bicalho 1, São Cristovão, tel. 21/3213-1800, www.novorio.com.br) is a major

transportation hub. Buses arrive from and depart to all points of Brazil as well as to other South American countries. It is located in a run-down dockside area of Centro on the edge of the Zona Norte. Despite its importance, the station itself is also pretty run-down, which is why a (long overdue) major renovation is underway to transform it into a spankingly modern station filled with shops, restaurants, bookstores, and cafés.

Getting to and from the Rodoviária from anywhere in the city is very easy: Just hop on any bus with Rodoviária posted as its destination on the front. A taxi from the bus station will set you back around R$15 to Centro and R$40 to Copacabana.

International

Although it's possible to drive or travel by bus to Rio from all neighboring countries, in most cases distances are quite enormous. Apart from Santa Elena de Uairén in Venezuela, the most accessible and common entry points are from Brazil's neighbors to the south, including Argentina and Paraguay at Foz do Iguaçu and Uruguay at Jaguarão. There is frequent bus service between Rio, São Paulo, and the capitals of the south, Montevideo (Uruguay), Buenos Aires (Argentina), Asunción (Paraguay), and even Santiago (Chile). Roads are generally quite good. International bus companies include **Pluma** (tel. 0800/646-0300 throughout Brazil, www.pluma.com.br) and **Crucero del Norte** (tel. 11/5258-5000 in Buenos Aires, www.crucerodelnorte.com.ar).

Domestic

Brazil has an excellent bus system covering the entire country. Service between Rio and major cities throughout Brazil is usually very efficient and will cost less than half of plane fare. Long-distance buses leave punctually (don't be late) and the comfortable vehicles themselves (often Mercedes-Benzes) are equipped with plush reclining seats, air-conditioning, bathrooms, TVs, and coolers with free mineral water. Although bathrooms start out clean, by the end of the trip they are usually less so. When you buy your ticket, you can reserve your seat—choose one at the front or the middle of the bus (the bathroom is at the back). Also beware that air-conditioning can be very heavy duty. Make sure you have a sweater and long pants (or a towel or light blanket). On overnight buses between major cities, you can opt for a deluxe *leito* bus. *Leito* means bed, and there are large, fully reclining seats and sheets and pillows to make it easier to sleep. *Leitos* usually cost two to three times more than a regular bus, but are still cheaper than flying.

Buses are operated by hundreds of private companies (national, regional, and local), but prices are comparable between rivals. More and more companies have websites where you can check schedules and prices and even purchase tickets in advance. For shorter trips, advance purchase isn't necessary, but for inter-state travel, especially during high season or holiday periods, it's recommended you purchase your ticket in advance. Although major companies sell tickets via travel agents, often your best (and only) option is to purchase them at the *rodoviária,* or bus terminal, where all companies have kiosks with schedules. When purchasing a ticket, specify you want it *sem seguro* (without insurance), an added fee that bequeaths a small sum of money to your loved ones should you be involved in a fatal bus crash (not likely).

Traveling by bus in Brazil is safe, but do keep an eye on your belongings at all times. Luggage stowed beneath the bus is quite secure (it can only be retrieved with a baggage claim). Otherwise, keep valuables close by, particularly at night, and take them with you at rest stops. Except for *leitos,* most long-distance buses will make stops every two to three hours. This will give you a chance to stretch your legs, grab some food or a drink, and use a clean bathroom. It's nonetheless advisable to bring some mineral water and a snack such as biscuits, fruit, or nuts.

Getting Around

Rio has a very extensive and inexpensive public transportation system consisting of a limited but efficient Metrô and far-reaching, if slightly more confusing, bus system that boasts over 400 lines. For everywhere else—and nighttime—there are taxis.

METRÔ

Rio's Metrô (tel. 21/3211-6300, www.metro-rio.com.br) system is clean, efficient, and safe (not to mention gloriously air-conditioned). The only problem is its size: To date, there are only two lines. Parts of the Zona Norte (Maracanã, for instance) are well serviced, as is Centro. In terms of the Zona Sul, however, Linha 1 (to date) only goes as far as Cantagalo station in Copacabana. To get to Ipanema, Leblon, Gávea, or Barra from Copacabana, *Integração Expressa* shuttle buses ferry passengers to and from Siqueira Campos station. This combination subway-bus system (the buses are optimistically referred to as a "surface Metrô") is efficient, but doesn't prevent you from getting stuck in traffic. Metrô tickets can be purchased in the stations as *unitários* (singles, R$2.80), *duplos* (two-way, R$5.60) or *múltiplos* (10 trips for R$28). If you're going to be taking the Integração express bus at your final Metrô stop, you can save money by purchasing a combined *integrado* ticket (R$3.80), which is less expensive than paying for two separate fares. The Metrô runs Monday–Saturday 5 A.M.–midnight and Sunday 7 A.M.–11 P.M.

BUS

Buses go everywhere in Rio. Except when they're mired in rush-hour traffic (usually 7–9 A.M. and 5–7 P.M.), they tend to go very, very fast—which, depending on your thrill factor, can either prove exhilarating or hairraising. The other drawback to Rio's municipal buses is that they're not the safest form of

Largo do Machado Metrô station

locomotion going, due to pickpockets and occasional armed holdups. That said, if you leave your valuables at the hotel and limit yourself to daytime trips between points in the Centro, Zona Sul, and the western beaches of Barra and Recreio, you'll be fine. Do take care to have your change counted out beforehand and always keep bags (including knapsacks) or other belongings closed (with a zipper or button) and close to your chest, especially when it's crowded. By day, buses run with great frequency. By night, you can risk taking buses between main stops in Flamengo, Botafogo, Copacabana, Ipanema, and Leblon, which are usually quite busy until around 9 or 10 P.M. Otherwise, however, stick to taxis.

Final destinations are written on the front of the bus, and along the side are the main stops along the routes—make sure you check this out. From the Centro, for example, buses whose final destination is Leblon careen along the coast through Copacabana and Ipanema, while others go inland via Botafogo and Jardim Botânico. After paying your fare (R$2.20) to

the *cobrador* at the back of the bus, make your way to the front, so you can make an easy exit when you get to your stop. If a bus stop is not clearly marked, look for a clump of people waiting. From the street you can signal for a bus to stop by sticking out your arm.

TAXIS

Taxis are often the best way to get around Rio. Taxi service is reasonably priced and for specific trips you can often bargain a fixed price with your driver (if language is a problem ask someone at your hotel or hostel for help as well as approximate prices). There are two kinds of taxis in Rio. Yellow cabs with blue stripes are the most common. They can be hailed in the street and are cheaper. Large white air-conditioned radio cabs are usually ordered by phone and are more expensive. Two reliable companies are **Centro de Taxis** (tel. 21/2593-2598) and **Coopacarioca** (tel. 21/2518-1818). Most Carioca cab drivers are friendly and honest (although very few speak English), but there are a few who specialize in scamming gringo tourists. Unless you've agreed on a set fare, check to make sure the meter is always running. During the daytime until 8 P.M. the cheaper Bandeira 1 rate is used; at night, holidays, and weekends the rate is Bandeira 2.

CAR RENTAL

Quite frankly, unless you're a daredevil with a lot of patience, driving in Rio de Janeiro itself is not exactly recommended. It's not that Cariocas are poor drivers, but they tend to forget they're not at the Indie 5000. Then there are the rush-hour traffic jams, which are not only stressful but also stiflingly hot with the tropical sun beating down. One-way streets, poorly marked turnoffs, and holdups—at stoplights and when you're parked—are further dissuading factors. In truth, renting a car only makes sense for *outside* of the city.

Until recently, drunk driving was a major problem throughout Brazil. However, in July 2008, the nation's lamentable record for having one of the highest vehicle accident death tolls caused the government to enact a law of zero tolerance. This has resulted in police-organized blitzes around the country, where drivers are stopped arbitrarily and must take a breathalyzer test. If even the slightest amount of alcohol is detected, you're looking at a R$955 fine and a suspension from driving for one year. Whether this law will actually be enforced universally over the long run remains to be seen, and it's always best to be on your guard when driving back from a long day at the beach (where it's a Brazilian tradition to knock back more than a few).

Despite the pitfalls, if you want to visit natural attractions around Rio having a car gives you much more freedom to hit off-the-beaten-track places where buses don't go (and if they do go, it's likely they'll make 200 local stops on the way). Cars can come in very handy for beach-hopping, since you can hit secluded coves not accessible by bus. If you do rent a car, try to avoid traveling on big holiday weekends, when traffic is guaranteed to be atrocious. Also avoid driving at night. When parking, whether you need help or not, you'll usually be guided into a space by an informal parking attendant. Aside from helping you back in or out, he'll promise to watch over your car as well. Whether he does or not, it's customary to tip him R$1–2 since he makes his living this way. Nonetheless, don't leave any valuables in the car, even in the trunk.

In Rio, major rental companies include **Avis** (www.avis.com.br) in Copacabana (Av. Princesa Isabel 350, tel. 21/2543-8481); **Hertz** (www.hertz.com.br) with agencies at Galeão (tel. 21/3398-4339), Santos Dumont (tel. 21/2262-0612), and Copacabana (Av. Princesa Isabel 334, tel. 21/2275-7248); and **Localiza Rent a Car** (www.localiza.com.br) with agencies at Galeão (tel. 21/3398-5445), Santos Dumont (tel. 21/2240-9181), and in Copacabana (Av. Princesa Isabel 214, tel. 21/2275-3440). An international driver's license is more widely recognized than a foreign license, but the latter is valid for up to six months. Rates for unlimited mileage range R$100–150 a day. Prices don't necessarily include insurance, so check beforehand.

© MICHAEL SOMMERS

taxi stand

Visas and Officialdom

VISAS

In terms of foreigners entering the country, Brazil practices a policy of reciprocity. This means that if your country requires Brazilians to have travel visas, you will have to get a visa from the nearest Brazilian consulate before entering Brazil. To date, citizens of Canada, the United States, and Australia require visas. Citizens of Great Britain (and other E.U. countries) and New Zealand don't need visas, but do need a passport that is valid for six months and a return ticket. Upon arrival, they'll be given a 90-day tourist visa.

Various types of visas are available. What differs is the cost, processing time, and documentation necessary. Currently, a single-entry tourist visa that has a validity of 90 days costs US$100 for Americans, CDN$90 for Canadians, and A$90 for Australians. Count on one to two weeks for processing. You'll need to submit a passport photo, show proof of a return ticket, and can often only pay with a money order.

All visitors who arrive in Brazil and go through customs will receive an entry form, which you should *not* lose. You'll need to hand it back to the Polícia Federal when leaving the country. Should you want to extend your stay, you can renew your visa, 15 days before it expires, at the visa section of the Polícia Federal headquarters in any major city. The fee for renewal is the equivalent of US$10. If you overextend the 180-day limit, you won't be deported, but you will pay a fine. The federal police is also where you should head if your passport is lost or stolen. You'll need to make a report in order to get a temporary travel document from your consulate. Then you'll need to return once again to the Polícia Federal to receive an official stamp.

Artists and/or academics who are coming to Brazil for a short time are better off traveling on a tourist visa. Those with a long-term research or study project will need to apply for a *visto temporário,* which can be issued for six months,

one year, or even two years. To get one, you'll need to be sponsored by a recognized Brazilian educational institution confirming your project. Processing can take several months.

Before coming to Brazil, make copies of your passport. Also bring a second photo ID with you. By law, in Brazil you are always required to have a picture ID. In many circumstances— from renting headphones in a museum to entering an office building—you will need to show or even leave your ID.

CUSTOMS

At Brazilian customs *(alfândega)* officials are generally more interested in Brazilians who went on major shopping sprees abroad than they are in foreign visitors. However, since checks are random, you might find your luggage being inspected. Visitors can bring in objects for their own personal use, including cameras and laptop. If it is new, you may be asked to register the item to make sure you take it with you when you leave. (It's a good idea to bring receipts for new items.) If you're bringing things for Brazilian friends, keep them to a minimum (i.e., don't show up with four digital cameras, five iPods, and two laptops). Should you be discovered, you will end up paying duty on them. Gifts purchased overseas that are worth more than US$500 should be declared.

Before heading to customs, you might want to start shopping at the airport duty-free shops (yes, you can purchase duty-free upon arrival as well as prior to departure), where you can indulge in up to US$500 of purchases. Prices are quite competitive, particularly items such as alcohol and perfume. Should you be visiting with any Brazilians on your trip, the gift of a fine bottle of imported whiskey will earn you their undying gratitude.

BRAZILIAN EMBASSIES AND CONSULATES

The Brazilian Embassy in the **United States** is in Washington, D.C. (tel. 202/238-2700, www.brasilemb.org). You'll also find main consulates in New York (tel. 917/777-7777, www.brazilny.org), Miami (tel. 305/285-6200, www.brazilmiami.org), and Los Angeles (tel. 323/651-2664, www.brazilianconsulate.org). In **Canada,** the Brazilian Embassy is in Ottawa (tel. 613/237-1090, www.brasembottawa.com) and the main consulate is in Toronto (tel. 416/922-2503, www.consbrastoronto.org). In **Britain,** the embassy is in London (tel. 020/7499-0877, www.brazil.org.uk). In **Australia,** it is in Canberra (tel. 02/6273-2372, www.brazil.org.au).

FOREIGN CONSULATES AND EMBASSIES IN BRAZIL

Foreign embassies are all located in Brasília, while major consulates are found in both Rio de Janeiro and São Paulo. For specific numbers and listings, check the main embassy web pages.

Consulates in Rio de Janeiro: **Australia** (Av. Presidente Wilson 231, Suite 23, tel. 21/3824-4624), **Canada** (Av. Atlântica 1130, 5th fl., tel. 21/2543-3004), **United States** (Av. Presidente Wilson 147, tel. 21/3823-2000), and **Great Britain** (Praia do Flamengo 284, tel. 21/2555-9600).

Conduct and Customs

Overall, Brazil is a very relaxed and casual place, although sometimes appearances can be deceiving. Underneath the freewheeling, sensual vibe, you'll sometimes find a conservative core. Brazil has the largest Catholic population on the planet, and though the practice of Catholicism in Brazil is considered to be much less rigid and conservative than in other Latin American countries, a great many people do take it seriously. If you're entering a place of worship—Christian or otherwise—take care to dress and behave with a certain degree of modesty. In some official buildings, among them government buildings as well as municipal theaters and even libraries and archives, similar forms of decorum apply: Women should not wear shorts or micro-skirts, men should wear long pants, and flip-flops should be avoided.

GREETINGS

Brazilians are extremely warm and friendly and this is apparent in the way they greet each other. If you're meeting a woman—whether a long-lost friend or a stranger—you'll greet her with two kisses *(beijos),* one on each cheek. Women kiss men as well, while with each other men do the more manly thing and shake hands. However, among younger men as well as male friends and family members, back slapping, hugging *(abraços),* and other forms of friendly

physical contact are quite common. When taking leave of each other, the same hugging and kissing rituals apply. If anything, they are much warmer on account of intimacies (and alcohols) shared.

PUBLIC DISPLAYS OF AFFECTION

Brazilians are naturally very affectionate, which can sometimes cause confusion for foreigners. A lot of friendly hugging and kissing goes on in public, and the sense of privacy and personal space is quite different than in North America. Brazilians not only love to be together (Garbo's "I want to be alone" is a very foreign concept), but when they're together they sit close and touch one another a great deal. In general, such behavior merely demonstrates a natural playfulness and lack of hang-ups about expressing affection, and you shouldn't treat it as sexual. When they want to be, Brazilians can be great and thoroughly effective flirts; to *jogar o charme* (cast your charm) is commonly accepted (both seriously and tongue-in-cheek) as a way of getting something (a discount, a restaurant table, a favor).

Another thing about Brazilians is that they tend to be far less hung up about their bodies (and revealing them in public), and about sex matters in general, than North Americans.

However, it's a serious mistake to confuse sensuality with licentiousness or with an "anything goes" attitude. And someone's looking sexy should not be equated with him or her wanting to have sex.

JEITO BRASILEIRO (THE BRAZILIAN WAY)

Dar um jeito or *um jeitinho* is a common Brazilian expression that sums up a quintessentially Brazilian philosophy as well as an art form and a way of life. Literally (and inadequately) translated, it means "give a way," which doesn't begin to do justice to the rich and subtle inferences the expression embraces. *Dar um jeito* is a Brazilian's typical recourse when confronted with the many *pepinos* (cucumbers, i.e. problems) that daily life throws their way. When faced with an awkward situation or a difficult problem, Brazilians rarely confront it head on—usually a futile tactic since the *pepino* is often the result of inflexible and sometimes absurd rules or government bureaucracy. Instead, they rely on a wide range of indirect *jeitos* or strategies, among them diplomacy, craftiness, flexibility, and charm, to get around an obstacle or extricate oneself from a predicament. The whole point is not to lose your cool and make a big scene, which Brazilians, a nonconfrontational people, only resort to *in extremis*. When they do make a scene it's known as *um escândalo,* and involves an impressive display of melodrama.

Tips for Travelers

TRAVELERS WITH DISABILITIES

For the most part, Brazil is very poorly equipped to deal with travelers with disabilities. In Rio the number of hotels, restaurants, public buildings, and tourist attractions with wheelchair access and ramps is growing, but they are the minority. Moreover, getting to them is very difficult: Sidewalks and streets are often uneven, traffic is chaotic, and there are almost no ramps. Very few buses, and no taxis, are equipped to deal with wheelchairs. For more information about traveling overseas with a disability contact Access-able (303/232-2979, www.access-able.com), based in Wheat Ridge, Colorado.

TRAVELING WITH CHILDREN

If a trip is well planned, kids usually love Brazil. And, indeed, Brazilians really love kids. In fact, families are generally more welcome in Brazil, than in North America. On beaches, it's easy for your kids to meet and play with Brazilian kids, who, like their parents, are usually outgoing and friendly. Often kids playing together breaks the ice for parents to get to know each other as well.

In hotels, children under six can usually stay for free in their parents' room—an extra bed is often provided. For older children often only a supplement is charged. If you're going to make trips outside the city, know that children cost the full fare on buses, but on planes fares are half price for ages 2–12. If you plan on renting a car and you have an infant, consider bringing a baby seat. Rental companies usually don't have them, and they are expensive in Brazil.

Perhaps the biggest threat to children is the sun. Make sure you bring plenty of sunscreen from home since it's outrageously expensive in Brazil, and make sure that on the beach you always have access to shade. In terms of disposable diapers for babies, you'll find Pampers and other brands in most supermarkets and pharmacies.

With the great variety of food in Rio, even picky young eaters should have no problem. If all else fails, there's *comida a quilo* and the food courts at the local *shoppings*. Most restaurants have high chairs—if not, they can improvise. Although few restaurants have

WHAT TO TAKE

Rio is a famously casual place in terms of **clothing.** To blend in and minimize hassles from insistent vendors or thieves, it helps to dress down. You won't find many baggy cargo shorts or oversized T-shirts, though. The jeans worn by men and women alike are fitted and stylish. Colors rule – black is far less popular than in North America and Europe, and during the day dark colors soak up heat.

Brazilians take great pride in their **beachwear.** You won't find men wearing Speedos or surfing shorts (unless they're surfers) or women wearing one-piece bathing suits. Consider purchasing swimwear in Rio so as not to stand out too much. If you plan to do some snorkeling, it's a good idea to bring your own **snorkeling gear.**

Even during the summer, bring a long-sleeved shirt or light jacket to keep you warm in intensely air-conditioned environments.

A **money belt** is a must in Rio. You never want to carry cash or cards in easy-to-pick pockets.

children's menus or portions, regular portions are often so large that kids can share with adults.

WOMEN TRAVELERS

Machismo has a strong hold in Brazil, however it's generally a more tepid version than in other Latin American countries. Although Brazilians respect women, North American notions of political correctness have never caught on here. And the definition of what constitutes sexual harassment is far more lax in Brazil (although an increasing number of cities have a *delegacia de mulheres,* where an all-female staff specializes in crimes against women). Flirting is a way of life in Brazil and is usually harmless. A *gringa,* whether traveling alone or with other women, will definitely incite curiosity and inevitably receive some intense stares and/

or come-ons. For the most part these are harmless, and can actually be flattering if you're in the right frame of mind. The problem is that you might feel targeted if you're being bothered every time you go out for a drink (women by themselves in bars is a rarity) or to the beach. If that's the case, try to join a group, or at least stick close to one (on the beach, for example). If saying a firm *"não"* and walking away isn't dissuading an insistent suitor, head immediately to a safe place (a hotel or restaurant). Avoid deserted areas by day, and always take taxis at night.

SENIOR TRAVELERS

Brazil is known for having a strong youth culture, and as a result many activities and venues tend to be geared towards a younger public. It's rather uncommon to see groups of elderly Brazilians traveling the way you would in North America and Europe. While in most major cities older Brazilians are not very visible, Rio is somewhat of an exception. Copacabana, in particular, has a very large population of elderly residents that takes full advantage of the neighborhoods's beach, boardwalk, and many cafés. However, the hassle and discomfort of public transportation coupled with messy traffic, crowds, and uneven sidewalks can make getting around the city a daunting experience. The overbearing heat and strong sun often exacerbates matters. On the upside, taxis are cheap and abundant, and many places have air-conditioning. Moreover, Brazilians are generally sensitive to the needs of seniors. Although discounts for seniors on public transportation and at museums and movies are generally accorded based on showing Brazilian ID, if you have proof of age (60 or 65) you can receive *um desconto para idosos* as well.

GAY AND LESBIAN TRAVELERS

A lot of gay and lesbian foreigners associate Rio with images of transvestites, Carnaval drag queens, and the muscle boys of Ipanema, and allow themselves to think that the city is a very gay place indeed. In reality, it is and it isn't. Brazil is more tolerant of gays and lesbians than many other Latin American countries. You'll see both gay and lesbian romances played out on nightly *novelas* and there are openly gay and lesbian celebrities (although they are hardly activists). Rio has an intense gay scene (though almost nonexistent lesbian scene)—particularly in the Zona Sul—with a wide range of bars, clubs, and strips of beach *barracas* that cater primarily to a gay and lesbian public. As with straight people, gays and lesbians can also be much more open about flirting in public. However, aside from a few specific gay enclaves, overall the scene is much more GLS (gay, lesbian, and sympathizers) than exclusively gay and lesbian. Straight, gay, and lesbian folks mix much more, and the result is a less overt and politicized gay and lesbian presence than in North America or Europe.

Ultimately, many Brazilians don't mind if you're gay or lesbian, but they don't want to be reminded of it. That is, they can deal with the fact of a same-sex romance in theory, but don't want to see signs of it (like public kissing or hand-holding) or hear you referring explicitly to your homosexuality. Two men or women living together, traveling together, or sharing a hotel room is not a problem, but often the implicit agreement is that you're two friends (even if deep down, people may suspect you're not). Although the drag queen and flamboyant queen is very much an accepted part of the culture, there is a distinction between spectacle and humor, and the reality of day-to-day life. Brazil is ultimately a macho culture, and explicit signs of homosexuality can incite insults and even violence. Even in cosmopolitan Rio, violence against gays is not unheard-of. For more information about the gay and lesbian scene in Brazil, in Portuguese, check out www.guiagaybrasil.com.br, which has GSL listings for cities all over Brazil. If you're traveling to Rio, check out the English-language Rio Gay Guide (www.riogayguide.com).

Health and Safety

BEFORE YOU GO

Before your trip, it's always a good idea to check with your country's travel health recommendations for Brazil, available online: Australia (www.dfat.gov.au/travel/), Canada (www.phac-aspc.gc.ca/tmp-pmv/pub-eng.php), Great Britain (www.direct.gov.uk/en/TravelAndTransport/TravellingAbroad/index.htm), United States (www.cdc.gov/travel/). Another good source is the **MD Travel Health** website (www.mdtravelhealth.com), which has complete travel health information, updated daily, for both physicians and travelers.

Vaccinations

No vaccines are necessary if you're visiting Rio. However, if you're going to be traveling around other parts of Brazil **yellow fever** is recommended, and in some cases, required. It is absolutely essential for visiting the Amazon region, but there have been isolated, yet recent, occurrences in the Pantanal, Brasília, and even Minas Gerais and Bahia. Other recommended vaccines include **hepatitis A, hepatitis B, typhoid,** and **rabies shots.**

What to Bring

Bring any prescription medication that you're taking, in its original packaging. Just in case, ask your pharmacist or doctor to give you the generic names for any medication. You will usually be able to purchase the same drug at any Brazilian pharmacy (although the brand name will be different). Not only can you get many prescription drugs over the counter in Brazil, but they're often a lot cheaper than in North America or Europe. Do, however, bring plenty of mosquito repellent, sunscreen, and aspirin or Tylenol (which are more expensive in Brazil). Aloe vera or other relief for sunburn is also a good idea, as is calamine lotion or witch hazel to take the irritating itch out of any mosquito bites.

Insurance

If you have medical coverage, check to see if it covers you for expenses incurred overseas. If not, you might want to consider buying travel insurance. In either case, find out if the insurer will make payments directly or reimburse you afterwards—most insurers tend to do the latter. Regardless, most of the best Brazilian clinics and hospitals (which are private) will make you pay for service up-front.

HEALTH PRECAUTIONS

Tropical heat and humidity favor the growth of bacteria, and cause food and organic matter in general to spoil and rot very quickly. As a result, hygiene standards in Brazil are quite high. Nevertheless, it's wise to take certain precautions so as not to spend your trip with an upset stomach or diarrhea.

In terms of food, be attentive to the conditions of any food you purchase on the street. Fruit with a peel (banana, mango, papaya) is safer than fruit without (which should be carefully washed). Similarly, boiled vegetables are safer than raw ones (unless you know they've been well washed) or vegetables that have been sitting around in mayonnaise. You should also be careful with seafood (such as shrimp). If something looks poorly cooked, or smells or tastes slightly off, spit it out and stop eating.

It is supposedly safe to drink the tap water in Rio, although few people actually do (in part due to the heavy chlorine taste). Most Brazilians drink filtered water or mineral water; either *natural* or *com gas* (carbonated), and you should too (although brushing your teeth or rinsing fruit with tap water is perfectly fine). Mineral water is inexpensive and available everywhere: at restaurants, bars, bus stations, gas stations, supermarkets, and pharmacies. And you should really stick to it, or soft drinks. Ice is usually made from filtered water as well. However, if you're in an out-of-the-

IVO PITANGUY

If Brazil is the plastic-surgery capital of the world, then Ivo Pitanguy is the celebrity surgeon who put it on the map. Pitanguy, whose father was a surgeon, began his pioneering techniques in reconstructive surgery by working on wounded WWII soldiers and, later on, burn victims. When he opened his own private clinic in Rio de Janeiro, he set the stage for what would become one of Brazil's most renowned industries. With cutting-edge technology and rock-bottom prices – not to mention an idyllic location for recuperation – Rio, always a city where appearances mattered enormously, became a mecca for celebrities from around Brazil and the world in search of a little nip or tuck. Recently, the city has become a prime destination for "cosmetic vacationers" – a new breed of tourist who combines going under the scalpel with post-operative trips to beaches and mountain retreats.

way place that seems a bit dodgy, you might want to order your drink without it (*sem gelo*). Also make a habit of using a straw when drinking from cans (one will invariably be offered to you). If drinking beer from a can, make sure you wipe the top off with a napkin (or even your shirt).

PHARMACIES

Pharmacies are everywhere in Rio. Most are open seven days a week, until 10 P.M. Many take turns staying open for 24 hours. Two locations of **Drogaria Pacheco** that never close are in Copacabana (Av. Nossa Senhora de Copacabana 534-A/B, tel. 21/2548-1525) and Catete (Rua do Catete 248, tel. 21/2556-6792). All *farmácias* have at least one licensed pharmacist trained to deal with minor medical problems and emergencies, which could save you a trip to a clinic or hospital (the only problem is it's very unlikely that they'll speak any English). You'll be able to find good medicine for whatever ails you (upset stomach, diarrhea, headache, rashes, a cold or cough), even though you probably won't recognize the names.

CLINICS AND HOSPITALS

Brazil has a very good health system—as long as you can pay for it. All Brazilians have access to public hospitals for free. In theory, this is fantastic. In practice, the state of many public hospitals is truly frightening. There is a saying among Brazilians that a sick person who goes into a public hospital usually gets worse instead of cured. While doctors and nurses are often qualified, lack of funds often makes public hospitals precarious. Moreover, the sight of sick and suffering people lining up on the sidewalk as early as 2 A.M. and then waiting for hours, in the hot sun, to get medical attention is truly tragic. For all these reasons, unless you have a real emergency, should you require medical attention it's best to head to a private clinic. Middle-class and wealthy Brazilians usually pay high health-insurance premiums that give them access to state-of-the-art First World–style clinics, particularly in major cities. You can have access to them as well, but it will cost you. Consulates can recommend good hospitals, clinics, or specialists, although English-speaking doctors are rare.

In the event of a medical emergency, dial **193** for Pronto Socorro (First Aid). If you need to visit a hospital, **Clínica Galdino Campos** (Av. Nossa Senhora de Copacabana, tel. 21/2548-9966, www.galdinocampos.com.br) in Copacabana is a private clinic that has a tradition of treating foreigners. It is open 24 hours and has English-speaking staff. In Ipanema, **Hospital Ipanema** (Rua Antônio Parreiras 67, tel. 21/2287-2322) is a public hospital with emergency services. For non-emergencies, contact the **Rio Health Collective** (Av. das Américas 4430, tel. 21/3325-9300). By phone, they can provide you with names of qualified specialists who speak English.

TRAVELER'S DIARRHEA

To avoid diarrhea, be careful about the source of the water you drink and the food you eat. Even so, you might get diarrhea simply as a result of being exposed to different types of bacteria. In the event you do get sick, make sure to drink lots of fluids. Particularly good for diarrhea and upset stomachs are *água de coco* (fresh coconut water) and *suco de lima,* a juice made from a citrus fruit that is a cross between an orange and a lime. If your diarrhea is still serious after two to three days, you should go to a pharmacy and ask for an antibiotic and an antidiarrheal drug. If you see blood and have a fever, chills, or strong abdominal pains, seek medical treatment.

DENGUE

Dengue fever is a viral infection that, like many tropical diseases—including malaria and yellow fever—is transmitted by mosquitoes. Dengue isn't caused by just any old mosquito, but by a species known as *aedes* that breeds in stagnant water, usually in densely populated urban areas with improper drainage. Plant containers and abandoned rubber tires are particularly common breeding grounds. Dengue mosquitos usually attack during the daytime, and are most common during hot, humid rainy periods. In recent years, Rio de Janeiro has had a large dengue epidemic during its rainy summer months. Although rarely fatal, dengue is like having a really debilitating case of flu. Symptoms include fever, aching muscles, headaches, nausea, weakness, vomiting, and a rash. In general, the worst symptoms last for five to seven days, but full recuperation can take longer. Diagnosis is via a blood test. There is no vaccine for dengue nor is there treatment aside from rest, plenty of liquids, and acetaminophen (Tylenol)—do not take aspirin. Only severe cases require hospitalization. The best thing you can do to avoid infection is to take precautions to avoid getting bitten in the first place.

AIDS AND STDS

Brazil has one of the highest numbers of people living with HIV. According to statistics, more than 20 percent of infected people are women. Although Brazil has one of the world's most highly respected and effective AIDS policies—aside from creating low-cost generic drugs, the Brazilian government's fight against AIDS involves free medication and medical follow-up for all patients for life—it doesn't prevent people from getting HIV in the first place. Condoms—known as *camisinhas* ("little shirts")—are widespread (you'll find them in all pharmacies and many supermarkets) and there is not so much a stigma as a resistance to using them. As a result, you really have to be careful about HIV and STDs. Whether you're with a man or a woman, always insist upon using a condom.

SUN EXPOSURE

When you arrive in Rio from the cold and gray Northern Hemisphere, your first instinct will be to sprawl on the sand for a day, but try to exercise some self-control and expose yourself to the sun gradually. The tropical sun, particularly during the summer months, can cause a lot of damage. Brazilians (many of whom don't use sunscreen due to its exorbitant cost) have the highest rate of skin cancer in the world. Using a strong sunscreen (bring it from home) that filters out UVA and UVB rays is essential; SPF 30 is the minimum you should use. Even with SPF 30, if you're foolish enough to stay in the sun between the deadliest hours of 11 A.M. and 2 P.M. you will get burned. On many beaches, you can rent a parasol or head to a thatched *barraca* for shade come high noon. Children and those with fair, sensitive skin should use a much higher SPF. A hat is always essential, whether you're on the beach or practicing any outdoor sport, and you'll be practically blinded without a pair of sunglasses with a protective filter. Remember to drink lots of liquids all the time, even if you're not thirsty. Beer and *caipirinhas* might be refreshing, but alcohol actually dehydrates. An ideal replenishing drink is *água de coco*.

MOSQUITOS

Mosquitos can be very irritating. They can also be carriers of diseases such as yellow fever, dengue fever, and malaria. They are especially a problem in urban areas during hot rainy seasons (in which dengue can be a problem). Aside from getting necessary vaccines, the best way to prevent mosquito bites is to wear effective repellent (containing DEET) as well as long pants, long sleeves, and closed shoes. Be careful not to get repellent close to your eyes or mouth. Sleep with mosquito netting and if your windows don't have screens, make sure you close them. Mosquitos don't like wind, so if you have a fan in your room keep it on. Burning mosquito coils helps, but you might still hear a bit of buzzing, and the odor can be somewhat overwhelming.

SAFETY

The subject of crime and security in Brazil is an extremely important and complex one. Violent crime, holdups, robberies, and drug warfare in major cities dominate the Brazilian news media (often in a sensationalist manner) and have a major social impact. An increasing number of middle-class Brazilians are moving to closed condominium complexes with electric fences and 24-hour security. Wealthy Brazilians are also the leading buyers of security systems and of bulletproof cars in the world. Meanwhile, poorer Brazilians who reside in peripheral neighborhoods or *favelas* live in fear of bus holdups, stray bullets, or drug traffickers. If you come into contact with Brazilians, read the papers, or watch TV, you will definitely hear such stories, and while the tone may be alarmist or melodramatic, the occurrences themselves are true. There's no need for paranoia, but don't let yourself be complacent.

Having lived in Brazil for 10 years, I don't know *anybody* who has never been robbed. I myself have been robbed on various occasions. I have had my apartment broken into (someone climbed up my building and in through the window); on the other occasions, I have to admit that I was in the wrong place at the wrong time: a deserted, if central street at night (7 P.M.), and in the midst of a multitude of drunk and celebrating people (upon the occasion of a popular street festival)—during which someone succeeded in sliding their hand into my pocket and making off with the contents.

Safety Tips

My experiences are typical of instances in which traveling foreigners might find themselves at risk. However, such situations are easy to avoid. Unless you're on a very busy or major street in a good neighborhood, don't walk around at night in a city you don't know. While Rio's downtown commercial centers may hum with energy by day, at night and on weekends (especially Sundays) they turn into ghost towns and should be avoided. If you're going to be amidst a crowd (at an outdoor performance, a parade, or during Carnaval) leave all valuables and original documents in your hotel. Carry a small change purse around your neck or a money belt.

Public transportation is safe enough during the day, but at night (when holdups are more likely), outside of the Zona Sul beach neighborhoods—which are quite busy and safe until around 10 P.M.—take a taxi, even if it's just a few blocks to your destination. If you've rented a car, be careful where you park. Particularly at night, you don't want to be on a dark or isolated side street. If you're at a stoplight, keep your windows rolled up: Stuck in traffic, you can easily be held up. In fact, in major cities throughout Brazil, drivers slow down at stoplights, but don't actually stop their cars (a practice sanctioned by law).

You should never be walking around (night or day) with a lot of cash in a purse or pocket. Do, however, keep a few small bills in a location that you can easily access. Fumbling around for money in public (on a bus or at a market) leaves you exposed to robbery. Similarly, when you go to the beach, don't bring any valuables with you. Bring enough cash for drinks or snacks and that's it. Keep all your possessions with you, in a neat pile or a cheap (preferably local) beach bag, within your line of vision (there are tales of tourists dozing in the sun and waking up to find their possessions gone—a good trick is to tie your bag around your beach chair). If you're on your own and want to go swimming, ask someone to watch your stuff. This is very common on Brazilian beaches.

If you're going to be taking money out of an ATM, make sure nobody is watching you. Even though ATMs are open until 10 P.M., the best time to take out money is during the day, in a busy area (preferably in an airport or shopping mall). Be careful on Sundays, when commercial areas can be quiet. Once again, if you're withdrawing a lot of cash, put it in a money belt.

Although Rio has a lot of crime, in recent years the city has taken great pains to make sure major tourist areas—particularly the beaches of the Zona Sul—are heavily policed. Nonetheless, always have your wits about you. If you travel outside of Rio to small towns or beach resorts, you will definitely feel more relaxed. Crime is much lower, and you can let your guard down somewhat (although don't be lulled into complete carelessness).

Gringos are uniformly considered easy targets, not only because they are all thought to be rich, but because they are often careless. One thing that may help is to try to camouflage yourself: Get a bit of a tan, don't talk loudly in a foreign language, and try to dress like the locals (i.e., casually, but smartly, with no flashy jewelry, expensive footwear, or fashionable designer duds). Also be careful about where you flash your camera, particularly if it has a big zoom lens. The smaller and more compact your camera, the better. Don't unfold big maps in public or look lost or unsure of where you're going. Without being neurotic, try to always be aware of where you are and what's going on around you. Trust your instincts. If a bar, street, or neighborhood feels dodgy, make a fast exit. If you feel someone is watching you or following you, speed up your pace, cross the street, or enter a shop or public building. Be aware of possible scams such as being approached by so-called officials at airports who want you to go with them (after you've come out of the arrivals section). Another notorious *golpe* is Boa Noite Cinderela (Good Night Cinderella), in which someone slips a drug into your drink and, while you're knocked out, robs you blind. This trick usually befalls unsuspecting romantics (particularly gays) who hook up with a potential conquest in a bar. If you find yourself in this situation, don't leave your drink unguarded (such as when you go to the bathroom).

Police

The North American or European view of police as (for the most part) symbols of law and order doesn't hold true in Brazil. When trouble occurs, most Brazilians avoid the police, who are grossly underpaid and subject to corruption and violence. It is sometimes difficult to distinguish police from the bandits and drug traffickers they are supposedly battling. This is, of course, a generalization, and there are exceptions to the rule.

In Brazil, there are various types of police. The most efficient (and well paid, and thus less corrupt) of the bunch are the Polícia Federal, who deal with all matters concerning passports, visas, and immigration. They have offices at all international airports as well as at frontier posts and in state capitals, and are generally helpful. The Polícia Militar are a hangover from the era of military dictatorship. They dress in soldier-like khaki uniforms accessorized with tough lace-up boots and berets (even in the tropical heat). You'll often see them supposedly keeping the peace on street corners. Although they can be rough with Brazilian indolents, they leave foreigners alone. The plain-clothes Polícia Civil deal with solving crimes. If you're robbed and want to report the crime, in many places you'll need to go to the nearest *delegacia,* or station. Be prepared if you want an official report: You'll need to wait in line, and nobody will speak English. Unless you really need a report for insurance purposes, you might want to just let it go. You'll have better luck if you go to the *delegacia de turismo,* located in Leblon (Av. Afrânio de Melo Franco 159, tel. 21/3399-7170). This special police force specializes in crimes against foreign tourists and some of their agents speak English.

Theft

Most crime in Brazil takes place in poorer neighborhoods that you'll probably never see. If you take the necessary precautions, it's not that likely that you'll be robbed. Even if you are, in most cases it will consist of a *furto* in which your pockets are picked or someone grabs your bag and takes off. However, *assaltos* (holdups) do occur. In the event that you are held up by someone, do not resist. Outside of *favelas,* which are often controlled by drug traffickers, armed robbery is somewhat rare, but you could find yourself being threatened by a knife or a broken bottle. Quickly and calmly hand over whatever the thief wants. It is a no-brainer between your money, watch, jewelry, or documents and your life. Accidents happen when people get very upset or try to resist, making the robber nervous and prone to act impulsively.

In the event of an emergency, call **190** to reach the police. Meanwhile, if you are robbed, seek out the **Delegácia Especial de Atendimento ao Turista** (Tourist Police) unit whose Leblon headquarters (Av. Afrânio de Melo Franco 159, tel. 21/3399-7170) is open 24 hours a day. Agents are generally helpful and speak English. Even if you do report a robbery, it's extremely unlikely you'll get your possessions back.

Information and Services

MONEY

Brazil's currency is the *real* (pronounced "ray-all"; the plural, *reais,* is pronounced "ray-eyes"). One *real* (R$1) can be divided into 100 *centavos.* In terms of denominations, you'll come across 1, 2, 5, 10, 20, 50, and 100 *real* bills (although R$1 bills are rare, having been replaced by a two-toned R$1 coin). Bills are easy to distinguish since each is a different color. Coins are trickier, since some have several versions, but you'll find 5, 10, 25, and 50 *centavo* coins. Due to the fact that they were virtually worthless, there are no longer any 1 *centavo* coins. When you purchase something, the total will be rounded up or down (e.g., if the total comes to R$4.37 the cashier will expect R$4.35; if it comes to R$1.38, you'll get change for R$1.40).

Exchanging Money

You might want to bring some U.S. dollars for an emergency (in the event you can't get cash from an ATM or if your card gets lost or stolen). However, you'll usually lose money exchanging dollars at a bank, a *casa de câmbio* (exchange house), a major hotel, or an airport bank (open 7 days a week; regular banking hours are Mon.–Fri. 10 A.M.–4 P.M.). Since the Brazilian *real* has stabilized in recent years, U.S. dollars (which were hoarded by all Brazilians in the face of rampant inflation) have become less coveted. Dollars are not accepted in many places these days, and attractive black-market exchange rates are a thing of the past. Likewise, don't bother with travelers checks, which very few places will exchange. The most advantageous place to exchange currency is at major branches of **Banco do Brasil**. There is a branch at Aeroporto Internacional Tom Jobim as well as in Centro (Rua Senador Dantas 105, tel. 21/3808-2689) and Copacabana (Av. Nossa Senhora da Copacabana 1292, tel. 21/2523-1441). There is an **American Express** at the Copacabana Palace (Av. Atlântica 1702-B, tel. 21/2548-2148 or 0/800-702-0777).

ATMs

The best way to deal with money concerns in Rio is to bring an international Visa or MasterCard (or both, to give you more options) and withdraw cash from bank machines. Not only is this the most secure method, but you'll get the best exchange rate. Most major branches of Banco do Brasil and Bradesco will have at least one ATM that accepts Visa/PLUS cards, while Bradesco, HSBC, and Citibank accept MasterCard/Cirrus. Meanwhile, red Banco 24 Horas ATMs accept all cards, all of the time. In all cases, you need to have a 4-digit PIN. All ATMs have an option in English. More and more ATMs accept international cards. If you're going to a small town or somewhere off the beaten track, it's best to stock up on cash beforehand, although credit cards will be accepted by most hotels and larger restaurants. The largest concentrations of banks are on Avenida Rio Branco (Centro), Avenida Nossa Senhora de Copacabana (Copacabana), and Rua Visconde de Pirajá (Ipanema), but you'll usually find them in all major *shoppings* as well as at the airports and *rodoviária.*

For security reasons, bank ATMs are open daily 6 A.M.–10 P.M. Most have a withdrawal limit of R$1,000 (although Bradesco's is R$600). To check out locations online in advance, consult the sites for Visa/PLUS (www.visa.com) and MasterCard/Cirrus (www.mastercard.com.) During big holidays, such as New Year's, Carnaval, and any long weekend, it's wise to stock up on cash in advance since sometimes the machines run dry.

Credit Cards

Most hotels, restaurants, and stores in Rio accept international credit cards. Using a card not only alleviates carrying around big wads of cash, but also offers the most advantageous exchange rate. The only thing it won't get you is the discounts (usually of 10 percent) that you can ask for (and usually get) if you pay for accommodations or shopping items in cash (*em dinheiro*). Visa and MasterCard are the most widely accepted cards (once again, bring both to increase your payment possibilities), although many places will take American Express and Diners Club.

Money Wires

Should you have an emergency and require a money wire, Banco do Brasil has a partnership with Western Union. A person can send you money from North America, via Western Union (www.westernunion.com), to any Banco do Brasil branch. Once you've specified the city you're in, all you need to do (aside from standing in a long line) is show up with your passport and the wire transaction code and get your cash.

MAPS AND TOURIST INFORMATION
Tourist Information

Before traveling to Rio, it's helpful to check out some of the books and Internet resources listed at the back of this book. Once you're in Rio, you'll find several **Riotur** (www.riotur.com .br) information kiosks scattered throughout the city, operated by the municipal secretary of tourism. The main branch is in Centro (Praça Pio X 119, 9th fl., Mon.–Fri. 9 A.M.–6 P.M., tel. 21/2271-7000), but there are also branches in Copacabana (Av. Princesa Isabel 183, tel. 21/2541-7522, daily 9 A.M.–6 P.M.) and at the Aeroporto Internacional Tom Jobim (6 A.M.–midnight) and the Rodoviária Novo Rio (daily 8 A.M.–8 P.M.). Aside from a free map, Riotur publishes a very thorough bilingual bimonthly city guide that includes descriptions of sights and attractions as well as hotel, restaurant, nightlife, entertainment, sports, leisure, and events listings. It's very up-to-date and extremely handy (not to mention unobtrusive). In general, Riotur staff are helpful and usually speak some English. For up-to-date information or listings in English, you can make a free call to their tourist hotline, **Alô Rio** (tel. 0/800-285-0555, daily 9 A.M.–6 P.M.). For (scant) information about the rest of Rio de Janeiro

state, you can visit **TurisRio** (www.turisrio .rj.gov.br), with offices at the international airport (daily 10 A.M.–9 P.M.) and in Centro (Rua México 125, tel. 0/800-282-2007, Mon.–Fri. 9 A.M.–6 P.M.).

Maps

Aside from the maps offered by Riotur, most *bancas de revista* (newsstands) and bookstores will sell city maps for around R$5. The best maps are produced by Quatro Rodas, which sells regional maps for all of Brazil as well as highway maps and a detailed fold-out map of Brazil that is free with its annually published *Guia Quatro Rodas* (a Brazilian equivalent of France's Michelin).

The Quatro Rodas website (www.via-jeaqui.abril.com.br/g4r)—which is only in Portuguese, but quite easy to navigate—has an option where you can type in a street name and number and pinpoint an exact address on a map that also permits zooming in and out. For long-distance travel, there is an option that allows you to type in the city of origin and the destination city, and you'll be shown a map indicating possible routes. Google Maps (www .maps.google.com) now covers Brazil and is easier for English speakers to navigate.

COMMUNICATIONS AND MEDIA
Postal Service

The main post office is in Centro (Rua Primeiro de Março 64, tel. 21/2219-5315), but there are numerous agencies throughout the city, including one at Aeroporto Internacional Tom Jobim (24 hours) and branches in Copacabana (Av. Nossa Senhora de Copacabana 540) and Ipanema (Rua Visconde de Pirajá 452). Major *shoppings* also usually have small branches. (Hours are Monday–Friday 8 A.M.–6 P.M., Sat. 8 A.M.–noon.) It's easy to identify post offices (Correios) by their bright yellow-and-blue marquees.

When sending a letter or parcel, you can send it *simples* (regular mail) or *registrada* (registered). Sedex is Correios's version of FedEx and is quite efficient. Correios sells cardboard

© MICHAEL SOMMERS

mailbox

boxes of various sizes as well as postcards and very beautiful aerograms. For envelopes, you'll often have to go to a *papelaria* (stationery store). There are no adhesive envelopes in Brazil, but the Correios will always have a pot of glue and a brush and you can proceed to make a big mess. Postage within Brazil is very inexpensive, but sending letters or packages abroad can be expensive depending on weight. On the bright side, intensely colorful Brazilian postage stamps *(selos)* are quite stunning.

Telephones

Brazilian phone service is quite efficient, if not exactly cheap. Local calls are charged by the minute. Calls within Brazil have become somewhat cheaper in recent years with the privatization of the phone industry, but the cost of international calls is pretty astronomical, and unless it's essential to call you're better off emailing or Skype-ing with loved ones at home. If you make an international call from a hotel, it will be even more exorbitant (it will be much cheaper if you ask people back home to call you).

Throughout Brazil, you will see dome-shaped phone booths known as *orelhões* ("big ears") where you can make local calls as well as long-distance calls throughout Brazil. There used to be considerable lineups at *orelhões*, but now that cell phones are so popular you'll find them abandoned (and often not working). To use an *orelhão*, you'll need to purchase a phone card *(cartão telefônica)*, sold at any *banca de revistas* or by vendors in busy streets. They usually come in 40 and 60 units *(unidades)*. A quick local call will use up one or two units. A short long-distance call will quickly use up an entire card.

Brazil has several telephone companies, or *operadoras,* and whenever you make a long-distance call outside of your area code (known as a DDD), you'll have to precede the number with a two-digit number belonging to one of them. Embratur (21) is the biggest one, with national and international coverage. Other *operadoras* are Intelig (23) and Oi (31). When calling a number throughout Brazil, you'll need to dial 0 followed by the *operadora* code 21 (for example), followed by the DDD, followed by the number. An example of a call from Rio to São Paulo (whose area code is 11) would be: 0/21-11-3333-3333. An example of an international call to Canada or the United States (whose country code is 1) would be: 00/21-1-416-999-9999. It is also possible to make a collect call *(uma chamada a cobrar)* from Brazil via the Embratel operator. To do so, call 0/800-703-2111.

For international telephone calls, Rio has quite a few international calling centers, which also have Internet access. **Central Fone** (www.centralfone.com.br) has many locations throughout the city including Centro (Av. Rio Branco 156, Mon.–Fri. 9 A.M.–9 P.M., Sat. 10 A.M.–4 P.M.) and Ipanema (Rua Vinicius de Moraes 129, Mon.–Fri. 9:30 A.M.–8 P.M., Sat.–Sun. 11 A.M.–6 P.M.). There are many call centers/cyber cafés in Copacabana, among them **Locutório** (Rua Francisco Sá 26, daily 8 A.M.–2 A.M.) and **Telerede** (Av. Nossa Senhora da Copacabana 209, daily 8 A.M.–midnight).

Cell phones are immensely popular throughout Brazil. In fact, many poorer Brazilians prefer to have a cell phone rather than a more expensive home phone that carries hefty monthly rates. Calling to or from a cell phone, however, is more expensive than calling from a fixed phone. If you're calling long distance, charges are extremely steep. You'll find cell phone coverage in most places throughout Brazil. Your own cell phone should work in Brazil if it is compatible with international GSM standards; contact your provider before your trip to confirm. However, since roaming charges will be really high, you're much better off buying a Brazilian SIM chip with TIM (www.tim.com.br), the only provider that provides nationwide service. Or, you can rent a cell phone at the airports with a company such as **PressCell** (tel. 21/3322-2692, www.presscell .com.br).

Internet

Internet service has spread through Brazil like wildfire. Although only around 10 percent of the population has Internet at home, cyber cafés in bookstores, bars, and *shoppings* are ubiquitous, as are LAN houses—dark (but air-conditioned) dens where adolescents while away the day playing games and blogging (Brazilians comprise the second-biggest population of bloggers in the world after Americans). Prices are roughly R$3–10 an hour, depending on location (tourists areas are usually more expensive), but service (via broadband) is uniformly quite rapid. Headphones and microphones are often provide to allow you to Skype. More and more places (cafés and shopping malls) also have free wireless access in the event you have a laptop or cell phone with Internet. Moreover, most hotels, *pousadas,* and even youth hostels in Rio have invested in Internet, not only for themselves, but for their guests as well (although it's often provided for free, in some large hotels you'll sometimes have to pay an exorbitant hourly rate). As a result, no matter where you are, you'll have no trouble checking your email or uploading digital photos.

Newspapers and Magazines

Rio's two main daily newspapers are the *Jornal do Brasil* and *O Globo. Jornal do Brasil* is slightly conservative and *O Globo* is owned by the Globo media giant that also owns radio stations, a record company, and the famous Globo television network. Even if you don't read Portuguese, both publish good arts and entertainment listings.

Brazil has magazines galore. The three weekly news magazines along the lines of *Time* and *Newsweek* are *Istoé, Época* (owned by Globo), and *Veja.* None of them are quite as hard-hitting and high-quality as they were in the pre-Internet age. If you buy *Veja* in Rio, you'll receive a free *Time Out*–style city guide with the upcoming week's cultural and arts listings and events along with shopping news, restaurant reviews, and articles about various Carioca hot topics and personalities. If you're interested in Brazilian food and restaurants, *Gula* is a great magazine (similar to *Gourmet*). *Bravo* is an intelligent and attractive magazine devoted to the Brazilian and international art world. *Trip* and *TPM* are two funky magazines aimed at hipster twentysomething females. Brazilian *Vogue* is fun for visiting fashionistas. Meanwhile, curious travelers might want to check out *Viagem e Turismo,* a gorgeously photographed monthly travel mag that always puts out interesting special editions on different Brazilian regions (it is published by Abril, which also publishes the Quatro Rodas maps and guides).

At Rio's main *livrarias,* you can get your hands on major English-language papers and all sorts of international magazines as well as English-language guidebooks and fiction. Large *bancas de revistas* in the Zona Sul also carry foreign press. Because these items are imported, they will cost a lot more than you would pay for them back home.

Television

Brazilian TV is a great unifier: No matter how much the landscape, temperature, or accents change, you'll see people all over the country watching the same soccer games, *novelas,* newscasts, reality shows, and plethora of live-audience shows animated by grating, unctuous, and plastic surgery–enhanced hosts and hostesses. For the most part, Brazilian TV is also pretty terrible.

The major networks beamed across the nation are SBT, Record, Bandeirantes, MTV (a Brazilian version of the American music network), Globo, and TV Educadora, a state-owned educational network that has a mix of high-brow roundtables, films, and very good cultural programming (including great live-music performances). Based in Rio's Jardim Botânico neighborhood, the all-powerful Globo is the leading network. Its nightly *novelas* (which air Mon.–Sat. 7 P.M., 8 P.M., and 9 P.M.) are the most watched of all nightly programs. These soap operas go all-out in terms of sets, costumes, lighting, and production and star a roster of gorgeous (and usually pretty talented) actors, actresses, and models. Known as Globais, they're all part of a permanent stable of stars that hearkens back to the Hollywood studio system. When these Globais aren't participating in a *novela,* miniseries, or other Globo productions, they make commercials and give the paparazzi and gossip columnists endless fodder. If you don't speak Portuguese, you will find *novelas* cheesy and melodramatic. If you do understand the language, you will still find them cheesy and melodramatic, but you'll easily get drawn in, and perhaps become addicted. Otherwise, you don't need to understand much Portuguese to watch the broadcast of a live *jogo de futebol.* The machine-gun fire of words rattled off by Brazilian sports commentators with jacked-up fervor and excitement will have you alternately biting your nails and cheering for joy, even if you've never been much of a soccer fan.

In basic hotels you'll usually receive these basic Brazilian channels. In moderate to luxury lodgings you'll be treated to cable with BBC, CNN, some superior Brazilian cable channels, and lots of American cable series.

WEIGHTS AND MEASURES

Brazil uses the metric system. Throughout this book, measurements are given in both standard and metric. However, you'll also find a conversion chart at the back of this guide.

Depending on where in the country you're located, the electric current varies from 100 to 240 volts, although most common is 110 volts, meaning you won't have problems with electronic devices from North America—most laptops and battery chargers come equipped with adaptors and power units that convert automatically to changes in voltage. Most outlets in Brazil have two flat prongs, the same type of prong you would find in the United States. Should you need a cheap adaptor, you'll find one easily at any hardware store or larger supermarket.

Until June 2008, Brazil had four different time zones; now it only has three. The main time zone includes Rio, São Paulo, and the entire coastline going inland as far as Brasília. Westward, the states of Mato Grosso and Mato Grosso do Sul (containing the Pantanal) and the entire Amazon region (excluding Pará) are one hour behind Rio time. During the Brazilian summer (North American winter) most of the country (with the exception of the Northeast) goes on daylight saving time (which makes the days longer). During this time, Rio, São Paulo, Minas, and the south spring forward, and they are two hours ahead of New York City. Otherwise, the time difference between New York and Rio is only one hour (i.e., when it's noon in New York, it's 1 P.M. in Rio).

RESOURCES

Glossary

açaí a high-energy deep purple Amazonian fruit

acarajé a crunchy bean fritter cooked in palm oil and filled with dried shrimp, pepper, *vatapá*, and *caruru* that is a favorite snack in Bahia

água de coco milk from a green coconut (great for a hangover)

artesanato popular art and handicrafts

azulejo Portuguese glazed ceramic tile

baía bay

bairro neighborhood

barraca small rustic kiosk or beach bar

bloco large Carnaval group

botequim/boteco (singular) laid-back traditional neighborhood-style bar, mostly associated with Rio

botequins (plural) more than one neighborhood-style bar

caboclo person of mixed race (Indian and European), often used to describe residents of the Amazon region

cachaça distilled sugarcane, the Brazilian equivalent of rum

cachoeira waterfall

caipirinha classic Brazilian cocktail made with *cachaça*, crushed ice, lime, and sugar

caipiroska *caipirinha* in which vodka substitutes for the *cachaça*

camarão shrimp

Candomblé Afro-Brazilian religion, whose practice is particularly strong in Bahia

capoeira Afro-Brazilian mixture of martial art and dance

Carioca person or thing from Rio de Janeiro

Carnaval Carnival

carne-de-sol sun-dried meat

caruru a traditional Afro-Bahian dish of diced okra flavored with *dendê* and dried shrimp

chope draft beer

choro/chorinho type of instrumental music from the Northeast

comida por quilo popular self-service buffet restaurant where you pay for food by weight (per kilo)

costa coast

cupuaçu deliciously sweet milky-white Amazonian fruit

dendê palm oil used in Bahian cooking

doce sweet; often *doces* refer to candies or preserved fruit such as *doce de goiaba* (preserved guava)

doce de leite creamy fudge-like pudding

empada empanada

farinha flour (generally manioc flour, which is dusted over meals)

farofa manioc flour toasted with butter and other seasonings as an accompaniment to meals in the Northeast

favela urban slum

fazenda ranch, farm, country estate

feijão beans

feijoada classic Brazilian stew of beans and salted pork and beef

feira open-air market

ferroviária train station

festa celebration, party

forró country-style type of music and dance from the Northeast

fortaleza fortress

Globo Brazil's biggest television and media conglomerate; its stable of glamorous soap stars are known as Globais

gringo foreigner

guaraná Amazonian berry used as a pick-me-up; in small doses it flavors Brazil's national cola

Iemanjá popular Afro-Brazilian goddess of the seas

igreja church

ilha island

kanga a rectangular piece of thin, brightly colored cotton that can be worn as a beach wrap or used as a beach towel

lanchonete snack bar, food stand

largo small square or plaza

litoral coastline

mangue mangrove swamp

Mata Atlântica native Atlantic rainforest, whose remaining patches can still be found along the Brazilian coast, mostly in Bahia and the Southeast

mercado market

Metrô subway

Mineiro a person from Minas Gerais

mineiro a thing from Minas Gerais

moqueca typical Bahian stew of fish and or seafood cooked with tomatoes and green peppers in palm oil and coconut milk

morro hill, small mountain

mosteiro monastery

MPB Música Popular Brasileiro, i.e., classic Brazilian pop

mulato person of mixed African and European heritage

Nordeste the Northeast of Brazil

novelas popular nightly television soap operas

orixá a Candomblé divinity

orla oceanfront

pastel a deep-fried pastry stuffed with a variety of fillings (especially popular in São Paulo)

pau-brasil brazilwood tree, coveted by early colonial explorers, which inspired Brazil's name

Paulistano a person or thing from the city of São Paulo

petiscos nibbles or appetizers (usually served in bars)

pousada an inn, guesthouse, or bed-and-breakfast

praça square or plaza

praia beach

restinga a mixture of native vegetation that includes various species of trees, bushes, vines, bromeliads, and ferns and is typical of the coastal area surrounding the Zona Oeste beaches of Barra and Recreio

rodízio a type of restaurant service in which you pay a fixed price and then can choose from a rotating selection of items (usually *churrasco* or pizza)

rodovia highway

rodoviária bus terminal

rua street

salgado any savory type of pastry

samba a fast rhythmic, drum-based Brazilian style of music with strong African influences

serra mountain range

Sertão the poor, desert-like, and often drought-ridden interior of the Northeast

shopping shopping mall

sorveteria ice cream parlor

terreiro house and surrounding area where Candomblé rituals are performed

tira-gosto appetizer

Tupi Indian people and language that thrived along coastal Brazil before the arrival of European explorers

vatapá a traditional Afro-Bahian dish in which cashews, dried shrimp, palm oil, and coconut milk are combined into a thick puree

Portuguese Phrasebook

Although most Brazilians are taught English at school, the quality of the teaching is generally so poor that it's hard to get more out of them than "Hi.... How are you?...The book is on the table." In Rio, English may be spoken in places that receive heavy tourist traffic as well as more upscale hotels and restaurants. Generally, younger and/or wealthier Cariocas have some knowledge of English. Speaking Spanish, which is similar in many ways to Portuguese, can come in handy (although never assume that this is Brazilians' mother tongue – a common gringo faux pas that doesn't go over well), but while Brazilians might understand you, you'll have a more difficult time understanding their replies. It's highly recommended that you learn a few basic expressions in Portuguese. Although pronunciation can be tricky, Brazilians will love the fact that you are making an effort and will usually be very encouraging. Brazilian Portuguese is quite different from the Portuguese spoken in Portugal. In terms of speaking and comprehension, Brazilian Portuguese is easier, since Brazilians pronounce words as they are written (while the Portuguese tend to distort certain sounds). A wonderfully innovative language, Brazilian Portuguese is full of colorful expressions and sayings as well as borrowed words from diverse idioms.

PRONUNCIATION

Portuguese is spoken as it is written. However, things take a turn for the complex when confronted with the challenging vowel sounds.

Vowels

So-called non-nasal vowels are fairly straight-forward:

a   is pronounced "ah," as in "father" in words like *garota* (girl).

e   is pronounced "eh," as in "hey" in words like *fé* (faith). At the end of a word, such as *fome* (hunger), it is pronounced "ee," as in "free."

i   is pronounced "ee," as in "free," in words such as *polícia* (police).

o   is pronounced "aw" as in "dog," in words

such as *loja* (shop). At the end of a word, such as *minuto* (minute), it veers from "oh," as in "go," to "oo" as in "too."

Much more complicated are the nasal vowels. Nasal vowels are signaled by a tilde accent (~) as in *não* (no), or by the presence of the letters **m** or **n** following the vowel, such as *bem* (good) or *ponte* (bridge). When pronouncing them, it helps to exaggerate the sound, focus on your nose and not your mouth, and pretend there is an hidden "ng" on the end.

Consonants

Portuguese consonant sounds are a breeze compared with the nasal vowels. There are, however, a few exceptions to be aware of.

c   is pronounced "k," as in "catch," in words like *casa* (house). However, when followed by the vowel **e** or **i,** or when sporting a cedilha accent (¸), as in *caçar* (to hunt) it is pronounced "s," as in "soft," in words like *cidade* (city).

ch   is pronounced "sh," as in "shy," in words like *chá* (tea).

d   is usually pronounced as in English. The exception is when it is followed by the vowel **e** or **i** – in words such as *parede* (wall) – it acquires a "j" sound similar to "jump."

g   is pronounced "g," as in "go," in words like *gado* (cattle). However, when followed by the vowel **e** or **i,** it is pronounced like the "s" in "vision" in words like *gigante* (giant).

h   is always silent. Words like *horário* (schedule) are pronouned like "hour" in English.

j   is pronounced like the "s" in "vision," in words like *jogo* (game).

n   is usually pronounced as in English. The exception is when it is followed by **h** – in words such as *banho* (bath) – when it acquires a "ny" sound similar to "new."

r   can be pretty complicated. At the beginning of a word, such as Rio de Janeiro, or when found in twos, such as *carro* (car), it is pronounced as a very guttural "h" as in "home."

t is usually pronounced as in English. The exception is when it is followed by the vowel **e** or **i** – in words such as *morte* (death) – when it acquires a "ch" sound similar to "chalk."

x is pronounced like "sh," as in "shy," when found at the beginning of words such as *xadres* (chess). Otherwise, it is pronounced "z" as in "zoo," in words such as *exercício* (exercise).

Stress

Most Portuguese words carry stress on the second-to-last syllable. *Janeiro* (January), for example, is pronounced "ja-NEI-ro." There are, however, some exceptions. The stress falls on the last syllable with words that end in r – *falar* (to talk) is pronounced "fa-LAR" – as well as words ending in nasal vowels – *mamão* (papaya) is pronounced "ma-MAO." Vowels with accents over them – ~, ´, `, ^ – indicate that the stress falls on the syllable containing the vowel. As such, *inglês* (English) is pronounced "ing-LES" and *cardápio* (menu) is pronounced "car-DA-pi-o."

PLURAL NOUNS AND ADJECTIVES

In Portuguese, the general rule for making a noun or adjective plural is to simply add a "s." For example, the plural of *casa branca* (white house) is *casas brancas*. However, there are various exceptions. For instance, words that end in nasal consonants such as "m" or "l" change to "ns" and "is," respectively. The plural of *botequim* (bar) is *botequins*, while the plural of *hotel* (hotel) is *hotéis*. Words that end in nasal vowels also undergo changes. "Ão" becomes "ãos," "ães," or "ões," as in the case of *mão* (hand) which becomes *mãos* and *pão* (bread) which becomes *pães*.

GENDER

Like French, Spanish, and Italian, all Portuguese words have masculine and feminine forms of nouns and adjectives. In general, nouns ending in **o** or consonants, such as *cavalo* (horse) and *sol* (sun) are masculine, while those ending in **a,** such as *terra* (earth) are feminine. Many words have both masculine and feminine versions determined by their *o/a* ending, such as *menino* (boy) and *menina* (girl). Nouns are always preceded by articles – *o* and *a* (definite) and *um* and *uma* (indefinite) that announce their gender. For example, *o menino* means "the boy" while *a menina* means "the girl." Um menino is "a boy," while *uma menina* is "a girl."

DIMINUTIVES

Brazilians have a great fondness for using the *diminutivo* (diminutive), which accounts for the flood of *"inhos"* and *"zinhos"* attached to most words. Although the diminutive's true function is to indicate smallness in size – a *cafezinho* is an espresso-sized coffee, a *casinha* refers to a modest house – in Brazil, the diminutive is first and foremost used as a sign of affection between friends and family members. Since Brazilians are very affectionate, these are used more often than are standard names. Men named Luiz are inevitably called Luizinho and women named Ana become Aninha. A *filho* (son) is a *filhinho*, a *mãe* (mother) is *mãezinha*, and a *namorado* (boyfriend) is a *namoradinho*, and even a beloved *cachorro* (dog) is often a *cachorrinho*. Moreover, Brazilians possess a great talent for recounting everything from *historinhas* (stories) to *fofoquinhas* (gossip), and in the recounting the diminutive is often used for emphasis. It can also be used to downplay an event – a *joguinho* is a *jogo* (game) without importance – or to placate someone (asking a client to wait just a *minutinho* for service is somehow less onerous than having to wait an entire *minuto*). There are, however, some instances in which a diminutive might refer to something quite different. A *camishinha* is not a small *camisa* (shirt), but a condom. An *abóbora* is a pumpkin, while an *abobrinha* is a zucchini.

BASIC AND COURTEOUS EXPRESSIONS

Hello *Olá*
Hi *Oi*
Good morning *Bom dia*
Good afternoon/evening *Boa tarde*
Good night *Boa noite*
See you later *Até mais tarde, até breve*

Goodbye *Tschau*
How are you? *Como vai?/Tudo bem?*
Fine, and you? *Tudo bem, e você?*
So so *Mais ou menos*
Not so good *Meio ruim*
Nice to meet you. *Um prazer.*
You're very kind. *Você é muito(a) simpático(a)*
Yes *Sim*
No *Não*
I don't know. *Não sei.*
Please *Por favor*
Thank you *Obrigado (if you're male),*
Obrigada (if you're female)
You're welcome. *De nada.*
Excuse me. *Com licença.*
Sorry *Desculpa*
What's your name? *Como se chama?/Qual é*
seu nome?
My name is... *Meu nome é...*
Where are you from? *De onde vem?*
I'm from... *Sou de...*
Do you speak English? *Fala inglês?*
I don't speak Portuguese. *Não falo*
Portuguese.
I only speak a little bit. *Só falo um*
pouquinho.
I don't understand. *Não entendo*
Can you please repeat that? *Por favor,*
pode repetir?
What's it called? *Como se chama?*
What time is it? *Que horas são?*
Would you like . . . ? *Gostaria de . . . ?*

TERMS OF ADDRESS

I *eu*
you *você*
he/him *ele*
she/her *ela*
we/us *nós*
you (plural) *vocês*
they/them *eles/elas*
Mr./Sir *Senhor*
Mrs./Madame *Senhora or Dona*
young man *moço or rapaz*
young woman *moça*
guy/fellow *rapaz, cara*
boy/girl *garoto/garota*
child *criança*

brother/sister *irmão/irmã*
father/mother *pai/mãe*
son/daughter *filho/filha*
husband/wife *marido/mulher*
uncle/aunt *tio/tia*
grandfather/grandmother *avô, avó*
friend *amigo/amiga*
colleague *colega*
boyfriend/girlfriend *namorado/namorada*
single *solteiro/a*
divorced *divorciado/a*

TRANSPORTATION

Where is . . . ? *Onde é/Onde fica . . . ?*
How far away is . . . ? *Qual é a distância*
até . . . ?
Which is the quickest way? *Qual é o*
caminho mais rápido?
How can I get to . . . ? *Como eu posso*
chegar . . . ?
Is it far? *É longe?*
Is it close? *É perto?*
bus *ônibus*
the bus station *a rodoviária*
the bus stop *a parada de ônibus*
How much does a ticket cost? *Quanto*
custa uma passagem?
What is the schedule? *Qual é o horário?*
When is the next departure? *Quando é a*
próxima saida?
What time do we leave? *Á que horas vamos*
sair?
What time do we arrive? *Á que horas vamos*
chegar?
first *primeiro*
last *último*
next *próximo*
Are there many stops? *Tem muitas*
paradas?
plane *avião*
Is the flight on time? *O vôo está na hora?*
Is it late? *Está atrasado?*
I'd like a round-trip ticket. *Quero uma*
passagem ida e volta.
I have a lot of luggage. *Tenho muita*
bagagem.
Is there a baggage check? *Tem guarda*
volumes?

boat *barco*
ship *návio*
ferry boat *ferry, balsa*
port *porto*
Is the sea calm or rough? *O mar está calmo ou turbulento?*
Are there many waves? *Tem muitas ondas?*
I want to rent a car. *Quero alugar um carro.*
Is it safe to drive here? *É seguro dirigir aqui?*
gas station *posto de gasolina*
Can you fill up the gas tank? *Pode encher o tanque?*
To drive fast/slowly *dirigir rapidamente/ devagar*
parking lot *estacionamento*
stoplight *o sinal*
toll *pedágio*
at the corner *na esquina*
sidewalk *a calçada*
dead-end street *rua sem saida*
one-way *mão unica*
The car broke down. *O carro quebrou.*
I need a mechanic. *Preciso dum mecânico.*
Can you fix it? *Pode consertar?*
The tire burst. *O pneu furou.*
Where can I get a taxi? *Onde posso achar um taxi?*
Is this taxi free? *Está livre?*
Can you take me to this address? *Pode me levar para este endereço?*
Can you stop here, please? *Pode parar aqui, por favor?*
north *norte*
south *sul*
east *este*
west *oeste*
left/right *esquerda/direita*
straight ahead *tudo direito*

ACCOMMODATIONS

To stay in a hotel *Ficar num hotel*
Is there a guesthouse nearby? *Tem pousada perto daqui?*
Are there any rooms available? *Tem quartos disponivéis?*
For today? *Para hoje?*
I'd like to make a reservation. *Queria fazer uma reserva.*

I want a single room. *Quero um quarto simples.*
Is there a double room? *Tem quarto duplo?*
With a double bed or two singles? *Com cama de casal ou duas camas solteiras?*
With a fan or air-conditioned? *Com ventilador ou ar condicionado?*
Is there a view? *Tem vista?*
private bathroom *banheiro privado*
shower *chuveiro*
key *chave*
Is breakfast included? *O café de manhã é incluido?*
How much does it cost? *Quanto custa?*
Can you give me a discount? *É possivel ter um desconto?*
It's too expensive. *É muito caro.*
Is there something cheaper? *Tem algo mais barato?*
for just one night *para uma noite só*
for three days *para três dias.*
Can I see it first? *Posso dar uma olhada primeiro?*
quiet/noisy *tranquilo/barulhento*
comfortable *confortável*
change the sheets/towels *trocar os lençóis/toalhas*
soap *sabão*
toilet tissue *papel higiênico*
Could you please wake me up? *Por favor, pode me acordar?*

FOOD

to eat *comer*
to drink *beber*
I'm hungry. *Estou com fome.*
I'm thirsty. *Estou com sede.*
breakfast *café de manhã*
lunch *almoço*
dinner *jantar*
a snack *um lanche*
a light meal *uma comida leve*
I just want to nibble. *Só quero beliscar.*
Are the portions large? *As porções são grandes?*
Is it enough for two? *Dá para duas pessoas?*
Can I order a half portion? *Posso pedir uma meia-porção?*

Can I see the menu? *Pode dar uma olhada no cardápio?*
Is it all-you-can-eat? *Pode comer a vontade?*
Can you call the waiter over? *Pode chamar o garçom?*
Is there a free table? *Tem mesa livre?*
I'd like a cold beer. *Quero uma cerveja gelada.*
Another, please. *Mais uma, por favor.*
Do you have wine? *Tem vinho?*
Red or white? *Tinto ou branco?*
I'd like more ice please. *Quero mais gelo, por favor.*
This glass is dirty. *Este copo está sujo.*
Can you bring me another? *Pode me trazer outro?*
Do you have juice? *Tem suco?*
I'd like it without sugar. *Quero sem açúcar.*
Do you have sweetener? *Tem adocante?*
carbonated mineral water *água mineral com gaz*
I'm a vegetarian. *Sou vegetariano.*
I'm ready to order. *Estou pronto para pedir.*
Can I have some more time? *Pode me dar mais um tempinho?*
well done *bem passado*
medium *ao ponto*
rare *mal passado*
hot *quente*
cold *frio*
sweet *doce*
salty *salgado*
sour *azedo*
flatware *talheres*
fork *garfo*
knife *faca*
soup spoon *colher de sopa*
tea spoon *colher de chá*
dessert *sobremesa*
Can you bring coffee please? *Pode trazer um cafezinho?*
with milk *com leite*
Can you bring the bill please? *Pode trazer a conta por favor.*
It was delicious. *Foi deliciosa.*

Meat
red meat *carne*
chicken *frango, galinha*
pork *porco, leitão*
ham *presunto*
turkey *peru*
sausage *salsicha*

Fish and Seafood
fish *peixe*
seafood *frutas do mar, mariscos*
freshwater *água doce*
tuna *atum*
shrimp *camarão*
crab *caranguejo, siri*
squid *lula*
octopus *polvo*
lobster *lagosta*

Eggs and Dairy
eggs *ovos*
hard-boiled egg *ovo cozido*
scrambled eggs *ovos mexidos*
whole milk *leite integrado*
skim milk *leite desnatado*
powdered milk *leite em pó*
cream *creme de leite*
butter *manteiga*
cheese *queijo*
yogurt *iogurte*
ice cream *sorvete*

Vegetables
vegetables *verduras/legumes*
salad *salada*
lettuce *alface*
carrot *cenoura*
tomato *tomate*
potato *batata*
cucumber *pepino*
zucchini *abobrinha*
couve *kale*
cabbage *repolho*

Fruits
mango *manga*
papaya *mamão*

passion fruit *maracujá*
apple *macã*
orange *laranja*
lime *limão*
pineapple *abacaxi*
grape *uva*
strawberry *morango*
watermelon *melância*
guava *goiaba*
jackfruit *jaca*
cashew fruit *cajú*

Seasoning and Spices
salt *sal*
black pepper *pimenta do reino*
hot pepper *pimenta*
cilantro *coentro*
parsley *salsa*
ginger *gengibre*
mint *hortelã*
basil *manjeiricão*
onion *cebola*
green onion *cebolinha*
garlic *alho*
cooking oil *óleo*
olive oil *azeite*
vinegar *vinagre*
brown sugar *açúcar mascavo*
cinnamon *canela*
clove *cravo*
nutmeg *noz moscada*
vanilla *baunilha*

Baked Goods
bread *pão*
whole wheat bread *pão integral*
cookies *biscoitos*
cake *bolo, torta*
flour *farinha*

Cooking
roasted, baked *assado*
boiled *cozido*
steamed *a vapor*
grilled *grelhado*
barbecue *churrasco*

fried *frito*
breaded *à milanesa*

Drinks
water *água*
milk *leite*
soft drink *refrigerante*
juice *suco*
ice *gelo*
beer *cerveja*
wine *vinho*

MONEY AND SHOPPING
to buy *comprar*
to spend a lot of money *gastar muito dinheiro*
to shop *fazer compras*
for sale *à venda*
Until what time does the bank stay open? *Até que horas o banco fica aberto?*
I'm out of money. *Estou sem dinheiro.*
I don't have change. *Estou sem troco.*
ATM *caixa automática*
Do you accept credit cards? *Aceita cartão de crédito?*
Can I exchange money? *Posso trocar dinheiro?*
money exchange *câmbio*
Is there a discount if I pay in cash? *Tem desconto se pagar em dinheiro?*
That's too expensive. *É caro demais.*
That's very cheap. *É muito barato.*
more *mais*
less *menos*
a good price *Um preço bom.*
Let's bargain. *Vamos negociar.*
Is it on sale? *Está em promoção?*
It's a good deal. *É um bom negócio.*
What time does the store close? *A que horas fecha a loja?*
salesperson *vendedor/a*
Can I try it on? *Posso provar?*
It doesn't fit. *Não cabe bem.*
too tight *muito apertado*
too big *grande demais*
Can I exchange it? *Posso trocar?*

HEALTH
Can you help me? *Pode me ajudar?*
I don't feel well. *Não me sinto bem.*
I'm nauseous. *Estou com nausea.*
I've got a headache. *Estou com dor de cabeça.*
I've got a stomachache. *Estou com dor de barriga.*
fever *um febre*
pain *uma dor*
infection *uma infeção*
cut *um corte*
burn *uma queimadura*
vomiting *vomitando*
I can't breathe. *Não posso respirar.*
I'm sick. *Estou doente.*
Is there a pharmacy close by? *Tem uma farmácia perto daqui?*
Can you call a doctor? *Pode ligar para um médico?*
I need to go to a hospital. *Preciso ir para o hospital.*
pill *pílula*
medicine *remédio/medicamento*
antibiotic *antibiótico*
ointment *pomada/creme*
cotton *algodão*
toothpaste *pasta de dentes*
toothbrush *escova de dentes*
condom *preservativo/camisinha*

SAFETY
Is this neighborhood safe? *Este bairro é seguro?*
dangerous *perigoso*
roubo *robbery*
thief *ladrão*
mugging *assalto*
mugger *assaltante*
Call the police! *Chame a polícia!*
Help! *Socorro!*

COMMUNICATIONS
to talk, speak *falar*
to say *dizer*
to hear *ouvir*
to listen *escutar*
to shout *gritar*

to make a phone call *fazer um telefonema/ ligar*
What's your phone number? *Qual é seu numero de telefone?*
the wrong number *o numero errado*
collect call *uma chamada a cobrar*
international call *uma chamada internacional*
Do you have Internet here? *Tem Internet aqui?*
I want to send an email. *Quero mandar um email.*
What's your email address? *Qual é seu endereço de email?*
post office *os correios*
letter *carta*
postcard *postal*
package *um pacote*
box *uma caixa*
to send *enviar*
to deliver *entregar*
stamp *selo*
weight *peso*

NUMBERS
1 *um, uma*
2 *dois, duas*
3 *três*
4 *quatro*
5 *cinco*
6 *seis*
7 *sete*
8 *oito*
9 *novo*
10 *dez*
11 *onze*
12 *doze*
13 *treze*
14 *quatorze*
15 *quinze*
16 *dezesseis*
17 *dezessete*
18 *dezoito*
19 *dezenove*
20 *vinte*
21 *vinte e um*
30 *trinta*
40 *quarenta*

50 *cinquenta*
60 *sessenta*
70 *setenta*
80 *oitenta*
90 *noventa*
100 *cem*
101 *cento e um*
200 *duzentos*
500 *quinhentos*
1,000 *mil*
2,000 *dois mil*

TIME
What time is it? *Que horas são?*
It's 3 o'clock. *São três horas.*
It's 3:15. *São três e quinze.*
It's 3:30. *São três e meia.*
It's 3:45. *São três e quarenta-cinco.*
In two hours. *Daqui a duas horas.*
Sorry for being late. *Desculpe o atraso.*
Did I arrive early? *Cheguei cedo?*
before *antes*
after *depois*

DAYS AND MONTHS
day *dia*
morning *manhã*
afternoon *tarde*
night *noite*
today *hoje*
yesterday *ontém*
tomorrow *amanhã*
week *semana*
month *mês*
year *ano*
century *século*
Monday *segunda-feira*
Tuesday *terça-feira*

Wednesday *quarta-feira*
Thursday *quinta-feira*
Friday *sexta-feira*
Saturday *sábado*
Sunday *domingo*
January *janeiro*
February *fevereiro*
March *março*
April *abril*
May *maio*
June *junho*
July *julho*
August *agosto*
September *setembro*
October *outubro*
November *novembro*
December *dezembro*

SEASONS AND WEATHER
season *estação*
spring *primavera*
summer *verão*
autumn *outuno*
winter *inverno*
weather *o tempo*
sun *sol*
It's sunny. *Está fazendo sol.*
rain *chuva*
Is it going to rain? *Vai chover?*
clouds *nuvens*
cloudy *nublado*
It's hot. *Faz calor.*
It's cold. *Faz frio.*
a cool breeze *uma brisa fresca*
a strong wind *um vento forte*
dry air *ar seco*
wet *molhado*

Suggested Reading

TRAVEL LITERATURE

Bishop, Elizabeth. *One Art.* New York: Farrar, Strauss and Giroux, 1995. America's poet laureate in 1949—1950, Elizabeth Bishop was also a steadfast and elegant letter writer. On a South American cruise, Bishop stopped off in Rio de Janeiro, fell ill after eating a cashew fruit, and was nursed back to health by Lota Macedo Soares, a wealthy and very clever Carioca with whom she fell in love. The subsequent years she spent in Brazil are chronicled with sharpness and affection in the letters published in this tome.

Haddad, Annette, and Scott Doggett, eds. *Travelers' Tales Brazil: True Stories.* New York: Travelers' Tales Guides, 2004. This great collection of travel essays—penned by a variety of writers and excerpted from books and magazines—offers a multifaceted view of Brazil through many lenses.

Page, P. K. *Brazilian Journal.* Toronto: L.& O. Dennys, 1987. In the 1950s, Canadian poet P. K. Page found herself in Rio when her husband became Canada's ambassador to Brazil. Despite bouts of culture shock, Page fell in love with Brazil. Her descriptions of Rio's glamorous last days as the nation's capital are simple, lyrical, and ultimately moving.

Toussaint-Samson, Adèle. *A Parisian in Brazil.* Wilmington, DE: SR Books, 2001. In the 1850s, feeling the urge to expand her horizons, well-to-do Parisian Toussaint-Samson traveled to Rio, where she spent the next 10 years of her life. The account of her experiences was originally published in France in the 19th century and offers a fascinating insight into imperial Rio as well as what it was like to be a *gringa* on the loose in the Cidade Maravilhosa.

HISTORY AND SOCIETY

De Jesus, Carolina Maria. *Child of the Dark.* New York: Signet, 2003. Written between 1955 and 1960, these intimate journal entries by Carolina de Jesus offer a rare first-hand glimpse of the life of a single black mother of three who lived in a São Paulo *favela* and earned a living picking garbage. Through a chance encounter with a journalist, her diary was published in 1960 and de Jesus became somewhat of a celebrity.

Fausto, Boris. *A Concise History of Brazil.* Cambridge, MA: Cambridge University, 1999. One of Brazil's leading historians and a professor at the University of São Paulo, Fausto does an admirable job of condensing five centuries of events and outsized personalities into one comprehensive and highly readable narrative.

Levine, Robert M., and John Crocitti, eds. *The Brazil Reader: History, Culture, Politics.* New York: Duke University Press, 1999. An intelligently edited volume of essays on myriad and often subtle aspects of Brazilian history, society, and daily life. The texts range from academic to alternative, but all are thought-provoking and do a fine job at tackling Brazil's overwhelming diversity and complexity.

Mattoso, Katia M. de Queiroz. *To Be a Slave in Brazil, 1550–1888.* New York: Rutgers, 1987. Mattoso provides Balzac-ian details that movingly bring to life the harrowing existence of slaves in colonial Brazil as seen through the eyes of both slaves and their masters.

Page, Joseph A. *The Brazilians.* New York: Da Capo Press, 1996. In an attempt to explain "Brazilian-ness," this highly readable cultural history of Brazil draws on politics, economics, sports, literature, pop culture, religion, and historical events and figures.

CULTURE AND MUSIC

Bellos, Alex. *Futebol: The Brazilian Way of Life.* London: Bloomsbury, 2002. A compelling look at Brazil's national pastime (some would say religion) that traces the fascinating history of soccer from its humble beginnings to its overblown present. Bellos is an accomplished journalist and mixes insightful reporting with highly entertaining anecdotes.

Castro, Ruy. *Bossa Nova—The Story of the Brazilian Music that Seduced the World.* Chicago: Chicago Review Press, 2003. One of Brazil's most prolific journalists, Castro conjures up the heady days of Ipanema in the late 1950s and early '60s when fascinating characters such as João Gilberto and Tom Jobim pioneered the cool syncopated sound that took the world by storm. Aside from detailing the history of bossa nova, the book offers a slice of Carioca life from that time.

Guillermoprieto, Alma. *Samba.* New York: Vintage, 1991. A former dancer and contributor to the *New Yorker,* Guillermoprieto spent a year in Rio de Janeiro's Zona Norte neighborhood with Mangueira, one of the city's most traditional samba schools, as its 5,000 members prepared for Carnaval. This result is a vibrant, passionate, and beautifully written backstage narrative.

McGowan, Chris, and Ricard Pessanha. *The Brazilian Sound: Samba, Bossa Nova, and the Popular Music of Brazil.* Philadelphia: Temple University Press, 1998. A thorough and well-written compendium of popular Brazilian music styles and major performing artists,

this book serves as a useful introduction to Brazil's rich musical world. The text is accompanied by photos and a vast discography.

Peterson, Joan, and David Peterson. *Eat Smart in Brazil: How to Decipher the Menu, Know the Market Foods & Embark on a Tasting Adventure.* Corte Madera, CA: Gingko Press, 2006. Illustrated with mouthwatering photos, this highly readable book acts as a culinary companion, introducing you to the ingredients, recipes, and diverse regional cooking traditions of Brazil.

Sullivan, Edward J., ed. *Brazil Body and Soul.* New York: Guggenheim Museum, 2003. Published to coincide with Brazil's 500-year anniversary and the subsequent "best of" survey exhibited by the Guggenheim Museum, this massive catalog provides a mesmerizing overview of Brazilian art. Included are early explorer's depictions of "paradise," Aleijadinho's baroque marvels, modernism, folk art from throughout the Northeast, and interesting sections on indigenous and Afro-Brazilian art. The thoughtful essays are illustrated with stunning high-quality photos.

Veloso, Caetano. *Tropical Truth: A Story of Music and Revolution in Brazil.* New York: Da Capo Press, 2003. Brilliant, charming, and sometimes aggravating, Bahian singer-composer Caetano Veloso is one of MPB's most creative figures. In this colorful memoir he provides an insider's look at the generation-defining musical movement of the late '60s and '70s that became known as Tropicália.

Internet Resources

Adventures of a Gringa in Rio
www.riogringa.typepad.com
This lively blog written by a nice Jewish girl from New York is entertaining and offers a diary of life as an expat in Rio, with some interesting links and tips from a foreign insider.

Agenda do Samba & Choro
www.samba-choro.com.br
This Portuguese site is a great reference for aficionados of samba and *choro* where you can download music and also check out events throughout Brazil. Rio receives special emphasis with an easy-to-read calendar of all samba and *choro* performances taking place in the city.

Brazil.com
www.brazil.com
This practical site is a decent general guide with information on major destinations as well as samples of airfares and hotel rates (with links). Also offers Brazil basics and tips for planning your trip.

BrazilMax
www.brazilmax.com
Billing itself as the "hip guide to Brazil," BrazilMax is operated by award-winning American journalist Bill Hinchberger, who has lived and worked in Brazil for over 20 years. Hinchberger and a stable of other talented expats pen the succinct travel articles and travel-related features that are regularly updated.

Brasil Sabor
www.brasilsabor.com.br
This site takes you on a detailed and mouth-watering journey throughout Brazil with itineraries whose focus is food in all its forms. Organized by region, everything from native ingredients and local markets to hidden-away restaurants, street *barracas,* and vanguard chefs are described in vivid prose, accompanied by sumptuous photographs.

Brazil Travel Blog
www.braziltravelblog.com
This engagingly written and highly informative blog is written by Tony Galvez, a Spanish expatriate living in São Paulo. Published in English and Spanish, his discriminating traveler's tips and information are spot-on. Illustrated with captivating photographs, the accounts of his many journeys (which include trips to Rio city and state) make for enticing reading.

Brazzil Magazine
www.brazzil.com
Brazzil Magazine features informative and concise articles, essays, and news pieces about various elements of Brazilian political, economic, social, and cultural life, largely written by English-speaking Brazilian specialists as well as savvy gringos living in Brazil. The site features some useful links and classified ads.

Cena Carioca
www.cenacarioca.com.br
This website is produced by and for alternative young Carioca clubbers who want to keep up with Rio's underground nocturnal scene. Aside from up-to-date info about DJs, clubs, *festas,* cultural events, and trends, there is a daily calendar of events and lots of pics for those whose Portuguese is sketchy.

Copacabana.com
www.copacabana.com
Find out what the weather's like in Copa, watch videos of live beach shows, and find exhaustive listings of every hotel, bar, and restaurant as well as their locations and architectural and historical facts about *every single* street in the *bairro.*

Embratur
www.braziltour.com
Embratur, the Brazilian ministry of tourism, has a well-organized multilingual site that allows you to browse potential journeys

according to region, itinerary, or interest (ec-otourism, beaches, culture, sports, business travel) and covers both the city and state of Rio de Janeiro. It also has up-to-date tips and resources for travelers concerning travel logistics (visas, vaccinations, airports, etc.).

Federação Brasileira dos Albergues de Juventude
www.hostel.org.br
Brazil's youth-hostel association offers information on 90 hostels throughout the country associated with the International Youth Hostel Association. Listings include amenities, photos, and rates.

Federação de Futebol do Estado do Rio de Janeiro
www.fferj.com.br
Soccer fans who want to bone up on local teams and scores should check out the site of Rio's pro and amateur teams, which includes game schedules and links to all teams as well as video broadcasts.

Gay Travel Brazil
www.gaytravelbrazil.com
This small but informative site concentrates mainly on Rio and São Paulo (with gay-friendly hotel recommendations), but also provides general info and tips to all the major cities. Apart from booking flights, Gay Travel Brazil works with gay-friendly tour operators and guides in Rio who can organize customized excursions.

Ipanema.com
www.ipanema.com
Billing itself as an insider's guide to Rio, this English-language website is user friendly and contains lots of interesting detail. Although it's not always completely up-to-date, it covers a lot of territory—not just Ipanema—and offers walking itineraries and maps.

Jornal do Brasil
http://jbonline.terra.com.br
The online version of Rio's most reputed daily paper includes news features and arts and entertainment reviews and listings.

Lá Na Lapa
www.lanalapa.com.br
This lively site (in Portuguese) is your best source for up-to-the-moment info about nightlife and cultural life in Rio's most bohemian *bairro*.

Latin American Network Information Center (LANIC)
www.lanic.utexas.edu
The University of Texas at Austin has one of the best departments of Latin American and Brazilian Studies in North America. This site has great links to a wide variety of Brazilian-related themes and issues.

Leblon.com
www.leblon.com.br
Rio's chicest *bairro* has a website all its own where you can watch live on video, read how many babies are born daily, and check out the largest quantity of Leblon photos on the 'net (including some interesting old ones). For those who read Portuguese, there's an interesting history page and a service guide.

Liga Independente das Escolas de Samba do Rio de Janeiro (LIESA)
www.liesa.globo.com
The league of Rio's samba schools' site has everything you need to know about *escola de sambas* rehearsals as well as Carnaval itself.

Made in Brazil
www.madeinbrazil.typepad.com
Made in Brazil is a freewheeling blog with a decidedly gay flavor that riffs on Brazilian fashion, celebrity gossip, and travel (with an emphasis on hipster clubs, restaurants, and

bars). It has some good travel info as well as interesting pop culture tidbits.

Maria Brazil
www.maria-brazil.org
Maria Brazil is a welcoming travel site for lovers of Brazil and all things Brazilian that is operated by an American expat who divides her time between Rio and Miami. Aside from a little black book of great insider Rio listings, "Maria" shares Brazilian recipes and information on music and festivals.

Metrô Rio
www.metrorio.com.br
On the site of Rio's subway system, you can type in your destination and receive directions on how to get there by Metrô and/or the special *integração* express bus system.

O Globo
www.oglobo.globo.com
The online version of one of Rio's most popular dailies, owned by the Globo media giant, offers up-to-the-moment news and cultural listings.

Quatro Rodas
www.viajeaqui.abril.com.br/g4r/
Quatro Rodas publishes the best maps and guidebooks in Brazil. On their website are travel articles published in *Viagem* magazine. And if you click on "Guia de Ruas" under "Mapas," you can pinpoint specific places in Rio (or any other city) by typing in the name or the address.

Rio Convention Bureau
www.rioconventionbureau.com.br
This bilingual site operated by Rio's convention and visitors' bureau has a lot of basic but useful information, for business travelers in particular. An archive with articles published in English-language press makes for interesting reading.

Rio Gay Life
www.riogaylife.com
This English-language guide to Rio's gay scene provides listings of beaches, bars, clubs, and saunas as well as travelers' tips. There's also an online forum.

Riotur
www.riodejaneiro-turismo.com.br
The City of Rio's tourism secretary offers very good up-to-date information about all attractions and events going on in the city, in both English and Portuguese, along with hotel and restaurant listings.

Rio This Week
www.riothisweek.com.br
Published in English and Portuguese, this fashion-forward website and accompanying monthly online magazine (downloadable in PDF) has tourism-related articles and listings, lusciously arty photographs, and even apartments available for vacation rentals.

Veja Rio
www.vejario.com
The digital version of the *Veja Rio* weekly magazine has up-to-date restaurant and bar reviews as well as complete listings of what's going on in the city. Many of the articles published in the print version are available online and provide insight into city news and trends—as long as you can read Portuguese.

Waves
www.waves.com.br
No *surfista* worth his or her board leaves the house without logging on to this virtual surfers' community, which shows up-to-the-minute wave conditions for all of Rio's (and Brazil's) beaches.

Index

Restaurants Index

Nightlife Index

Shops Index

Hotels Index

Acknowledgments

Just as Rio is a city of infinite layers and textures, this book, appropriately, is the sum of many journeys, moments, and most of all, people whose kindness, generosity, and companionship provided me with opportunities to discover and get to know the Cidade Maravilhosa on a more intimate level.

In this respect, I want to thank Helen and Monty for the first-ever trip back in 1970, which set the stage for so many more. Tinny, *você me deu meu primeiro* Rio *adulto; um* Rio *fundo do nosso amor, um* Rio *na companhia da família* Martins *que eu nunca vou esquecer.* Little Bet, *só você para achar uma cobertura tão maravilhosamente Copacabanistica e me convidar ("Vem pra cá!") para morar lá com você e dividir tantas deliciosas aventuras* Cariocas. Anne, over the years, Rio became our playground and we always managed to live it up like nobody's business—and always will.

Pelas dicas, gentileza, e hospitalidade, quero agradecer particularmente a Roberto e Dirk, Otto Suarez, Cornelius Rohr, *e* Paula Bezerra de Mello.

Agradecimentos também á Embratur (particularmente a Renata Braga de Faria) *pelas fotos.*

At Avalon Travel, thanks to publisher Bill Newlin for the continuing opportunities, and to acquisitions editor Jehan Seirafi for bringing everything together. Thank you Lucie Ericksen for photographic feedback and encouragement, and Mike Morgenfeld for sensitivity and professionalism regarding maps. Most of all, thank you to Erin Raber: Our ongoing writer-editor relationship has been not only a source of support, but of pleasure as well.

Finally—and this is crazy, but true—thanks to Jesse L. for the ocular solidarity.

www.moon.com

DESTINATIONS | ACTIVITIES | BLOGS | MAPS | BOOKS

MOON.COM is all new, and ready to help plan your next trip! Filled with fresh trip ideas and strategies, author interviews, informative blogs, a detailed map library, and descriptions of all the Moon guidebooks, Moon.com is all you need to get out and explore the world—or even places in your own backyard. As always, when you travel with Moon, expect an experience that is uncommon and truly unique.